Lecture Notes in Computer Science 15507

Founding Editors

Gerhard Goos
Juris Hartmanis

The series Lecture Notes in Computer Science (LNCS), including its subseries Lecture Notes in Artificial Intelligence (LNAI) and Lecture Notes in Bioinformatics (LNBI), has established itself as a medium for the publication of new developments in computer science and information technology research, teaching, and education.

LNCS enjoys close cooperation with the computer science R & D community, the series counts many renowned academics among its volume editors and paper authors, and collaborates with prestigious societies. Its mission is to serve this international community by providing an invaluable service, mainly focused on the publication of conference and workshop proceedings and postproceedings. LNCS commenced publication in 1973.

Quentin Bramas · Bapi Chatterjee ·
Stéphane Devismes · Malcolm Egan ·
Partha Sarathi Mandal ·
Krishnendu Mukhopadhyaya · V. Vijaya Saradhi
Editors

Distributed Computing and Intelligent Technology

21st International Conference, ICDCIT 2025
Bhubaneswar, India, January 8–11, 2025
Proceedings

Springer

Editors
Quentin Bramas ⓘ
Université de Strasbourg
Strasbourg, France

Stéphane Devismes ⓘ
University of Picardie Jules Verne
Amiens, France

Partha Sarathi Mandal ⓘ
Indian Institute of Technology Guwahati
Guwahati, Assam, India

V. Vijaya Saradhi
Indian Institute of Technology Guwahati
Guwahati, Assam, India

Bapi Chatterjee ⓘ
IIIT Delhi
New Delhi, Delhi, India

Malcolm Egan ⓘ
Inria
Villeurbanne, France

Krishnendu Mukhopadhyaya ⓘ
ISI Kolkata
Kolkata, West Bengal, India

ISSN 0302-9743   ISSN 1611-3349 (electronic)
Lecture Notes in Computer Science
ISBN 978-3-031-81403-7   ISBN 978-3-031-81404-4 (eBook)
https://doi.org/10.1007/978-3-031-81404-4

This Springer imprint is published by the registered company Springer Nature Switzerland AG
The registered company address is: Gewerbestrasse 11, 6330 Cham, Switzerland

If disposing of this product, please recycle the paper.

Preface

This volume contains the papers selected for presentation at the 21th International Conference on Distributed Computing and Intelligent Technology (ICDCIT 2025), held during January 8–11, 2025, in Kalinga Institute of Industrial Technology (KIIT), Bhubaneswar, India.

Starting from its first edition in 2004, the ICDCIT conference series has grown to an annual conference of international repute and has become a global platform for computer science researchers to exchange research results and ideas on the foundations and applications of distributed computing and intelligent technology. ICDCIT 2025 was the 21th meeting in the series. ICDCIT strives to provide an opportunity for students and young researchers to get exposed to topical research directions of distributed computing and intelligent technology.

ICDCIT is organized into two tracks: Distributed Computing (DC) and Intelligent Technology (IT). The DC track solicits original research papers contributing to the foundations and applications of distributed computing, whereas the IT track solicits original research papers contributing to the foundations and applications of Intelligent Technology. Each track has a separate program committee (PC) including PC chairs, who evaluate the papers submitted to that track.

This year we received 93 full paper submissions; 30 papers in the DC track and 63 papers in the IT track. Each submission considered for publication was reviewed by at least three PC members, with the help of reviewers outside of the PC. Based on the reviews, the PC decided to accept 18 papers for presentation at the conference, with an acceptance rate of 19%. The DC track PC accepted 10 papers (7 regular papers and 3 short papers), with an acceptance rate of 33%.The IT track PC accepted 8 regular papers, with an acceptance rate of 12%.

ICDCIT 2025 adopted a double-blind review process to help PC members and external reviewers come to a judgment about each submitted paper without possible bias. Additionally, each paper that was in conflict with a chair/PC member was handled/reviewed by another chair/PC member who had no conflict with the paper.

We also invited several distinguished people from the distributed computing and intelligent technology fields to propose position papers related to hot topics of their research fields. Three such papers are included in this volume.

We would like to express our gratitude to all the researchers who submitted their work to the conference. Our special thanks go to all colleagues who served on the PC, as well as the external reviewers, who generously offered their expertise and time which helped us select the papers and prepare the strong conference program.

This year, we were able to award best paper as well as best student paper awards in both DC and IT tracks. The awards were announced during the conference. Notice that the best paper awardee in each track received 50,000 Indian Rupees in total and the best student paper awardee in each track received 25,000 Indian Rupees in total. We congratulate the authors of the selected papers for their outstanding research.

We were fortunate to have six distinguished keynote speakers: Debasish Das (Amazon, India), Jean-Marie Gorce (INSA-Lyon, France), Giuseppe F. Italiano (LUISS University, Italy), Michel Raynal (University of Rennes, France), G. Narahari Sastry (Indian Institute of Technology Hyderabad, India), and Raj Kumar Buyya (University of Melbourne, Australia). Their talks provided us with the unique opportunity to hear research advances in various fields of DC and IT from leaders in those respective fields. The abstracts of the keynote talks are also included in this volume.

We wish to express our thanks to the local organizing committee who worked hard to make this conference a success, especially our organizing chair, Bindu Agarwalla. We also wish to thank the organizers of the satellite events as well as the many student volunteers. The School of Computer Engineering of KIIT, the host of the conference, provided various support and facilities for organizing the conference and its associated events.

Finally, we enjoyed institutional and financial support from KIIT for which we are indebted. We express our appreciation to all the Steering/Advisory Committee members, and in particular Sandeep Kulkarni, Samaresh Mishra, Anisur Rahaman Molla, Sathya Peri and Gokarna P. Sharma, whose counsel we frequently relied on. Thanks are also due to the faculty members and staff of the School of Computer Engineering of KIIT for their timely support.

January 2025

Quentin Bramas
Bapi Chatterjee
Stéphane Devismes
Malcolm Egan
Partha Sarathi Mandal
Krishnendu Mukhopadhyaya
V. Vijaya Saradhi

Organization

Chief Patron

Achyuta Samanta   KIIT & KISS, India

General Chairs

Stéphane Devismes   Université de Picardie Jules Verne, France
Partha Sarathi Mandal   IIT Guwahati, India
V. Vijaya Saradhi   IIT Guwahati, India

Program Committee Chairs

Quentin Bramas (DC Track)   University of Strasbourg, France
Bapi Chatterjee (IT Track)   IIIT Delhi, India
Malcom Egan (IT Track)   Inria, France
Krishnendu Mukhopadhyaya (DC   ISI Kolkata, India
    Track)

Conference Management Chair

Hrudaya Kumar Tripathy   KIIT, India

Organizing Chair

Bindu Agarwalla   KIIT, India

Finance Chairs

Jagannath Singh   KIIT, India
Subhasis Dash   KIIT, India

Publicity Chairs

William K. Moses Jr.   Durham University, UK
Lipika Mohanty   KIIT, India
Rabi Shaw   KIIT, India

Registration Chairs

Adyasha Dash   KIIT, India
Junali Jasmine Jenna   KIIT, India

Session Management Chairs

Satarupa Mohanty   KIIT, India
Prasenjeet Maity   KIIT, India
Abhishek Raj   KIIT, India

Publications Chairs

Mainak Bandyopadhyay   KIIT, India
Leena Das   KIIT, India

Student Symposium Chairs

Manjusha Pandey   KIIT, India
Anjan Bandyopadhyay   KIIT, India

Industry Symposium Chairs

Abhishek Ray   KIIT, India
Krishna Chakravarty   KIIT, India

Project Innovation Chairs

Satya Ranjan Dash	KIIT, India
Lalit Kumar Vashishtha	KIIT, India
Pratyusa Mukherjee	KIIT, India

Workshop Chairs

Sushruta Mishra	KIIT, India
Kunal Anand	KIIT, India
Abhaya Kumar Sahoo	KIIT, India

Ph.D. Symposium Chairs

Chittaranjan Pradhan	KIIT, India
Himanshu Das	KIIT, India

Hackathon Chairs

Siddharth Swarup Rautaray	KIIT, India
Rajat Behera	KIIT, India
Saurabh Jha	KIIT, India
Bhaswati Sahoo	KIIT, India

Advisory Committee

Saranjit Singh	KIIT, India
D. N. Dwivedy	KIIT, India
Jnyana Ranjan Mohanty	KIIT, India
Raj Bhatnagar	University of Cincinnati, USA
Rajkumar Buyya	University of Melbourne, Australia
Diganta Goswami	IIT Guwahati, India
Biswajit Sahoo	KIIT, India
Samresh Mishra	KIIT, India

Steering Committee

Sathya Peri	IIT Hyderabad, India
Anisur Rahaman Molla	ISI Kolkata, India
Gokarna P. Sharma	Kent State University, USA
Sandeep Kulkarni	Michigan State University, USA

Program Committee

Distributed Computing Track

Ansuman Banerjee	Indian Statistical Institute, India
Doina Bein	California State University, USA
Andrew Berns	University of Northern Iowa, USA
Subhash Bhagat	Indian Institute of Technology Jodhpur, India
Quentin Bramas	University of Strasbourg, France
Sandip Chakraborty	Indian Institute of Technology Kharagpur, India
Joshua Daymude	Arizona State University, USA
Giuseppe Antonio Di Luna	University of Rome - Sapienza, Italy
Anaïs Durand	LIMOS, Université Clermont Auvergne, France
Ayan Dutta	University of North Florida, USA
Romaric Duvignau	Chalmers University of Technology, Sweden
Barun Gorain	Indian Institute of Technology Bhilai, India
Sayaka Kamei	Hiroshima University, Japan
Anissa Lamani	Université de Strasbourg, France
Krishnendu Mukhopadhyaya	ISI Kolkata, India
Srabani Mukhopadhyaya	BIT, Mesra, India
Himadri Sekhar Paul	TCS Research and Innovation, India
Gokarna Sharma	Kent State University, USA
Yuichi Sudo	Hosei University, Japan
Amitabh Trehan	Durham University, UK

Intelligent Technology Track

Vinayak Abrol	IIIT Delhi, India
B. Ashwini	IIIT Delhi, India
Sumit Bhatia	Adobe Inc., India
Bapi Chatterjee	IIIT Delhi, India
Rachit Chhaya	IIT Gandhinagar, India
Malcolm Egan	Inria, France

Vyacheslav Kungurtsev	CTU Prague, Czech Republic
Farnaz Moradi	Ericsson Research, Sweden
Raghava Mutharaju	IIIT Delhi, India
Nir Oren	University of Aberdeen, UK
Samir Perlaza	Inria, France
Ranjitha Prasad	IIIT Delhi, India
Jyoti Sahni	Victoria University of Wellington, New Zealand
Supratim Shit	IIIT Delhi, India
Jainendra Shukla	IIIT Delhi, India

Additional Reviewers

Aujla, Gagangeet Singh
Chakraborty, Abhinav
Das, Debendranath
Eguchi, Ryota
Goyal, Nidhi
Johnen, Colette
Karati, Sabyasachi
Kitamura, Naoki
Lafourcade, Pascal
Maiti, Animesh
Maitra, Subhamoy
Miller, Loïc

Moldt, Daniel
Mondal, Kaushik
Mukherjee, Kuntal
Pattanayak, Debasish
Poudel, Pavan
Puys, Maxime
Shaban, Zubair
Shah, Nazreen
Shukla, Prakhar
Singh, Rishi Ranjan
Southern, Karl

Keynotes

Neoteric Frontiers in Cloud and Quantum Computing

Rajkumar Buyya

University of Melbourne, Australia

Abstract. The twenty-first-century digital infrastructure and applications are driven by Cloud computing and Internet of Things paradigms. The Cloud computing paradigm has been transforming computing into the 5th utility wherein "computing utilities" are commoditized and delivered to consumers like traditional utilities such as water, electricity, gas, and telephony. It offers infrastructure, platform, and software as services, which are made available to consumers as subscription-oriented services on a pay-as-you-go basis over the Internet. Its use is growing exponentially with the continued development of new classes of applications such as AI-powered models (e.g., ChatGPT) and the mining of crypto currencies such as Bitcoins. To make Clouds pervasive, Cloud application platforms need to offer (1) APIs and tools for rapid creation of scalable and elastic applications and (2) a runtime system for deployment of applications on geographically distributed Data Centre infrastructures (with Quantum computing nodes) in a seamless manner.

The Internet of Things (IoT) paradigm enables seamless integration of cyber-and-physical worlds and opening opportunities for creating new classes of realtime applications such as smart cities, smart robotics, and smart healthcare. The emerging Fog/Edge computing models support latency sensitive/real-time IoT applications with a seamless integration of network-wide resources all the way from edge to the Cloud.

This keynote presentation will cover (a) 21st century vision of computing and identifies various emerging IT paradigms that make it easy to realize the vision of computing utilities; (b) innovative architecture for creating elastic Clouds integrating edge resources and managed Clouds, (c) Aneka 6G, a 6th generation Cloud Application Platform, for rapid development of Big Data/AI applications and their deployment on private/public Clouds driven by user requirements, (d) a novel FogBus software framework with Blockchain-based data-integrity management for end-to-end IoT-Fog/Edge-Cloud integration for execution of realtime IoT applications, (e) experimental results on deploying Big Data/IoT applications in engineering, health care (e.g., COVID-19), deep learning/Artificial intelligence (AI), satellite image processing, and natural language processing (mining COVID-19 literature for new insights) on elastic Clouds, (f) QFaaS: A Serverless Function-as-a-Service Framework for Quantum Computing, and (g) new directions for emerging research in Cloud, Edge, and Quantum computing.

Keywords: Cloud Computing · Quantum Computing · Application Development Platforms · Resource Management and Scheduling · Internet of Things (IoT) Applications · Big Data applications

Designing High-Performance Distributed Systems in Cloud

Debasish Das

Amazon, India

Abstract. Building high performance distributed systems is complex and needs the application of rigour and time tested practices. Today, we would discuss the common pitfalls of building such systems, more so in the cloud, which can't be overcome by applying anecdotes, hearsay and just the work experience. In the first part of the discussion we would focus on the principles and design patterns involved in building a large-scale high performance system and in the second part we would bring in the complexity of building it in the cloud (using commodity hardware) where failure of the individual components or network partition is a common occurrence. In this discussion, we won't focus on a specific application, but we will explain the concepts using 1) a simple web application which depends on a datastore and needs synchronous response 2) an asynchronous (off-line) data processing job. We will discuss the theoretical issues of Scalability, Data Consistency and Robustness in the first part and focus on the problems created by the Faulty Hardware and Network Latency in the next. We would also discuss the Security issues in the cloud, if time permits. We will introduce the CAP theorem, Split Brain problem, Distributed Caching, Leader Election and Consensus algorithms, Gossip protocol and Clock Synchronisation (if time permits). The goal of this discussion is to shift the failure discussions to the left, while the architecture of the system is defined rather than doing it as an afterthought while the system starts failing in the production environment.

Keywords: CAP Theorem · Spilt Brain Problem · Leader Election · Gossip Protocol

Learning Networks: How to Combine Protocols, Distributed Algorithms and Machine Learning?

Jean-Marie Gorce

NSA-Lyon, Inria, France

Abstract. While machine learning has revolutionized the digital world, both in its applications and in its foundations, the deep interactions between network protocol design and decentralized algorithms are still under-explored. In this presentation, we study the problem from two complementary angles: the use of machine learning for networks, and the optimization of networks for learning. We will discuss some recent results related to distributed and federated learning, as well as the use of machine learning algorithms to control and optimize wireless networks.

Keywords: Wireless Cellular Networks · 6G · Federated Learning · Distributed Learning · Channel State Information

The Linearizability Hierarchy: An Example-Based Introduction

Michel Raynal[1,2]

[1] Univ Rennes, IRISA, Inria, CNRS, 35042 Rennes, France
[2] Department of Computing, Hong Kong Polytechnic University

Abstract. This talk is neither a survey nor a research paper in the classical sense, but an example-based introduction to the linearizability hierarchy. Its aim is to explain it in an "as simple as possible" way. While linearizability is a consistency condition that addresses objects defined by a sequential specification, set-linearizability and interval-linearizability are consistency conditions that have been introduced to take into account objects defined by a concurrent specification. So, they naturally extend linearizability (and its fundamental composability property) from sequential to concurrent objects specification. The aim of the talk is not to present the theoretical foundations of set-linearizability and interval-linearizability, but to explain concurrency patterns allowed by concurrent specifications, and show how these consistency conditions report on them. This is done in a very simple way with the help of three objects that define a family of snapshot objects. In addition to the fact that it constitutes a pedagogical introduction to the topic, this talk has also.

Keywords: Asynchrony · Concurrent Object · Concurrent Specification · Contention Point · Contention Interval · Crash Failure · Interval Linearizability · Linearizability Hierarchy · Object Specification, Modular Programming · Read/Write Register · Set-linearizability · Read/Write-Based Communication · Simultaneity, Snapshot Object · Time Ubiquity

Machine Learning and AI Applications in Drug Discovery and Healthcare

G. Narahari Sastry

Indian Institute of Technology Hyderabad, India

Abstract. Technological revolution being witnessed today largely owes to the emergence of Artificial Intelligence, and particularly machine learning, which impacted both basic and applied sciences. The ability to ask scientific questions and probing the new technological space was greatly enhanced due to the new roads made by intelligent technologies. In this talk I would like to focus on two areas, drug discovery and health care, and how these emerging technologies have metamorphosed the research practices in these fields. The impact of the AI driven technologies in hit and lead identification, lead optimization, animal and clinical trails will be analyzed with some illustrative case studies. Examples will be given where the top-niche human skills are being slowly replaced by machine learning and chatbots. Drug discovery and healthcare appear to be two different areas, but AI and ML techniques are able to bring some unusual correlations between these areas. Some of the fundamental questions on aging, metabolic disorders, degenerative diseases and geriatric care will be addressed. Importantly, how these questions can be effectively addressed by using AI and ML approaches will be explained.

Contents

Invited Paper: Security and Privacy in Large Language and Foundation Models: A Survey on GenAI Attacks

Giuseppe Francesco Italiano$^{(\boxtimes)}$ (iD), Alessio Martino (iD), and Giorgio Piccardo (iD)

LUISS Guido Carli University, Rome, Italy
{gitaliano,amartino,gpiccardo}@luiss.it

Abstract. As Large Language Models and Foundation Models continue to evolve and integrate into various aspects of our society, understanding their capabilities, limitations, and potential vulnerabilities becomes of the utmost importance. In this paper, we aim at exploring the security and privacy landscape surrounding those models in a systematic way.

Keywords: Large Language Models · Generative Artificial Intelligence · Foundation Models · Privacy · Security · Cyberattacks

1 Introduction

Large Language Models (LLMs) and Foundation Models (FMs) have revolutionized the field of Natural Language Processing (NLP), enabling remarkable advancements in language understanding and generation. The rapid progress of LLMs has been a double-edged sword: while they have demonstrated remarkable capabilities across a wide range of tasks, their deployment also raises critical concerns around data privacy, adversarial attacks, and the potential for misuse. Researchers have explored various security and privacy issues, including vulnerabilities to adversarial attacks, potential harms caused by malicious uses, and the need for robust mitigation strategies [1].

One key area of focus is the risk of private data leakage from these large models. Previous studies have shown that LLMs can be vulnerable to privacy attacks, where attackers can generate sequences from the trained model and identify those memorized from the training set. This vulnerability has been attributed to the presence of duplicated data in commonly used web-scraped training sets, as sequences that appear multiple times in the training data are more likely to be generated. In addition to data privacy concerns, LLMs are also susceptible to adversarial attacks, where malicious actors can manipulate the inputs to the model to generate harmful or misleading outputs. These vulnerabilities could be exploited to spread disinformation, generate abusive content, or even impersonate individuals. To address these challenges, researchers have proposed various

Q. Bramas et al. (Eds.): ICDCIT 2025, LNCS 15507, pp. 1–17, 2025.
https://doi.org/10.1007/978-3-031-81404-4_1

mitigation strategies, such as improved data curation, robust model training, and the development of security-focused evaluation frameworks.

As LLMs and FMs continue to evolve and integrate into various aspects of our society, understanding their capabilities, limitations, and potential vulnerabilities becomes crucial. This survey aims to explore the security and privacy landscape surrounding those models. We focus on the perspectives and guidelines provided by the NIST framework for categorizing threats and vulnerabilities in Generative AI (GenAI) systems, which provides a structured approach to analyzing the security landscape in this domain [48].

The remainder of the paper is organized as follows. In Sect. 2 we provide a quick overview of the NIST taxonomy, which will serve as a backbone for the subsequent sections. In Sect. 3 we compare to previous work in related areas. In Sect. 4 we dive into the collection of resources in this area, which will be crucial for defining a taxonomy of attacks in Sect. 5. Finally, Sect. 6 lists some concluding remarks.

2   Attacks on Generative AI Systems: A NIST Perspective

NIST has emerged as a leading authority in establishing guidelines and standards for the security and privacy of AI systems, including LLMs and FMs. In particular, the NIST framework for categorizing threats and vulnerabilities in GenAI systems offers a valuable lens through which to analyze the security and privacy landscape of LLMs and FMs. The framework identifies four main categories of attacks:

Privacy attacks: can involve the exploitation of model vulnerabilities to extract sensitive information from the training data, such as personal details or proprietary content. This type of attack poses a significant threat to the privacy of individuals and organizations whose data was used to train the models;

Integrity attacks: can involve the manipulation of model inputs or outputs to generate misinformation, abusive content, or impersonate individuals. This type of attack could undermine the trustworthiness and reliability of these models, with potentially far-reaching consequences;

Availability attacks: can target the underlying infrastructure or resources that support GenAI systems, potentially disrupting their functionality and denying access to legitimate users;

Abuse attacks: involve the exploitation of GenAI systems for malicious purposes, such as automating the creation of spam, phishing messages, or other harmful content at scale.

To address these threats, NIST has emphasized the importance of a comprehensive approach to AI security, including robust model training, secure data management, and the development of security-focused evaluation frameworks.

3   Related Work

Our survey tries to offer a unique and comprehensive contribution to the field of security and privacy in GenAI by analyzing both FMs and LLMs within the same framework. Existing surveys often focus on either FMs or LLMs, treating them as distinct research areas. Additionally, many of these surveys limit their scope to specific aspects such as performance, efficiency, or ethical concerns, rather than providing a comprehensive overview of security-related issues across both types of models. One notable exception is the survey by Fan et al. [12], which investigates the trustworthiness of state-of-the-art generative models across four dimensions: privacy, security, fairness, and responsibility, and the work by Barret et al. [5] which presents a broad overview of the security risks associated with GenAI, including LLMs. A recent survey by Yao et al. [55], provides a comprehensive overview of the security and privacy issues surrounding LLMs and FMs. It examines how these models can both enhance and threaten cybersecurity, highlighting their positive impacts, potential risks and threats, and inherent vulnerabilities. The survey categorizes the literature into "The Good", "The Bad" and "The Ugl" indicating that while LLMs have improved certain aspects like code security and data privacy, they can also be exploited for various attacks due to their advanced language capabilities.

Differently from previous work, we introduce a hierarchical taxonomy that enables a multi-faceted analysis of security incidents in LLMs and FMs. This taxonomy allows one to analyze incidents from the perspective of their impact, in terms of the consequences they can generate. This hierarchical approach can be particularly valuable in the context of risk analysis activities that characterize European regulations, from Regulation 2016/679 (GDPR) onwards. By providing a framework that aligns with these regulatory requirements, our taxonomy serves not only as a tool for understanding the technical aspects of attacks but also as a bridge between technical vulnerabilities and their broader implications for privacy, data protection, and risk management in AI systems. This addition to our work enhances its practical applicability, making it a valuable resource for both technical experts and policymakers grappling with the security challenges posed by advanced AI systems in a rapidly evolving regulatory landscape.

4   Methodology

Our methodology adheres to the Preferred Reporting Items for Systematic Reviews and Meta-Analyses (PRISMA) 2020 guidelines [35]. To ensure comprehensive coverage of the relevant literature, we conducted an extensive search across major academic databases and digital libraries, including IEEE Xplore, ACM Digital Library, arXiv, Google Scholar, and Scopus. Our search employed a carefully crafted combination of keywords related to security, privacy, LLMs, and FMs. Further, we analyzed the reference lists of included studies to identify additional relevant papers (snowballing) and conducted a forward citation search on key included papers in order to capture the most recent developments. We included very recent work (e.g., arXiv preprints), recognizing the rapidly evolving nature of the field. This allowed us to capture cutting-edge research and emerging trends that may not yet have undergone extensive peer review but could show significant promise in addressing critical security and privacy challenges in LLMs and FMs. We focused on papers and technical reports published between 2018 and 2024, with an emphasis on the most recent developments. Conversely, we excluded studies that focused solely on traditional machine learning without relevance to LLMs or FMs, lacked substantial technical depth or presented only very preliminary results.

We developed a standardized approach to extract relevant data from the included studies. The extracted information encompassed study characteristics, research objectives and methodologies, types of attacks or vulnerabilities addressed, proposed defense mechanisms or mitigation strategies, key findings and conclusions, and relevance to NIST guidelines or standards. We then synthesized this data qualitatively, focusing on identifying common themes, trends, and gaps in the current research landscape. Following the NIST framework (see Sect. 2), we classified the included studies into four main categories: Availability, Integrity, Privacy, and Abuse. Studies addressing threats to the operational continuity and performance of LLMs and FMs were classified under Availability. Research focused on preserving the correctness and trustworthiness of model outputs fell under Integrity. Studies addressing the protection of sensitive information in both training data and models were categorized under Privacy. Lastly, research on detecting and preventing the malicious use of LLMs and FMs was classified under Abuse. Within each category, we further clustered papers based on specific attack vectors and methodological approaches.

5   Taxonomy of Attacks on Generative AI Systems

This section presents a systematic analysis of security vulnerabilities in GenAI systems, with a focus on LLMs and FMs.

5.1   Availability Attacks

Availability attacks seek to disrupt the regular operation of GenAI systems, rendering them unreliable or unusable. These attacks are particularly concerning as LLMs and FMs become increasingly integrated into critical infrastructures and decision-making processes [28]. Existing research on real-world security vulnerabilities in machine learning highlights the need for a comprehensive security approach, covering software, data and model supply chains, as well as network and storage systems [2]. Since AI systems are software-based, they inherit vulnerabilities associated with traditional software supply chains. However, many GenAI tasks begin with using open-source models or data that have often been outside the scope of traditional cybersecurity efforts. For instance, prominent machine learning repositories like TensorFlow and OpenCV exhibit significant software vulnerability exposure as the resulting models are often stored in formats which allow for serialization and deserialization mechanisms that could potentially enable critical vulnerabilities such as arbitrary code execution [45]. Attackers can also disrupt the availability of GenAI systems by providing them with maliciously crafted inputs that increase computational demands or overwhelm the system, leading to denial of service. These attacks are particularly concerning when executed indirectly, where a resource rather than a registered user is the source of the availability violation. Availability attacks that increase computation can cause the model or service to perform unusually slowly [16]. This has been typically achieved by optimizing "sponge examples" [44], but with current LLMs, it could also be done by instructing the model to perform a time-intensive task in the background.

Recent advancements in autonomous agents built on LLMs have led to their increased deployment in real-world applications. These agents can enhance the capabilities of their base LLM models in various ways. Given the practical applications of these agents and their ability to perform consequential actions, it is critical to assess their potential vulnerabilities. A recent study by Tu et al. [47] introduces a new type of attack that can induce malfunctions by misleading the agent into executing repetitive or irrelevant actions. The researchers conducted comprehensive evaluations using diverse attack methods, surfaces, and properties to identify susceptible areas. Their experiments reveal that these attacks can result in failure rates exceeding 80% across multiple scenarios. By targeting implemented and deployable agents in multi-agent settings, the authors emphasize the realistic risks associated with these vulnerabilities.

One common availability attack is the model poisoning attack, where adversaries intentionally introduce harmful data into the training process. This can lead to the model producing undesirable or incorrect outputs, or even completely failing. Developers often gather data from a wide range of unvetted online sources, which can introduce vulnerabilities. Dataset providers typically only provide a list of URLs, and these hosting domains can be modified or taken over by attackers, allowing them to replace the original content. Adversaries can insert carefully crafted perturbations or corruptions into the training data, resulting in model instability, performance decline, or total model failure. This can be achieved by manipulating the data sources used to train the models or by directly injecting malicious content into the training pipeline. Researchers have investigated the vulnerabilities of LLMs and FMs to such data poisoning attacks [41]. Multimodal models that leverage both visual and linguistic inputs have also been found vulnerable to data poisoning attacks. Zang et al. [54] suggest that the linguistic modality is susceptible to such attacks, and the poisoning effect can vary across modalities. However, data poisoning attacks are often more closely linked to integrity breaches, as they seek to undermine the trustworthiness and reliability of GenAI systems by manipulating their training data.

5.2 Integrity Attacks

Integrity attacks on GenAI systems pose significant threats to their trustworthiness and reliability, particularly in critical decision-making contexts. These attacks aim to manipulate model outputs or decision-making processes, potentially leading to far-reaching consequences across various application domains.

As anticipated, data poisoning has emerged as a key vector for integrity attacks. Wallace et al. [49] introduced a novel concealed data poisoning attack that allows adversaries to control model predictions when specific trigger phrases are present in the input, without the poisoned examples explicitly containing these triggers. Their study demonstrated that inserting just 50 carefully crafted poison examples into a sentiment model's training set could cause it to frequently predict "Positive" whenever the input contained phrases like "James Bond". This attack extends beyond sentiment analysis to language modeling and machine translation tasks, highlighting its broad applicability across NLP domains. The threat of data poisoning extends to more complex AI systems, as demonstrated by PoisonedRAG attack of Zou et al. [60]. This knowledge corruption attack specifically targets Retrieval-Augmented Generation (RAG) systems, achieving high success rates across different LLMs and RAG setups under various threat models. PoisonedRAG can achieve a 90% success rate with just 5 malicious texts per target question, highlighting the efficiency and potency of this attack vector.

Adversarial examples, a well-established concept in traditional machine learning, also pose a significant threat to GenAI systems. Some works have explored imperceptible NLP attacks that use encoding-specific perturbations like invisible characters, homoglyphs, reordering, or deletions to manipulate model outputs without visible changes to the inputs [7]. These attacks can significantly degrade model performance or even functionally break most models with just a few injections. Multimodal systems are not immune to integrity attacks. Vision-Language Models (VLMs) have been shown to be susceptible to a stealthy attack method called Shadowcast [51], which uses visually indistinguishable poison samples with matching text to manipulate VLM responses. This technique has demonstrated high effectiveness in causing misidentification of class labels and crafting deceptive narratives, remaining effective across various prompts and transferable across different VLM architectures. Another example of adversarial attack, known as image hijacking, controls the behavior of VLMs at runtime and has been proposed in [4]. These images, with only small perturbations, can force the VLM to generate arbitrary outputs, leak information, override safety training, and even accept false statements. Bailey et al. [4] introduce the "Behavior Matching" algorithm to train these image hijacks, allowing them to match the behavior of an arbitrary text prompt, such as making the model believe and propagate false information ("the Eiffel Tower is now located in Rome"). This method expands the attack surface significantly, showing that adversarial images can be crafted to force VLMs to comply with harmful instructions, perform actions against the user's intentions, or produce misleading outputs. These image hijacks are shown to achieve a success rate of over 80% in various attack scenarios, indicating the robustness and effectiveness of this attack vector.

Backdoor attacks represent another critical integrity threat. Huang et al. [21] introduce a sophisticated attack that combines multiple triggers to exploit language model vulnerabilities. This approach makes it difficult to detect the malicious behavior, posing a serious threat to the integrity of LLM outputs. The complexity of these composite backdoors underscores the evolving nature of integrity attacks and the challenges in developing effective countermeasures. More advanced strategies, such as Virtual Prompt Injection (VPI), mark a significant evolution in the sophistication of attacks against LLMs. As detailed by Yan et al. [53], VPI introduces novel backdoor attack methods where the model is manipulated to respond as if an attacker-specified virtual prompt was appended to the user's input under specific trigger conditions. This approach does not require explicit intervention during inference, making it particularly insidious. By subtly poisoning the model's instruction-tuning data, an attacker can influence the model's responses to produce seemingly correct but biased or false information in targeted scenarios, while maintaining normal behavior in other contexts to evade detection.

Another family of attacks that can affect the integrity of the models are Prompt injection attacks, both direct and indirect. Direct attacks, which exploit a model's foundational instructions through malicious input injection, represent a significant threat to the intended behavior of LLMs. These attacks effectively hijack the model's decision-making process, compelling it to generate responses that breach its predefined safety boundaries [16]. Recent comprehensive surveys [25,29] have meticulously cataloged an array of attack vectors, underscoring the escalating complexity and diversity of methodologies employed to manipulate LLMs. These studies emphasize the potential for such attacks to compromise the model's integrity, resulting in the production of intentionally erroneous or misleading outputs. Among the plethora of direct attack techniques, jailbreaking stands out as a particularly notorious method. This approach grants the attacker unfettered control over the LLM for an entire interaction session, effectively circumventing filters designed to inhibit harmful content generation. Through carefully crafted prompts, malicious actors can coerce the model into producing unsafe outputs. A prime example of this is the "Do Anything Now" (DAN) attack [42], which exploits the model's instruction-following capabilities to generate toxic or misleading information by bypassing built-in safety protocols. Qi et al. [38] also explore the concept of jailbreaking through visual adversarial examples. It demonstrates how a single visual adversarial example can universally jailbreak an aligned LLM, compelling it to follow harmful instructions that it would otherwise refuse.

Roleplay variations represent another sophisticated form of direct attack. In this scenario, the model is prompted to assume the persona of a specific agent, such as a malicious hacker. This technique exploits the model's contextual adaptability, inducing it to generate false or harmful responses under the guise of a simulated scenario. The model, when tricked into adopting a nefarious role, may provide instructions or responses that it would typically refuse to generate, thereby compromising its ethical boundaries. One example is the IntentObfuscator framework [40], which is a novel black-box technique that can obscure the true intent behind user prompts for LLMs, enabling the generation of restricted or undesirable content.

Obfuscation techniques involve the strategic masking of critical input components to evade filters and induce the model to generate inappropriate content. Attackers leverage tokens like <mask>, which many LLMs are trained to reconstruct, to craft prompts that appear innocuous but lead the model to regenerate harmful or misleading content. This method allows for the circumvention of safety mechanisms, guiding the model towards producing responses that would otherwise be blocked. Payload splitting represents a more subtle approach, where a malicious input is fragmented into seemingly benign components. When processed by the LLM, these fragments coalesce into a prompt that compels the model to generate unsafe outputs. This technique exploits the model's ability to interpret and combine contextual information, allowing attackers to bypass traditional filtering mechanisms.

Indirect attacks involve manipulating the model's interactions with external tools and data sources to influence its behavior. Unlike direct attacks that target the model's alignment through crafted prompts, indirect attacks leverage the model's reliance on external elements, leading to breaches in system integrity. One common indirect attack is Indirect Prompt Injection, where adversaries strategically plant prompts in data sources likely to be accessed by the model during inference, allowing them to control the model remotely without direct interface access and causing it to produce erroneous or misleading outputs. Greshake et al. [16] explore how adversaries can exploit these interactions to compromise system integrity. Key indirect attack techniques include Token Smuggling, where an LLM is manipulated to use external interpreters to bypass safety mechanisms and reconstruct obfuscated prompts. Attackers can also embed malicious prompts in web content to influence the behavior of LLMs with browsing capabilities, leading to corrupted outputs. Another approach involves introducing hidden prompts into internal organizational tools like code-completion engines, contaminating the LLM's suggestions and altering the intended application functions. Those attacks can extend to real-world applications that integrate LLMs [9,56], such as Bing Chat [20] and code-completion engines [23]. This poses various security risks, including data theft, denial of service, and system control. For example, adversaries may manipulate the information retrieval process of an LLM by poisoning search engine results or public websites, leading to the dissemination of disinformation or biased content. Through indirect control, attackers can compel the model to execute arbitrary instructions, transform benign tools into harmful vectors, or even propagate the attack across multiple systems. In this context Wu et al. [50] show how the use of uncontrolled inputs in open-domain chatbots can be leveraged to manipulate language models, leading to unexpected or undesirable outputs.

5.3   Privacy Attacks

Privacy attacks on LLMs have emerged as a critical concern in the rapidly evolving landscape of GenAI [15,27,31]. As these models process and generate vast amounts of potentially sensitive information, they have become attractive targets for adversaries seeking to exploit vulnerabilities and extract private data.

One of the primary privacy risks associated with LLMs is the potential for data extraction. Carlini et al. [8] demonstrated that it is possible for adversaries to extract specific training data from language models, including personal and sensitive information. This vulnerability stems from the models' ability to memorize and reproduce snippets from their training data, which can include email addresses, phone numbers, and other private details. The risk is particularly acute in models trained on large, uncurated datasets scraped from the internet. The broader implications of these privacy risks are thoroughly examined by Yan et al. [52], who provide a panoramic view of the privacy threats facing LLMs, ranging from passive information leakage to more active, targeted attacks. It also offers valuable insights into the current state of privacy protection mechanisms employed in these models, highlighting both their strengths and limitations. Further contributing to our understanding of these risks, Pan et al. [36] delve into the specific ways in which LLMs may leak sensitive information about individuals represented in their training data.

Membership Inference Attacks (MIAs), which aim to determine whether a particular data point was used in training the model, represent another significant privacy threat. The work by Shokri et al. [43] has been instrumental in highlighting the feasibility of such attacks, even in black-box settings where an attacker only has query access to the model. While LLMs have shown a certain level of robustness against simple probing methods, there remain significant privacy risks when MIAs are tailored specifically for these models. Previous research, such as that by Jagielski et al. [22], suggests that basic MIAs may have limited success, often barely outperforming random guessing. However, more recent studies such as [14,30,32] have demonstrated that MIAs can achieve varying degrees of success when adapted for LLMs. For instance, the approach proposed in [30] has exhibited higher success rates, nearly doubling the effectiveness of previous methods, especially when targeting models like GPT-2. These findings indicate that while LLMs may benefit from some degree of inherent protection due to their large training datasets and the typical single-pass training regimes that encourage "forgetting", they are not completely resilient to well-crafted MIAs. In the realm of diffusion models, which have become increasingly popular in industrial applications due to their superior image generation capabilities, Pang et al. [37] designed MIAs tailored specifically for these models. Their findings indicate that white-box attacks are highly applicable in real-world scenarios and are currently the most effective. Furthermore, their attacks demonstrated commendable resilience against common defense mechanisms.

Information Gathering Attacks (IGAs) represent a broader category of privacy threats that encompass various techniques to extract sensitive information from LLMs. These attacks aim to glean private or proprietary data by exploiting the model's responses to carefully crafted queries. Unlike MIAs, which focus specifically on determining whether a particular data point was used in training, IGAs cast a wider net, seeking to extract any valuable information the model might have learned during training. This is particularly concerning when LLMs are applied within Information Retrieval (IR) systems, as highlighted by Zhu et al. [59]. LLMs used in IR systems, such as query rewriters or retrievers, process massive amounts of data and generate semantically rich results. Adversaries can exploit these advanced capabilities by crafting queries designed to extract sensitive or proprietary information. Zhu et al. discuss how LLMs' natural language generation and comprehension capabilities significantly improve the efficiency and accuracy of IR systems, but these very strengths also heighten the risk of privacy attacks. IGAs, for instance, could manipulate the model into revealing more than what a traditional IR system would disclose, inadvertently exposing confidential or proprietary data in the process.

While earlier studies have concentrated on attacks like membership inference and data extraction, recent works have expanded to include "prompt stealing" attacks, as explored by Sha and Zhang [39]. These attacks target the intricate process of prompt engineering, aiming to reconstruct original prompts used in LLMs based solely on the generated outputs. Sha and Zhang introduce a methodology that leverages a two-fold mechanism, parameter extraction and prompt reconstruction, to effectively reverse-engineer prompts. Their findings reveal that this form of attack is not only feasible but it can also achieve high accuracy, adding a new dimension to the privacy concerns surrounding LLMs. Zhang et al. [58] further examined this vulnerability in their work on prompt extraction attacks, demonstrating that these attacks can succeed even when attackers have limited access to the model. They systematically measured the effectiveness of such attacks across various models, including GPT-4 and Llama-2-chat, finding that larger and more capable models tend to have a broader attack surface, making prompt extraction more feasible.

A particularly concerning development is the emergence of attacks that can compromise privacy in federated learning settings for language models. Federated learning has long been regarded as a privacy-enhancing technique, as it enables model training across decentralized data sources without directly sharing the data itself. However, recent research indicates that even in federated settings, language models remain vulnerable to privacy attacks, challenging the assumption that federated learning alone is sufficient to protect sensitive information. The "Decepticons" attack introduced by Fowl et al. [13] demonstrates the ability to expose private user text by deploying malicious parameter vectors, even with mini-batches, multiple users, and long sequences. This attack exploits characteristics of the Transformer architecture and embeddings to extract tokens and positional information, enabling the exposure of private data.

While privacy risks associated with LLMs are diverse and significant, some researchers argue that the overall privacy risk of LLMs may be lower than that of traditional machine learning models [33]. This argument is based on LLMs' ability to capture broader distributions in their training data, which can reduce the likelihood of memorizing specific data points. Recent studies such as [22] have suggested that LLMs have an inherent tendency to "forget" training data over time, especially when data points are encountered early in the training process.

5.4   Abuse Attacks

Unlike privacy or integrity attacks, which often target the model or its training data directly, abuse attacks operate within the model's designed parameters, exploiting its outputs for nefarious ends. This distinction is significant because it implies that even a "perfectly" trained model with robust privacy protections and high integrity could still be vulnerable to abuse. The potential for misuse stems from the very capabilities that make LLMs powerful and useful, creating a unique challenge at the intersection of AI ethics, security, and societal impact [12,26,28]. Abuse attacks encompass a wide range of malicious activities, from generating sophisticated phishing content and spreading misinformation [57] to automating social engineering tactics and creating malicious code. These attacks are particularly concerning due to their potential to amplify existing cybersecurity threats and create new ones, leveraging the advanced language understanding and generation abilities of LLMs to operate at unprecedented scales and levels of sophistication.

One particularly concerning aspect of abuse attacks is their potential to amplify and streamline existing cybersecurity threats. For instance, recent research has demonstrated how LLMs can be exploited to generate highly convincing phishing emails that are personalized and contextually relevant, significantly increasing their effectiveness compared to traditional methods [19]. As shown by Bethany et al. [6] LLM-generated phishing emails pose significant challenges for current detection infrastructures. This study explores the use of LLMs to create highly targeted spear-phishing campaigns in a university setting, demonstrating that these attacks bypass existing email filters due to their human-like text and personalized content. Moreover, the ability of LLMs to generate human-like text at scale presents unprecedented challenges in combating misinformation and disinformation campaigns. Malicious actors can potentially use these models to flood online platforms with seemingly diverse but artificially generated content, manipulating public opinion or spreading false narratives with unprecedented efficiency. Tsamados et al. [46] underscore the urgency of addressing these risks, emphasizing the need for robust cybersecurity practices specifically tailored to manage LLM-related threats.

Another critical area of concern is the potential misuse of LLMs for generating malicious code or automating the creation of malware. While LLMs have shown promise in assisting with code generation and vulnerability detection, this capability can be double-edged. Attackers might leverage these models to rapidly prototype malware, create polymorphic variants, or even discover and exploit new vulnerabilities in software systems. For instance, Gupta et al. [18] highlight the alarming capability of LLMs like ChatGPT to automate hacking processes, generate malware, and assist in creating polymorphic malware, which can evade traditional detection mechanisms. The authors demonstrate how jail-breaking techniques can bypass model safeguards, allowing malicious code to be generated, including examples of ransomware and other malicious payloads. On the other side, Deng et al. [10] introduce the MASTERKEY framework, which systematically explores jailbreak attacks and potential countermeasures. The framework features a novel approach for automatically generating jailbreak prompts aimed at bypassing the defenses of well-secured chatbots. Notably, the framework achieved a 21.58% success rate in circumventing chatbot safeguards.

We note that malicious exploitation is not limited to text generation models. As highlighted by Bagdasaryan et al. [3] attackers can manipulate images or audio clips to covertly instruct the model to produce harmful or manipulated responses without the user's awareness. This type of attack takes advantage of the context-sensitive nature of multi-modal LLMs, bypassing traditional content filters and safeguards designed to detect malicious activity, thereby enabling the generation of harmful outputs. Similarity, Niu et al. [34] outline a technique to circumvent the safety mechanisms of multimodal LLMs, enabling the generation of potentially harmful responses to user inputs. The authors propose a maximum likelihood-based algorithm to construct an "image jailbreaking prompt" that can be used to bypass the safeguards implemented in various multimodal LLMs.

The ethical implications of abuse attacks extend beyond immediate security concerns, touching on issues of privacy, consent, and the societal impact of GenAI technologies. As highlighted by Kumar et al. [24], there is a pressing need to develop ethical frameworks and assessment tools to guide the development and deployment of LLMs, ensuring they respect user privacy and dignity while mitigating potential for abuse. Additionally, Guo et al. [17] elaborate on the broader public safety concerns that arise from the misuse of GenAI technologies like ChatGPT. It highlights that advanced AI models can not only create malicious content but also threaten societal structures through the production of deceptive or dangerous materials that could compromise public trust, governance, and security. Recent research has also explored confidentiality issues in LLM-integrated systems. For instance, Evertz et al. [11] explore how LLMs, when integrated with external services, are vulnerable to leaking sensitive information due to their interaction with malicious tools. These confidentiality risks highlight the necessity for robust security measures that go beyond protecting the model's training data and extend to its operational environment.

6   Conclusions

This survey has highlighted the complex and rapidly evolving landscape of security and privacy in LLMs and FMs. By examining these issues through the prism of the NIST, we have uncovered several critical insights and implications for the field. Foremost, the survey underscores the dual nature of LLMs and FMs in the context of cybersecurity. These powerful AI systems have demonstrated significant potential to enhance various security aspects, including code vulnerability detection, data privacy protection, and automated security analysis. Concurrently, they introduce novel and formidable security challenges beyond those associated with traditional machine learning systems. The ability of these models to generate human-like text and multi-modal content at scale presents unique risks, such as sophisticated social engineering attacks, misinformation generation, and potential leakage of sensitive information. Our taxonomy of attacks reveals the multifaceted nature of threats facing GenAI systems. Following the NIST framework, we have categorized these threats into four main areas: availability, integrity, privacy, and abuse. Availability attacks, such as data poisoning and denial of service, threaten the operational continuity of these models. Integrity attacks, including backdoor poisoning and prompt injection, undermine the trustworthiness of model outputs. Privacy attacks demonstrate the potential for unauthorized access to training data and model information. Abuse attacks highlight the dual-use nature of these powerful AI systems, showcasing how their intended functionalities can be exploited for malicious purposes. Looking ahead, the field of security and privacy in GenAI is likely to remain dynamic and challenging. As these models become more powerful and widely deployed, the potential impact of security breaches or misuse is expected to grow exponentially in the near future.

Acknowledgments. Giuseppe F. Italiano was partially supported by the Italian Ministry of University and Research under PRIN Project n. 2022TS4Y3N - EXPAND: scalable algorithms for EXPloratory Analyses of heterogeneous and dynamic Networked Data.

Disclosure of Interests. The authors have no competing interests to declare that are relevant to the content of this article.

References

1. Abdali, S., Anarfi, R., Barberan, C., et al.: Securing Large Language Models: Threats, Vulnerabilities and Responsible Practices. arXiv preprint arXiv:2403.12503 (2024)
2. Apruzzese, G., Anderson, H.S., Dambra, S., et al.: "Real attackers don't compute gradients": bridging the gap between adversarial ML research and practice. In: 2023 IEEE Conference on Secure and Trustworthy Machine Learning (SaTML), pp. 339–364 (2023)
3. Bagdasaryan, E., Hsieh, T.Y., Nassi, B., et al.: (Ab)using Images and Sounds for Indirect Instruction Injection in Multi-Modal LLMs. arXiv preprint arXiv:2307.10490 (2023)
4. Bailey, L., Ong, E., Russell, S., et al.: Image hijacks: adversarial images can control generative models at runtime. arXiv preprint arXiv:2309.00236 (2023)
5. Barrett, C., Boyd, B., Bursztein, E., et al.: Identifying and mitigating the security risks of generative AI. Found. Trends® Priv. Secur. **6**(1), 1–52 (2023)
6. Bethany, M., Galiopoulos, A., Bethany, E., et al.: Large language model lateral spear phishing: a comparative study in large-scale organizational settings. arXiv preprint arXiv:2401.09727 (2024)

7. Boucher, N., Shumailov, I., Anderson, R., et al.: Bad characters: imperceptible NLP attacks. In: 2022 IEEE Symposium on Security and Privacy (SP), pp. 1987–2004. IEEE (2022)
8. Carlini, N., Jagielski, M., Zhang, C., et al.: The privacy onion effect: memorization is relative. In: Koyejo, S., Mohamed, S., Agarwal, A., Belgrave, D., Cho, K., Oh, A. (eds.) Advances in Neural Information Processing Systems, vol. 35, pp. 13263–13276. Curran Associates, Inc. (2022)
9. Chen, B., Wang, G., Guo, H., et al.: Understanding multi-turn toxic behaviors in open-domain chatbots. In: Proceedings of the 26th International Symposium on Research in Attacks, Intrusions and Defenses, RAID 2023, pp. 282–296. ACM, New York (2023)
10. Deng, G., Liu, Y., Li, Y., et al.: Masterkey: automated jailbreaking of large language model chatbots. In: Proceedings 2024 Network and Distributed System Security Symposium. NDSS 2024, Internet Society (2024)
11. Evertz, J., Chlosta, M., Schönherr, L., et al.: Whispers in the machine: confidentiality in LLM-integrated systems. arXiv preprint arXiv:2402.06922 (2024)
12. Fan, M., Chen, C., Wang, C., et al.: On the trustworthiness landscape of state-of-the-art generative models: a comprehensive survey. arXiv preprint arXiv:2307.16680 (2023)
13. Fowl, L.H., Geiping, J., Reich, S., et al.: Decepticons: corrupted transformers breach privacy in federated learning for language models. In: The 11th International Conference on Learning Representations, pp. 1–23 (2023)
14. Fu, W., Wang, H., Gao, C., et al.: Practical membership inference attacks against fine-tuned large language models via self-prompt calibration. arXiv preprint arXiv:2311.06062 (2023)
15. Golda, A., Mekonen, K., Pandey, A., et al.: Privacy and security concerns in generative AI: a comprehensive survey. IEEE Access **12**, 48126–48144 (2024)
16. Greshake, K., Abdelnabi, S., Mishra, S., et al.: Not what you've signed up for: compromising real-world LLM-integrated applications with indirect prompt injection. In: Proceedings of the 16th ACM Workshop on Artificial Intelligence and Security, AISec 2023, pp. 79–90. ACM, New York (2023)
17. Guo, D., Chen, H., Wu, R., et al.: AIGC challenges and opportunities related to public safety: a case study of ChatGPT. J. Saf. Sci. Resil. **4**(4), 329–339 (2023)
18. Gupta, M., Akiri, C., Aryal, K., et al.: From ChatGPT to ThreatGPT: impact of generative AI in cybersecurity and privacy. IEEE Access **11**, 80218–80245 (2023)
19. Heiding, F., Schneier, B., Vishwanath, A., et al.: Devising and detecting phishing emails using large language models. IEEE Access **12**, 42131–42146 (2024)
20. Hines, K., Lopez, G., Hall, M., et al.: Defending against indirect prompt injection attacks with spotlighting. arXiv preprint arXiv:2403.14720 (2024)
21. Huang, H., Zhao, Z., Backes, M., et al.: Composite backdoor attacks against large language models. In: Duh, K., Gomez, H., Bethard, S. (eds.) Findings of the Association for Computational Linguistics: NAACL 2024, pp. 1459–1472. Association for Computational Linguistics, Mexico City, Mexico (2024)
22. Jagielski, M., Thakkar, O., Tramer, F., et al.: Measuring forgetting of memorized training examples. In: The 11th International Conference on Learning Representations, pp. 1–22 (2023)
23. Kang, D., Li, X., Stoica, I., et al.: Exploiting programmatic behavior of LLMs: dual-use through standard security attacks. In: 2024 IEEE Security and Privacy Workshops (SPW), pp. 132–143. IEEE, Los Alamitos, CA, USA (2024)
24. Kumar, A., Singh, S., Murty, S.V., et al.: The ethics of interaction: mitigating security threats in LLMs. arXiv preprint arXiv:2401.12273 (2024)

25. Kumar, S.S., Cummings, M.L., Stimpson, A.: Strengthening LLM trust boundaries: a survey of prompt injection attacks. In: 2024 IEEE 4th International Conference on Human-Machine Systems (ICHMS), pp. 1–6 (2024)
26. Le, T.N., Nguyen, H.H., Yamagishi, J., et al.: Robust deepfake on unrestricted media: generation and detection. In: Khosravy, M., Echizen, I., Babaguchi, N. (eds.) Frontiers in Fake Media Generation and Detection, pp. 81–107. Springer, Singapore (2022)
27. Li, H., Chen, Y., Luo, J., et al.: Privacy in large language models: attacks, defenses and future directions. arXiv preprint arXiv:2310.10383 (2023)
28. Liao, Q.V., Wortman Vaughan, J.: AI Transparency in the Age of LLMs: A Human-Centered Research Roadmap. Harvard Data Science Review (Special Issue 5) (2024)
29. Liu, Y., Deng, G., Li, Y., et al.: Prompt Injection attack against LLM-integrated Applications. arXiv preprint arXiv:2306.05499 (2023)
30. Mattern, J., Mireshghallah, F., Jin, Z., et al.: Membership inference attacks against language models via neighbourhood comparison. In: Rogers, A., Boyd-Graber, J., Okazaki, N. (eds.) Findings of the Association for Computational Linguistics: ACL 2023, pp. 11330–11343. Association for Computational Linguistics, Toronto, Canada (2023)
31. Miranda, M., Ruzzetti, E.S., Santilli, A., et al.: Preserving privacy in large language models: a survey on current threats and solutions. arXiv preprint arXiv:2408.05212 (2024)
32. Mireshghallah, F., Goyal, K., Uniyal, A., et al.: Quantifying privacy risks of masked language models using membership inference attacks. In: Goldberg, Y., Kozareva, Z., Zhang, Y. (eds.) Proceedings of the 2022 Conference on Empirical Methods in Natural Language Processing, pp. 8332–8347. Association for Computational Linguistics, Abu Dhabi, United Arab Emirates (2022)
33. Neel, S., Chang, P.: Privacy issues in large language models: a survey. arXiv preprint arXiv:2312.06717 (2023)
34. Niu, Z., Ren, H., Gao, X., et al.: Jailbreaking attack against multimodal large language model. arXiv preprint arXiv:2402.02309 (2024)
35. Page, M.J., Moher, D., Bossuyt, P.M., et al.: PRISMA 2020 explanation and elaboration: updated guidance and exemplars for reporting systematic reviews. BMJ **372** (2021)
36. Pan, X., Zhang, M., Ji, S., et al.: Privacy risks of general-purpose language models. In: 2020 IEEE Symposium on Security and Privacy (SP), pp. 1314–1331 (2020)
37. Pang, Y., Wang, T., Kang, X., et al.: White-box membership inference attacks against diffusion models. arXiv preprint arXiv:2308.06405 (2023)
38. Qi, X., Huang, K., Panda, A., et al.: Visual adversarial examples jailbreak aligned large language models. In: The 38th AAAI Conference on Artificial Intelligence (AAAI 2024), pp. 21527–21536 (2024)
39. Sha, Z., Zhang, Y.: Prompt stealing attacks against large language models. arXiv preprint arXiv:2402.12959 (2024)
40. Shang, S., Yao, Z., Yao, Y., et al.: Intentobfuscator: a jailbreaking method via confusing LLM with prompts. In: Garcia-Alfaro, J., Kozik, R., Choraś, M., Katsikas, S. (eds.) Computer Security - ESORICS 2024, pp. 146–165. Springer, Cham (2024)
41. Shayegani, E., Mamun, M.A.A., Fu, Y., et al.: Survey of vulnerabilities in large language models revealed by adversarial attacks. arXiv preprint arXiv:2310.10844 (2023)

42. Shen, X., Chen, Z., Backes, M., et al.: "Do Anything Now": Characterizing and Evaluating In-The-Wild Jailbreak Prompts on Large Language Models. arXiv preprint arXiv:2308.03825 (2023)
43. Shokri, R., Stronati, M., Song, C., et al.: Membership inference attacks against machine learning models. In: 2017 IEEE Symposium on Security and Privacy (SP), pp. 3–18 (2017)
44. Shumailov, I., Zhao, Y., Bates, D., et al.: Sponge examples: energy-latency attacks on neural networks. In: 2021 IEEE European Symposium on Security and Privacy (EuroS&P), pp. 212–231 (2021)
45. Tidjon, L.N., Khomh, F.: Threat Assessment in Machine Learning based Systems. arXiv preprint arXiv:2207.00091 (2022)
46. Tsamados, A., Floridi, L., Taddeo, M.: The cybersecurity crisis of artificial intelligence: unrestrained adoption and natural language-based attacks. arXiv preprint arXiv:2311.09224 (2023)
47. Tu, J., Wang, T., Wang, J., et al.: Adversarial attacks on multi-agent communication. In: 2021 IEEE/CVF International Conference on Computer Vision (ICCV), pp. 7748–7757. IEEE Computer Society, Los Alamitos, CA, USA (2021)
48. Vassilev, A., Oprea, A., Fordyce, A., et al.: Adversarial machine learning: a taxonomy and terminology of attacks and mitigations. Technical report, National Institute of Standards and Technology (2023)
49. Wallace, E., Zhao, T., Feng, S., et al.: Concealed data poisoning attacks on NLP models. In: Toutanova, K., Rumshisky, A., Zettlemoyer, L., et al. (eds.) Proceedings of the 2021 Conference of the North American Chapter of the Association for Computational Linguistics: Human Language Technologies, pp. 139–150. Association for Computational Linguistics (2021)
50. Wu, F., Zhang, N., Jha, S., et al.: A New Era in LLM Security: Exploring Security Concerns in Real-World LLM-based Systems. arXiv preprint arXiv:2402.18649 (2024)
51. Xu, Y., Yao, J., Shu, M., et al.: Shadowcast: stealthy data poisoning attacks against vision-language models. arXiv preprint arXiv:2402.06659 (2024)
52. Yan, B., Li, K., Xu, M., et al.: On Protecting the Data Privacy of Large Language Models (LLMs): A Survey. arXiv preprint arXiv:2403.05156 (2024)
53. Yan, J., Yadav, V., Li, S., et al.: Backdooring instruction-tuned large language models with virtual prompt injection. In: Duh, K., Gomez, H., Bethard, S. (eds.) Proceedings of the 2024 Conference of the North American Chapter of the Association for Computational Linguistics: Human Language Technologies (Volume 1: Long Papers), pp. 6065–6086. Association for Computational Linguistics, Mexico City, Mexico (2024)
54. Yang, Z., He, X., Li, Z., et al.: Data poisoning attacks against multimodal encoders. In: Proceedings of the 40th International Conference on Machine Learning. ICML 2023. JMLR.org (2023)
55. Yao, Y., Duan, J., Xu, K., et al.: A survey on large language model (LLM) security and privacy: the good, the bad, and the ugly. High-Confidence Comput. 4(2), 100211 (2024)
56. Yu, J., Wu, Y., Shu, D., et al.: Assessing prompt injection risks in 200+ custom GPTs. arXiv preprint arXiv:2311.11538 (2023)
57. Yu, X., Wang, Y., Chen, Y., et al.: Fake Artificial Intelligence Generated Contents (FAIGC): A Survey of Theories, Detection Methods, and Opportunities. arXiv preprint arXiv:2405.00711 (2024)
58. Zhang, Y., Carlini, N., Ippolito, D.: Effective prompt extraction from language models. In: First Conference on Language Modeling, pp. 1–26 (2024)

59. Zhu, Y., Yuan, H., Wang, S., et al.: Large Language Models for Information Retrieval: A Survey. arXiv preprint arXiv:2308.07107 (2023)
60. Zou, W., Geng, R., Wang, B., et al.: PoisonedRAG: Knowledge Corruption Attacks to Retrieval-Augmented Generation of Large Language Models. arXiv preprint arXiv:2402.07867 (2024)

Invited Paper: Application of Physics-Based and Data-Driven Approaches for Drug-Like Property Prediction

Natarajan Arul Murugan[1(✉)] and Garikapati Narahari Sastry[1,2]

[1] Department of Computational Biology, Indraprastha Institute of Information Technology, Okhla Phase III Industrial Area, New Delhi 110020, New Delhi, India
arul.murugan@iiitd.ac.in, gnsastry@bt.iith.ac.in
[2] Department of Biotechnology, Indian Institute of Technology, Hyderabad, Hyderabad 10587, Telangana, India .

Abstract. Drug discovery projects involve the identification of hits or lead compounds having favorable drug-like properties. In other words, it is a multivariate optimization problem and the properties to be optimized are binding affinity, binding specificity, ADMET properties, solubility, and bioavailability. Computationally these properties can be estimated using physics-based and data-driven models. In the physics based models, the drug-like properties are computed as free energy differences. In data-driven models, the molecules are described numerically using various descriptors and finger-prints and machine learning and deep learning models can be built using dataset of descriptors/finger-prints and corresponding drug-like properties available from experiments. The physics-based models are usually computationally demanding and so are limited to smaller chemical space. However ML/DL models, can be applied to compute the drug-like properties of huge chemical libraries such as GDB17, Real Enamine DB, ZINC having more than billion compounds. The implementation, merits and demerits of these two approaches will be discussed in some detail in this paper.

Keywords: Machine learning · Deep Learning · Molecular Graph Representation · Druggability prediction · Physics based models

1 Introduction

The earlier predictive models in physics, chemistry, biology and materials science were physics based models where the systems' structure, dynamics and properties were dictated by equations governed by classical machanics or quantum mechanics. As per classical mechanics, any systems' structure and dynamics can be predicted by solving Newton's equation of motion given that initial configuration at a time zero along with the force-field describing the interactions of the system is known. Similarly, in quantum mechanics any properties is computable

Q. Bramas et al. (Eds.): ICDCIT 2025, LNCS 15507, pp. 18–23, 2025.
https://doi.org/10.1007/978-3-031-81404-4_2

once the molecular or all-electron wavefunction or the electron density is known for the given molecular system. The application of quantum mechanics for large sized systems such as molecular crystals, protein, protein-ligand, protein-protein complexes becomes difficult as the time complexity grows as much as N^3 to N^9 (here N refers to the number of one electron wavefunction or orbital) depending upon the level of theory employed [1]. Even in the classical mechanics driven computational approaches such as molecular dynamics, the time complexity goes as N^2 and in this case N refers to number of atoms in the system [2]. Alternatively, the machine learning (ML) and deep learning (DL) approaches were employed where the properties can be written as the dependent variable which depends on the numerous features and finger-prints of chemicals. In general, the descriptors and finger-prints carry information on the bioactivity, chemical, physico-chemical properties of the chemicals. Earlier, simplified machine learning models were referred to as quantitative structure activity relationship (QSAR) [3] which related the drug-like properties to various physico-chemical properties such as lipophilicity through simple or multiple linear regression models. The recent ML and DL models [4,5] can capture complex dependence of the drug-like properties to various physico-chemical properties, descriptors and finger-prints of the molecules. Unless like the physics based models, the data driven approaches which include QSAR, ML and DL require the dataset relating the chemical entities to drug-like properties such as binding affinity, binding specificity, ADMET properties, solubility, permeability, bio-availability. The time complexity of ML and DL models during the training depends on the number of epochs (number of iterations used for building models on training dataset). However, during the test phase, the time complexity grows as $N \times M$ where N refers to number of samples and M refers to number of features. Further, the size of the features and finger-prints is prefixed and does not change with the size of the molecules itself. These features are highly advantageous over the physics based models where the time complexity grows as N^2 to N^9.

2 Applications of Physics-Based and Data-Driven Approaches for Druggability Prediction

The use of machine learning and deep learning methods has revolutionized many areas in science, engineering, medicine and technology. The application of deep learning models for diagnosis [6] of various diseases in their early and advanced stages based on the medical images from fMRI, CT and PET-scans can be alternative and more reliable approach when compared to human counterpart. Advantageously, the deep-learning based diagnosis can be free from human bias due to subjective perception of reality or emotional or mental status of the observer [7]. Similarly, the domain of drug discovery can also benefit enormously from the use of machine learning and deep learning models. In this paper, our main objective is to discuss the applications of both physics based and machine learning and deep learning based approaches to drug discovery applications. The drug discovery in general is multivariate optimization problem where various properties such as binding affinity, binding specificity, absorption, distribution, metabolism, excretion, toxicity, solubility, bio-availability need to be optimized simultaneously. Among these the properties such as binding affinity, binding specificity, toxicity are of paramount importance to be optimal, while the solubility and permeability can be compromised to certain extend through alternative drug-delivery routes such as intravenous injection or nanoparticle mediated drug-delivery. All these drug-like properties can be computed using physics-based methods such as molecular docking, molecular dynamics, and free energy calculations. These properties can be related to free energy difference of the ligands in biological, polar and non-polar solvent and crystalline environments [8]. The binding affinity can be computed as the free energy difference of the ligand in target biomolecule and water medium. The permeability and partition coefficient can be computed from the free energy difference of the ligand in membrane and water environments. Similarly, solubility can be estimated from the free energy difference of the ligand in crystalline and water environments. So, the reliability of the physics based models in predicting various drug-like properties is dependent on chemical accuracy of the computed free energies of the ligands in different environments. The physics based approaches rely on the parametrization of the force-field which describes the interaction between the subsystems and intramolecular dynamics within the subsystems. Due to various approximation involved in the force-field parametrization, the chemical accuracies cannot be lowered down to a few kcal/mol. This has been the main reason why the drug-like properties are often difficult to compute accurately using force-field based methods. More over, the absolute free energies are not of any relevance but the difference in free energies between the ligands and so their relative difference in binding affinities or other drug-like properties are important in these studies. There are numerous bench-marking studies on predicting the binding affinities which employ different scoring functions as implemented in softwares such as Autodock4.0, Autdock Vina, Dock6, Glide. The docking energies (which is proportional to binding affinities and association constants) as obtained from these molecular docking softwares generally account for van der Walls, electrostatic, hydrogen bonding, solvation energies and entropic contributions due to torsional degrees of freedom. However, the docking energies are computed for the most stable protein-ligand complex structure and so does not account for contributions due to thermally weighted configurations of the protein-ligand complex. The molecular mechanics-Generalized Born(Poisson Boltzmann) surface area (MM-GB(PB)SA) [9] approaches consider these contributions as well which have shown to be better in ranking the protein-ligand complexes in certain studies. These studies use the configurations for the protein-ligand complexes from molecular dynamics simulations and employ implicit solvent description for estimating the solvation energies. There were many benchmark studies to evaluate the performance of these physics based approaches in predicting the binding affinity and binding pose of the ligands when they are bound to biomolecular targets. It was concluded that certain molecular docking software is more suited for binding affinity prediction while other for binding pose prediction [10]. In addition, the performance results also depend on the target proteins. Recently, through the elegant use of fragmentation scheme, quantum mechanics was employed for the free energy calculations for protein-ligand complexes. Due to the computational demand, QM fragmentation or DFT/MM calculations were employed for limited number of systems but shown promising results when compared to force-field based approaches.

2.1 Various Biological and Chemical Databases for ML/DL Model Building

There has been enormous progress in the field of experimental biology and chemistry focusing on studying various protein-protein and protein-ligand interactions and measuring various physicochemical properties of ligands (such as partition coefficient, lipophilicity, hydrophilicity and so on), and this has generated rich amount of experimental data available for developing ML/DL models for various drug-like properties. To mention a few, the GeneBank contains about 0.25 Billion DNA sequences which are annotated based on the organism of origin, function, and mutations which can be used to develop machine learning models for characterizing the protein/gene function based on the sequence information. The protein databank contains about 227111 structures for proteins, protein-protein, protein-dna, protein-rna and protein-ligand complexes which can be used to develop ML/DL models for binding affinity and binding specificity prediction. The BindingDB [11] and PDBBind [12] are the other two databases with known association constants and 3D structures for protein-ligand complexes and so can be used to build structure based ML/DL models for binding affinity prediction. The ChEMBL database contains the activity and physicochemical properties of 2.4 M compounds, which can be exploited for developing models for bioactivity, permeability, toxicity, and so on. The Cambridge structure database contains about 1.25 M 3D structures for organic molecules and inorganic complexes which eventually can be used to build models for solubility and bio-availability. The DrugBank database contains information about drugs, protein-drug interactions and can be utilized to build models on binding affinity and binding specificity (Table 1).

Table 1. List of chemical and biological databases for ML/DL models for druggability prediction

Database	Nature of database	Drug-like property
GeneBank	Biological	Binding affinity/specificity
Protein databank	Biological and chemical	Binding affinity, specificity
Cambridge crystallographic DB	Chemical	Solubility, bio-availability
ChEMBL	Biological and chemical	Binding affinity, specificity, permeability
DrugBank	Biological and chemical	Binding affinity, specificity, toxicity
PDBBind, BindingDB	Biological and chemical	Binding affinity, specificity

Using the aforementioned databases such as GeneBank, CSD, PDB, Bind-ingDB, PDBBind, DrugBank DB which are associating the chemicals to various biological activity and properties, one can develop different machine learning and deep learning models for predicting various drug-like properties. Here, one can use two different representations for molecules to develop these models. The databases usually contain the molecules in the SMILES (refers to Simplified Molecular Input Line Entry System) representation which is linear (1D) string representation. In this representation even the aromatic structures are repre-sented linearly by opening along a chemical bond and the atoms involved in the bonding are numerically labeled. Further, the molecules in SMILES format are converted into mol (2D) and mol2 (3D) formats, which then were used to esti-mate various molecular descriptors (which are characterized as 1D, 2D, and 3D) based on their dimensionalities. In stead of the descriptors which adopt contin-uous values, molecules also can be represented as fingerprints which are binary representation of chemical structures. A fixed size array with binary values is used for the finger-print representation and 0 and 1 represents the presence or absence of functional group or substructure within the molecule. These features and finger-prints were used to develop various machine-learning models. Alter-natively, the molecules can be represented as molecular graphs, which were then used for developing graph neural network-based models (which are similar to convolutional neural network models built on images). The graph representa-tion also include the node features, and edge-features to describe the chemical nature of the atoms in molecules in a more realistic way. There are various studies on the druggability prediction using descriptors, finger-prints and molec-ular graph representations. There are very limited studies which compare the performance of descriptors/finger-prints based models to molecular graph based representation [13].

3 Discussion

The main objectives in the drug discovery projects is the identification of hits and lead compounds which should exhibit superior drug-like properties such as binding affinity, specificity and favorable pharmacokinetic and pharmacody-namic properties. The current paper discusses about the different computational models available for estimating various drug-like properties. In particular, dif-ferent physics-based and data-driven approaches are discussed along with their merits and limitations. The time complexity of the physics based approaches is in the order of N^2 to N^9 and so can be challenging to apply for a larger biological or chemical databases. The data-driven approach can be very handy to develop predictive models for drug-like properties and then can be used to screen chem-ical libraries having more than billion compounds. Care should be taken that the experimental results may have errors associated due to difference in mea-surement conditions and this may affect the accuracy of the models. The main advantage of physics-based model is that the prediction can be made for any new molecular entities but the data-driven approach requires a dataset which relates the chemical entities to properties.

4 Conclusion

The high-throughput experimental screening to identify hits or leads for the drug-discovery can be very demanding in terms of cost, use of human resources and time. It is necessary to employ the predictive models to optimize the drug-like properties in these compounds. Once the search space can be narrowed down to a few hundreds compounds, the wet-lab validation can be carried out. We have discussed about the merits, and limitations of various physics-based on data-driven approaches for druggability prediction. Data-driven and physics-based models can be employed in a sequential manner so that the success rate in the computational screening is significantly improved.

References

1. Ratcliff, L.E., Mohr, S., Huhs, G., Deutsch, T., Masella, M., Genovese, L.: Challenges in large scale quantum mechanical calculations. Wiley Interdisc. Rev. Comput. Mol. Sci. **7**(1), 1290 (2017)
2. Zhou, K., Liu, B.: Molecular Dynamics Simulation: Fundamentals and Applications. Academic Press (2022)
3. Tropsha, A., Isayev, O., Varnek, A., Schneider, G., Cherkasov, A.: Integrating QSAR modelling and deep learning in drug discovery: the emergence of deep QSAR. Nat. Rev. Drug Discov. **23**(2), 141–155 (2024)
4. Elbadawi, M., Gaisford, S., Basit, A.W.: Advanced machine-learning techniques in drug discovery. Drug Discov. Today **26**(3), 769–777 (2021)
5. Murugan, N.A., Priya, G.R., Sastry, G.N., Markidis, S.: Artificial intelligence in virtual screening: models versus experiments. Drug Discov. Today **27**(7), 1913–1923 (2022)
6. Aggarwal, R., et al.: Diagnostic accuracy of deep learning in medical imaging: a systematic review and meta-analysis. NPJ Digit. Med. **4**(1), 65 (2021)
7. Topol, E.J.: High-performance medicine: the convergence of human and artificial intelligence. Nat. Med. **25**(1), 44–56 (2019)
8. Cheng, A.C.: Predicting selectivity and druggability in drug discovery. Annu. Rep. Comput. Chem **4**, 23–37 (2008)
9. Genheden, S., Ryde, U.: The MM/PBSA and MM/GBSA methods to estimate ligand-binding affinities. Expert Opin. Drug Discov. **10**(5), 449–461 (2015)
10. Nguyen, N.T., et al.: Autodock vina adopts more accurate binding poses but autodock4 forms better binding affinity. J. Chem. Inf. Model. **60**(1), 204–211 (2019)
11. Liu, T., Lin, Y., Wen, X., Jorissen, R.N., Gilson, M.K.: BindingDB: a web-accessible database of experimentally determined protein-ligand binding affinities. Nucleic Acids Res. **35**(suppl_1), 198–201 (2006)
12. Liu, Z., et al.: PDB-wide collection of binding data: current status of the PDB-bind database. Bioinformatics **31**(3), 405–412 (2014). https://doi.org/10.1093/bioinformatics/btu626
13. Jiang, D., et al.: Could graph neural networks learn better molecular representation for drug discovery? A comparison study of descriptor-based and graph-based models. J. Cheminform. **13**, 1–23 (2021)

Invited Paper: Distributed Computability: A Few Results Masters Students Should Know

Michel Raynal[1,2]([⊠])

[1] Univ Rennes, IRISA, Inria, CNRS, 35042 Rennes, France
[2] Department of Computing, Hong Kong Polytechnic University, Hung Hom, Hong Kong
michel.raynal@irisa.fr

Abstract. As today Informatics is more and more (~~driven~~) eaten by its applications, it becomes more and more important to know what can be done and what cannot be done. For a long time now, this is well known in sequential computing. But today the world becomes more and more distributed, and consequently more and more applications are distributed. As a result, it becomes important, or even crucial, to understand what is distributed computing and which are its power and its limits. This article is a step in this direction when looking from an agreement-oriented fault-tolerance point of view.

> Teaching is not an accumulation of facts.
> L. Lamport [59]

> Correctness may be theoretical, ... but incorrectness has practical impact.
> M. Herlihy

> - Don't you have a more recent newspaper? I've known these news for two days.
> - Read them again. In a few days they will be new again.
> *La Marca del viento* (2019), Eduardo Fernando Valera

1 Introduction

1.1 Sequential and Parallel Computing

Sequential Computing. All curricula in informatics have a section devoted to computability in sequential computing. It follows that students know fundamental results such as

- the automata hierarchy, namely: Finite State automata $\subsetneq$ Pushdown automata $\subsetneq$ Turing machine,
- the Church-Turing *thesis* stating that everything that can be mechanically computed can be computed by a Turing machine,

© The Author(s), under exclusive license to Springer Nature Switzerland AG 2025
Q. Bramas et al. (Eds.): ICDCIT 2025, LNCS 15507, pp. 24–44, 2025.
https://doi.org/10.1007/978-3-031-81404-4_3

- the impossibility to solve some well-defined problems (such that the halting problem [96]),
- The impossibility to bypass some bounds (for example design a comparison-based sorting algorithm whose number of comparisons is always smaller than $O(n \ \log n)$, where n is the number of elements to sort).
- The notion of non-determinism and the P $\neq$ NP conjecture.

This basic theoretical knowledge, together with algorithms and programming, constitutes the pillars on which stands sequential computing.

Parallel Computing. Parallel computing was introduced to solve *efficiency* issues [98]. As in the recursive thinking, the idea is to decompose a problem Pb in independent sub-problems, and then recompose their solutions to obtain a solution to Pb. Said in an other way, the key of parallel computing is *data independence*. It consists in making data (or blocs of data) independent of each other, so that they can be processed independently the ones from the others –i.e. without interactions–, which, from an efficiency point of view, means processing them simultaneously.

The decomposition of the set of input data in independent data is under the control of the programmer and constitutes the core of the design of parallel algorithms. Put it differently, if efficiency was not the issue, the problems addressed in parallel computing could be solved with a sequential algorithm.

1.2   Distributed Computing

An Informal View (from [80]). Distributed computing was born in the late 1970s when researchers and practitioners started taking into account the intrinsic characteristic of physically distributed systems. The field then emerged as a specialized research area distinct from networking, operating systems, and parallel computing.

Distributed Computing arises when one has to solve a problem in terms of pre-defined distributed entities (usually called processors, nodes, processes, actors, agents, sensors, peers, etc.) such that   *each entity has only a partial knowledge* of the many parameters involved in the problem that has to be solved. While parallel computing and real-time computing can be characterized, respectively, by the terms *efficiency* and *on-time computing*, distributed computing can be characterized by the term *coordination in the presence of uncertainty*. In distributed computing, the computing entities are not defined by the programmer but *imposed* to her, who has to allow them to correctly *cooperate*.

This uncertainty is created by asynchrony, multiplicity of control flows, absence of shared memory and global time, failure, dynamicity, mobility, etc., all called *adversaries*. The set of the adversaries defines what is called the *environment*. Let us notice that the environment constitutes an implicit and unknown input of any distributed execution (in the sense it can affect the result produced by the execution).

Mastering one form or another of uncertainty is pervasive in all distributed computing problems. A main difficulty in designing distributed algorithms comes from the fact that no entity cooperating in the achievement of a common goal can have an instantaneous knowledge of the current state of the other entities, it can only know some of their past local states.

As we can see, the aim of parallel computing and distributed computing can be seen as being orthogonal: parallel computing is looking for data independence in order to split the computation in independent computing entities to obtain efficient algorithms, while the aim of distributed computing is to allow computing entities to cooperate in the presence of adversaries.

Two Quotations. Here are two quotes that can help the reader capture the spirit of distributed computing. The first one is an humorous quote from L. Lamport [57]:

> A distributed system is one in which the failure of a computer you didn't even know existed can render your own computer unusable.

This quote can be seen as a funny version of the FLP theorem (presented below). The second one (from [45]) stresses the fundamental difference between sequential computing and distributed computing when looking at computability.

> In sequential systems, computability is understood through the Church-Turing Thesis: anything that can be computed, can be computed by a Turing Machine. In distributed systems, where computations require coordination among multiple participants, computability questions have a different flavor. Here, too, there are many problems which are not computable, but these limits to computability reflect the difficulty of making decisions in the face of ambiguity, and have little to do with the inherent computational power of individual participants.

2   Preliminaries

2.1   Computing Models

The reader interested in the notion of *model* can consult [91].

Computing Eentities. In the following we consider a static system is made up of a set of n asynchronous computing entities (called processes in the following), denoted p_1, ..., p_n. The local power of a process is the one of a Turing machine. "Asynchronous" means that each process progresses at its own speed, which can vary with time, and remains always unknown to the other processes.

Process Failures. Two types of process failures are considered.

– Crash failure model. A crash is a premature unanticipated halt by a process. Moreover once crashed, a process remains crashed forever. It is important to notice that a process behaves correctly until it crashes (if it ever crashes).

– Byzantine failure model. This type of failure was introduced in the early eighties [60,73]. A Byzantine process is a process that does not follow the behavior defined by the algorithm it is assumed to execute. Such an incorrect behavior can be intentional or not. When intentional, it is sometimes called "malicious". In this model a crash is considered as a Byzantine failure.

Given a run and according to the failure model, a process that does not commit a failure is a *correct* (or *non-faulty*) process. Otherwise it is a *faulty* process. The fact we do not know in advance which are the correct and the faulty processes is one of main sources of non-determinism that distributed algorithms have to master.

Let us also notice that these are more sophisticated Byzantine failure models –not addressed in this article– that distinguish crash failures from Byzantine failures (the former being less severe than the latter).

Communication Model. We consider two communication models.

– Shared memory model. In this model the processes communicate through atomic registers. According to the primitive operations the processes can use to access these registers, two sub-models can be defined.
  • In the basic read/write (RW) model, the only operations a process can invoke to access a register are read and write.
  • In the read/modify/write (RMW) model, in addition to read and write primitive operations, a process can invoke one or more sophisticated primitive operations such as Test&Set(), Fetch&Add(), Compare&Swap(), or LL/SC (linked load/store conditional). According to the operations enriching the basic RW model, there are many RMW models. The model enriched with the primitive operation op is denoted RMW+op. As an example let us consider the model RMW+Compare&Swap. As LL/SC, the operation Compare&Swap, is an atomic conditional write. The effect of Compare&Swap(R, old, new) where R is a shared register and old and new are two values is the following. If $R = old$, the operation assigns new to R and returns true. If $R \neq old$, R is not modified and the operation returns false.
– Message-passing model. In this model the processes exchange message on top of a communication network. In this case, in addition to the local power provided by a Turing machine, the processes can send and receive messages. It is assumed that the network is reliable (i.e., there is neither loss, creation, nor alteration of messages).

2.2 Progress Conditions

Case of the Failure-Free Model. In a failure-free context, two progress conditions have been defined for the high level operations invoked on shared objects defined by the programmer or supplied by a library (e.g., the operations push() and pop() associated with a stack). According to the underlying communication model, these objects are implemented on top of registers of the shared memory, or on top of the local memories of the processes (in this case, the communication medium can be message-passing or shared memory). *Deadlock-freedom* states that if one or more processes invoke an high level operation on a shared object, at least one invocation will succeed. *Starvation-freedom* is a stronger progress condition, namely it states that if any process invokes an operation on a shared object, its invocation will succeed. Deadlock-free and starvation-free mutual exclusions are a classical techniques used to protect accesses to shared objects [76].

Case of the Shared Memory Crash-Prone Model. In this context, the situation is different. The crash of a process p while it is accessing a shared object can prevent other processes from forever accessing the object. Intuitively, this is due to the fact that no process can know if p crashed or is only very slow. As a consequence, since the early nineties, progress conditions suited to asynchronous crash-prone systems have been proposed.

- Obstruction-freedom [44]. An object operation is *obstruction-free* if, assuming the invoking process p does not crash and executes in isolation for a long enough period, its invocation terminates. "In isolation" means that, if any, the concurrent invocations of operations on the same object by other processes have stopped their execution -maybe in the middle of their code- and remain pending until p returns from its invocation).
- Non-blocking [48]. An object operation is *non-blocking* if, whatever the number of concurrent invocations, at least one of them terminates. Non-blocking extends deadlock-freedom to process crash failures.
- Wait-freedom [43]. An object operation is *wait-free* if all its invocations by processes that do not crash terminate. Wait-freedom extends starvation-freedom to process crash-failures.

In the case of Byzantine failures, the progress condition states that the invocation of an operation by a correct process must terminate if the number of Byzantine processes doe not bypass a pre-defined threshold.

Case of the Asynchronous Message-Passing Model. In this context, according to the problem (object to implement) that is solved, the previous progress conditions may apply in the case of crash failures.

But this not true for all the problems. As for Byzantine failures in shared memory systems, in many cases, the progress condition that is considered states that an operation invoked by a correct process must terminate if some assumptions are satisfied. These assumptions usually involve the maximum number of processes that can be faulty [46].

3   Asynchronous Crash-Prone Shared Memory

3.1   The Consensus Object

A Notion of Universality. Considering the asynchronous crash-prone shared memory model, M. Herlihy introduced the notions of a *universal object* and a *universal construction* [43]. This notion of universality concerns the *wait-free implementation* of the objects defined by a sequential specification ("wait-free implementation" means that all the operations of the object that is built must be wait-free). To this end, he introduced the notion of a *universal object type*. An object type T is universal if a universal construction can be built from

- any number of objects of type T, and
- any number of atomic read/write registers.

It is shown in [43] that the *consensus* object type (defined below) is universal.

The Consensus Object. Consensus is a one-shot object that provides the processes with a single operation denoted propose(). (One-shot" means that a process may invoke d propose() at most once). When a process p_i invokes propose(v_i) we say " p_i proposes the value v_i". Such an invocation returns a value v and, when this occurs, we say "p_i decides v". In the context of process crah failures, *consensus* is defined by the three following properties (validity and agreement are safety properties, while wait-freedom is a liveness property).

- Validity: The value decided by a process is a proposed value.
- Agreement: No two processes decide different values.
- Wait-freedom: The invocation of propose() by a non-faulty process terminates.

Principles Underlying Universal Constructions. The universality of the consensus object comes from the fact that it allows the processes to *agree on a unique order* to apply the operations invoked on the object O that is built. On the client side each process can invoke an operation on O by announcing it to all the processes. On the server side, the processes execute a sequence of rounds, each using a new consensus object. During each round, each process proposes to the consensus object the operations it sees as being proposed and not yet applied to O. The proposal output by the consensus object is the winner proposal for the corresponding round, and the sequence of operations it contains is applied by each process to its local copy of the object (if the state machine replication –SMR– paradigm is used [56,81,90]), or to the unique copy of the object in the case where the object O is stored in a shared memory [43]. All the universal constructions rely on a helping mechanism [22], which ensures that the operations invoked by processes that crash during their invocations are applied by all or none the non-crashed processes.

More Advanced Topic: Yet More Universal Constructions. The previous constructions consider the construction of a single object. A more general construction is described in [39], that considers the case where, not only one, but k objects are built and the wait-freedom property is satisfied for at least one of them. This construction relies on k-set agreement, a generalization of consensus [25].

A yet more general construction is described in [87], that considers the simultaneous construction of k objects such that the wait-freedom property is satisfied for at least ℓ of them, $1 \le \ell \le k$. Such a construction relies on the k-simultaneous consensus object defined in [4].

3.2   The Consensus Hierarchy

The Consensus Number Notion. This notion was introduced in [43]. The consensus number of an object type T is the greatest integer n such that, despite asynchrony and any number of process crashes, it is possible to build a consensus object from atomic read/write registers and objects of type T in a system of n processes. If there is no such finite n, the consensus number of T is $+\infty$.

It is shown in [43] that the consensus numbers defines an infinite hierarchy such that

- Read/write registers have consensus number 1. (The first proof showing that consensus cannot be wait-free implemented on top of read/write registers in the presence of asynchrony and any number of process crashes appeared in [61].)
- Test&Set registers, Fetch&Add registers, stacks, queues have consensus number 2.
- Compare&Swap registers, LL/SC (linked load/store conditional) registers, Memory-to-Memory swap registers have consensus number $+\infty$.

A Simple Object Family Covering the Full Hierarchy. The *k-sliding read/write register* object, in short RW(k) was introduced in [65] (a similar object was independently introduced in [35]). This object is a natural generalization of an atomic read/write register, which corresponds to the case $k = 1$). This object is an (initially empty) sequence of values such that the write of a value v adds v at the end of the sequence, and a read returns the sub-sequence of the last k written values (if only $x < k$ values have been written, the read return these x values). It is easy to see that the type RW(1)is the read/write register type, while RW($+\infty$) is nothing else than a ledger [80].

Universal Constructions. Universal constructions based on consensus objects or on operations whose consensus number is $+\infty$ (such as LL/SC), are described in many articles, e.g. [34, 36, 43, 77, 79], and and in textbooks such as [10, 47, 77, 93].

Objects at Level 1 of the Hierarchy. It follows from the previous hierarchy that, as they have consensus number 2, objects such as stacks and queues cannot be wait-free implemented on top of read/write registers only. Differently, important objects such as snapshot [1, 6, 52], renaming [8, 18], immediate snapshot [13], and approximate agreement [29] have consensus number 1 and can consequently be wait-free built on top of read/write registers only, despite asynchrony and any number of process crashes. The interested reader can consult textbooks such as [47, 77, 93] where are described wait-free implementation of such objects. The family of the CRDT objects (Conflict-free Replicated Data Types [92]) is a sub-class of the objects at level 1 of the consensus hierarchy.

Implication of the Hierarchy for Consensus Number > 1. It follows from Herlihy's infinite hierarchy, that no object with consensus number $x > 1$ can be wait-free implemented on top of an object whose consensus number is smaller than x.

It follows from this observation that, while a shared stack (or a queue) can be implemented on top of atomic read/write atomic registers in an asynchronous failure-free systems (whatever the number of processes), this is impossible in a crash-prone system. This, which at first glance may seem surprising and counter-intuitive, is due to the fact their consensus number is 2, while the consensus number of read/write registers is 1.

It follows that, differently from what occurs in sequential computing (where read/write registers are the cells of a Turing machine) and more generally in failure-free concurrent computing, read/write registers are not universal in asynchronous crash-prone systems, where consensus is needed to cope with the non-determinism created by the environment (net effect of asynchrony and crash failures).

Read/Write with Respect to Read/Modify/Write. An important point lies in the fact that a write operation not only defines a new value for the register R to which it is applied, but also erases its past which is then lost forever. Differently, while operations such as Fetch&Add(R) or Test&Set(R) (whose consensus number is 2) are unconditional writes, they return the previous value of the register R to which they are applied (and consequently this value is not lost forever and can used by the invoking process). More, the operation Compare&Swap(R, old, new) (whose consensus number is $+\infty$) is a conditional write (it modifies the register R to which it is applied only if its current value is equal to the parameter value old).

Domain of Consensus Numbers. The notion of consensus number has been defined in the context of the asynchronous shared memory model in which any number of processes may crash. Such a notion cannot be directly applied to message-passing systems or Byzantine failures.

Advanced Topics. The multiplicative power of consensus numbers has been investigated in [50]. An extension of the consensus number hierarchy to multi-threaded systems is presented in [74]. It has been shown in [2,28] that given any integer $x \geq 1$, there is an infinite number of objects $O(x,1)$, $O(x,2)$, etc., such that, while they all have consensus number x, it is possible to build $O(x,y)$ from $O(x,y-1)$ but $O(x,y-1)$ cannot be built from $O(x,y)$ (hence, there is an infinite computability-related sub-hierarchy between any two consecutive consensus numbers). An exhaustive survey of the consensus number land is presented in [82] and an in-depth study of related topics is presented in [83].

A notion close but different from consensus numbers, called d-solo executions, is presented in [46]. A process runs solo when it computes its local output without receiving any information from other processes, either because they crashed or they are too slow. While in wait-free shared memory models at most one process may run solo in an execution, any number of processes may have to run solo in an asynchronous wait-free message-passing model. In the d-solo model, $1 \leq d \leq n$, up to d processes may run solo. A hierarchy of wait-free models is described in [46] that, while weaker than the basic crash-prone read/write model, are nevertheless strong enough to solve non-trivial tasks.

4 Synchronous Message-Passing Systems

From now on, we assume the inter-process communication is through message-passing. Moreover, each pair of processes is connected by a reliable bidirectional channel.

4.1 Round-Based Communication

In a synchronous message-passing system the processes execute a sequence of rounds whose progress is governed by an external clock, the progress of which defines a sequence of *rounds*. Each round r is composed three phases.

- Phase 1: at the beginning of a round r each process sends a message to the other processes. If a process crashes during this sending phase, an arbitrary subset of processes receives the message.
- Phase 2: a process receives messages sent by the other processes.
- Phase 3: according to its current local state and the messages it has received, a process does local computations that modifies its local state.

The Synchrony Property. The fundamental synchrony property (provided for free) of the synchronous message-passing system model lies in the fact that a message sent by a process during a round r is received by its destination process during the very same round r.

If follows from the synchrony property that, if a process p crashes during round r, a non-crashed processes learns it during round r or round $(r + 1)$ (because it does not receive a message from p). As we can see, this synchrony property drastically reduces the non-determinism due to environment.

4.2 Consensus in the Round-Based Synchronous Communication Model

Let t, $1 \leq t < n$, be a model parameter denoting the maximum number of processes that may be faulty in a run. It is assumed that t is known by the processes. Moreover, given a run, let f, $0 \leq f \leq t$ be the number of faulty processes in this run. We have the following results concerning consensus [5, 30, 37].

The Case of Process Crashes. In the synchronous failure-prone message-passing model, the synchrony assumption is strong enough to allow consensus to be solved. More precisely, we have the following.

- Consensus can be solved for any value of $t < n$.
- The maximal number of rounds to solve consensus is $\min(f + 2, t + 1)$.

The Case of Byzantine Processes. As a Byzantine process can never decide or can decide any value, and the non-Byzantine processes can propose different values, the definition of consensus must be appropriately modified in order an algorithm can be designed. We consider here the following classical definition [10, 30, 80].

– Validity: If all the non-faulty processes propose the same value, this value is decided. In the other cases any value can be decided.
– Agreement: No two non-faulty processes decide different values.
– Wait-freedom: The invocation of propose() by a non-faulty process terminates.

Let us observe that, in the case of binary consensus (only two values can be proposed), it follows from the validity property that the value decided by the non-faulty processes is always a value proposed by one of them [80].

A stronger validity property is used in some articles, namely: If $(t+1)$ non-faulty processes propose the same value, this value is decided. In the other cases any value can be decided. This does not change the following results.

Considering the round-based communication model, we have the following results.

– Consensus can be solved if and only if $t < n/3$ [60,73].
– The maximal number of rounds needed to solve Byzantine consensus is $\min(f + 2, t + 1)$ [30].
– If the model is enriched with message authentication, the previous necessary and sufficient condition $(t < n/3)$ becomes $t < n/2$.

Remark 1. Let us notice that there are algorithms that (at the additional cost of two synchronous rounds) reduce multi-valued synchronous consensus to binary synchronous consensus in the presence of $t < n/3$ Byzantine processes [69,80, 97].

Remark 2. As far as synchrony assumptions are concerned, it is important to say that the synchrony offered by the round-based synchronous communication model is not the weakest synchrony assumption that allows consensus to be solved. In other words, the synchronous communication model is stronger than necessary. This point is addressed in Sect. 5.4 for the case of Byzantine failures.

5   Asynchronous Message-Passing Systems

An asynchronous message-passing distributed system is such that both the processes and the communication channels are asynchronous. An asynchronous channel is such that there is no assumption of the transfer delay of each message, except it is finite.

In the following we consider three problems, and for each of them consider the case of crash failures an the case of Byzantine processes. As previously, t denotes the maximal number of processes that may commit failures.

5.1   Construction of an Atomic Read/Write Register

As a read/write register is the most basic object of sequential computing, and, more generally, a file is nothing else than a "big" read/write register, it is natural to try to build a such a register on top of an synchronous message-passing system prone to process (crash or Byzantine) failures.

The Case of Process Crashes. The most important result, due to [7], is the following necessary and sufficient condition:

- $t < n/2$ is a necessary and sufficient condition to build an atomic read/write register in asynchronous n-process system prone to process crash failures.

Intuitively, this is due to the following reason. If $t \geq n/2$, the processes can be partitioned in two subsets $Q1$ and $Q2$ such that the communication inside each partition is rapid while the communication between the two partitions is arbitrarily slow. In this case, the processes of $Q1$ (reps. $Q2$) cannot distinguish the case were the processes $Q2$ (reps. $Q1$) have crashed or are arbitrarily slow. This is called an *indistinguishability argument* [9]. Differently, if $t < n/2$, it is possible for a process to communicate with a majority of processes without risking to become blocked forever. As any two majorities intersect, we have then $Q1 \cap Q2 \neq \emptyset$, from which portioning can be prevented.

The efficiency of algorithms implementing read/write registers in the presence of asynchrony and a majority of processes that do not crash has been addressed in [32,71]. It is shown in [69] that, in addition to the value of the register, messages have to carry two bits of control information.

The Case of Byzantine Processes. As a Byzantine process can pollute each register it writes, the shared memory must be restricted to be an array $M[1..n]$ of single-writer multi-reader (SWMR) atomic registers. Hence, $M[i]$ can read by all the processes but written only by p_i. Considering such a context, the following necessary and sufficient condition is proved in [49]:

- $t < n/3$ is a necessary and sufficient condition to build a shared memory made up SWMR atomic registers in an asynchronous n-process system in which up to t process may be Byzantine.

Algorithms building such a Byzantine-tolerant shared memory are presented in [49,66].

An Intuitive Explanation of the $t < n/3$ Assumption. Let us consider the worst case, namely $n = 3t+1$. So, there are at least $n-t = 2t+1$ non-faulty processes. Let us partition the processes in four sets: $Q1$, $Q2$, $Q3$, and $Q4$, so that each of $Q1$, $Q2$, and $Q3$ contains t processes, $Q4$ contains a single process, and all the up to t Byzantine processes are in $Q3$. As there are $n - t = 2t + 1$ non-faulty processes, a process can communicate with this number of processes without risking to be blocked. But, due to asynchrony, it is possible that, inside the set of $n-t = 2t+1$ processes with which it communicates, t processes are Byzantine, each of them sending different values to distinct processes (while it is assumed to send the same value). Given any two non-faulty processes p_i and p_j, let $P_i = Q1 \cup Q3 \cup Q4$ the set of processes the set of processes communicating with p_i, and $P_j = Q2 \cup Q3 \cup Q4$. We have then $|P_i \cap P_j| = t + 1$, when means that there is at least one non-faulty that communicate with both p_i and p_j.

5.2   Consensus in the Presence of Asynchrony and Process Crashes

Consensus Impossibility. One of most important results of asynchronous crash-prone message-passing rums i the following one, known under the name FLP, according to its the name of its authors (Fischer, Lynch, and Paterson [38]).

- There is no deterministic algorithm that solves consensus in asynchronous message-passing systems in which even a single process may crash.

To prove their theorem, the authors considered binary consensus and, assuming an algorithm can solve consensus, they introduced a new notion that revealed to be extremely simple and powerful, namely the notion of *valence* of a global state (also called configuration) of the algorithm assumed to solve consensus.

A state in 0-valent (resp.,1-valent), if only 0 (resp. 1) can be decided from this state (maybe no one knows it, but in such a state "the dices are thrown"). 0-valent states and 1-valent states are called mono-valent states. A bi-valent state in a state in which nothing has yet been decided (maybe no one knows it, but in such a state "the dices are not yet thrown").

The proof is then made up of two parts. The first consists in showing that among all possible global states, at least one of them is bi-valent. The second part consists in showing, that given any algorithm assumed to solve consensus, if it is in a bi-valent state there is a execution of it that moves it in a new bi-valent state, from which follows that the algorithm will never terminate.

How to Circumvent FLP? Several approaches have proposed to circumvent the impossibility of consensus in asynchronous crash-prone systems.

- Add scheduling assumptions restricting the set of possible behaviors [16,31, 33,64].
- Provide the processes with information on failures [24]. It has been shown in [23] that the weakest information on crash failures that allows consensus to be solved is captured by the failure detector, called *eventual leader* and denoted Ω [23]. Such a failure detector provides each process p_i with a read-only variable $leader_i$, which always contains a process identity, and these local variables are such that there is an unknown but finite time τ after which they all contain the same identity, which is the identity of a process that does not crash.
- Restriction on the sets of input vectors. An input vector is the vector (unknown by the processes) of size n, the entry i containing the value proposed by p_i. This approach, called condition-based, was introduced in [67].
- Use randomization. For crash failures, this approach was introduced in [11].

Several algorithms based on each of the previous assumptions are described in [80].

Advanced Topic. Computability-related equivalences between round-based synchronous models constrained by message adversaries and asynchronous crash-prone message-passing models enriched with failure detectors are presented in [3,86].

5.3   Consensus in the Presence of Asynchrony and Byzantine Processes

As Byzantine failures are more severe than crash failures The FLP impossibility remains valid in the Byzantine failure model. Many Byzantine-tolerant consensus algorithms have been proposed. They are based on asynchronous rounds, which –differently from the synchronous model– must be explicitly built by the algorithm. The major part of these algorithms consider binary consensus.

Starting with an early article by M. Rabin [75], these algorithms use randomization to circumvent the consensus impossibility. Among the existing algorithms the one described in [63] is optimal in several respects. More precisely:

- It requires $t < n/3$ and is consequently optimal with respect to t.
- It uses a constant number of communication steps per round.
- The expected number of rounds to decide is constant.
- The message complexity is $O(n^2)$ messages per round.
- Each message carries its type, a round number plus a constant number of bits.
- The algorithm uses a weak common coin. Weak means here that there is a constant probability that, at every round, the coin returns different values to distinct processes.
- Finally, the algorithm does not assume a computationally limited adversary (and consequently it does not rely on signed messages).

Algorithms that reduce Byzantine multi-valued consensus to Byzantine binary consensus are described in [12,68,70].

Remark. The necessary and sufficient condition $t < n/3$ can be weakened into $t < n/2$ if the underlying asynchronous architecture is enriched with an appropriate temperproof distributed component such as TTCB (Trusted Timely Computing Base). As an example, the interested reader will find in [26,27,89] the development of such an approach.

5.4   Byzantine Consensus: The Minimal Synchrony Assumption

While consensus can be solved in the round-based synchronous message-passing system model where up to $t < n/3$ processes can be Byzantine, it cannot be solved in fully asynchronous process model where up to $t < n/3$ processes can be Byzantine. Hence, the question: which is the weakest synchrony assumption that allows consensus to be solved in the presence of up to $t < n/3$ Byzantine processes. This question has been answered in [14], where it is shown that the following synchrony assumption is necessary and sufficient condition.

Uni-directional Channels. Let us assume that each pair of processes is connected by two uni-directional communication channels. (This is to be as general as possible as it becomes possible to associate different transfer delays to each direction of a bi-directional channel.)

Eventually Timely Channel. Let us consider the channel connecting a process p to a process q. This channel is *eventually timely* if there is a finite time τ and a bound δ, such that any message sent by p to q at time $\tau' \geq \tau$ is received by q by time $\tau' + \delta$. Let us observe that neither τ nor δ are known by the processes.

Eventual $\langle t + 1 \rangle Bisource.$ An *eventual $\langle t + 1 \rangle bisource$* is a non-faulty process p that has (a) eventually timely input channels from t correct processes and (b) eventually timely output channels to t correct processes (these input and output channels can connect p to different subsets of processes).

It is shown in [14] that the existence of an eventual $\langle t + 1 \rangle$bisource is the weakest synchrony assumption that allows Byzantine-tolerant consensus to be solved. This article presents also an algorithm based on this assumption.

6   Reliable Broadcast

Reliable broadcast belongs to the family of fundamental problems of fault-tolerant distributed computing [15,16]. As previously, it comes in two versions according to the process failure model. *Reliable* means here that the set of the messages that are delivered satisfy well-defined properties, which are crucial to the design of provably correct distributed software.

Reliable Broadcast in the Presence of Crash Failures. This communication abstraction, that provides the processes with two operations denoted R_broadcast() and R_deliver(), is defined by the following properties. When a process invokes R_broadcast(m), we say that it "r-broadcasts m". Similarly, when it issues R_deliver() and obtains the message m, we say that it "r-delivers m".

- Validity. If a process p_i r-delivers a message m from a process p_j, m has previously been r-broadcast by p_j.
- Integrity. Assuming all the messages are different, no process r-delivers twice the same message (no duplication).
- Termination-1. If a non-faulty process r-broadcasts a message m, it r-delivers m.
- Termination-2. If a process r-delivers a message m, every non-faulty process r-delivers the message m.

Let us notice that in the last item, the process that r-delivers m can be faulty or non-faulty. It is easy to see that this communication abstraction satisfies the following properties.

- The non-faulty processes r-deliver the same set M of messages, which includes all the messages they r-broadcast and a subset of the messages r-broadcast by faulty processes.
- A faulty process r-delivers a subset of the messages in M.

This abstraction is easy to implement. When a process invokes R_broadcast(m), it sends a copy of m to each process, and when a process receives a message m for the first time it forwards it to the other processes (except its sender). It is easy to see that an invocation of R_broadcast() generates at most $O(n^2)$ sending of m.

Reliable Broadcast in the Presence of Byzantine Processes (BRB). In the Byzantine failure context, it is not possible to control the message r-deliveries of the Byzantine process. The definition becomes the following one.

– If a non-faulty process p_i r-delivers a message m from a non-faulty process p_j, m has previously been r-broadcast by p_j.
– Integrity. Assuming all the messages are different, no non-faulty process r-delivers twice the same message (no duplication).
– Termination-1. If a non-faulty process r-broadcasts a message m, it r-delivers m.
– Termination-2. If a non-faulty process r-delivers a message m, (whatever the sender of m) every non-faulty process r-delivers the message m.

Similarly to the case of crash failures, the following agreement property follows from the previous properties: the non-faulty processes delivers the same set of messages M, which contains (at least) all the messages they r-broadcast.

On Byzantine Reliable Broadcast Algorithms. Bracha presented in [15] an elegant signature-free algorithm, which implements the reliable broadcast abstraction in the presence of asynchrony and up to $t < n/3$ Byzantine processes. It is proved in [15,16] that $t < n/3$ is an upper bound for the number of Byzantine processes, hence Bracha's algorithm is optimal from a t-resilience point of view. From an operational point of view, this algorithm is based on a *double echo* mechanism of the value broadcast by the sender process. For each application message, this algorithm requires three consecutive communication steps, and generates $(n-1)(2n+1)$ implementation messages.

It is natural that, as it is a fundamental communication abstraction, Byzantine reliable broadcast has been addressed by many authors. Here are a few recent results.

– The BRB algorithm presented in [53], implements the broadcast of an application message with only two communication steps (*single echo* mechanism), two message types, and n^2-1 protocol messages. The price to pay for this gain in efficiency is a weaker t-resilience, namely $t < n/5$. Hence, this algorithm and Bracha's algorithm differ in the trade-off t-resilience versus message/time efficiency.
– Scalable BRB is addressed in [42]. The issue is here not to pay the $O(n^2)$ message complexity cost. To this end, the authors use a non-trivial message-gossiping approach which allows them to design a sophisticated BRB algorithm satisfying fixed probability-dependent properties.
– BRB in *dynamic* systems is addressed [41]. Dynamic means that a process can enter and leave the system at any time. In their article the authors present an efficient BRB algorithm for such a context. This algorithm assumes that, at any time, the number of Byzantine processes present in the system is less than one third of total number of processes present in the system.

– An efficient algorithm for BRB with long inputs of ℓ bits using lower costs than ℓ single-bit instances is presented in [72]. This algorithm, which assumes $t < n/3$, achieves the best possible communication complexity of $\Theta(n\ell)$ input sizes. This article also presents an authenticated extension of the previous algorithm.

7 Further Readings

The reader interested in dissymetric progress conditions will consult [51,54,94]. A tutorial on the notion of universality in crash-prone asynchronous message-passing systems is presented in [81]. There are several textbooks entirely devoted to fault-tolerant distributed computing, e.g. [10,17,40,47,55,58,62,77,78,80,88, 93] to cite a few. Differently, the textbook [78] is entirely devoted to algorithms for failure-free asynchronous distributed systems. Let us obseve that, in the today blockchain-dominated technology, the previous readings could help better understand what can be done and which are the assumptions needed to obtain provably reliable distributed software.

Finally, on the important side of the specification and consistency conditions suited to distributed objects, the reader interested in the *linearizability hierarchy* is invited to have a look at the following articles [20,21,48,76]. Concerning the spirit of distributed computing the reader will consult [84,85].

Acknowledgments. I want to thank the program chairs of the distributed computing track of ICDCIT 2025, namely Quentin Bramas (University of Strasbourg, France) and Krishendu Mukhopadhya (ISI Kolkata, India), for their kind invitation to write this article.

This work was partially supported by the French ANR project ByBLoS (ANR-20-CE25-0002-01) devoted to the modular design of building blocks for large-scale trustless multi-users distributed applications.

References

1. Afek, Y., Attiya, H., Dolev, D., Gafni, E., Merritt, M., Shavit, N.: Atomic snapshots of shared memory. J. ACM **40**(4), 873–890 (1993)
2. Afek, Y., Ellen, F., Gafni, E.: Deterministic objects: life beyond consensus. In: Proceedings of the 35th ACM Symposium on Principles of Distributed Computing (PODC 2016), pp. 97–106. ACM Press (2016)
3. Afek, Y., Gafni, E.: A simple characterization of asynchronous computations. Theoret. Comput. Sci. **561**, 88–95 (2015)
4. Afek, Y., Gafni, E., Rajsbaum, S., Raynal, M., Travers, C.: The k-simultaneous consensus problem. Distrib. Comput. **22**(3), 185–195 (2010)
5. Aguilera, M.K., Toueg, S.: A simple bi-valency proof that t-resilient consensus requires $t+1$ rounds. Inf. Process. Lett. **71**, 155–158 (1999)
6. Anderson, J.H.: Multi-writer composite registers. Distrib. Comput. **7**(4), 175–195 (1994)
7. Attiya, H., Bar-Noy, A., Dolev, D.: Sharing memory robustly in message passing systems. J. ACM **42**(1), 121–132 (1995)

8. Attiya, H., Bar-Noy, A., Dolev, D., Peleg, D., Reischuk, R.: Renaming in an asynchronous environment. J. ACM **37**(3), 524–548 (1990)
9. Attiya, H., Rajsbaum, S.: Indistinguishability. Commun. ACM **63**(5), 90–99 (2020)
10. Attiya H., Welch J.L.: Distributed computing: fundamentals, simulations and advanced topics, 2nd edn, 414p. Wiley-Interscience (2004). ISBN 0-471-45324-2
11. Ben-Or, M., Another advantage of free choice: completely asynchronous agreement protocols. In: Proceedings of the 2nd ACM Symposium on Principles of Distributed Computing (PODC 1983), pp. 27–30 (1983)
12. Ben-Or, M., Kelmer, B., Rabin, T.: Asynchronous secure computations with optimal resilience. In: Proceedings of the 13th ACM Symposium on Principles of Distributed Computing (PODC 1994), pp. 183–192. ACM Press (1994)
13. Borowsky, E., Gafni, E.: Immediate atomic snapshots and fast renaming. In: Proceedings of the 12th ACM Symposium on Principles of Distributed Computing (PODC 1993), pp. 41–51. ACM Press (1993)
14. Bouzid, Z., Mostéfaoui, Raynal, M.: Minimal synchrony for Byzantine consensus. In: Proceeding of the 34th ACM Symposium on Principles of Distributed Computing (PODC 2015), pp. 461–470. ACM Press (2015)
15. Bracha, G.: Asynchronous Byzantine agreement protocols. Inf. Comput. **75**(2), 130–143 (1987)
16. Bracha, G., Toueg, S.: Asynchronous consensus and broadcast protocols. J. ACM **32**(4), 824–840 (1985)
17. Cachin, Ch., Guerraoui, R., Rodrigues, L.: Reliable and Secure Distributed Programming, 367p. Springer (2011). ISBN 978-3-642-15259-7
18. Castañeda, A., Rajsbaum, S., Raynal, M.: The renaming problem in shared memory systems: an introduction. Elsevier Comput. Sci. Rev. **5**, 229–251 (2011)
19. Castañeda, A., Rajsbaum, S., Raynal, M.: Unifying concurrent objects and distributed tasks: interval-linearizability. J. ACM **65**(6), 45 (2018). 42 pages
20. Castañeda, A., Rajsbaum, S., Raynal, M.: A linearizability-based hierarchy for concurrent specifications. Commun. ACM **66**(1), 86–97 (2023)
21. Castañeda, A., Rajsbaum, S., Raynal, M.: Sets, fetch&increment, stacks and queues with multiplicity: a relaxation that allows set-linearizable implementations from read/write operations. Distrib. Comput. **36**(2), 89–106 (2023)
22. Censor-Hillel, K., Petrank, E., Timnat, S.: Help! In: Proceedings of the 34th Symposium on Principles of Distributed Computing (PODC 2015), pp. 241–250. ACM Press (2015)
23. Chandra, T.D., Hadzilacos, V., Toueg, S.: The weakest failure detector for solving consensus. J. ACM **43**(4), 685–722 (1996)
24. Chandra, T.D., Toueg, S.: Unreliable failure detectors for reliable distributed systems. J. ACM **43**(2), 225–267 (1996)
25. Chaudhuri, S.: More choices allow more faults: set consensus problems in totally asynchronous systems. Inf. Comput. **105**(1), 132–158 (1993)
26. Correia, M., Ferreira Neves, N., Veríssimo, P.: How to tolerate half less one Byzantine nodes in practical distributed systems. In: Proceedings of the 23rd International Symposium on Reliable Distributed Systems (SRDS 2004), pp. 174–183. IEEE Press (2004)
27. Correia, M., Ferreira, N.N., Veríssimo, P.: BFT-TO: intrusion tolerance with less replicas. Comput. J. **56**(6), 693–715 (2013)
28. Daian, E., Losa, G., Afek, Y., Gafni, E.: A wealth of sub-consensus deterministic objects. In: Proceedings of the 32nd International Symposium on Distributed Computing (DISC 2018), LIPICS 121, 17p (2018)

29. Dolev, D., Lynch, N.A., Pinter, S.H., Stark, E.W., Weihl, W.E.: Reaching approximate agreement in the presence of failures. J. ACM **33**(3), 499–516 (1986)
30. Dolev, D., Reischuk, R.S., H.R.,: Early stopping in Byzantine agreement. J. ACM **37**(4), 720–741 (1990)
31. Dolev, D., Dwork, C., Stockmeyer, L.: On the minimal synchronism needed for distributed consensus. J. ACM **34**(1), 77–97 (1987)
32. Dutta, P., Guerraoui, R., Levy, R., Vukolic, M.: Fast access to distributed atomic memory. SIAM Journal of Computing **39**(8), 3752–3783 (2010)
33. Dwork, C., Lynch, N., Stockmeyer, L.: Consensus in the presence of partial synchrony. J. ACM **35**(2), 288–323 (1988)
34. Ellen, F., Fatourou, P., Kosmas, E., Milani, A., Travers, C.: Universal constructions that ensure disjoint-access parallelism and wait-freedom. Distrib. Comput. **29**, 251–277 (2016)
35. Ellen, F., Gelashvili, G., Shavit, N., Zhu, L.: A complexity-based hierarchy for multiprocessor synchronization. In: Proceedings of the 35th ACM Symposium on Principles of Distributed Computing (PODC 2016), pp. 289–298. ACM Press (2016)
36. Fatourou, P., Kallimanis, N.D.: Highly-efficient wait-free synchronization. Theory Comput. Syst. **55**, 475–520 (2014)
37. Fischer, M.J., Lynch, N.A.: A lower bound for the time to ensure interactive consistency. Inf. Process. Lett. **14**, 183–186 (1982)
38. Fischer, M.J., Lynch, N.A., Paterson, M.S.: Impossibility of distributed consensus with one faulty process. J. ACM **32**(2), 374–382 (1985)
39. Gafni, E., Guerraoui, R.: Generalizing universality. In: Proceedings of the 22nd International Conference on Concurrency Theory (CONCUR 2011), LNCS, vol. 6901, pp. 17–27. Springer (2011)
40. Garg, V.K.: Elements of Distributed Computing, 423p. Wiley-Interscience (2002)
41. Guerraoui, G., Komatovic, J., Kuznetsov, P., Pignolet, P.A., Seredinschi, D.-A., Tonkikh, A.: Dynamic Byzantine reliable broadcast. In: Proceedings of the 24th International Conference on Principles of Distributed Systems (OPODIS 2020), Lipics, vol. 184, Article 23, 18 pages (2020)
42. Guerraoui, G., Kuznetsov, P., Monti, M., Pavlovic, M., Seredinschi, D.-A.: Scalable Byzantine reliable broadcast. In: Proceedings of the 33rd International Symposium on Distributed Computing (DISC 2019), LIPIcs, vol. 146, Article 22, 16 pages (2019)
43. Herlihy, M.P.: Wait-free synchronization. ACM Trans. Program. Lang. Syst. **13**(1), 124–149 (1991)
44. Herlihy, M.P., Luchangco, V., Moir, M.: Obstruction-free synchronization: double-ended queues as an example. In: Proceedings of the 23th International IEEE Conference on Distributed Computing Systems (ICDCS 2003), pp. 522–529. IEEE Press (2003)
45. Herlihy, M., Rajsbaum, S., Raynal, M.: Power and limits of distributed computing shared memory models. Theoret. Comput. Sci. **509**, 3–24 (2013)
46. Herlihy, M., Rajsbaum, S., Raynal, M., Stainer, J.: From wait-free to arbitrary concurrent solo executions in colorless distributed computing. Theoret. Comput. Sci. **683**, 1–21 (2017)
47. Herlihy, M., Shavit, N.: The Art of Multiprocessor Programming, 508p. Morgan Kaufmann (2008). ISBN 978-0-12-370591-4
48. Herlihy, M.P., Wing, J.M.: Linearizability: a correctness condition for concurrent objects. ACM Trans. Program. Lang. Syst. **12**(3), 463–492 (1990)

49. Imbs, S., Rajsbaum, S., Raynal, M., Stainer, J.: Read/Write shared memory abstraction on top of an asynchronous Byzantine message-passing system. J. Parallel Distrib. Comput. **93–94**, 1–9 (2016)
50. Imbs, D., Raynal, M.: The multiplicative power of consensus numbers. In: Proceedings of the 29th ACM Symposium on Principles of Distributed Computing (PODC 2010), pp. 26–35. ACM Press (2010)
51. Imbs, D., Raynal, M.: A liveness condition for concurrent objects: x-wait-freedom. Concurr. Comput.: Pract. Exp. **23**, 2154–2166 (2011)
52. Imbs, D., Raynal, M.: Help when needed, but no more: efficient read/write partial snapshot. J. Parall. Distrib. Comput. **72**(1), 1–13 (2012)
53. Imbs, D., Raynal, M.: Trading t-resilience for efficiency in asynchronous Byzantine reliable broadcast. Parall. Process. Lett. **26**(4), 8 (2016)
54. Imbs, D., Raynal, M., Taubenfeld, G.: On asymmetric progress conditions. Proceedings of the 29th ACM Symposium on Principles of Distributed Computing (PODC 2010), pp. 55–64. ACM Press (2010)
55. Kshemkalyani, A.D., Singhal, M.: Distributed Computing: Principles, Algorithms and Systems, 736p. Cambridge University Press (2008)
56. Lamport, L.: Time, clocks, and the ordering of events in a distributed system. Commun. ACM **21**(7), 558–565 (1978)
57. Lamport, L., Message-Id: <8705281923.AA09105@jumbo.dec.com>, Thu, 28 May 1987 12:23:29
58. Lamport, L.: Specifying Systems, 364p. Addison-Wesley, Pearson Education (2003)
59. Lamport, L.: Teaching concurrency. ACM Sigact NEWS **40**(1), 58–62 (2009)
60. Lamport, L., Shostack, R., Pease, M.: The Byzantine generals problem. ACM Trans. Program. Lang. Syst. **4**(3), 382–401 (1982)
61. Loui, M., Abu-Amara, H.: Memory requirements for agreement among unreliable asynchronous processes. Adv. Comput. Res. **4**, 163–183 (1987). JAI Press
62. Lynch, N.A.: Distributed Algorithms, 872p. Morgan Kaufmann Publication, San Francisco (1996). ISBN 1-55860-384-4
63. Mostéfaoui, A., Moumen, H., Raynal, M.: Signature-free asynchronous binary Byzantine consensus with $t<n/3$, $O(n^2)$ messages, and $O(1)$ expected time. J. ACM **62**(4), 31 (2015). 21 pages
64. Mostéfaoui, A., Mourgaya, E., Raynal, M.: Asynchronous implementation of failure detectors. In: Proceedings of the International IEEE Conference on Dependable Systems and Networks (DSN 2003), pp. 351–360. IEEE Computer Society Press (2003)
65. Mostéfaoui, A., Perrin, M., Raynal, M.: A simple object that spans the whole consensus hierarchy. Parall. Process. Lett. **28**(2), 1850006:1–1850006:9 (2018)
66. Mostéfaoui, A., Petrolia, M., Raynal, M., Jard, C.: Atomic read/write memory in signature-free Byzantine asynchronous message-passing systems. Theory Comput. Syst. **60**(4), 677–694 (2017). Springer
67. Mostéfaoui, A., Rajsbaum, S., Raynal, M.: Conditions on input vectors for consensus solvability in asynchronous distributed systems. J. ACM **50**(6), 922–954 (2003)
68. Mostéfaoui, A., Raynal, M.: Intrusion-tolerant broadcast and agreement abstractions in the presence of Byzantine processes. IEEE Trans. Parallel Distrib. Syst. **27**(4), 1085–1098 (2016)
69. Mostéfaoui, A., Raynal, M.: Two-bit messages are sufficient to implement atomic read/write registers in crash-prone systems. In: Proceedings of the 35th ACM Symposium on Principles of Distributed Computing (PODC 2016), pp. 381–390. ACM Press (2016)

70. Mostéfaoui, A., Raynal, M.: Signature-free asynchronous Byzantine systems: from multivalued to binary consensus with $t<n/3$, $O(n^2)$ messages, and constant time. Acta Informatica **54**, 501–520 (2017)
71. Mostéfaoui, A., Raynal, M., Roy, M.: Time-efficient read/write register in crash-prone asynchronous message-passing systems. Springer Comput. **101**, 3–17 (2018)
72. Nayak, K., Ren, L., Shi, E., Vaidya, N.H., Xiang, Z.: Improved extension protocols for Byzantine broadcast and agreement. In: Proceedings of the 34th International Symposium on Distributed Computing (DISC 2020), LIPIcs, vol. 179, 16p, Article 28 (2020)
73. Pease, M., Shostak, R., Lamport, L.: Reaching agreement in the presence of faults. J. ACM **27**, 228–234 (1980)
74. Perrin, M., Mostéfaoui, A., Bonin, G.: Extending the wait-free hierarchy to multi-threaded systems. In: Proceedings of the 39th ACM Symposium on Principles of Distributed Computing (PODC 2020), pp. 21–30. ACM Press (2020)
75. Rabin, M.: Randomized Byzantine generals. In: Proceedings of the 24th IEEE Symposium on Foundations of Computer Science (FOCS 1983), pp. 116–124. IEEE Computer Society Press (1983)
76. Rajsbaum, S., Raynal, M.: Mastering concurrent computing through sequential thinking: a half-century evolution. Commun. ACM **63**(1), 78–87 (2020)
77. Raynal, M.: Concurrent Programming: Algorithms, Principles and Foundations, 515p. Springer (2013). ISBN 978-3-642-32026-2
78. Raynal, M.: Distributed Algorithms for Message-Passing Systems, 515p. Springer (2013). ISBN: 978-3-642-38122-5
79. Raynal, M.: Distributed universal constructions: a guided tour. Electron. Bullet. EATCS (Eur. Assoc. Theor. Comput. Sci.) **121**, 65–96 (2017)
80. Raynal, M.: Fault-Tolerant Message-Passing Distributed Systems: An Algorithmic Approach, 550p. Springer (2018). ISBN: 978-3-319-94140-0
81. Raynal, M.: The notion of universality in crash-prone asynchronous message-passing systems: a tutorial. In: Proceedings of the 38th International Symposium on Reliable Distributed Systems (SRDS 2019), 17p. IEEE Press (2019)
82. Raynal, M.: An Informal visit to the wonderful land of consensus numbers and beyond. Bullet. Eur. Assoc. Theor. Comput. Sci. **129**, 168–192 (2019)
83. Raynal, M.: Concurrent Crash-Prone Shared Memory Systems: A Few Theoretical Notions, 139p. Morgan & Claypool Publishers (2022). https://doi.org/10.2200/S01165ED1V01Y202202DCT018. ISBN 9781636393315
84. Raynal, M.: About informatics, distributed computing and our job: a personal view. (Invited Talk). In: Proceedings of the 30th International Colloquium on Structural Information and Communication Complexity (SIROCCO 2023), LNCS, vol. 13892, pp. 44–56. Springer (2023)
85. Raynal, M.: On distributed computing: a view, from physical objects to logical objects, and a look at fully anonymous. Keynote Talk. In: Proceedings of the 26th International Symposium on Stabilization, Safety, and Security of Distributed Systems (SSS 2024), LNCS. Springer (2024)
86. Raynal, M., Stainer, J.: Round-based synchrony weakened by message adversaries vs asynchrony enriched with failure detectors. In: 32th ACM Symposium on Principles of Distributed Computing (PODC 2013), pp. 166–175. ACM Press (2013)
87. Raynal, M., Stainer, J., Taubenfeld, G.: Distributed universality. Algorithmica **76**(2), 502–535 (2016)
88. Santoro, N.: Design and Analysis of Distributed Algorithms, 589p. Wiley-Interscience (2007). ISBN 0-471-71997-8

89. Santos, V.G., Correia, M., Bessani, A., Lung, C.L., Veríssimo, P.: Efficient Byzantine fault-tolerance. IEEE Trans. Comput. **62**(1), 16–30 (2013)

90. Schneider, F.B.: Implementing fault-tolerant services using the state machine approach. ACM Comput. Surv. **22**(4), 299–319 (1990)

91. Schneider, F.B.: What good are models, and what models are good? In: Distributed Systems, 2nd edn, pp. 17–26. Adddison-Wesley/ACM Press (1993)

92. Shapiro, M., Preguiça, N.M., Baquero, C., Zawirski, M.: Conflict-free replicated data YYPES. In: Proceedings of the 13th International Symposium on Stabilization, Safety, and Security of Distributed Systems (SSS 2011), LNCS, vol. 6976, pp. 386–400. Springer (2011)

93. Taubenfeld, G.: Synchronization Algorithms and Concurrent Programming, 423p. Pearson Education/Prentice Hall (2006). ISBN 0-131-97259-6

94. Taubenfeld, G.: The computational structure of progress conditions and shared objects. Distrib. Comput. **33**(2), 103–123 (2020)

95. Toueg, S.: Randomized Byzantine agreement. Proceedings of the 3rd Annual ACM Symposium on Principles of Distributed Computing (PODC 1984), pp. 163–178. ACM Press (1984)

96. Turing, A.M.: On computable numbers with an application to the Entscheidungsproblem. Proc. Lond. Math. Soc. **42**, 230–265 (1936)

97. Turpin, R., Coan, B.A.: Extending binary Byzantine agreement to multivalued Byzantine agreement. Inf. Process. Lett. **18**, 73–76 (1984)

98. Parallel Computing. https://en.wikipedia.org/wiki/Parallel_computing

IoT-Based Service Allocation in Edge Computing Using Game Theory

Kushagra Agrawal[1] , Polat Goktas[2] , Biswajit Sahoo[1] , Sujata Swain[1] ,
and Anjan Bandyopadhyay[1(✉)]

[1] School of Computer Engineering, KIIT Deemed to be University, Bhubaneswar,
India
anjan.bandyopadhyayfcs@kiit.ac.in
[2] School of Computer Science, University College Dublin, Dublin, Ireland

Abstract. The rapid growth of the Internet of Things (IoT) has created a pressing need for efficient service allocation methods to manage the multitude of connected devices. Edge computing has become
essential to fulfill the low-latency and high-bandwidth demands of IoT
applications. This paper investigates the use of game theory as a framework for optimizing service allocation in edge computing environments.
By treating the interactions between IoT devices and edge servers as a
strategic game, we propose strategies to achieve optimal allocation and
resource utilization. Our approach tackles key challenges such as minimizing latency, improving energy efficiency, and balancing load. Experimental results indicate that game-theoretic methods greatly improve the
performance and scalability of IoT systems in edge computing, positioning them a promising solution for future applications.

Keywords: Edge Computing · Internet of Things (IoT) · Game
Theory

1 Introduction

The proliferation of Internet of Things (IoT) devices has accelerated markedly in
recent years, leading to the interconnection of billions of devices globally. These
devices generate vast quantities of data that necessitate real-time processing
for a wide array of applications, including smart cities, healthcare, autonomous
vehicles, and industrial automation. Despite the extensive capabilities of traditional cloud services offered by providers such as Amazon and Microsoft,
including significant resources in memory, storage, computing power, and bandwidth (BW), these solutions have inherent limitations. While cloud services can
improve the energy efficiency of edge devices by offloading computational tasks to
distant servers, they introduce significant latency due to the physical separation
between data sources and processing centers. Applications requiring ultra-low
latency, such as high-quality video streaming, are especially affected, as cloud
data centers located across multiple continents fail to meet the stringent latency
requirements [1].

© The Author(s), under exclusive license to Springer Nature Switzerland AG 2025
Q. Bramas et al. (Eds.): ICDCIT 2025, LNCS 15507, pp. 45–60, 2025.
https://doi.org/10.1007/978-3-031-81404-4_4

To address these challenges, edge computing systems have been introduced. Positioned between end devices and cloud servers, the edge layer brings computing resources closer to the data sources at the network's edge. This proximity reduces latency and provides adequate resources for processing data from mobile terminals, thereby extending the battery life of devices by offloading computationally intensive tasks. Nevertheless, the computational resources available in edge computing are significantly constrained when compared to those in cloud data centers [2]. Consequently, it is imperative to develop efficient resource management techniques to address the limitations at the edge and meet the dynamic demands of end devices [1]. Traditional cloud computing's reliance on centralized data centers often fails to meet the low-latency and high-bandwidth requirements of many IoT applications due to the considerable distance between data generation and processing locations [3,4].

Edge computing thus addresses some of the critical limitations of traditional cloud computing, particularly in terms of latency and BW requirements. By processing data nearer to its source, edge computing not only meets the low-latency demands of many IoT applications but also offers enhanced scalability and system resilience [5]. Nonetheless, the heterogeneity and dynamic nature of IoT environments present substantial challenges for resource management and service allocation at the edge [6].

Efficient service allocation in edge computing environments is crucial for enhancing the performance of IoT applications. Key challenges include (see Fig. 1).

Fig. 1. Key challenges in efficient resource allocation for edge computing.

- **Latency Minimization:** IoT applications often have stringent latency requirements. Allocating tasks to edge servers based on proximity and current load is essential for reducing response times.
- **Energy Efficiency:** IoT devices and edge servers are frequently resource constrained, particularly in terms of energy. Optimizing service allocation to

minimize energy consumption while preserving performance is vital for the long-term viability of IoT systems.

- **Load Balancing:** The dynamic nature of IoT environments, with varying numbers and types of devices, requires effective load balancing strategies to prevent any single edge server from becoming a bottleneck.
- **Scalability:** The continuous growth in the number of IoT devices necessitates scalable solutions for service allocation to manage the increasing volume and diversity of data and processing demands.

To address these challenges, game theory provides a comprehensive framework for modeling and analyzing strategic interactions among various entities. By conceptualizing IoT devices and edge servers as participants in a strategic game, researchers can develop sophisticated algorithms that optimize service allocation and resource utilization. This approach takes into account a variety of crucial factors, including latency minimization, energy efficiency, and load balancing [7]. By carefully integrating these elements, game theory facilitates the design of strategies that not only enhance individual components but also improve overall system performance. This makes it a robust solution for the complex dynamics inherent in edge computing environments.

Here, this paper explores the application of game theory to optimize service allocation in edge computing environments for IoT applications. Our approach aims to tackle key challenges such as latency minimization, energy efficiency, and load balancing, while ensuring optimal resource allocation and utilization. Through rigorous experimental evaluations, we demonstrate the efficacy of game-theoretic methods in enhancing the performance and scalability of IoT systems in edge computing, highlighting their potential as a promising solution for future applications.

The structure of this paper is organized as follows: Sect. 2 provides a comprehensive review of the literature, covering topics such as IoT and Edge Computing, the application of Game Theory in resource allocation, and existing methodologies. Section 3 details the methodology, including the game-theoretic framework and the system model. This section also explains the notations, definitions, and utility functions for IoT devices and edge servers, leading to the development of strategies and the introduction of the algorithm. Section 4 presents the simulation results and assesses their significance. Finally, Sect. 5 concludes the paper by summarizing the findings and suggesting directions for future research.

2 Literature Review

2.1 IoT and Edge Computing

Traditional cloud computing often falls short in meeting the stringent latency and BW requirements of IoT applications due to the physical distance between data sources and cloud data centers [8]. Edge computing mitigates these limitations by bringing computational resources closer to the data sources, thereby reducing latency and improving response times. For latency-sensitive applications such as autonomous vehicles, smart healthcare, and industrial IoT, edge computing provides substantial benefits by enabling fast data processing and timely decision-making [8,9]. By processing data at the network edge, it not only accelerates response times but also reduces the volume of data that must be transferred to central cloud servers, thereby alleviating BW constraints [10,11].

Numerous studies underline the synergy between edge computing and emerging technologies like 5G/6G networks, which significantly enhance the capabilities of IoT applications [12]. The integration of edge computing with these advanced networks allows for ultra-low latency and high-speed data transmission, supporting sophisticated IoT applications such as augmented reality, virtual reality, and real-time analytics [10]. In addition, edge computing contributes to energy efficiency and extends the battery life of IoT devices. By offloading intensive computational tasks to edge servers, these devices conserve energy, which is particularly crucial for battery-operated IoT devices in remote or inaccessible locations [10,11].

Despite its numerous advantages, edge computing also faces challenges, including resource constraints, security concerns, and the need for efficient resource management. Given their typically limited computational and storage capacities, edge devices require well-designed resource allocation strategies to achieve optimal performance, in contrast to the more robust centralized cloud data centers [11,13].

2.2 Game Theory in Resource Allocation

Game theory has proven to be a powerful framework for optimizing service allocation in edge computing environments, particularly for IoT applications. In these scenarios, the allocation of virtual service providers (VSPs) to users can be modeled using preference-based game-theoretic approaches [14]. By representing the interactions between IoT devices and edge servers as a strategic game, researchers have developed efficient algorithms that address critical challenges such as latency minimization, energy efficiency, and load balancing [3,4,15].

Numerous studies have demonstrated the effectiveness of game theory in optimizing IoT-based service allocation. Techniques such as Stackelberg games and potential games have been utilized to tackle issues including task offloading, resource allocation, and service delay minimization [16–20]. These models take into account various factors such as energy consumption, task delay, and user satisfaction, providing a comprehensive approach to task offloading in complex networks of IoT devices and edge servers. Strategies like the Optimal Pricing and Best Response Algorithm have been particularly successful in maximizing the revenues of base stations and the utility for IoT devices. These approaches ensure equilibrium and rapid convergence in simulations, making them highly effective for real-world applications.

Recent research has also explored the integration of game-theoretic models with data-driven approaches and dynamic resource pricing mechanisms, enhancing the efficiency of IoT service allocation in edge computing environments. For example, a study proposed a game-theoretic framework that jointly optimizes task offloading and resource allocation, resulting in significant improvements in energy efficiency and load balancing within mobile edge computing systems [21]. Another study demonstrated the benefits of using a joint task offloading and resource allocation algorithm in scenarios involving energy harvesting and load balancing [22]. Furthermore, the use of deep reinforcement learning combined with game-theoretic models has been explored to minimize latency and balance the load in mobile edge computing, showing promising results in complex and dynamic environments [23].

Besides these strategies, there has been research focused on particular use cases like an unmanned aerial vehicle (UAV)-assisted mobile edge computing, where game theory helps to fine-tune UAV trajectories and resource allocation to cut down latency and increase energy efficiency [24]. Game theory has also been applied in emerging areas such as Fog Computing [9] and the Metaverse [13]. In Fog Computing, it addresses resource allocation challenges, while in the Metaverse, it optimizes the allocation of resources like medical surgery rooms based on user preferences, surpassing the efficiency of random allocation methods. Overall, the integration of game theory-based strategies for energy-efficient task offloading, load balancing, and resource allocation has significantly improved the performance and scalability of IoT networks in mobile edge computing environments [24]. These advances underline the pivotal role of game theory in enhancing the efficiency and effectiveness of next-generation computing systems.

2.3   Current Approaches to Service Allocation in Edge Computing

We review the prevailing strategies for service allocation in edge computing, encompassing heuristic methods, optimization algorithms, and machine learning-driven solutions. One approach employs distributed game theory to achieve cost-efficiency and quality of service awareness, reaching a pure Nash equilibrium as the optimal stable outcome for resource allocation among users [3]. In the context of distributed edge computing for IoT-powered smart cities, a multi-criteria optimization approach utilizes an auction-based resource allocation system to effectively manage time-sensitive tasks [4].

To address the issues of energy efficiency and workload delay guarantees within IoT-edge-cloud computing systems, a workload allocation problem is defined, focusing on the optimal distribution of workloads across local edge servers, neighboring edge servers, and the cloud to minimize energy consumption and ensure delay constraints [15]. A mixed-integer nonlinear program has been developed to jointly optimize computing offloading and service caching in edge computing for smart grids, aiming to minimize system task costs through a collaborative approach to computing offloading and resource allocation [5]. Resource allocation for nonorthogonal multiple access (NOMA)-edge computing in power IoT, characterized by extensive connectivity, is examined using a multi-timescale, multi-dimensional approach. By leveraging Lyapunov optimization, the complex problem of long-term stochastic optimization is broken down into three distinct short-term deterministic subproblems: resource allocation on large timescales, task division on small timescales, and computation resource allocation [6].

Additionally, various other strategies have been explored in scholarly research. For example, an extensive review of task distribution strategies and optimization techniques in edge computing highlights the critical need to manage energy consumption, latency, and the trade-offs related to quality of service [25]. Dynamic service placement in multi-access edge computing has also been investigated, focusing on improving user experience through the flexible deployment of application services on edge servers [26]. Utility theory has been applied to the problem of selecting optimal services, resource allocation, and task offloading in Mobile Edge Computing. This approach is framed as a mixed-integer nonlinear programming problem, with the objective of maximizing user Quality of Experience [27]. There is also growing interest in optimization strategies for service allocation under budget constraints, with the use of Lyapunov optimization techniques to allocate resources effectively within financial limitations [28].

The incorporation of machine learning techniques into resource allocation has been increasingly recognized, as research has demonstrated the substantial enhancements in efficacy and flexibility within edge computing settings. The examination of auction-based approaches has also been acknowledged, with the objective of enhancing resource distribution to achieve higher user contentment and profitability for service providers [29].

3   Methodology

3.1   Game Theory

Game theory, a branch of applied mathematics, offers tools for analyzing a variety of situations and has widespread applications in fields such as economics, medicine, engineering, military, and business [30]. It encompasses both cooperative and non-cooperative games, providing insights into decision-making processes and strategic interactions among different parties [31]. The discipline covers diverse game models like the prisoner's dilemma, median voter theorem, Gounod model, and Bertrand model, showcasing its versatility in understanding complex scenarios and predicting outcomes [30]. Additionally, game theory plays a crucial role in game design, ensuring balance and strategic depth in games like Rock-Paper-Scissors and First-Person Shooter games [32]. Overall, the evolution and practical applications of game theory underscore its significance in analyzing competition, decision-making, and strategic interactions across various domains, making it a valuable tool for understanding complex real-world scenarios.

In engineering, game theory contributes significantly to system design and process optimization by developing strategies for efficient resource allocation and coordination in complex systems such as smart grids and transportation networks. A notable application is in flight safety, where game theory helps avoid collisions. By employing a decentralized approach based on satisficing game theory, aircraft can navigate free-flight airspace, effectively eliminating conflicts with other aircraft and avoiding obstacles, including special use airspace and severe weather regions. This method ensures optimal decision-making and stability, enhancing overall operational efficiency and safety in aviation [33].

Furthermore, game theory's principles are leveraged in social sciences to design effective policies and understand social dynamics. It assists in conflict resolution and decision-making processes involving multiple stakeholders with different interests. For example, in political science, game theory is used to analyze voting systems and coalition formations, helping to predict and explain the behaviors of political entities [34].

3.2   Our System Model

Overview: In this section, we introduce a detailed mathematical model that addresses the service allocation problem in an IoT-based edge computing environment, utilizing game theory as the foundational framework. This model is designed to capture the complex interactions between IoT devices and edge servers, considering key factors such as latency, energy consumption, and server load. By applying game theory, our objective is to develop a robust framework that optimizes resource allocation in a distributed and dynamic setting. Our current model assumes constant latency and energy consumption for simplicity. Future work will extend this to include dynamic models that account for variations due to load and network conditions. A schematic representation of the model is illustrated in Fig. 2.

Notations and Definitions: To establish a precise mathematical model, we first define the notations and key parameters involved. Let $D = \{D_1, D_2, \ldots, D_N\}$ denote the set of IoT devices, each of which generates tasks that require processing. Similarly, let $S = \{S_1, S_2, \ldots, S_M\}$ denote the set of edge servers tasked with processing these offloaded tasks. We define the task arrival rate for IoT device D_i as λ_i, and the service rate of edge server S_j by μ_j. The latency L_{ij} experienced by D_i when its task is processed by S_j includes both communication delay and processing delays. The energy consumption E_{ij} for D_i when its task is processed by S_j encompasses the energy used for transmitting the task to the server and any related overheads. Finally, the capacity of edge server S_j, which is the maximum number of tasks it can handle simultaneously, is denoted by C_j.

Utility Functions: Utility functions are fundamental in game theory as they represent the preferences and priorities of the players-in this context, the IoT devices and edge servers.

Utility Function for IoT Devices: Each IoT device seeks to minimize its latency and energy consumption. Therefore, we define the utility function for an IoT

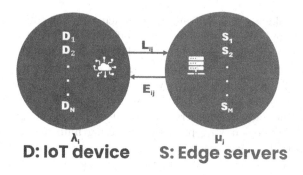

D: IoT device   S: Edge servers

Fig. 2. Schematic diagram of the system model.

device D_i as follows:

$$U_i(S_j) = -(w_L L_{ij} + w_E E_{ij})$$

where:

- w_L and w_E are weight factors representing the relative importance of latency and energy consumption for the IoT device D_i.
- L_{ij} denotes the latency experienced by D_i when its task is processed by the edge server S_j.
- E_{ij} represents the energy consumed by D_i for transmitting the task and any associated overhead.

These weights can be adjusted according to the specific needs or constraints of the IoT device, allowing for a customized approach to resource optimization.

Utility Function for Edge Servers: Edge servers aim to balance their load efficiently and manage their resources to prevent overloading, thereby ensuring timely task processing. The utility function for an edge server S_j is defined as:

$$U_j(D_j) = -\left(\frac{1}{C_j} \sum_{D_i \in D_j} \lambda_i L_{ij} + \gamma \left(\sum_{D_i \in D_j} \frac{\lambda_i}{\mu_j}\right)^2\right)$$

where:

- D_j represents the set of IoT devices assigned to the edge server S_j.
- C_j denotes the capacity of edge server S_j, indicating the maximum number of tasks it can handle simultaneously.
- γ is a weight factor that reflects the significance of load balancing for S_j.
- The term $\left(\sum_{D_i \in D_j} \frac{\lambda_i}{\mu_j}\right)^2$ penalizes high loads, thereby promoting an even distribution of tasks among servers.

This utility function helps edge servers optimize their operations by balancing the load and managing resources efficiently, ensuring a stable and effective service allocation system.

Game-Theoretic Model: The service allocation problem in this scenario is modeled as a non-cooperative game $G = (D, S, U)$, where:

- **Players:** The players in this game are the IoT devices and the edge servers.
- **Strategy Space for IoT Devices:** For each IoT device D_i has a strategy space consisting of the set of edge servers S. The device can choose any server from this set to offload its tasks.
- **Strategy Space for Edge Servers:** For each edge server S_j has a strategy space consisting of the set of IoT devices D. The server can decide which devices' tasks to accept based on its utility function.
- **Utility Functions:** The utility functions U_i and U_j represent the preferences of IoT devices and edge servers, respectively, as defined in previous sections.

Nash Equilibrium: A Nash equilibrium in this game is a set of strategies $(S_1^*, S_2^*, \ldots, S_N^*)$ such that no player can improve their utility by unilaterally changing their strategy. Formally, for each IoT device D_i and edge server S_j, the following conditions hold:

$$U_i(S_j^*) \geq U_i(S_j) \quad \forall S_j \in S,$$
$$U_j(D_j^*) \geq U_j(D_j) \quad \forall D_j \subseteq D.$$

While achieving Nash equilibrium is significant, our utility function also enhances load balancing and resource management, contributing to operational efficiency beyond equilibrium conditions.

Strategy Development: The strategies for IoT devices and edge servers are developed as follows:

- **IoT Device Strategy:** Each IoT device D_i selects the edge server S_j that maximizes its utility function U_i, taking into account factors such as latency and energy consumption.
- **Edge Server Strategy:** Each edge server S_j chooses to accept tasks from IoT devices D_j in a way that maximizes its utility function U_j, considering factors such as load balancing and resource availability.

These strategies ensure that both IoT devices and edge servers optimize their respective utilities, leading to an efficient allocation of resources in the edge computing environment.

Iterative Algorithm for Finding Nash Equilibrium: The algorithm described in this section iteratively finds the Nash Equilibrium in a system where IoT devices interact with edge serves, named as Iterative Resource Allocation algorithm. In this system, each IoT device selects an edge server, and each edge server decides which IoT devices' tasks to accept, with the goal of maximizing their respective utility functions. The process begins with each IoT device randomly choosing an edge server. Subsequently, the algorithm proceeds with iterative updates: each IoT device re-evaluates and selects the edge server that maximizes its utility, while each edge server updates its accepted set of IoT devices to optimize its utility. This iterative process continues until a state is reached where no IoT device or edge server can unilaterally improve their utility by changing their strategy. This results in a stable resource allocation corresponding to a Nash Equilibrium, where no player has an incentive to deviate from their current strategy.

Algorithm 1. Iterative Resource Allocation Algorithm

Require: Each IoT device D_i randomly selects an edge server S_j
 1: **repeat**
 2:     **for** each IoT device D_i **do**
 3:         D_i selects S_j that maximizes U_i
 4:     **end for**
 5:     **for** each edge server S_j **do**
 6:         S_j accepts tasks from D_j that maximize U_j
 7:     **end for**
 8: **until** no D_i or S_j can improve their utility

Theorem 1. *The iterative algorithm described by Iterative Resource Allocation Algorithm converges to a Nash Equilibrium of the IoT-edge server system. At this equilibrium, the allocation of IoT devices to edge servers and the task acceptance strategy of edge servers are such that no IoT device D_i can increase its utility by switching edge servers, and no edge server S_j can improve its utility by altering its set of accepted IoT devices. Formally, this equilibrium is characterized by:*

$$U_i(S_j^*) \geq U_i(S_j) \quad \forall S_j \in S,$$
$$U_j(D_j^*) \geq U_j(D_j) \quad \forall D_j \subseteq D.$$

where $(S_1^*, S_2^*, \ldots, S_N^*)$ *is the set of strategies for IoT devices and* $(D_1^*, D_2^*, \ldots, D_M^*)$ *is the set of strategies for edge servers at equilibrium.*

4   Simulation and Results

In this section, we present the simulation results of *Iterative Resource Allocation Algorithm*, designed to optimize resource allocation among a network of 10 IoT devices and 5 edge servers over 100 iterations. The primary objective was to enhance the utility of each device and server through iterative strategy updates. Initially, utility matrices for devices and servers were randomly initialized, and each device was assigned to a server randomly. During each iteration, the algorithm updated device strategies by assigning each device to the server offering the highest utility. Simultaneously, server strategies were adjusted to prioritize devices that maximized the server's overall utility. Our framework's robustness is demonstrated through simulations showing consistent performance under varying conditions. Detailed results are provided in the simulation section.

The simulation results demonstrated a diverse assignment of devices to servers based on the highest utility values. The utilities of the devices varied widely, ranging from 0.0019 to 0.979, reflecting a customized approach that aligns device needs with server capabilities. Notably, some devices achieved high utility scores, indicating effective optimization, while others had lower scores, showcasing the algorithm's ability to adapt to various performance requirements.

For server utilities, Server 4 achieved the highest utility of 2.341, suggesting it effectively served multiple devices. Other servers also showed substantial utility, indicating a balanced distribution of resources across the network. The plots of total device and server utilities over iterations illustrated convergence and improvement in performance, confirming that the algorithm progressively enhanced both device and server utilization (see, Fig. 3).

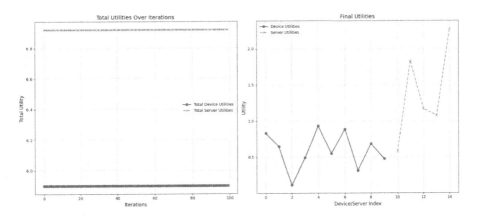

Fig. 3. Total and final utilities of devices and servers in device-edge server resource allocation.

4.1   Comparative Analysis with Wang et al.'s Resource Allocation Strategy

To evaluate the effectiveness of Iterative Resource Allocation Algorithm, we compared it with the resource allocation strategy proposed by Wang et al. 2022 [35]. The comparison highlighted several advantages of our Iterative Resource Allocation Algorithm over the approach by Wang et al.'s method:

Utility Distribution: Our algorithm employs a nuanced resource allocation mechanism, resulting in a wide range of device utilities from 0.0019 to 0.979. This range demonstrates the algorithm's ability to allocate resources based on individual device needs and performance, achieving a more balanced and effective distribution. In contrast, the method by Wang et al. 2022 shows a concentrated allocation of resources among a few users, with values reaching up to 9.387 [35]. This often leads to inefficient resource utilization and underutilization of remaining computational resources. Furthermore, the uniform task offloading policy in Wang et al.'s method, assigning a maximum value of 100 to all users (as detailed in Fig. 4), fails to account for individual user requirements and capabilities, potentially leading to suboptimal performance.

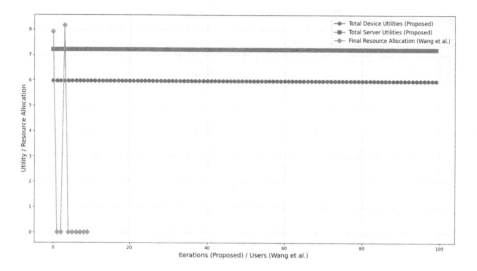

Fig. 4. Comparison of Metrics Between the Proposed Algorithm and Wang et al.'s Algorithm. [35].

Practical Utility and Efficiency: The diverse utility scores achieved by Iterative Resource Allocation Algorithm reflect its adaptability to various demands, making it highly practical for real-world applications. By dynamically adjusting server strategies in response to device needs, Iterative Resource Allocation Algorithm ensures efficient resource distribution, minimizing waste and optimizing utilization. In contrast, the uniform resource distribution approach by Wang et al. can lead to resource saturation, as it does not accommodate varying user demands, resulting in significant inefficiencies and wasted resources [35].

Flexibility and Adaptability: The iterative updating mechanism of Iterative Resource Allocation Algorithm allows it to adapt to changing conditions and preferences, continually enhancing its performance and resource allocation. This adaptability is a key strength, ensuring the algorithm's effectiveness in dynamic environments. Conversely, the fixed task offloading policy employed by Wang et al. lacks flexibility, offering a uniform allocation that does not consider individual user needs and performance characteristics, potentially leading to less effective resource management.

5   Conclusion

This study introduced a game-theoretic approach to optimize service allocation in edge computing for IoT applications. Our key contributions include:

- **Comprehensive Model Development:** We created a mathematical model to capture interactions between IoT devices and edge servers, considering latency, energy consumption, and server load.
- **Resource Allocation Algorithm:** We proposed an iterative algorithm to achieve Nash Equilibrium, ensuring efficient and stable resource allocation.
- **Comparative Analysis:** Our approach outperformed existing methods like Wang et al. (2022) in utility distribution, efficiency, and adaptability.

Future research directions and applications include:

- **Advanced Game-Theoretic Models:** Developing sophisticated models to address complex IoT environments, including security and privacy concerns.
- **AI and Machine Learning Integration:** Combining game theory with AI and machine learning for real-time learning and adaptation, enhancing resource allocation.
- **Scalability and Resilience:** Exploring scalable solutions and enhancing edge computing resilience against disruptions.
- **Emerging Applications:** Adapting our framework for 5G, augmented reality, virtual reality, and autonomous vehicles to ensure optimal performance and user satisfaction.

Our study advances the understanding and methodologies in IoT-based edge computing, opening new avenues for research and technological advancements to create more efficient, scalable, and resilient systems. Future research will focus on incorporating heterogeneous task requirements into our model, where tasks consume varying server capacities. Additionally, we aim to provide formal proofs for all theoretical claims made in this study, enhancing the rigor and credibility of our findings.

Acknowledgment. The authors express their gratitude to all researchers in Game Theory and Edge Computing for their invaluable contributions. They also extend their thanks to the School of Computer Engineering, KIIT Deemed to be University & School of Computer Science, University College Dublin for the support that they have provided throughout this study.

References

1. Zhou, S., Jadoon, W., Khan, I.A.: Computing offloading strategy in mobile edge computing environment: a comparison between adopted frameworks, challenges, and future directions. Electronics **12**(11) (2023). https://www.mdpi.com/2079-9292/12/11/2452
2. Zamzam, M., El-Shabrawy, T., Ashour, M.: Game theory for computation offloading and resource allocation in edge computing: a survey. In: 2020 2nd Novel Intelligent and Leading Emerging Sciences Conference (NILES), pp. 47–53 (2020)
3. Kumar, S., Goswami, A., Gupta, R., Singh, S.P., Lay-Ekuakille, A.: A cost-effective and QoS-aware user allocation approach for edge computing enabled IoT. IEEE Internet Things J. **10**(2), 1696–1710 (2023)
4. Mahmood, O.A., Abdellah, A.R., Muthanna, A., Koucheryavy, A.: Distributed edge computing for resource allocation in smart cities based on the IoT. Information **13**(7) (2022). https://www.mdpi.com/2078-2489/13/7/328
5. Zhou, H., Zhang, Z., Li, D., Su, Z.: Joint optimization of computing offloading and service caching in edge computing-based smart grid. IEEE Trans. Cloud Comput. **11**(2), 1122–1132 (2023)
6. Yu, H., Zhou, Z., Jia, Z., Zhao, X., Zhang, L., Wang, X.: Multi-timescale multi-dimension resource allocation for noma-edge computing-based power IoT with massive connectivity. IEEE Trans. Green Commun. Networking **5**(3), 1101–1113 (2021)
7. Jin, Z., Zhang, C., Jin, Y., Zhang, L., Su, J.: A resource allocation scheme for joint optimizing energy consumption and delay in collaborative edge computing-based industrial IoT. IEEE Trans. Industr. Inf. **18**(9), 6236–6243 (2022)
8. Hamdan, S., Ayyash, M., Almajali, S.: Edge-computing architectures for internet of things applications: a survey. Sensors **20**(22) (2020). https://www.mdpi.com/1424-8220/20/22/6441
9. Sinha, A., Mishra, V., Bandyopadhyay, A., Swain, S., Chakraborty, S.: Fair resource allocation in fog computing by using a game theoretic approach. In: Chaki, N., Roy, N.D., Debnath, P., Saeed, K. (eds.) Proceedings of International Conference on Data Analytics and Insights, ICDAI 2023, pp. 125–134. Springer, Singapore (2023)
10. Jazaeri, S.S., Jabbehdari, S., Asghari, P., et al.: Edge computing in SDN-IoT networks: a systematic review of issues, challenges and solutions. Clust. Comput. **24**(6), 3187–3228 (2021). https://doi.org/10.1007/s10586-021-03311-6
11. Bourechak, A., Zedadra, O., Kouahla, M.N., Guerrieri, A., Seridi, H., Fortino, G.: At the confluence of artificial intelligence and edge computing in IoT-based applications: a review and new perspectives. Sensors **23**(3) (2023). https://www.mdpi.com/1424-8220/23/3/1639
12. Ishtiaq, M., Saeed, N., Khan, M.A.: Edge computing in IoT: a 6G perspective. arXiv abs/2111.08943 (2021). https://api.semanticscholar.org/CorpusID:244269978
13. Sihna, A., Raj, H., Das, R., Bandyopadhyay, A., Swain, S., Chakrborty, S.: Medical education system based on metaverse platform: a game theoretic approach. In: 2023 4th International Conference on Intelligent Engineering and Management (ICIEM), pp. 1–6 (2023)
14. Bandyopadhyay, A., et al.: A game-theoretic approach for rendering immersive experiences in the metaverse. Mathematics **11**(6) (2023). https://www.mdpi.com/2227-7390/11/6/1286

15. Guo, M., Li, L., Guan, Q.: Energy-efficient and delay-guaranteed workload allocation in IoT-edge-cloud computing systems. IEEE Access **7**, 78685–78697 (2019)
16. Keshta, I., Soni, M., Deb, N., Singh, S., Saravanan, K., Khan, I.R.: Game theory-based optimization for efficient IoT task offloading in 6G network base stations (2024)
17. Yang, H., Zhang, H., Gong, Z.: Computation offloading and resource allocation in mobile edge computing-enabled IoT network (2024)
18. Bing-jie, L., Wang, H., Li, M., Ding, L., Li, F., Dong, P.: Dynamic pricing in edge computing resource allocation based on stackelberg dynamic game (2023)
19. Yin, T., Chen, X., Jiao, L., Xing, H., Min, G.: Game-based service requests and channel selection in mobile edge computing (2023)
20. Liu, X., Zheng, J., Zhang, M., Li, Y., Wang, R., He, Y.: A game-based computing resource allocation scheme of edge server in vehicular edge computing networks considering diverse task offloading modes. Sensors **24**(1) (2024). https://www.mdpi.com/1424-8220/24/1/69
21. Li, N., Yan, J., Zhang, Z., Martinez, J.F., Yuan, X.: Game theory based joint task offloading and resource allocation algorithm for mobile edge computing. In: 2020 16th International Conference on Mobility, Sensing and Networking (MSN), pp. 791–796 (2020)
22. Li, S., Zhang, N., Jiang, R., Zhang, Y., Han, T.: Joint task offloading and resource allocation in mobile edge computing with energy harvesting. J. Cloud Comput. **11**(1), 17 (2022). https://doi.org/10.1186/s13677-022-00290-w
23. Song, Q., Qu, L.: UAV-D2D assisted latency minimization and load balancing in mobile edge computing with deep reinforcement learning. In: Jin, H., Yu, Z., Yu, C., Zhou, X., Lu, Z., Song, X. (eds.) Green, Pervasive, and Cloud Computing, pp. 108–122. Springer, Singapore (2024)
24. Li, S., Zhai, D., Du, P., Han, T.: Energy-efficient task offloading, load balancing, and resource allocation in mobile edge computing enabled IoT networks. SCIENCE CHINA Inf. Sci. **62**(29), 307 (2019). https://doi.org/10.1007/s11432-017-9440-x
25. Patsias, V., Amanatidis, P., Karampatzakis, D., Lagkas, T., Michalakopoulou, K., Nikitas, A.: Task allocation methods and optimization techniques in edge computing: a systematic review of the literature. Future Internet **15**(8) (2023). https://www.mdpi.com/1999-5903/15/8/254
26. Tabatabaee Malazi, H., et al.: Dynamic service placement in multi-access edge computing: a systematic literature review. IEEE Access **10**, 32639–32688 (2022)
27. Chu, W., Yu, P., Yu, Z., Lui, J.C., Lin, Y.: Online optimal service selection, resource allocation and task offloading for multi-access edge computing: a utility-based approach. IEEE Trans. Mob. Comput. **22**(7), 4150–4167 (2023)
28. Ding, Y., Li, K., Liu, C., Tang, Z., Li, K.: Budget-constrained service allocation optimization for mobile edge computing. IEEE Trans. Serv. Comput. **16**(1), 147–161 (2023)
29. Hassannataj Joloudari, J., Mojrian, S., Saadatfar, H., et al.: Resource allocation problem and artificial intelligence: the state-of-the-art review (2009–2023) and open research challenges. Multimedia Tools Appl. **83**, 67953–67996 (2024). https://doi.org/10.1007/s11042-024-18123-0
30. Wu, W.K.: Theory and practical application based on game theory. BCP business & management (2023)
31. Li, Y.: Study and application of game theory. Highlights in Business, Economics and Management (2023)
32. Pi, J.: Game theory and game mechanics design (2024)

33. Xiaohui, J., Xuejun, Z., Xiangmin, G.: A collision avoidance method based on satisfying game theory. In: 2012 4th International Conference on Intelligent Human-Machine Systems and Cybernetics, vol. 2, pp. 96–99 (2012)
34. Munck, G.L.: Game theory and comparative politics: new perspectives and old concerns. World Politics **53**(2), 173–204 (2001)
35. Wang, S., Hu, Z., Deng, Y., Hu, L.: Game-theory-based task offloading and resource scheduling in cloud-edge collaborative systems. Appl. Sci. **12**(12) (2022). https://www.mdpi.com/2076-3417/12/12/6154

Exploring Hidden Behaviors in OpenMP Multi-threaded Applications for Anomaly Detection in HPC Environments

Biswajit Bhowmik$^{(\boxtimes)}$, K. K. Girish, Pawanesh Mishra, and Rishi Mishra

Maharshi Sushrut CAS Lab, BRICS Lab, Department of Computer Science and Engineering, National Institute of Technology, Mangalore, Karnataka, India
{brb,girishkk.217cs003,pawaneshmishra.232cs023,
rishimishra.232cs028}@nitk.edu.in

Abstract. In high-performance computing (HPC), multi-threaded applications using OpenMP face complex challenges in identifying hidden performance issues, often due to resource conflicts, software inefficiencies, and hardware anomalies. These subtle issues can significantly degrade performance and reduce system reliability. This paper introduces an innovative approach designed to address these concealed issues in OpenMP multi-threaded applications. The proposed method integrates a Random Forest classifier with anthropomorphic diagnosis to effectively identify and diagnose performance-affecting problems. The approach has demonstrated a remarkable ability to detect 90% of performance-affecting issues that are often obscured within complex HPC environments.

Keywords: High Performance Computing (HPC) · OpenMP · Random Forest · Anthropomorphic Diagnosis · Performance Issues · System Efficiency

1 Introduction

The rising demand for computational power in research and industry has driven technological progress, making parallel computing essential for enhancing efficiency and performance. HPC advances this by utilizing sophisticated hardware, large memory systems, and parallel processing techniques, facilitating fast simulations and addressing complex challenges [1]. Concurrently, parallel programming models, particularly OpenMP for shared-memory systems, have become crucial for maximizing modern architectures. OpenMP simplifies code parallelization for multi-core processors and enables efficient workload distribution through constructs like parallel loops, sections, and tasks [2].

OpenMP, despite its advantages, encounters challenges in extreme-scale computing, such as managing processes and threads, which impact performance. Issues like anomalous processes and memory leaks can lead to inefficiencies and system failures [3]. Studies [4–11] reveal that traditional diagnostics relying on

© The Author(s), under exclusive license to Springer Nature Switzerland AG 2025
Q. Bramas et al. (Eds.): ICDCIT 2025, LNCS 15507, pp. 61–67, 2025.
https://doi.org/10.1007/978-3-031-81404-4_5

manual analysis often struggle with system complexity. This paper introduces a novel framework combining anthropomorphic diagnosis with a Random Forest classifier, leveraging human-like reasoning and historical heartbeat data to detect complex behaviors missed by conventional methods. The rest of the paper is organized as follows: Section 2 presents the proposed methodology. Section 3 provides the experiments and results. Section 4 concludes the paper.

2   Proposed Methodology

The proposed method introduces a cutting-edge framework called openMP-Anomaly Detect, that synergistically combines Anthropomorphic Diagnosis with a Random Forest classifier. By incorporating human-like reasoning and analyzing historical heartbeat data from OpenMP applications, this approach enhances the detection and resolution of performance-related issues that traditional methods often overlook. Figure 1 illustrates the framework of proposed methodology.

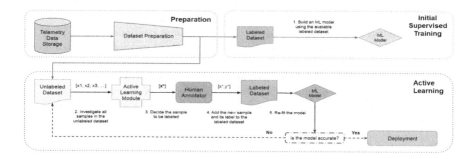

Fig. 1. Proposed Framework for Detection of Hidden Behaviors in HPC Systems

2.1   Extraction of Statistical Features

In the OpenMP-AnomalyDetect framework, extracting and selecting statistical features from telemetry data is essential for accurate anomaly detection in OpenMP applications. This process involves collecting comprehensive heartbeat data, including metrics like CPU usage, memory allocation, and execution times. Advanced features are derived using time series characterization to identify performance patterns and anomalies, along with descriptive statistics for insights into data distribution. This combined approach offers a detailed view of application performance under varying conditions. To optimize model performance, the Chi-Square feature selection technique [12] reduces data dimensionality, enhancing detection efficiency and accuracy by evaluating each feature's relevance to the target variable. Algorithm 1 illustrates the application of this technique in the framework.

Algorithm 1. Chi-Square Feature Selection

Input: Dataset X with features $[x_1, x_2, \ldots, x_m]$, target variable Y, number of features to select k
Output: Top k selected features based on Chi-Square scores

1: Initialize an empty list S to store Chi-Square scores for each feature
2: **for** each feature x_i in X **do**
3:     Construct contingency table T for feature x_i and target variable Y
4:     Compute observed frequencies O_{ij} for each cell (i, j) in T
5:     Compute expected frequencies E_{ij} for each cell (i, j):

$$E_{ij} = \frac{R_i \cdot C_j}{N}$$

6:     Compute Chi-Square statistic χ_i^2 for feature x_i:

$$\chi_i^2 = \sum_{(i,j)} \frac{(O_{ij} - E_{ij})^2}{E_{ij}}$$

7:     Append χ_i^2 to list S
8: **end for**
9: Rank all features based on their Chi-Square scores in list S
10: Select the top k features with the highest Chi-Square scores from list S
11: **Return:** The top k selected features

2.2 Supervised Training

After feature selection, the OpenMP-AnomalyDetect framework optimizes model performance through hyperparameter searching via grid search and cross validation [13]. Predefined hyperparameter values are tested and evaluated on accuracy, precision, recall, and F1-score to determine optimal settings. Following this, supervised training uses labeled samples to establish a baseline understanding of normal versus anomalous behavior, setting the stage for the active learning phase. This phase refines detection capabilities through iterative data integration and real-time feedback. Active learning enhances sample labeling by adaptively selecting the most informative samples, reducing the need for extensive manual annotation. As shown in Algorithm 2, three query strategies are employed: Classification Entropy for measuring prediction uncertainty, Classification Margin for assessing the probability gap between top predictions, and Classification Uncertainty for quantifying overall ambiguity through variance.

3 Experiments and Results

This section offers a comprehensive overview of the experiments conducted to evaluate the proposed framework.

3.1 HPC Systems and Dataset

The HPC setup for anomaly detection in OpenMP applications features an Intel Core i5 multi-core processor, an NVIDIA Tesla K80 GPU, and 512 GB DDR4 RAM for strong parallel processing capabilities, complemented by a 4 TB NVMe

Algorithm 2. Active Learning for OpenMP- AnomalyDetect

Input: Initial labeled dataset D_{init}, unlabeled dataset $D_{unlabeled}$, anomaly detection model M, and query number Q.

Output: Updated model M with improved anomaly detection.

1: **Initialize:**
2:   Train M with D_{init}
3:   Set $D_{labeled} \leftarrow D_{init}$ and $D_{unlabeled} \leftarrow D_{unlabeled}$
4:   Initialize $t \leftarrow 0$
5: **while** not stopping criterion met **do**
6:     **Uncertainty Sampling:**
7:     **for** each $x_i \in D_{unlabeled}$ **do**
8:         Compute uncertainty $U(x_i)$ using M:

   Classification Entropy: $H(x_i)$
   Margin Sampling: $\Delta(x_i)$
   Least Confident Sampling: $C(x_i)$

9:     **end for**
10:    **Select Top Q Samples:**
11:    Choose Q samples with highest $U(x_i)$
12:    **Query Oracle:**
13:    Obtain labels for selected samples from oracle
14:    **Update Datasets:**
15:    Add new labeled samples to $D_{labeled}$
16:    Remove queried samples from $D_{unlabeled}$
17:    **Re-train Model:**
18:    Train M with updated $D_{labeled}$
19:    Increment $t \leftarrow t + 1$
20: **end while**
21: **Return:** Updated model M

SSD for storage and a 100 Gbps Infiniband network for fast data transfers. The software stack includes Python 3.8, TensorFlow, and OpenMP, facilitating efficient algorithm development, while the SLURM Workload Manager optimizes resource allocation and job scheduling, making the configuration ideal for intensive anomaly detection tasks. To simulate diverse telemetry scenarios, a synthetic dataset named `X_hidden_behaviors` was generated using NumPy from human heartbeat data, comprising 100 samples with 794 features to replicate real-world system behaviors and potential anomalies. This dataset is used to test and validate the anomaly detection framework in various operational conditions.

3.2   Supervised Training with Hyperparameter Tuning

To test the anomaly detection framework effectively, the dataset is created with simulated anomalies using the `introduce_anomalies` function, which perturbed synthetic samples to emulate issues like memory leaks and thread contention, labeling instances as normal (0) or anomalous (1). The dataset is split into training (`X_train`, `y_train`) and testing (`X_test`, `y_test`) subsets using scikit-learn's `train_test_split` function, as shown in Figure 2. The methodology employs a Random Forest classifier with hyperparameter tuning to optimize performance, focusing on key parameters such as `n_estimators=100`, `max_depth=None`, and `n_jobs=-1` to improve sensitivity to subtle anomalies. Although accuracy initially increased with the number of trees, further additions led to diminishing returns, illustrated in Figure 3. Additionally, an active learning approach guided by classification entropy iteratively selects high-uncertainty instances, enhancing the model's anomaly detection capabilities.

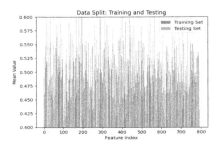

Fig. 2. Train Test Split   **Fig. 3.** Hyperparameter Tuning

3.3   Model Evaluation and Results

The final evaluation of the model on the testing set showed high effectiveness, achieving 90% accuracy and precision, with a recall of 98%, indicating excellent detection of positive cases. An F1-score of 94% highlighted the model's balanced performance, confirming its robustness. Additionally, the framework was assessed for heartbeat diagnosis using several supervised machine learning methods, including logistic regression (LR), decision tree (DT), random forest (RF), naive bayes (NB), SGDC classifier, and heartbeat sequence analysis (HSA). Heartbeat samples were categorized into three groups: normal (N), memory leak/abnormal (A), and shutdown (S), with macro F-scores calculated for each group. As shown in Table 1, the proposed method outperformed other techniques across multiple OpenMP benchmarks, such as NPB-sp, NPB-lu, NPB-bt, NPB-cg, and EPCC-array.

Table 1. Comparison Between Different OpenMP Anomaly Detection Frameworks

Method	NPB-sp			NPB-lu			NPB-bt			NPB-cg			EPCC-Array		
	N	A	S	N	A	S	N	A	S	N	A	S	N	A	S
LR	0.55	0.87	0.91	0.63	0.88	0.58	0.44	0	0	0.65	0	0.84	0.64	0.90	0
DT	0.86	0.91	0.92	0.42	0.79	0.62	0.45	0.70	0.55	0.94	0.94	1.00	1.00	0.31	0.83
RF	0.67	0.81	0.63	0.46	0.93	0.53	0.43	0.66	0.40	0.94	0.93	1.00	1.00	0.93	0.95
NB	0.49	0.88	0	0.52	0.71	0.08	0.37	0	0	0.50	0	0	0.53	0	0
SGDC	0	0.81	0.87	0.53	0.73	0.12	0.46	0	0.12	0.86	0	0.74	0	0.68	0.48
HSA	0.93	0.89	0.91	0.86	0.90	0.85	0.83	0.78	0.90	1.00	0.86	1.00	1.00	0.90	1.00
Proposed	0.94	0.90	0.93	0.89	0.93	0.89	0.89	0.82	0.93	0.92	0.87	0.92	1.00	0.91	0.92

4   Conclusion

In the evolving field of HPC, optimizing application performance is crucial for user satisfaction and system efficiency. This paper introduces a novel active learning-based framework designed to address performance anomalies in HPC systems. Utilizing automated telemetry data and a robust active learning mechanism, the framework achieves 90% accuracy in detecting both known and novel anomalies. Its successful testing on both production and testbed HPC systems demonstrates practical utility and resilience. By significantly reducing reliance on labeled data while maintaining high performance, the framework offers a valuable tool for managing HPC complexities and improving system reliability and efficiency.

References

1. Wang, J., Wang, L., Zhao, X., Miao, Z.: Optimization problems and maintenance policy for a parallel computing system with dependent components. Ann. Oper. Res. 1–26 (2024)
2. Bhowmik, B., Biswas, S., Deka, J.K., Bhattacharya, B.B.: Reliability-aware test methodology for detecting short-channel faults in on-chip networks. IEEE Trans. Very Large Scale Integr. (VLSI) Syst. **26**(6), 1026–1039 (2018)
3. Mishra, A., Malik, A.M., Lin, M., Chapman, B.: OpenMP advisor: a compiler tool for heterogeneous architectures. In: International Workshop on OpenMP, pp. 34–48, Springer (2023)
4. Tuncer, O., et al.: Online diagnosis of performance variation in HPC systems using machine learning. IEEE Trans. Parallel Distrib. Syst. **30**(4), 883–896 (2018)
5. da Rosa, F.R., Garibotti, R., Ost, L., Reis, R.: Using machine learning techniques to evaluate multicore soft error reliability. IEEE Trans. Circuits Syst. I Regul. Pap. **66**(6), 2151–2164 (2019)
6. Shen, Y., Peng, M., Wu, Q., Li, R.: A machine learning method to variable classification in OpenMP. Futur. Gener. Comput. Syst. **140**, 67–78 (2023)
7. Yamazaki, I., Kurzak, J., Wu, P., Zounon, M., Dongarra, J.: Symmetric indefinite linear solver using OpenMP task on multicore architectures. IEEE Trans. Parallel Distrib. Syst. **29**(8), 1879–1892 (2018)
8. Agullo, E., Aumage, O., Bramas, B., Coulaud, O., Pitoiset, S.: Bridging the gap between OpenMP and task-based runtime systems for the fast multipole method. IEEE Trans. Parallel Distrib. Syst. **28**(10), 2794–2807 (2017)
9. Vargas-Pérez, S., Saeed, F.: A hybrid MPI-OpenMP strategy to speedup the compression of big next-generation sequencing datasets. IEEE Trans. Parallel Distrib. Syst. **28**(10), 2760–2769 (2017)
10. González-Domínguez, J., Bolón-Canedo, V., Freire, B., Touriño, J.: Parallel feature selection for distributed-memory clusters. Inf. Sci. **496**, 399–409 (2019)
11. Aldea López, S., Estébanez López, Á., González Escribano, A., Llanos Ferraris, D.R., et al.: An OpenMP extension that supports thread-level speculation. Information Sciences (2017)

12. Ahakonye, L.A.C., Nwakanma, C.I., Lee, J.-M., Kim, D.-S.: Scada intrusion detection scheme exploiting the fusion of modified decision tree and chi-square feature selection. Internet Things **21**, 100676 (2023)
13. Sukamto, S., Hadiyanto, H., Kurnianingsih, K.: KNN optimization using grid search algorithm for preeclampsia imbalance class. In: E3S Web of Conferences, vol. 448, p. 02057, EDP Sciences (2023)

A "Symbolic" Representation of Object-Nets

Michael Köhler-Bußmeier[1] and Lorenzo Capra[2]

[1] University of Applied Science, Hamburg Berliner Tor 7, 20099 Hamburg, Germany
michael.koehler-bussmeier@haw-hamburg.de
[2] Dipartimento di Informatica, Università degli Studi di Milano, Via Celoria 18, Milan, Italy
capra@di.unimi.it

Abstract. In this contribution, we extend the concept of a Petri net morphism to Elementary Object Systems (Eos). Eos are a net-within-nets formalism, that is, we allow the tokens of a Petri net to be Petri nets again. This nested structure has the consequence that even systems defined by very small Petri nets have a quite huge reachability graph. In this contribution, we use automorphism to describe symmetries of the Petri net topology. Since these symmetries carry over to markings as well, this leads to a condensed state space, too.

Keywords: Automorphism · canonical representation · nets within nets · symmetry · state space reductions

1 Exploiting Symmetry and Canonical Representations

In this paper, we study *Elementary Object Systems* (Eos) [5] a Nets-within-Nets formalism as proposed by Valk [9], that is, we allow the tokens of a Petri net to be Petri nets again. Due to the nesting structure, many of the classical decision problems, such as reachability and liveness, become undecidable for Eos.

From a complexity perspective, we have studied these problems for *safe* Eos [5,7,8] where markings are restricted to *sets* (i.e., places are marked or unmarked). More precisely: All problems that are expressible in LTL or CTL, including reachability and liveness, are PSPACE-complete. This means that in terms of complexity theory, safe Eos are not more complex than safe place transition (P/T) nets. But, a look at the details shows a difference that is practically relevant: For safe p/t nets, it is known that whenever there are n places, the number of reachable states is bounded by $O(2^n)$; but for safe Eos the number of reachable states is in $O(2^{(n^2)})$ – a quite drastic increase. Therefore, our main goal is to derive a *condensed* state space for Eos, where 'condensed' is expressed as factorization modulo equivalence.

In this contribution, we extend the concept of a Petri net morphism to Eos. Here, we use automorphism to describe symmetries of the Petri net topology.

Q. Bramas et al. (Eds.): ICDCIT 2025, LNCS 15507, pp. 68–74, 2025.
https://doi.org/10.1007/978-3-031-81404-4_6

Since these symmetries carry over to markings as well, this leads to a condensed state space, too. In our approach, these symmetries are introduced very naturally to the representation of the state space using *canonical representatives* of equivalent (automorphic) markings.

2   Eos-Automorphism and Canonical Representation

The pseudo-symbolic representation of EOS that we will introduce relies on established concepts like graph (auto)morphism and canonical representative. In what follows, we implicitly employ multiset homomorphism.

A *place/transition net (p/t net)* N is a tuple $N = (P, T, \mathbf{pre}, \mathbf{post})$, such that P is a set of places, T is a set of transitions, with $P \cap T = \emptyset$, and $\mathbf{pre}, \mathbf{post} : T \to MS(P)$ are the pre- and post-condition functions. A marking of N is a multiset of places: $\mathbf{m} \in MS(P)$.

Definition 1. *Given p/t nets N and N', a morphism between N and N' is a pair $\varphi = (\varphi_t, \varphi_p)$ of bijective maps $\varphi_t : T_N \to T_{N'}, \varphi_p : P_N \to P_{N'}$ such that*

$$\forall t \in T_N : \ \mathbf{pre}_{N'}(\varphi_t(t)) = \varphi_p(\mathbf{pre}_N(t)) \land \mathbf{post}_{N'}(\varphi_t(t)) = \varphi_p(\mathbf{post}_N(t))$$

We use the notation $\varphi : N \to N'$, and $N \cong N'$ means there exists $\varphi : N \to N'$. A morphism between marked p/t nets $(N, \mathbf{m})$ and $(N', \mathbf{m}')$ is a p/t morphism $\varphi : N \to N'$ such that $\varphi_p(\mathbf{m}) = \mathbf{m}'$.
(We extend the notation introduced above to marked nets' morphism.)

A morphism $\varphi : N \to N$ is referred to as an automorphism: φ_p, φ_t are permutations. The markings $\mathbf{m}_1$ and $\mathbf{m}_2$ of N are said equivalent if and only if there exists a morphism $\varphi : (N, \mathbf{m}_1) \to (N, \mathbf{m}_2)$. We denote this by $\mathbf{m}_1 \cong \mathbf{m}_2$. Furthermore, $\cong$ establishes an equivalence relation on the set of markings of N.

It is well known that a p/t morphism $\varphi : N \to N'$ maintains the firing rule:

$$\mathbf{m}_1 \xrightarrow[N]{t} \mathbf{m}_2 \ \implies \ \varphi_p(\mathbf{m}_1) \xrightarrow[N']{\varphi_t(t)} \varphi_p(\mathbf{m}_2) \tag{1}$$

The equivalence relation $\cong$ on the markings of a *p/t net* N is thus a congruence when considering transition firing.

2.1   Eos-Automorphism

We provide a natural extension of automorphisms to EOS [5]. An elementary object system (EOS) $OS = (\widehat{N}, \mathcal{N}, d, \Theta)$ is composed of a *system net* $\widehat{N} = (\widehat{P}, \widehat{T}, \mathbf{pre}, \mathbf{post})$ and a set of *object nets* $\mathcal{N} = \{N_1, \dots, N_n\}$, such that each $N \in \mathcal{N}$ is given as $N = (P_N, T_N, \mathbf{pre}_N, \mathbf{post}_N)$. The system net places are typed by the mapping $d : \widehat{P} \to \mathcal{N}$ with the meaning, that a place $\widehat{p} \in \widehat{P}$ of the system net with $d(\widehat{p}) = N$ may contain only net-tokens of the type N.

For nets-within-nets events in the set Θ are nested, too. An Eos allows three different kinds of events – as illustrated by the following Eos.

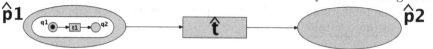

1. System-autonomous: The system net transition $\widehat{t}$ fires autonomously which moves the net-token from $\widehat{p}_1$ to $\widehat{p}_2$ without changing its marking.
2. Object-autonomous: The object net fires transition t_1, which "moves" the black token from q_1 to q_2. The object net itself remains at its location $\widehat{p}_1$.
3. Synchronisation: The system net transition $\widehat{t}$ fires synchronously with t_1 in the object net. Whenever synchronisation is demanded, autonomous actions are forbidden.

Definition 2. *An* Eos*-automorphism* φ_{OS} *is a collection of p/t automorphisms* $\varphi_{OS} = \left(\varphi_{\widehat{N}} : \widehat{N} \to \widehat{N},\ (\varphi_N : N \to N)_{N \in \mathcal{N}}\right)$ *that preserve d and* Θ:

1. $\forall \widehat{p} \in P_{\widehat{N}} :\ d(\varphi_{\widehat{N}}(\widehat{p})) = d(\widehat{p})$
2. $\forall \widehat{\tau}[\vartheta] \in \Theta :\ \exists \vartheta' : \varphi_{\widehat{N}}(\widehat{\tau})[\vartheta'] \in \Theta\ \wedge \forall N \in \mathcal{N} : \vartheta'(N) = \varphi_N(\vartheta(N))$

Observe that the second condition in Definition 2 implicitly establishes a permutation within the events in Θ.

A *marking* of an Eos is a *nested* multiset, denoted $\mu = \sum_{k=1}^{|\mu|} \widehat{p}_k[M_k]$, where $\widehat{p}_k$ is a place of the system net marked with a net-token and $M_k \in MS(P_{d(\widehat{p}_k)})$ is the net-token's marking. The set of all markings is denoted $\mathcal{M}$. We naturally extend the concept of Eos-automorphism to *marked* Eos.

Definition 3. *An automorphism between* (OS, μ) *and* (OS, μ') *is an* Eos-*automorphism* φ_{OS} *such that:*
If $\mu = \sum_{k=1}^{|\mu|} \widehat{p}_k[M_k]$ *then* $\mu' = \varphi_{OS}(\mu) := \sum_{k=1}^{|\mu|} \varphi_{\widehat{N}}(\widehat{p}_k)[\varphi_{d(\widehat{p}_k)}(M_k)]$.
The markings μ_1 *and* μ_2 *of OS are said to be* equivalent *if and only if there exist* $\varphi_{OS} : (OS, \mu_1) \to (OS, \mu_2)$. *We write (abusing notation)* $\mu_1 \cong \mu_2$.

Again, $\cong$ defines an equivalence relation on the set of markings of OS.

2.2   Eos-Events and Eos-Automorphism

The analogy of p/t automorphism and Eos-automorphism also holds for the firing rule. It is convenient to treat all three kinds of events uniformly as synchronisations (where autonomous events synchronise with "dummy" transitions). Then events are written in the form $\widehat{\tau}[\vartheta]$, where $\widehat{\tau}$ is a system net transition and ϑ is a function such that $\vartheta(N)$ is the multiset of transitions, which have to fire synchronously with $\widehat{\tau}$. Informally speaking, each event removes a nested multiset λ from the current marking μ (i.e. $\lambda \sqsubseteq \mu$) and then replaces λ with ρ; when firing $\mu \xrightarrow[OS]{\widehat{\tau}[\vartheta](\lambda,\rho)} \mu'$ the resulting successor marking is defined as $\mu' = \mu - \lambda + \rho$.

We use a *firing predicate* $\phi(\widehat{\tau}[\vartheta], \lambda, \rho)$ to specify that (i) all net-tokens are removed and added as specified by the system net transition $\widehat{\tau}$ and that (ii) all net-tokens are modified as specified by the synchronised transitions $\vartheta(N)$. For a formal definition of the firing rule the reader is referred to [5].

Observe that an automorphism φ_{OS} maintains the firing predicate.

Lemma 1. *The firing predicate ϕ is invariant w.r.t. an automorphism φ_{OS}:*

$$\phi(\widehat{\tau}[\vartheta], \lambda, \rho) \quad \implies \quad \phi(\varphi_{OS}(\widehat{\tau}[\vartheta]), \varphi_{OS}(\lambda), \varphi_{OS}(\rho)) \tag{2}$$

Here, $\varphi_{OS}(.)$ is the congruent homomorphic application of φ_{OS} components to Eos *events and markings.*

Proof. The proof is given in the extended version [6] of this paper.

From this Lemma we immediately obtain the invariance of the firing rule.

Proposition 1. *The firing rule is invariant w.r.t. an automorphism φ_{OS}:*

$$\mu \xrightarrow[OS]{\widehat{\tau}[\vartheta](\lambda, \rho)} \mu' \quad \implies \quad \varphi_{OS}(\mu) \xrightarrow[OS]{\varphi_{OS}(\widehat{\tau}[\vartheta])(\varphi_{OS}(\lambda), \varphi_{OS}(\rho))} \varphi_{OS}(\mu') \tag{3}$$

Proof. The proof follows from the previous Lemma and is given in [6].

Example 1. In the forthcoming example, we demonstrate our methodology. Our Eos represents a kitchen environment featuring two workstations, S_1 and S_2, which are areas (places) designated for performing various tasks. The whole scenario can be seen as a metaphor for flexible manufacturing systems, where the kitchen is the plant and the recipe is the workflow. We have a cook, akin to a robot, following a straightforward recipe: Initially, separate the eggs (action a); subsequently, mix the egg yolks with sugar (action b) and the egg whites with wine (action c) separately; finally, layer the white cream onto the pudding (action d). In process-algebra notation the recipe is denoted as $a; (b\|c); d$, where $\_;\_$ denotes sequential composition, and $\_\|\_$ denotes an and-split (parallel execution).

The corresponding Eos is shown in Fig. 1. The system-net has two places S_1 and S_2 for kitchen stations. Each station has side transitions to execute the actions that are possible at each station. The cook/recipe can move freely between the two stations. We have only one object net that models the recipe. In the initial marking the recipe starts at the station S_1. The symmetry of the locations is captured by the automorphism: $\varphi_{OS}(S_1) = S_2$, $\varphi_{OS}(p_1) = p_2$, and $\varphi_{OS}(p_3) = p_4$.

The resulting state space mainly describes the following execution: The recipe moves from the kitchen station S_1 where a is possible to the station S_2, where it is possible to execute both b and c (in any order). Finally, the recipe returns to station S_1 to execute d. In between of all these steps the recipe may moves 'erratically' between the two locations without making any progress to the recipe.

2.3   Canonical Representations of Eos

Our basic idea is to provide some pseudo-symbolic state representation based on automorphism. We use canonical representatives, that is, a most minimal representation of an equivalence class (corresponding to an automorphism group)

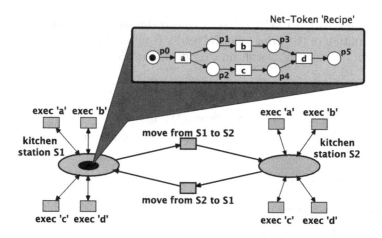

Fig. 1. Eos: A Kitchen with a Recipe as a Net-Token

considering a total order on nodes: for example, we assume that for any p/t net N there are two bijections $P_N \rightarrow \{1, \ldots, |P_N|\}$ and $T_N \rightarrow \{1, \ldots, |T_N|\}$. We derive the Eos automorphism from the canonical representative of the p/t components (net tokens and system net).

Example 2. Let us illustrate the main concepts using Fig. 1 (here $\widehat{p}_1$ means kitchen station S_1, $\widehat{p}_2$ means S_2). The following markings:

$$\mu = \widehat{p}_1[p_1 + p_4] + \widehat{p}_1[p_2 + p_3] + \widehat{p}_2[p_2 + p_3]$$

$$\mu' = \widehat{p}_1[p_2 + p_3] + \widehat{p}_2[p_1 + p_4] + \widehat{p}_2[p_2 + p_3]$$

are actually automorphic, their canonical representative is (we use weights for clarity):

$$\mu_c = \widehat{p}_1[p_1 + p_4] + 2 \cdot \widehat{p}_2[p_1 + p_4]$$

In this example, the state aggregation obtained through Eos automorphism and canonization grows exponentially with the quantity of net-tokens.

We integrate the formalization of canonization for Eos along the results for Rewritable Petri Nets as given in previous work [1,3]. There we used the well established **Maude** system [4] to define canonical representation of *Rewritable p/t* Nets. This formalization utilizes a multiset-based algebraic definition of mutable p/t nets. Whereas the method detailed in [1] is generic (similar to other graph canonization techniques), the one outlined in [3] is specific to modular p/t nets created and modified using selected composition operators and a structured node labelling, making it significantly more efficient for symmetric models. The two approaches can be seamlessly incorporated into the Eos formalism within **Maude**, which uses a consistent representation of p/t terms [2].

In theory, it is known that generating canonical representative is at least as complex as the graph automorphism problem (quasi polynomial). We hope for a more efficient canonization since for Eos the p/t structure does not change: the canonical representative of a marking must retain the net structure, which is a major source for efficiency. Although the exact effect on efficiency is still being studied, the application of the method [3] appears to be promising, when Eos components are built modularly.

Observe that the canonization approach in Maude is pseudo-symbolic from the operation point of view, because from a canonical representative (using the ordinary firing mode) we might reach equivalent markings through equivalent firing instances. For making the approach entirely symbolic, either canonical representative of firing modes should be calculated (through a uniform technique) or multiset terms containing variables (together with unification) should be used.

Conclusion In this paper, we have extended the concepts of automorphisms for Nets-within-Nets, here: Eos. In combination with canonical forms for representing the markings we have obtained a potential significant reduction of the size of the state space. We have integrated the approach in a Maude encoding of Eos. In future work, we plan to investigate the degree of state space reduction for a broader set of case studies. We further hypothesize that the automorphism concept for Eos can be readily extended to Object-nets with any level of net and channel nesting, allowing net-tokens to flow between different levels. We also aim to explore the practicality of less restrictive partial symmetry concepts.

References

1. Capra, L.: Canonization of reconfigurable PT nets in Maude. In: Lin, A.W., Zetzsche, G., Potapov, I. (eds.) Reachability Problems, pp. 160–177. Springer International Publishing, Cham (2022). https://doi.org/10.1007/978-3-031-19135-0_11
2. Capra, L., Köhler-Bußmeier, M.: Modelling adaptive systems with nets-within-nets in Maude. In: 18th International Conference on Evaluation of Novel Approaches to Software Engineering - ENASE, Prague, Czech Republic. pp. 487–496. INSTICC, SciTePress (2023). https://doi.org/10.5220/0011860000003464
3. Capra, L., Köhler-Bußmeier, M.: Modular rewritable Petri nets: an efficient model for dynamic distributed systems. Theor. Comput. Sci. **990**, 114397 (2024). https://doi.org/10.1016/j.tcs.2024.114397
4. Clavel, M., Durán, F., Eker, S., Lincoln, P., Martí-Oliet, N., Meseguer, J., Talcott, C.L. (eds.): All About Maude - A High-Performance Logical Framework, How to Specify, Program and Verify Systems in Rewriting Logic, Lecture Notes in Computer Science, vol. 4350. Springer-Verlag (2007)
5. Köhler-Bußmeier, M.: A survey on decidability results for elementary object systems. Fund. Inform. **130**(1), 99–123 (2014)
6. Köhler-Bußmeier, M., Capra, L.: A "symbolic" representation of object-nets (extended version). Tech. rep. (2024). http://arxiv.org/abs/2411.00149
7. Köhler-Bußmeier, M., Heitmann, F.: Safeness for object nets. Fund. Inform. **101**(1–2), 29–43 (2010)

8. Köhler-Bußmeier, M., Heitmann, F.: Liveness of safe object nets. Fund. Inform. **112**(1), 73–87 (2011)
9. Valk, R.: Object Petri nets: using the nets-within-nets paradigm. In: Desel, J., Reisig, W., Rozenberg, G. (eds.) Advanced Course on Petri Nets 2003. Lecture Notes in Computer Science, vol. 3098, pp. 819–848. Springer-Verlag (2003)

Optimal Dispersion in Triangular Grids: Achieving Efficiency Without Prior Knowledge

Himani and Supantha Pandit[✉]

Dhirubhai Ambani Institute of Information and Communication Technology,
Gandhinagar, Gujarat, India
202221003@daiict.ac.in, pantha.pandit@gmail.com

Abstract. In the dispersion problem, a group of $k \leq n$ mobile robots, initially placed on the vertices of an anonymous graph G with n vertices, must redistribute themselves so that each vertex hosts no more than one robot. We address this challenge on an anonymous triangular grid graph, where each vertex can connect to up to six adjacent vertices.

We propose a distributed deterministic algorithm that achieves dispersion on an unoriented triangular grid graph in $O(\sqrt{n})$ time, where n is the number of vertices. Each robot requires $O(\log n)$ bits of memory. The time complexity of our algorithm and the memory usage per robot are optimal. This work builds on previous studies by Kshemkalyani et al. [WALCOM 2020 [17]] and Banerjee et al. [ALGOWIN 2024 [3]]. Importantly, our algorithm terminates without requiring prior knowledge of n and resolves a question posed by Banerjee et al. [ALGOWIN 2024 [3]].

Keywords: Distributed algorithms · Mobile robots · Dispersion · Triangular grid · Deterministic algorithms

1 Introduction

The use of mobile robots to tackle global challenges in a distributed manner offers a unique and compelling approach to problem-solving. In this framework, each robot operates autonomously while coordinating with others to achieve objectives that may be difficult or impossible to accomplish through centralized methods. A key challenge in this domain is the dispersion of autonomous mobile robots evenly distributed across a region, which has garnered significant attention in the field of distributed robotics [11,12]. Recently, this challenge has been formalized in the context of graphs, where k robots, initially placed on the nodes of an n-node graph, autonomously reposition themselves until each robot occupies a distinct node [2]. This challenge, known as dispersion, has numerous practical applications, such as the relocation of self-driving electric cars to available charging stations, where cars, acting as robots, use smart communication to locate unoccupied stations [2,14]. The dispersion is closely related to other well-studied issues in autonomous robot coordination, including exploration [5,8,9], scattering [2,14], load balancing [6,21], and swarm robotics [11,12].

First, we distinguish between an oriented and an unoriented triangular grid. In an oriented grid (see Figs. 1(a) and 1(b)), the ports at each node (up to 6) are arranged in a specific sequence, allowing robots at that node to have full awareness of their direction. To move along a straight path, a robot selects the third port from its incoming port as the outgoing port and continues this process to maintain its straight trajectory. In contrast, in an unoriented grid (see Fig. 1(c)), the ports at each node are not organized in any particular order. This lack of structure makes it difficult for robots to discern the correct direction for straight-path movement, increasing the risk of becoming trapped in a cycle.

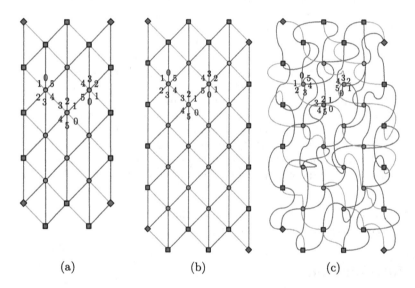

(a)   (b)   (c)

Fig. 1. Different triangular grid graphs. (a) Oriented with $n = 25$, (b) oriented with $n = 36$, (c) unoriented with $n = 36$

In this paper, we extend the work of Kshemkalyani et al. [17] and Banerjee et al. [3] by considering the dispersion problem in an unoriented triangular grid graph, a generalization of the square grid graph.

Definition 1. [Dispersion]: *Given any n-node unoriented triangular grid graph G, wherein a set of $k \leq n$ mobile robots positioned initially on the nodes of G, the robots reposition autonomously to reach a configuration where each robot is on a distinct node of G and terminate.*

1.1 Previous Work

Augustine and Moses Jr. [2] initially proposed the dispersion problem for $k = n$, demonstrating a time lower bound of $\Omega(n)$ and a memory lower bound of $\Omega(\log n)$ bits per robot. For $k \leq n$, these results were further improved in [14–16,18] across different models and configurations. In the context of local communication, the best-known algorithm for any arbitrary network operates in $O(\min\{m, k\Delta\} \cdot \log k)$ time, with each robot utilizing $O(\log n)$ bits of memory [15]. An algorithm achieving the same time bound but with an improved memory requirement of $O(\log(k + \Delta))$ bits was presented in [20], without the need for prior knowledge of m, k, or Δ. The dispersion problem is also examined under the global communication model in [16], where two deterministic algorithms are proposed: the first based on DFS traversal and the second on BFS traversal.

Our problem relates to the study of grid graphs, which have been the focus of previous research in areas such as exploration [1,13,19], and gathering [4,7,10] and dispersion [3,17]. The algorithm for the gathering problem with 1-hop vision and one-axis agreement on an infinite triangular grid presented in [10], where n robots can gather within $O(n)$ epochs under a semi-synchronous scheduler. In [17], two deterministic algorithms for dispersion were introduced: one for the local communication model and another for the global communication model on oriented square grids. The algorithm for the local communication model completes in $O(\min\{k, \sqrt{n}\})$ rounds, while the global communication model algorithm takes $O(\sqrt{k})$ rounds, with each robot using $O(\log k)$ bits of memory. This work was further extended in [3], where the dispersion problem on unoriented grids was explored, accounting for both faulty and non-faulty robots. The first two algorithms in their study address the dispersion of non-faulty and faulty robots, respectively, achieving dispersion in $O(\sqrt{n})$ rounds, with each robot requiring $O(\log n)$ bits of memory. The third approach, designed for faulty robots on an unoriented grid, completes in $O(\sqrt{n}\log n)$ time and requires $O(\sqrt{n}\log n)$ bits of memory per robot, with the assumption that the robots know n to terminate.

1.2 Proposed Results

We present a four-stage algorithm to address the dispersion problem on unoriented triangular grid graphs. Here, $k \leq n$ represents the number of robots, and our algorithm solves the problem in $O(\sqrt{n})$ rounds, using only $O(\log n)$ bits of memory per robot, without requiring any knowledge of n. Our solution is optimal in terms of both the number of rounds and memory requirements per robot.

1.3 Challenges

In existing algorithms for dispersion on grid graphs [3,17], robots need to know the value of n, the total number of nodes in the graph. In [3], the authors mention that n can be determined during the execution of the algorithm for the oriented square grid. However, this knowledge is particularly crucial for achieving efficient runtime in unoriented grid graphs. Specifically, for a single robot located at an internal node, it can be difficult to move in a straight path, with a risk of becoming trapped in a cycle. One option is for the robot to wait until other robots arrive to guide it before it becomes idle. This approach is used in [3], where knowing the value of n is essential because, without this knowledge, isolated robots cannot determine how long to wait before they become idle.

Another reason for n necessity is once all robots reach the corner, they disperse synchronously across the grid in the existing algorithm for unoriented grids [3]. Initially, robots are distributed at various nodes, and the time required to reach a corner node varies depending on their starting positions. Robots arriving at the corner earlier than others must know how long they need to wait to synchronize the remaining processes, where the knowledge of n is crucial.

We address these challenges by dynamically computing the value of n. First, if a node contains a single robot, that robot becomes idle. The other robots use a special counter variable, incrementing it with each round until the value of n is computed and communicated to all robots. We provide a guaranteed upper bound for this counter variable across all robots. Once n is determined, each robot uses the counter to calculate a wait time, wt, which is a constant multiple of $\sqrt{n}$. The robots then wait for wt rounds, ensuring that $wt \geq 0$ for all robots. After this, all robots will have knowledge of n and can proceed with the rest of the algorithm in a synchronized manner. Up to this point, the robots spend $O(\sqrt{n})$ rounds. We ensure that the remainder of the procedure also takes $O(\sqrt{n})$ rounds, resulting in an overall time complexity of $O(\sqrt{n})$.

2   Dispersion on Triangular Grid

2.1   Models and Definitions

Network: The underlying graph is an anonymous unoriented triangular grid graph G (see Fig. 1(c)). The nodes of the graph are unlabelled. The degree of each node is at most 6 and the edges incident on it are labeled by port numbers $\{0, 1, 2, 3, 4, 5\}$. There is no ordering among the ports. The port labels on two end vertices have no relationship for a particular edge. In this paper, we study the Dispersion problem on $(\sqrt{n} \times \sqrt{n})$ unoriented triangular grid. Depending on whether n is even or odd, there are two possible configurations of an unoriented triangular grid (Fig. 1(a) and 1(b) are the two types of oriented triangular grid, the unoriented version of Fig. 1(b) is depicted in Fig. 1(c)). The nodes of the graph are distinguished on the basis of their degrees. (i) *Internal node:* a node whose degree is 6 (see round shape nodes in Fig. 1), *Corner node:* a non-internal node is a corner node if either its degree is 2 or its degree is 3 and connected to a degree 4 vertex (see tilted-square shape nodes in Fig. 1), and (iii) *Boundary node:* a non-internal node is a boundary node if it is on some boundary of the graph. Specifically, the node is either degree 4, 5, or degree 3 and connected to a degree 5 vertex (see square shape nodes in Fig. 1).

The graph consists of 4 boundaries, namely, top, bottom, left, and right. For any top or bottom boundary, the degree of each boundary node is either 3 or 5. For a left/right boundary, the degree of each boundary node is 4.

Robot: There are $k \leq n$ robots $\{r_1, r_2, \ldots, r_k\}$ placed arbitrarily on the nodes of G. The robots are autonomous and homogeneous. Further, each robot has a unique ID of $O(\log k)$ bits. Robots have $O(\log n)$ bits of memory to store information. Assume that the computation performed by each robot during any round is negligible. No robot resides on any of the edges of G. Robots have no visibility. A robot remembers the port number from which it has entered a node.

Communication Model: The agents operate within a synchronous local communication model where only colocated robots can interact with each other and are active from the start. Time is divided into discrete global rounds. During each round, an agent positioned at a node undergoes a "communicate-compute-move" cycle. In the communicate phase, the agent exchanges information stored in its memory with other agents at the same node. During the compute phase, it processes the gathered information and its data to determine whether to remain at the current node or move to a neighbor through a specific port. In the move phase, the agent stores necessary information in its memory and exits the node via the computed port. Upon exiting, the agent always reaches another node (i.e., no agent resides on an edge).

3 Dispersion in an Unoriented Triangular Grid

This section presents a distributed deterministic algorithm for solving the dispersion problem on an unoriented triangular grid graph G with n nodes and $k \leq n$ robots. The time complexity of our algorithm is $O(\sqrt{n})$, and each robot requires only $O(\log n)$ bits of memory. Importantly, the algorithm executes under the assumption that the robots have no prior knowledge of n.

We begin by outlining the concept of our algorithm before delving into its detailed description. Let G represent a triangular grid graph with n nodes. Here, we mention a few variables and terminologies essential for understanding how the algorithm operates and how robots coordinate their actions to achieve dispersion. Each robot is equipped with a special counter variable, T, which increments by 1 with each passing round. A robot is considered *"alone"* if it is the only robot present at its current node; otherwise, it is classified as a *"non-alone"* robot. Each robot maintains a variable, *sqn*, which stores the number of columns on the grid graph. Some robots calculate *sqn* by counting the number of nodes along the top or bottom boundary and then share this information with other robots. This sharing process ensures that all robots have a consistent understanding of the grid's structure (i.e., $\sqrt{n}$) as the algorithm progresses.

3.1 High-Level Idea

Here, we give a high-level idea of our algorithm.

Stage 1: Moving *alone* robots to internal nodes. This stage is dedicated to robots that are *alone* and located on non-internal nodes of the graph G. During this stage, these robots move to an internal node. This ensures that no *alone* robot is present on some boundary or corner node of the graph G. This step is essential for the dispersion of robots in Stage 4.

Stage 2: Moving *non-alone* robots to a corner node. The *alone* robots, if they still exist, are located only on some internal nodes. They become *idle* and do not participate in any future computation. The *non-alone* robots may reside either on an internal, a boundary, or a corner node. Depending on the type of node residing, they perform specific tasks. Note that *non-alone* robots must be in a group of at least 2 on a node. Let a group g of at least 2 *non-alone* robots be present on a node u of G in the current round.

The node u is a corner node of G. If the robots in group g detect that there is no robot at node u, one of the robots (the minimum ID robot, say r) leaves the current node u and moves along the top/bottom boundary of the grid G. During each movement from one node to its neighboring node along the boundary, the robot increments the counter, sqn, by 1. When the robot r reaches the opposite corner, it determines the number of columns in G, which gives it knowledge of n. After acquiring this information, robot r returns to u, where the rest of its group members are waiting. Once robot r returns to node u, it shares the value of n that it has determined with the other robots in the group, as well as some other robots that reach u afterward during the movement of r. By this point, all robots in the group will have the knowledge of n. When a robot (including r) learns the value of n at node u for the first time, it stops incrementing its counter T and waits for rounds $wt = \alpha\sqrt{n} - T$, where α is a constant (a specific value for α will be provided later).

During robot r's movement, if other robots that are not part of group g arrive at node u, they will wait until the departing robot r returns. If r has already returned with the value of n, these newly arrived robots will also learn the value of n at node u. Once they have this information, they will wait for $wt = \alpha\sqrt{n} - T$ rounds, just like the other robots at u.

The node u is a boundary node of G. The robots of g move towards any of the corner nodes. There, they treat themselves as robots in a corner node and perform the procedure that a corner robot performs.

The node u is an internal node of G. The robots in group g move towards a boundary or corner node of G. Upon reaching their destination, they follow specific procedures: (i) if they reach a corner, they follow the procedure established for robots at a corner node; (ii) if they reach a boundary node, they adhere to the procedure designated for robots at a boundary node. Throughout their movement from an internal node to a boundary or corner node, robots ensure that they travel along a straight path to avoid being caught in a cycle. This straight-line movement is crucial for maintaining the efficiency and correctness of the algorithm.

In the end, every *non-alone* robot will have reached one of the four corner nodes of G and have obtained knowledge of n. Note that from the very start until the value of n is known, each robot increments the value of T by 1 with each passing round. Once the value of n is known, each robot computes a value $wt = \alpha\sqrt{n} - T$ and then wait for wt rounds before proceeding to the next stage. We will determine a value for α such that $wt \geq 0$, ensuring that all robots are synchronized at the beginning of the next stage. This synchronization is crucial for the coordinated progression of the algorithm.

Stage 3: Moving all *non-alone* robots to a specific corner. Note that all the *non-idle* robots are positioned at some corner node of G. At this point, one robot (the maximum ID robot) from each group moves along the grid boundaries to communicate and agree on a specific corner (where the minimum ID robot is located) as the gathering point for all robots. Once this corner is agreed upon, every robot proceeds towards the designated corner.

Stage 4: Disperse all *non-alone* robots. Once the robots reach a corner, say the top-left corner u, they determine the number k' of robots present at that corner, where $k' \leq k$. Now there are two situations:

[**Case S1: If $k' \leq 4\sqrt{n} - 4$**]: The robots then move along the boundaries of G to complete the dispersion. This is feasible because, as ensured by Stage 1, there are no *idle* robots on any boundary node.

[**Case S2: If $k' > 4\sqrt{n} - 4$**]: The robots first move along the top boundary of the grid, positioning two robots at each boundary node except at source node u where more than two robots are present. After this, each group of robots parallelly proceeds along their respective vertical paths, counting the number of robots needed on that path (i.e., number of nodes containing no *idle* robot) and reaching the bottom boundary. Once the robots reach the bottom boundary, the robots at the bottom-left corner, say v, begin the next phase of the process. First, the desired number of robots, i.e., $\sqrt{n}$, remains at v, while the remaining robots move to their immediate neighbor v' on the bottom boundary. At v', the desired number, if it exists, of robots stays, and the rest moves to the next immediate neighbor along the bottom boundary and continues iteratively until all nodes on the bottom boundary have, at most, the desired number of robots and at least a pair of robots.

Now, each group of robots aims to disperse the robots along their respective vertical paths in parallel. During the vertical movement, if an empty node is encountered, one robot will settle there and become *idle*. If an *idle* robot is already present at a node, the group ignores the node and moves to the next node along the vertical path. However, it is difficult to do so. In order to move a group vertically (and identify the correct exit port), at least two robots are required. Therefore, we maintain the invariant that during the dispersion along the vertical path, the group must contain at least 2 robots. To overcome this difficulty, the following procedure is employed. Initially, no robots are settled at the bottom boundary. During vertical movement, if an empty internal node is encountered, a robot is settled there and becomes *idle* only if the number of robots in the group does not fall below two. If the number of robots is reduced to two, or if an *idle* robot already occupies the current internal node, the group moves vertically toward the top boundary. A group of robots reaches the top boundary for each vertical path. These pairs then gather at a corner on the top boundary. Note that the number of robots in that corner is at most $4\sqrt{n} - 4$ (same as in Case S1). Finally, the robots disperse along the grid's boundaries.

3.2   Algorithm

Here, we provide a detailed description of the algorithm.

Stage 1 (Algorithm 1): First, every robot initializes its T value to 0 and increments it by 1 with each passing round (refer to line 1). In this stage, we will deal with the *alone* robots residing on some non-internal nodes. Every non-internal node has at least one neighboring node, which is internal, except the corner node, whose degree is 2. The corner node with degree 2 has two neighbors on two different boundaries. So, when there is a single robot on the corner whose degree is 2, then in the first round, it moves to one of the neighboring boundary node (refer to lines 2–3). After the first round, every *alone* robot on some non-internal node has a neighbor node, which is internal. So, an *alone* robot on the non-internal node visits its neighbors in some order (smallest to highest ports) and checks whether the visiting node is an internal node. If it is an internal node, then the robot stays there until this stage is finished. Otherwise, it returns and visits the next neighbor (refer to line 6–14). Note that a non-internal node has a maximum degree of 5, out of which at most 3 ports lead to another non-internal node (a corner and two boundary nodes). So, in at most 7 rounds, a robot on some non-internal node reaches an internal node. During this time, all other robots (either *alone* or reside on some internal node) stand still and do nothing.

Algorithm 1: MoveAloneToInternal(r)

```
1  each round the counter T of r increases by 1
2  if r is alone and on a corner node of degree 2 then
3  │   r moves to a neighbor node
4  else
5  │   r do nothing in this round
6  for the next 7 rounds {2, 3, 4, 5, 6, 7, 8} do
7  │   if r is alone and on some non-internal node v then
8  │   │   if round number is even then
9  │   │   │   r moves to a not-yet-visited neighbor u from v
10 │   │   if round number is odd then
11 │   │   │   if u is not an internal node then
12 │   │   │   │   return back to v
13 │   │   │   else if u is an internal node then
14 │   │   │   │   r stays there and wait
15 │   else
16 │   │   r do nothing
```

Stage 2 (Algorithm 2): The value T continues to increment by 1 for each robot as each round progresses (refer to line 1) until a robot first learns the value of n except those that are moving along the top/bottom boundaries to compute the value of n and stop incrementing their T values once they return to their starting corner from where it started moving. If a robot is still *alone* (on an internal node), it becomes *idle* in the first round and does not participate in any future computation (refer to lines 2–3). The *non-alone* robots in the first round (i.e., during round 9) identify themselves whether they are on an internal node, a boundary node with a degree of 4 or 5, or a corner node with a degree of 2. For the remaining robots (those on nodes with degree 3), up to 6 rounds are needed to ascertain whether they are on a boundary or a corner node by visiting each of their neighbors in order (refer to line 5). For a degree 3 corner node, one of its neighbors is a degree 4 boundary node. At this point, based on the type of node a robot resides on, they perform specific tasks. By now, the current T value will be 14 for each *non-idle* robot.

➤ **[A robot r is on a corner node:]** Let v_c be the current corner node, and g be the set of robots at v_c. Note that there are at least two robots at v_c. We will examine the perspective of a single robot, $r \in g$.

    Case 1: Robot r observes that no other robot is at the current corner node v_c to await the return of the robot that is supposed to share the value of n (i.e., no robot computing n in the previous round). Consequently, r understands that one of the robots present must compute the value of n (refer to line 7). There are two possible scenarios:

    [Case 1.1:] Let r have the minimum ID among the robots at the current corner node v_c. Robot r then begins the process of moving along the top boundary, say B, toward another corner node v_t (refer to lines 8–9). All other robots remain at v_c and do not take any action until r returns from v_t with the computed value of n (actually, $\sqrt{n}$) (refer to line 13).

    As r travels along B, it will visit some of the neighbors of a boundary node u (excluding the one from which it arrived) to determine the next node v on B towards v_t. The degree of node u can be 2, 3, or 5. The maximum degree of a boundary node is 5, and only one exit port leads to a neighbor towards v_t, including v_t. So at u, after visiting at most three neighbors in some order, r will inevitably encounter a non-internal node on B towards v_t. Moving from u to v on B requires at most 7 rounds: 2 rounds to visit a neighbor and return (if the neighbor is not v), plus 1 additional round to reach v. Upon reaching node v, robot r realizes whether v is a boundary node on B or the desired corner node v_t. If the degree of v is 2, then r has reached the desired corner node v_t. Alternatively, if v has a degree of 3 and the degree of its immediate preceding node (i.e., u) is also 3, then r is at the desired corner node v_t.

    Once r reaches v, this process is repeated and eventually arrives at v_t. During this journey, r determines the value of $\sqrt{n}$ by incrementing the counter sqn each time it moves from one boundary node to the next along B until reaching v_t. After reaching v_t, r returns via the same port through which it entered v_t and follows a similar route back to the original corner v_c. Upon returning to v_c, r shares the computed value of n with the other robots and stops incrementing T (refer to lines 10–11). It then waits for

$\alpha\sqrt{n} - T$ rounds before proceeding.

[**Case 1.2:**] If r's ID is not the minimum among the colocated robots. Then r will stay at that location and wait for the departing robot to return (line 13).

Case 2: If r is not initially at v_c and, upon arriving at v_c, discovers that another robot r_m has already left to compute $\sqrt{n}$, then r will remain at v_c and wait for r_m to return. During this time, r will increment the value of T in each round (refer to lines 14–15).

Case 3: r was not initially at v_c and, upon arriving at v_c, discovers that the robot that had left v_c to compute $\sqrt{n}$ has already returned, then r immediately learns the value of $\sqrt{n}$, stops incrementing T, and remains stationary for the next $\alpha\sqrt{n} - T$ rounds (refer to lines 16–17).

➤ [**A robot r is on a boundary node:**] Let g be a group of robots located at a node on the boundary B. Robot $r \in g$ (along with robots in g together) moves along the boundary B to reach a corner node, denoted v_c (refer to lines 18–19). From a node v_b on B, r proceeds to an immediate neighboring boundary node $v_{b'}$. The degree of v_b is either 3, 4, or 5. At v_b, r may visit some neighbors in a specific order before moving to $v_{b'}$. It takes at most 7 rounds for r to move from v_b to $v_{b'}$ (when v_b has degree 5 and r visits all its internal neighbors and returns before reaching $v_{b'}$). Upon arriving at $v_{b'}$, r must determine whether $v_{b'}$ is still a boundary node on B or if it is a corner node. If the degree of $v_{b'}$ is 4 or 5, then $v_{b'}$ is a boundary node. If the degree of $v_{b'}$ is 3 and the degree of the preceding node v_b is 3 or 4, then $v_{b'}$ is a corner node; otherwise, it is a boundary node. If $v_{b'}$ is a boundary node, r repeats this process. If $v_{b'}$ is identified as a corner, r follows the procedure designated for the corner node robots (refer to lines 20–21).

➤ [**A robot r is on an internal node:**] A group g consisting of at least 2 robots, including r, is currently at an internal node. Their objective is to collectively move to either a corner or a boundary node and: (i) if they reach a corner node, they will follow the procedures designed for robots at corner nodes, and (ii) if they reach a boundary node, they will follow the procedures designated for robots at boundary nodes (refer to lines 22–27). The robots in group g should ensure their movement is in a straight path, avoiding any cycles, to reach their target destination efficiently. Suppose the robots of g are currently at the internal node v_i. The robots identify the exit port at v_i, initially set to 0. The process begins with the maximum ID robot, say r_m, moving from v_i to a neighboring node $v_{i'}$ through the exit port. Meanwhile, all other robots remain at v_i. There are two cases to consider:

[**Case A: $v_{i'}$ is still an internal node**]: r_m computes the exit port q opposite to the entering port p at $v_{i'}$. We describe the procedure to find q.

Finding the exit port q of the entering port p at $v_{i'}$: r_m is now at $v_{i'}$ while the remaining robots in g remain at v_i. r_m begins by exploring all possible 3-length paths from $v_{i'}$. Out of the 5 ports at $v_{i'}$, excluding the one through which r_m entered, only one port (the desired one q) does not lead back to v_i. To identify the exit port, r_m tests each port in a specific order. When r_m selects a port, say s, it moves to the adjacent node $v_{i''}$. At

$v_{i''}$, r_m explores all possible 2-length paths. If r_m encounters v_i during this exploration, it recognizes that port s is not the desired exit port. In that case, r_m moves to $v_{i'}$ from v_i again and continues testing the next port in the sequence. If, however, r_m reaches $v_{i'}$ through port s and explores all possible 2-length paths without encountering v_i, it determines that s is indeed the desired exit port at $v_{i'}$ that the robot r_m looking for. After this realization, the entire group of robots $g \setminus \{r_m\}$ moves from v_i to $v_{i'}$. They all have the desired exit port information at $v_{i'}$. First, r_m moves from v_i to $v_{i'}$. Once there, r_m explores all possible 3-length paths by visiting each of the 5 ports. The total number of possible 3-length paths is at most $5 \times 5 \times 5 = 125$. Upon exploring all the paths and returns for r_m, the time required is at most 2×125. Finally, one round is dedicated to the robots in $g \setminus \{r_m\}$ to move to $v_{i'}$. The total time requirement is $2 + 2 \times 125 = 252$ rounds.

[**Case B: $v_{i'}$ is not an internal node**]: The robots $g \setminus \{r_m\}$ moves from v_i to $v_{i'}$. The next challenge for r_m is determining whether $v_{i'}$ is a boundary or corner node and shares with the remaining robots. If the degree of $v_{i'}$ is 3, it can be difficult for r_m to distinguish. To resolve this, r_m must visit both of the ports other than the one it used to enter $v_{i'}$ to understand whether $v_{i'}$ is a boundary or corner node, which takes at most 4 rounds. Once the robots of g reach a boundary or corner node, they proceed according to the appropriate procedures for boundary or corner nodes.

Eventually, each *non-alone* robot reaches a corner of G and follows the procedure designated for robots at a corner node. They then acquire the value of n and stop incrementing their corresponding T. With the value of n, they calculate $\alpha\sqrt{n}$ and wait for $wt = \alpha\sqrt{n} - T$ rounds before transitioning to the next stage. Note that the constant α is selected such that $wt \geq 0$ for all *non-alone* robots.

Stage 3 (Algorithm 3): At the end of Stage 2, all *non-alone* robots should be positioned at a corner node and have the knowledge of n. With this information, they can proceed in a synchronized manner for the remainder of their tasks. The objective of Stage 3 is to gather all *non-idle* robots at a single corner, specifically the corner where the robot with the minimum ID among all the robots is located.

Each robot is equipped with a variable called *cid*. Initially, robots in a corner set their *cid* to the ID of the robot with the minimum ID at that corner. The robot with the maximum ID at each corner (referred to as the local leader) then moves along the grid boundaries and eventually returns to its source corner (refer to lines 1–3). As the local leader moves, it brings the minimum *cid* from the other three corners. Moving from one node to its neighboring node along the boundary can take up to 7 rounds (in the case of a robot on a degree 5 boundary node). During these 7 rounds, each local leader moves in a synchronized manner. After $7 \times 4(\sqrt{n} - 1)$ rounds, each local leader will have completed a circuit of the grid's boundaries and returned to its source corner with the information about the minimum *cid*. During this time, the other robots in their respective corners remain inactive (refer to line 5). Once the local leaders have returned, all robots, except those in the corner with the minimum *cid*, begin to move toward the

---

Algorithm 2: Stage 2: MoveToACornerAndGetN(r)

---

1   each round the counter T of r increases // value of T starts from 8
2   **if** r is alone and $T = 9$ **then**
3 | r becomes idle
4   **else**
5 | in at most 6 rounds, r realize whether it is on an internal, corner, or boundary node.
6   **if** r is on a corner node **then**
7 | **if** r realize that no robot is waiting for the leaving robot to return **then**
8 | **if** the ID of r is the minimum among the colocated robots **then**
9 | move towards the other corner along the top/bottom boundary, incrementing *sqn* for each movement towards the corner, and return from the corner (no increment of *sqn* during return).
10 | after reaching the source corner, share *sqn* value with other co-located robots
11 | r stops incrementing T and waits for the next $273\sqrt{n} - T$ rounds
12   **else**
13 | stay at the current node until the minimum ID robot (the leaving robot) comes back
14   **else if** r realizes some robot has already left the current node to compute *sqn* **then**
15 | wait for the leaving robot to return to the current node
16   **else if** r realize that the leaving robot is at the current node **then**
17 | r gets the value *sqn*, stops incrementing T, waits for the next $273\sqrt{n} - T$ rounds
18   **else if** r is on a boundary node **then**
19 | r moves along the boundary towards any corner node
20   **if** during the movement r realizes that the current node is a corner **then**
21 | r now behaves like a robot on a corner node, i.e., execute line 6
22   **else if** r is on an internal node **then**
23 | r moves along a straight path (taking opposite to the entering port)
24   **if** at some node, r realize that the current node is a corner node **then**
25 | r now behaves like a robot on a corner node, i.e., execute line 6
26   **else if** at a node, r realize that the current node is a boundary node **then**
27 | r now behaves like a robot on a boundary node, i.e., execute line 18

---

corner where the robot with the minimum *cid* is located (refer to lines 6–9). It takes at most $7 \times 3(\sqrt{n} - 1)$ rounds for all robots to gather in that corner.

Algorithm 3: MoveToOneCorner(r)

---

1   **if** r is the highest ID robot in a corner **then**
2 | moves along the grid's boundaries
3 | at each corner, it updates its *cid* if required.
4   **else**
5 | do nothing except when the leader arrives, it communicates its *cid* with the leader
6   **if** *cid* of r matches with the minimum ID of colocated robots **then**
7 | wait there until all the other robots reach
8   **else**
9 | move along the boundary to gather at the corner where the robot with the minimum ID is located

---

Stage 4 (Algorithm 4): All *non-alone* robots are now located on a single corner node v_c, assumed to be the top-left corner of the grid G. If the number of robots at v_c is less than or equal to $4\sqrt{n} - 4$, the robots move along the grid's boundaries and become *idle* (refer to lines 1–2). This is feasible because no other robots reside on any boundary or corner node except at v_c. However, if the number of robots at v_c exceeds $4\sqrt{n} - 4$, the robots must move in pairs synchronously along the top boundary B of the grid. The degree of each node on B is either 3 or 5 until they reach the top-right corner node v_t, whose degree is 3 or 2. By the end of this process, each boundary node on B and the corner node v_t will contain a pair of robots, and v_c will contain more than 2 robots. The process begins with a pair of robots (highest and second highest ID robot) moving to a neighboring node u on B from v_c. The pair at u then moves to its neighboring node v on B. Meanwhile, another pair of robots (currently highest and second highest ID robots remaining at v_c) moves to u. This process continues until the first pair reaches the other corner node v_t; at this point, every node on B has received a pair of robots, and v_c contains the remaining robots (lines 4–5).

Each pair of robots takes at most 7 rounds (visiting neighbors in some order) to move from one node u to the next node v on B. Thus, the entire process is completed in $7(\sqrt{n} - 1)$ rounds. Afterward, each group moves along a vertical path to count the number of robots required, i.e., the number of unoccupied nodes (lines 6–7). Each group ensures that they move vertically, traversing through the opposite port from which they entered, except at the starting node. The robots follow the same procedure as those initially located at some internal node that moves to a boundary or corner; however, robots proceed in synchronization here. All groups of robots need to determine the correct exit port for vertical movement. Once identified, they will continue moving vertically through the opposite port corresponding to the entering point at some node until they reach a node on the bottom boundary. However, there is a challenge: consider a group located at a boundary node v_b with a degree of 3 and another group located at a boundary node $v_{b'}$ with a degree of 5, which is a neighbor of v_b. Each pair must ensure that their first move is vertical. The pair at v_b can easily identify the correct port for vertical movement, as the other two ports lead to the boundary nodes. However, the pair at $v_{b'}$ with a degree of 5 faces a challenge in determining which of the three ports leads to a vertical movement. To address this difficulty, the robot pairs at the degree 3 or 2 nodes in B will start the process first. Within at most 4 rounds, by visiting up to 2 neighbor nodes, pairs at the degree 3 or degree 2 nodes will determine the correct exit port that leads to their immediate neighbor in the vertical direction. In the fifth round, these pairs will move vertically to their respective neighbors in the vertical direction. Next, the pairs at the degree 5 nodes take their turn. Now, look carefully at the neighbors of such a degree 5 node. At most, three of the neighbors are boundary or corner nodes, and the rest of the neighbors contain a pair of robots except the neighbor towards the vertical direction that is empty. In at most 8 rounds, by visiting each of their neighbors (at most 3 of which are boundary nodes, and the rest have pairs of robots except towards vertical), these pairs will identify the correct exit port for vertical movement. In the 14th round, the group that moved in the 5th round will return to their respective source degree 3 boundary or corner nodes. Therefore, the total round required for the initial exit-port identification is at most 14. Once the correct initial exit port is identified, all pairs can move in parallel to the bottom boundary or corner node in the vertical direction. This procedure is identical to the procedure for the vertical movement of robots that are located on an internal node and move to a corner or boundary. During this movement, a leader of each pair is identified and counts the number of nodes required along vertical path. So, $252(\sqrt{n}-1)$ rounds are spent by robots to reach the boundary.

Once the robot groups reach the bottom boundary, the robots at the bottom-left corner node start processing. This process followed a similar process to how the pairs distributed along the top boundary. The desired number of robots stays at the bottom-left corner node, and the remaining robot moves to its immediate neighbor at the bottom boundary. This process continues iteratively until the desired number of robots, if any, reaches the bottom-right corner node (lines 8–9). The total time taken for this is at most $7(\sqrt{n}-1)$.

On each vertical path, the robots will move towards the top boundary as follows (lines 10–11). If the current node is an internal node, then a robot will settle there and become *idle* only if the number of robots there is more than 2 (lines 12–14). Otherwise, if either an *idle* robot is already present at the current node, or the number of robots at that node is 2, or the current node is a boundary node that is not part of the top boundary, all robots move to the immediate neighbor of the current node along their corresponding vertical direction (line 16). This ensures that at any point in time, there are at least 2 *non-idle* robots on the current node during the movement. The total time taken for this is at most $252(\sqrt{n}-1)$. After this, at the top boundary, at most $4\sqrt{n}-4$ robots will reach across all nodes. The robots then move towards a corner node on the top boundary and gather there (lines 17–18). Finally, the robots are dispersed across the boundaries of the grid and become *idle* since there are at most $4\sqrt{n}-4$ robots, and all the $4\sqrt{n}-4$ boundary and corner nodes are empty (lines 19–20). The total time taken for this is at most $4 \times 7(\sqrt{n}-1)$.

Algorithm 4: Dispersion

```
 1  if the number of robots at the corner is less than 4√n − 4 then
 2  │    the robots get dispersed along the boundary and become idle
 3  else
 4  │    for 7(√n − 1) rounds do
 5  │    │    a pair of robots move to each node along the top boundary
 6  │    for 252(√n − 1) rounds do
 7  │    │    each pair in parallel moves in a vertical path until reach the bottom boundary and
 8  │    │    computes the number of robots required in each vertical path
 8  │    for 7(√n − 1) rounds do
 9  │    │    robot disperse along the bottom boundary according to the requirement
10  │    for 252(√n − 1) rounds do
11  │    │    robots move in a vertical path toward the top boundary
12  │    │    if internal node is empty and the number of robots is more than 2 then
13  │    │    │    the minimum ID robot will become idle
14  │    │    │    remaining robots move to their neighbor along their vertical movement
15  │    │    else
16  │    │    │    robots move to their immediate neighbor along their vertical movement
17  │    for 7(√n − 1) rounds do
18  │    │    the non-idle robots move to a corner at top boundary
19  │    for 4 × 7(√n − 1) rounds do
20  │    │    the non-idle robots disperse along the boundary and became idle
```

4   Analysis of the Algorithm

After 8 rounds $(T = 8)$, any *alone* robot residing on an internal node becomes *idle* and no boundary or corner nodes contains an *alone* robot. An additional 6 rounds are required for the *non-alone* robots to identify the corner, boundary node, or internal node. We now establish the correctness of our algorithm and its complexity. Due to space constraints, the proofs are deferred to the full version.

Lemma 1. *After round 14, if a non-alone robot resides on any corner node, it correctly gathers the knowledge of n. In addition, it stops incrementing T with a value that must not exceed $14 + 14(\sqrt{n} - 1)$.*

Lemma 2. *After round 14, if a non-alone robot that resides on any boundary node must reach any corner node and correctly knows the value of n. In addition, it stops incrementing T with a value that must not exceed $14 + (7 + 14)(\sqrt{n} - 1)$.*

Lemma 3. *After round 14, if a non-alone robot that resides on any internal node must reach any corner node and correctly knows the value of n, it stops increasing T with a value that must not exceed $14 + (252 + 7 + 14)(\sqrt{n} - 1) + 4$.*

Lemma 4. *In at most $14+(252+7+14)(\sqrt{n}-1)+4$ rounds, all non-alone robots will have reached a corner node, acquired the knowledge of n, and stopped incrementing T. In addition, each robot requires $O(\log n)$ memory.*

Proof. Lemmas 1, 2, 3 ensure the maximum number of rounds needed for any robot to reach a corner and gather knowledge of n is $14+(252+7+14)(\sqrt{n}-1)+4$. Each robot maintains a constant number of variables. The maximum storage required for any variable is $O(\log n)$, sufficient to store values such as T or sqn.

Lemma 5. *For each robot, $wt \geq 0$ when α is set to 273.*

Proof. The robot waits for $wt = \alpha\sqrt{n} - T$ round, where $T = 18 + 273(\sqrt{n} - 1)$. Thus, by setting $\alpha = 273$, $wt \geq 0$ for all robots.   □

The following lemmas address gathering the robots in a single corner and then dispersing them. The robots possess knowledge of n and operate synchronously.

Lemma 6. *The non-idle robots, residing on various corner nodes and equipped with the knowledge of n, must converge at a single corner node within at most $49(\sqrt{n} - 1)$ rounds using $O(\log n)$ memory per robot.*

Lemma 7. *The robots, having gathered at a corner node and acquired the knowledge of n, disperse themselves across the triangular grid and become idle in at most $553(\sqrt{n} - 1) + 14$ rounds using $O(\log n)$ memory per robot.*

Lemmas 4, 6 and 7 together lead to the proof of the following theorem.

Theorem 1. *Consider any unoriented triangular grid of n nodes having k robots such that $k \leq n$ where each robot has memory $O(\log n)$ then Dispersion can be solved deterministically in $O(\sqrt{n})$ rounds.*

5   Conclusion

We presented a distributed algorithm for solving the dispersion problem in an unoriented triangular grid, achieving a runtime of $O(\sqrt{n})$ and using $O(\log n)$ bits of memory per robot, all without requiring prior knowledge of n. An interesting direction for future work would be to extend this algorithm to account for the presence of faulty robots while maintaining the same time and memory constraints. Additionally, exploring the adaptation of the dispersion algorithm to operate in semi-synchronous and asynchronous environments presents another promising area for further research.

References

1. Altshuler, Y., Bruckstein, A.M.: The complexity of grid coverage by swarm robotics. In: ANTS (2010)
2. Augustine, J., Moses Jr, W.K.: Dispersion of mobile robots: a study of memory-time trade-offs. In: ICDCN (2018)
3. Banerjee, R., Kumar, M., Molla, A.R.: Optimizing robot dispersion on unoriented grids: with and without fault tolerance. In: ALGOWIN (2024). arXiv:2405.02002
4. Castenow, J., Fischer, M., Harbig, J., Jung, D., auf der Heide, F.M.: Gathering anonymous, oblivious robots on a grid. Theor. Comput. Sci. **815**, 289–309 (2020)
5. Cohen, R., Fraigniaud, P., Ilcinkas, D., Korman, A., Peleg, D.: Label-guided graph exploration by a finite automaton. TALG **4**(4), 1–18 (2008)
6. Cybenko, G.: Dynamic load balancing for distributed memory multiprocessors. J. Parallel Distrib. Comput. **7**(2), 279–301 (1989)
7. d'Angelo, G., Di Stefano, G., Klasing, R., Navarra, A.: Gathering of robots on anonymous grids and trees without multiplicity detection. Theor. Comput. Sci. **610**, 158–168 (2016)
8. Fraigniaud, P., Gasieniec, L., Kowalski, D.R., Pelc, A.: Collective tree exploration. Netw. Int. J. **48**(3), 166–177 (2006)
9. Fraigniaud, P., Ilcinkas, D., Peer, G., Pelc, A., Peleg, D.: Graph exploration by a finite automaton. Theor. Comput. Sci. **345**(2–3), 331–344 (2005)
10. Goswami, P., Sharma, A., Ghosh, S., Sau, B.: Time optimal gathering of myopic robots on an infinite triangular grid. In: SSS (2022)
11. Hsiang, T., Arkin, E.M., Bender, M.A., Fekete, S.P., Mitchell, J.S.B.: Online dispersion algorithms for swarms of robots. In: SoCG (2003)
12. Hsiang, T.-R., Arkin, E.M., Bender, M.A., Fekete, S.P., Mitchell, J.S.B.: Algorithms for rapidly dispersing robot swarms in unknown environments. In: Boissonnat, J.-D., Burdick, J., Goldberg, K., Hutchinson, S. (eds.) Algorithmic Foundations of Robotics V. STAR, vol. 7, pp. 77–93. Springer, Heidelberg (2004). https://doi.org/10.1007/978-3-540-45058-0_6
13. Icking, C., Kamphans, T., Klein, R., Langetepe, E.: Exploring simple grid polygons. In: COCOON (2005)
14. Kshemkalyani, A.D., Ali, F.: Efficient dispersion of mobile robots on graphs. In: ICDCN (2019)
15. Kshemkalyani, A.D., Molla, A.R., Sharma, G.: Fast dispersion of mobile robots on arbitrary graphs. In: ALGOSENSORS (2019)
16. Kshemkalyani, A.D., Molla, A.R., Sharma, G.: Dispersion of mobile robots in the global communication model. In: ICDCN (2020)

17. Kshemkalyani, A.D., Molla, A.R., Sharma, G.: Dispersion of mobile robots on grids. In: WALCOM (2020)
18. Kshemkalyani, A.D., Sharma, G.: Near-optimal dispersion on arbitrary anonymous graphs. In: OPODIS (2022)
19. Sardar, M., Das, D., Mukhopadhyaya, S.: Grid exploration by a swarm of autonomous robots with minimum repetitions. Theor. Comput. Sci. **933**, 67–87 (2022)
20. Shintaku, T., Sudo, Y., Kakugawa, H., Masuzawa, T.: Efficient dispersion of mobile agents without global knowledge. In: SSS (2020)
21. Subramanian, R., Scherson, I.D.: An analysis of diffusive load-balancing. In: SPAA (1994)

Mobile Agents on Chordal Graphs: Maximum Independent Set and Beyond

Tanvir Kaur, Kaustav Paul, and Kaushik Mondal$^{(\boxtimes)}$

Indian Institute of Technology Ropar, Rupnagar, Punjab, India
{tanvir.20maz0001,kaustav.20maz0010,kaushik.mondal}@iitrpr.ac.in

Abstract. We consider the problem of finding a maximum independent set (MaxIS) of chordal graphs using mobile agents. Suppose n agents are initially placed arbitrarily on the nodes of an n-node chordal graph $G = (V, E)$. Agents need to find a maximum independent set M of G such that each node of M is occupied by at least one agent. Also, each of the n agents must know whether its occupied node is a part of M or not. Starting from both rooted and arbitrary initial configuration, we provide distributed algorithms for n mobile agents having $O(\log n)$ memory each to compute the MaxIS of G in $O(mn \log \Delta)$ time, where m denotes the number of edges in G and Δ is the maximum degree of the graph. Agents do not need prior knowledge of any parameters if the initial configuration is rooted. For arbitrary initial configuration, agents need to know few global parameters beforehand. We further show that using a similar approach it is possible to find the maximum clique in chordal graphs and color any chordal graph with the minimum number of colors. We also provide a dynamic programming-based approach to solve the MaxIS finding problem in trees in $O(n)$ time.

Keywords: Mobile agents · Maximum Independent Set · Distributed algorithms · Deterministic algorithms

1 Introduction

Graphs have been used to show connections between objects in diverse areas, like biology, the internet, social media, and computer programs. Extensive research has done to study and solve the problems using graph data. Many real-world problems can be modelled as graph optimization problems. One such problem is the maximum independent set (MaxIS) problem. Given a graph $G = (V, E)$, a set of vertices $S \subseteq V$ is said to be an *independent set* if the sub-graph induced by S, i.e. $G[S]$, has no edges. The problem of finding an independent set of maximum cardinality is known as the MaxIS problem. The independence number of G is the cardinality of a MaxIS of G, which is denoted by $\alpha(G)$. The *MaxIS* problem is a very well-known NP-hard problem in graph theory. The MaxIS problem has enormous real-world applications such as indexing techniques, collision detection, automated map-labelling, social network analysis, and association rule mining etc. [1–4]. Moreover, the MaxIS problem is related to very well-known algorithmic problems such as minimum vertex cover, maximum clique, graph coloring,

Q. Bramas et al. (Eds.): ICDCIT 2025, LNCS 15507, pp. 92–107, 2025.
https://doi.org/10.1007/978-3-031-81404-4_8

etc. The problem of maximal independent set (MIS) is one of the most fundamental and well-studied problems in the distributed message-passing model. Some seminal works in the distributed message-passing model to compute an MIS of a graph are [5–7]. To the best of our knowledge, there is no significant result in finding MaxIS in any class of graphs.

A distributed computing paradigm focuses on studying the computation and complexity of systems involving autonomous computational entities. These entities interact with each other to complete a task. This agent-based model has been gaining significant importance over the last decade. In recent years, the focus on studying multi-agent systems has increased as they can handle tasks that are too hard for just one agent. There are several existing works that use n mobile agents to solve various problems in a distributed setting [8–10]. Now the question is, is it possible to solve the MaxIS problem for some class of graphs using mobile agents? We affirmatively answer this question by proposing an algorithm to compute a MaxIS in chordal graphs. A chordal graph is one in which each cycle of length four or more has a chord. To the best of our knowledge, this is the first work providing an algorithm to solve the MaxIS problem on a significant class of graphs, such as chordal graphs, using a group of mobile agents. We show that the same technique can also be used to solve the problems of computing the maximum clique in a chordal graph and coloring the vertices of a chordal graph with the minimum number of colors in the same setting. Now we begin with a detailed description of our model assumptions.

1.1 The Model and the Problem

In this section, we present the graph and the agent model with their capabilities and restrictions followed by the problem definition.

Graph: A graph $G = (V, E)$ is an undirected connected graph where $|V| = n$ and $|E| = m$. The graph is port-labeled which implies that each edge associated with any node v has a distinct numbering from the range $[0, \delta(v) - 1]$ where $\delta(v)$ is the degree of node v. These port numbers associated with both ends of an edge are independent of each other. For any node v, we define $N[v, i]$ as the node u adjacent to v such that the port associated with the edge (v, u) at v is i. The nodes of the graph have no ID. The nodes of the graph have no storage.

Agent: There are n mobile agents which are initially co-located. Each agent is assigned a unique ID from the range $[1, n^c]$, where c is a constant. Each agent is equipped with $O(\log n)$ memory. Agents move through the edges. Whenever an agent moves from a node u to a node v, it knows the port number through which it exits the node u and the port number through which it enters into v. The agents that are co-located at a node in some round can communicate with each other in that round. This is known as the local communication model. The algorithm works in synchronous rounds. In each round, an agent performs one cycle of communicate-compute-move (CCM).

- Communicate: co-located agents can communicate with each other.
- Compute: based on the information an agent has, it computes the port number through which it will move or decides not to move at all. It may update its memory according to its computations.
- Move: agent moves through the computed port or stays at its current node.

The MaxIS Finding Problem: Let n agents be arbitrarily positioned on a chordal graph G. Agents need to find a maximum independent set M of G such that each node of M is occupied by at least one agent. Also, each of the n agents must know whether its occupied node is a part of M or not.

1.2 Our Contribution

In this work, we use mobile agents to solve the MaxIS problem in chordal graphs. Our results are as follows.

- Our Algorithm MaxIS_Chordal (refer Sect. 3) solves the MaxIS finding problem from rooted initial configuration in $O(mn \log \Delta)$ rounds where each agent is equipped with $O(\log n)$ memory. The agents have no prior knowledge of any of the parameters such as m, n, or Δ.
- Our Algorithm MaxIS_Chordal_AIC (refer Sect. 3) solves the MaxIS problem from arbitrary initial configuration in $O(mn \log \Delta)$ rounds where each agent has $O(\log n)$ memory. The agents require prior knowledge of parameters m, Δ, l, λ, where l is the number of nodes that have more than 1 agents in the initial configuration and λ is the maximum ID of agents.
- We present a dynamic programming based approach to find MaxIS in trees (refer Sect. 4) from the rooted initial configuration using n agents in $O(n)$ rounds with $O(\log n)$ bits of memory per agent. This shows the use of dynamic programming which is not used often in the distributed setting.
- We have shown that, using a similar approach as that of our Algorithm MaxIS_Chordal, it is possible to solve the maximum clique problem and also to do a vertex coloring of chordal graphs with minimum colors (Sect. 5).

2 Related Work

MIS is one of the most fundamental and well-studied problems in distributed computing in the message-passing model. Enormous work has been done in the literature that provides efficient randomized and/or parallel algorithms [5–7,11–15] to find MIS of graphs. However, finding an exact MaxIS is an NP-hard problem, so one can not expect to find an optimal solution for the problem in general graphs. Several approximation algorithms have been proposed for the MaxIS problem in [16–18]. In [16], authors gave an $O(n^\epsilon)$-approximation of MaxIS of general graphs that can be computed in $O(\frac{1}{\epsilon})$ rounds. In planar graphs, an $O(1 + \epsilon)$-approximation of MaxIS can be computed in $O(\log^* n)$ rounds [17]. In [19], authors designed an $O(\log^* n)$-time distributed algorithm to compute

MIS in bounded independence graphs. Another work [20] finds the MaxIS on unit interval graphs in $O(1)$ round in the $\mathcal{CONGEST}$ model.

However, solving the MIS problem using mobile agents was recently explored in [8,9]. Pattanayak et al. in [8] proposed an algorithm that produces an MIS for general graphs using n mobile agents from a rooted configuration in $O(n\Delta)$ rounds. Each agent requires $O(\log n)$ memory to execute their algorithm and does not require any prior knowledge of any global parameter. Further, they design an algorithm in which n mobile agents compute an MIS of a general graph from an arbitrary initial configuration in $O(n\Delta \log n)$ time complexity and $O(\log n)$ memory with each agent. However, to execute this algorithm, the agents require prior knowledge of global parameters such as n and Δ. In the same paper, the authors also proposed an algorithm to compute MIS in trees that runs in $O(n)$ rounds, where each agent requires $O(\Delta + \log n)$ memory and prior knowledge of n and Δ. In [9], the authors compute an MIS of a graph using $k > n$ mobile agents. The time required by the agents is $O(m)$ rounds and the agents do not require any prior knowledge of any global parameters. Another related work can be found in [21], where the authors presented a distributed algorithm to compute a minimum connected distance-k dominating set and maximum distance-$2k$ independent set of a tree. In a different model, using luminous[1] agents, Pramanick et al. [22] find MIS of any arbitrary connected graph where agents have prior knowledge of Δ, $O(\log \Delta)$ bits of persistent memory, and at least 3 hops visibility. The authors also used colors to represent different states and worked under semi-synchronous as well as asynchronous schedulers. On the contrary, we do not use any visibility or lights. In the same model as [22], Kamei et al. [23] solved MaxIS placement for grid networks. In their algorithm, asynchronous, anonymous, silent agents enter the graph via door and position on the MaxIS of grids. They use three lights and their visibility range is two. However, we solve a significantly harder problem than the MIS problem, that is, the MaxIS problem in this work without using luminous agents.

3 MaxIS in Chordal Graphs

Here we find MaxIS in chordal graphs using mobile agents. We solve the problem of MaxIS from both rooted and arbitrary initial configurations.

3.1 Rooted Initial Configuration

Our distributed algorithm uses n mobile agents with $O(\log n)$ memory per agent and computes a MaxIS of any chordal graph in $O(mn \log \Delta)$ time. We start with some preliminaries. Given a graph $G = (V, E)$, a *perfect elimination ordering* (PEO) in G is an ordering of the elements of V, such that, for each vertex v, v and the neighbors of v that occur after v in that ordering form a clique. Formally, if $v_1, v_2, \ldots, v_n$ is a PEO of G, then for each $i \in [n]$, $G[N_i[v_i]]$ is a clique, where $N_i[v_i] = \{v_j \in N[v_i] \mid j \geq i\}$. In [24], authors prove that a graph is chordal if

---

[1] Agents that posses externally visible persistent memory in form of lights.

and only if it admits a perfect elimination ordering. One way to find a PEO is as follows. A vertex u_1 whose closed neighborhood forms a clique can be the first element of the PEO. For $i \geq 2$, a vertex u_i, whose closed neighborhood forms a clique in the induced sub-graph formed by the nodes in $V \setminus \bigcup_{j=1}^{i-1} u_j$, is the i-th element of the PEO. This is used to find a PEO in [24]. Now we recall a method to compute a MaxIS in chordal graphs. Let $G = (V, E)$ be a chordal graph, $(v_1, v_2, \ldots, v_n)$ be a PEO of G. Define inductively a sequence of vertices $\{n_1, n_2, \ldots, n_t\}$ in the following way: $n_1 = v_1$ and n_k $(2 \leq k \leq t)$ is the smallest vertex greater than n_{k-1}, which is not in $N[n_1] \cup N[n_2] \cup \ldots \cup N[n_{k-1}]$. Stop when no such n_i is left to choose. The set $\{n_1, n_2, \ldots, n_t\}$ is a MaxIS (refer [25]).

Overview of Our Distributed Algorithm. Here we provide an overview of our algorithm. Firstly, agents achieve dispersion on the graph using [26]. After dispersion is achieved, the agent settled at the root node v_r, say r_r, starts to determine the PEO of the chordal graph. The agent r_r performs DFS traversal (which may be perpetual) starting from v_r. Whenever it reaches a node, say u, through u's parent pointer (stored during dispersion) and u does not belong to the PEO yet, it checks whether u and its eligible neighbors (the neighbors who are not in the PEO already) form a clique or not. If yes, r_r puts u in the PEO. More formally, let PEO$=(v_1, v_2, ..., v_{i-1})$ be computed till now and r_r reaches a node u. It checks whether u can be included in the PEO as v_i. If yes, it also puts u in the MaxIS if none of the neighbors of v have already been chosen as a part of the MaxIS. The agent r_r continues this until the PEO contains n elements (agents know n since the initial configuration is rooted). If the agent r_r completes one DFS traversal (it is back to v_r and all the edges associated with it are explored) while performing the above algorithm, it starts another DFS traversal again unless the PEO contains n elements.

For the sake of completeness, we provide a discussion on the rooted dispersion algorithm of [26]. Agents start from a node, say v_r. Initially, each agent a has $a.state = explore$ and $a.parent = \perp$. Initially, for each agent, a, the port $a.prt\_in$, through which it enters into the current node is -1. Whenever a enters a node through a port say x, it gets updated to x. The smallest ID agent, say r_r settles at v_r, marks itself settled, and updates $r_r.parent = -1$. The remaining agents move through port 0 in the $explore$ state. After entering a node u via port x, if u is vacant, the smallest ID agent, say a_u, from the group of unsettled agents, marks itself settled and updates its parent pointer $a_u.parent$ to x; each remaining unsettled agent a continues its DFS traversal in $explore$ state by moving through port $(a.prt\_in + 1) \mod degree(u)$. Also, in this case, the edge associated with node u corresponding to port x becomes a tree edge. Otherwise, if u is not vacant, the group of unsettled agents change their state to $backtrack$ and move back via the port x from u. Authors in [26] prove that this strategy disperses all the agents over the graph nodes within $4m$ synchronous rounds. We state and prove the following lemma which we use later in our analysis.

Lemma 1. *It is possible for r_r alone to repeat the same deterministic DFS traversal over the graph starting from the dispersed configuration achieved by the rooted dispersion algorithm of [26].*

Proof. Let r_r enter a node u via port x. If u is vacant, r_r understands it is v_r (the root node) and backtracks. Else, u contains an agent a_u. However, a_u can communicate with r_r and learn the parent pointer of a_u. If $a_u.parent$ is x, then r_r can understand that it has reached u via a tree edge. In this case, it continues DFS traversal in the *explore* state; else, it continues DFS traversal by backtracking from u. Hence, after entering a node, r_r can understand whether it entered via a tree edge or not. Thus, r_r alone can replicate the same DFS traversal over the graph achieved by the rooted dispersion algorithm of [26]. □

The Algorithm: MaxIS_Chordal. Let $G(V, E)$ be a chordal graph with $|V| = n$ and $|E| = m$ and n agents be positioned at a node, say v_r. They need to obtain a MaxIS of G. First agents achieve dispersion on the graph using [26] from the rooted initial configuration, which takes at most $4m \le 4n^2$ synchronous rounds. Recall that agents know n since the initial configuration is rooted. From $(4n^2+1)$-th round, r_r starts finding PEO and MaxIS via DFS traversal as per the following details. Each agent a maintains the following parameters.

- $a.prt\_in$- Port used by a to enter into the current node is stored in this parameter. It is initialized to -1.
- $a.prt\_out$- Port used by a to exit from the current node. Initialized to -1.
- $a.PEO$- This variable can take values from $[0, n]$. If $a.PEO = j$, then a is the jth member of the PEO, where $1 \le j \le n$. Initially $a.PEO = 0$.
- $a.return$- This parameter can take a value from $\{0, 1\}$. It is used as an indicator variable. This variable is initialized to -1.
- $a.selected$- This variable can take value either 0 or 1. If $a.selected = 1$, then a is a part of the MaxIS. Otherwise, it is not. It is initialized to 0.

The agent settled at the root node, say r_r, maintains another parameter $r_r.size$. This denotes the number of members of PEO that are already marked and the value of $r_r.size$ can be in $[0, n]$. Initially $r_r.size = 0$.

The agent r_r begins the traversal of the graph via the depth-first search traversal technique. If $r_r.size = s < n$ and r_r visit a node in *backtrack* state, it does nothing and continues its DFS traversal. Let $r_r.size = s < n$ and r_r visits a node v in *explore* state, where r_v is settled. If $r_r.prt\_in \ne r_v.parent$, then r_r backtracks and continues its DFS traversal. Else, in the case $r_r.prt\_in = r_v.parent$, if $r_v.PEO \ne 0$, it continues its DFS traversal (this implies r_v is already selected in PEO); else, if $r_v.PEO = 0$, r_r considers r_v to be a candidate for the next element of PEO. In this case r_v sets $r_v.update = 1$ and runs the subroutine Update(r_v). The details of the Update() function are provided later in this section. Agent r_r waits at the current node till the execution of Update() is completed. The function Update() either returns a 0 or a 1. If $r_v.return = 0$, this means r_v cannot be the next element of PEO. Thus, r_r proceeds according to its DFS traversal. However, if $r_v.return = 1$ then r_v is added to the PEO and $r_v.PEO$ is updated to $s + 1$. Also, $r_r.size$ is updated to $s + 1$. Now, r_r needs to check if r_v can also be added to the MaxIS. To check this, r_r moves through all the ports of node v and checks if any neighbor of r_v is already selected in MaxIS. If not, then r_v is selected to be a part of the MaxIS, and thus, $r_v.selected = 1$. Otherwise, $r_v.selected = 0$ that represents r_v is not included in the MaxIS. If $r_r.size = n$, then agent r_r understands that the MaxIS is computed. Thus, in this case, r_r returns to v_r by following the *parent* port of the settled agents. Finally, r_r can do another DFS traversal that requires $4m$ rounds to inform each agent that the MaxIS computation is over.

Now we provide the details of the algorithm Update(r_v) for an agent r_v that is settled at a node v and has $r_v.update = 1$. We first provide the parameters used by an agent a in the Update() function.

- $a.flag$- This variable can take values from $\{0, 1\}$. This is used as a marker of a node. If an agent a is marked (during the checking of a node if its closed neighborhood forms a clique), it sets $a.flag = 1$. Otherwise, it takes the value 0. It is initialized to 0.
- $a.checked$- It can take values from $\{0, 1, ..., \delta(v) - 1\}$ and is initialized to -1.
- $a.help$- This parameter can take values from $\{0, 1\}$. It is initialized to 0. This variable is used to distinguish an agent that is located at the current node to help in the execution of some task (known as a helper) from another agent (known as a non-helper).
- $a.help'$- This parameter can take values from $\{0, 1\}$. It is initialized to 0.
- $a_i.help''$- This parameter can take values from $\{0, 1\}$. It is initialized to 0.
- $a.delete$- An indicator variable where $a.delete = 1$ means a needs to unmark its neighboring nodes that were marked previously. It is initialized to 0.

The details of the algorithm are as follows. When $r_v.update = 1$, it updates $r_v.flag = 1$ and $r_v.help = 1$. It moves through port 0 and either meets with a settled agent, say a_0, or finds an empty node. If the visited node is empty, then r_v understands that it is the node where r_r is settled at. Thus, r_v returns to its original node and r_r updates $r_r.flag = 1$ if $r_r.PEO = 0$. However, if r_v finds a settled agent a_0 at the visited node then two cases are possible. If $a_0.PEO \neq 0$, then it updates $a_0.help = 1$. But if $a_0.PEO = 0$, then it updates $a_0.help = 1$ and $a_0.flag = 1$. In both scenarios, a_0 moves along with r_v to reach node v. Now, there are two agents r_v and a_0 at v that can simultaneously move through ports 1 and 2 respectively to help meet the settled neighbors of r_v. Let at a round t, the agents $a_1, a_2, ..., a_x$ are present at node v with $a_i.help = 1$, where $i \in \{1, 2, ..., x\}$. While $r_v.checked \neq \delta(v) - 1$, the agents $a_1, a_2, ..., a_x$ with $a_i.help = 1$ do the following. Let $\delta' = min\{x, \delta(v) - 1 - r_v.checked\}$. For $i = 1, 2, ..., \delta'$, the agent a_i is assigned to the neighboring node $u_i = N(v, i + r_v.checked)$. These agents a_i make a round trip as $v \rightarrow u_i \rightarrow v$. The agent r_v updates $r_v.checked = r_v.checked + \delta'$. We name this process of bringing settled agents from the neighborhood to explore multiple ports of the current node simultaneously as the *Helping process*. Note that, if at any round, an agent a_i does not bring any agent with it (the visited node was empty and hence it must

be the v_r), then the agent r_r updates $r_r.flag = 1$ if $r_r.PEO = 0$. This is because
the agent a_i in this case has visited node v_r. After, $r_v.checked = \delta(v) - 1$, the
total number of agents a_i that have $a_i.flag = 1$ is stored by r_v in the variable
$r_v.count$. Finally, the agents a_i with $a_i.help = 1$ reset $a_i.help$ to 0 and return to
their original positions. On the other hand, a settled agent r_j when meets with
such an agent a_i with $a_i.help = 1$, r_j checks if it is already selected in PEO or
not. If $r_j.PEO = 0$ (r_j is not selected in PEO yet), then it sets $r_j.flag = 1$,
$r_j.help = 1$. But if $r_j.PEO \neq 0$, then r_j sets $r_j.help = 1$. Since in both scenarios
$r_j.help = 1$, it moves through the port $a_i.prt\_in$, where a_i is the agent with
$a_i.help = 1$ and a_i has met with the agent r_j. In this way, the agent r_v marks
all its valid neighbors (the neighbors that are not yet selected in the PEO)
successfully after the execution of this algorithm.

All the neighbors of r_i with $flag = 1$ represent the marked neighborhood
of r_i. Now r_v needs to verify if this marked neighborhood of r_v including r_v
forms a clique. For this, r_v updates $r_v.verify = 1$ and $r_v.update = 0$ i.e., it calls
algorithm Verify(r_v). After executing the function Verify(r_v), it returns either
a 0 or a 1. The meaning of this indicator variable is explained in the function
Verify(). Now, the agent r_v has to delete its marked neighborhood, i.e. update
the $flag = 1$ values to 0. For this, the agent r_v updates $r_v.delete = 1$ and uses
Helping process as mentioned earlier for updating the values. The only difference
is that during updating the $flag$ values to 1, variable $help$ is used. But to update
$flag$ values to 0, variable $help'$ is used. Thus, a settled agent r when meets with
an agent a that has $a.help' = 1$, it understands that now it has to set $r.flag = 0$
(if $r.flag = 1$) and $r.help' = 1$ and moves through the port $a.prt\_in$.

We now provide the details of the algorithm Verify(r_v) whose objective is to
check whether the closed neighborhood of r_v that includes the agents with $flag =$
1 forms a clique or not. The agent r_v sets $r_v.verified = 0$. The variable $verified$
is used to store the port number corresponding to node v that is currently being
checked. It takes value from $\{0, 1, ..., \delta(v) - 1\}$ and is initialized to 0. While
$r_v.verified < \delta(v)$, the agent r_v moves through $r_v.verified$ port and meets
with either a settled agent say r_j or finds the visited node to be vacant. Let r_v
meet with a settled agent r_j. If $r_j.flag = 0$, then r_v returns to its original node
and increments the value of $r_v.verified$ by 1. However, if r_j has $r_j.flag = 1$,
then r_v needs to check if r_j's total number of neighbors with $flag = 1$ is the same
as $r_v.count$. For this, r_j runs the function Final_verify(r_j). If this value is same,
i.e., the total number of neighbors of r_j with $flag = 1$ is same as $r_v.count$ then r_j
returns $r_j.return = 1$. In this case, r_v returns to its original position, increments
$r_v.verified$ by 1 and moves through it. However, if r_j returns 0, then further
checking is no longer required. Thus, r_v sets $r_v.return = 0$, $r_v.verify = 0$,
and $r_v.delete = 1$. However, if r_v finds the visited node to be vacant, then it
understands that the visited node is the root node. Hence, r_v does the task
that r_r is supposed to do if it was here. Thus, it updates $r_v.port = r_v.prt\_in$
and initiates Final_verify(r_v). If the total number of neighbors with $flag = 1$
equals $r_v.count$ then r_v returns to its original position by moving via $r_v.port$,
increments $r_v.verified$ by 1 and further moves through it. But if this value is
not the same, then r_v sets $r_v.return = 0$, $r_v.verify = 0$, and $r_v.delete = 1$.

In the subroutine Final_verify(r_j), r_j updates $r_j.help'' = 1$ and $r_j.checked = 0$. The use of $help''$ is for the settled agent a to understand that it only needs to update $a.help'' = 1$ and move through the prt_in port of the agent that visited a. It does not alter its $flag$ variable. While $r_j.checked$ is less than the degree of the current node, *Helping process* is used to count the number of agents in neighborhood of r_j that have $flag = 1$. If this value is the same as $r_v.count$, then r_j returns 1. Otherwise, $r_j.return = 0$. This completes the checking part.

In this way, the agent r_r moves through the nodes of the graph one by one and checks if that node can be added to the MaxIS of the graph. Thus, with the execution of this algorithm, we obtain a MaxIS of a chordal graph. Below we present a flowchart that illustrates the overall execution of our algorithm (Fig. 1).

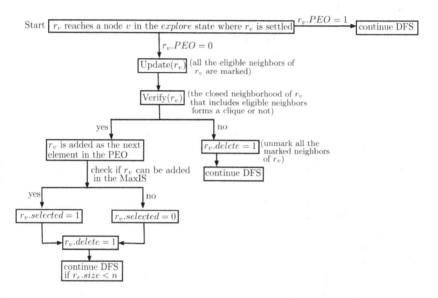

Fig. 1. Flowchart of our Algorithm MaxIS_Chordal when r_r is in explore state. Note that r_r simply continues its DFS if it is in backtrack state.

Correctness and Analysis: Below we prove the correctness and complexity analysis of our algorithm.

Theorem 1. *MaxIS_Chordal correctly computes the MaxIS of a chordal graph[2].*

Theorem 2. *The time taken by the agents to compute the Maximum Independent Set of a chordal graph with n nodes and m edges from a rooted initial configuration is $O(mn \log \Delta)$, where Δ is the maximum degree of the graph. The memory required by the agents to execute the algorithm is $O(\log n)$.*

Proof. The Algorithm MaxIS_Chordal begins with the dispersion of agents on the graph that requires $O(m)$ rounds (from [26]). The agent r_r i.e. the agent

---

[2] The proof can be found in the full version.

settled at the root node, repeats the DFS traversal of the graph (by virtue of Lemma 1). It moves through the nodes of the graph one by one to compute $PEO = (v_1, v_2, ..., v_n)$. This computation is done only when r_r reaches a node v in the *explore* state and v is not yet selected in the PEO. To check, whether this node v can be added as the next element in PEO, it runs Update() that further calls Verify() and Final_verify(). In Algorithm Update(), agent a settled at a node v requires $\log \delta(v)$ time to update the *flag* variable of all its neighbors. Then it calls Verify(a) in which agent a moves through all its neighbors one by one and for each marked neighbor, Final_verify() is invoked. The algorithm Final_verify() requires $\log \Delta$ time. Thus, sub-routine Verify() at node v takes $O(\delta(v) \log \Delta)$ time. Now, during one DFS traversal of the graph by r_r, at least one element of PEO is obtained. If during the first DFS traversal, the first element of PEO is not obtained, then it contradicts the theorem from [24] that a graph is chordal if and only if there exists a PEO of the graph. Hence, during the first DFS traversal, at least one element of PEO is obtained. In the worst case, the first element of PEO is obtained after visiting the last node of the DFS traversal. To find the first element of PEO, it takes at most $O(\sum_{i=1}^{n} \delta(v_i) \log \Delta)$ time. Then the next DFS traversal begins. Again during this DFS traversal, at least one element of PEO should be obtained. Hence, we may need to run at most n DFS traversals to obtain all the n elements of PEO. Thus, the agents require $O(n \cdot \sum_{i=1}^{n} \delta(v_i) \log \Delta)$ time tp obtain the PEO of the chordal graph. Each time we find an element of PEO, we also check if it can be added to MaxIS. Thus, after n elements of PEO are obtained, we also have a MaxIS of G. Thus, the time complexity to solve the MaxIS problem is $O(mn \log \Delta)$. Observe that each agent maintains constant many variables and each variable requires at most $O(\log n)$ memory. Thus, our algorithm requires $O(\log n)$ memory with each agent.   □

Remark 1. Tree is a subclass of chordal graphs. With minor modifications in the Algorithm MaxIS_Chordal, MaxIS in trees can be computed in $O(n)$ time in the same setting. The details can be found in the full version.

3.2   Arbitrary Initial Configuration

In this section, we provide an algorithm that solves MaxIS on a chordal graph using n agents that are initially positioned arbitrarily on the graph. Our objective is to achieve dispersion and to have a specific agent that can do the work that r_r was doing in MaxIS_Chordal starting from a rooted configuration. Note that, the configuration in the algorithm MaxIS_Chordal was rooted, due to which having such an agent r_r was simple. Thus, for an arbitrary initial configuration, we not only require a dispersed configuration where each agent is settled at a distinct node, but we also need a leader agent. To have such a dispersed configuration with an elected leader, we use the protocol given by Chand et al. in [10]. The authors in [10] start from an arbitrary initial configuration of n agents on an n-node and after achieving dispersion, one agent is elected as the leader. We denote this leader as r^* and the node that is occupied by r^* by the end of the algorithm of [10], as v^*. Now we provide our algorithm to solve the MaxIS finding problem.

Algorithm MaxIS_Chordal_AIC: The leader r^*, that is originally settled at v^*, initiates its own DFS. Whenever it enters a node, say v, for the first time where agent r_v is settled, r_v updates $r_v.parent$ to $r^*.prt\_in$. In this way, a new DFS tree rooted at v^* is formed. By the end of the DFS, r^* reaches v^*. Now the agent r^* can begin the execution of the algorithm MaxIS_Chordal (it skips the first $4n^2$ steps of MaxIS_Chordal as dispersion is already achieved here).

Correctness and Time Complexity: Correctness follows from the correctness of our Algorithm MaxIS_Chordal and from the correctness of the algorithm that we use from [10]. For the complexity analysis, the dispersion and leader election protocol from [10] takes $O(l\Delta \log \lambda + m)$ time, where l denotes the number of nodes with at least one agent in the initial configuration and λ denotes the maximum ID of an agent. The MaxIS_Chordal algorithm takes $O(mn \log \Delta)$ time complexity. As $O(mn \log \Delta)$ dominates $O(l\Delta \log \lambda)$ considering $\lambda \in [1, n^c]$ for some constant c (recall our agent model), our algorithm MaxIS_Chordal_AIC runs in $O(mn \log \Delta)$ rounds to solve MaxIS on a chordal graph from an arbitrary initial configuration. Now we have the following theorem.

Theorem 3. *The time taken by the agents to compute the Maximum Independent Set of a chordal graph with n nodes and m edges from an arbitrary initial configuration is $O(mn \log \Delta)$. Each agent has prior knowledge of the parameters n, Δ, l, and λ, where l denotes the number of nodes with at least one agent in the initial configuration and λ denotes the maximum ID of an agent. The memory required by the agents to execute the algorithm is $O(\log n)$.*

4   MaxIS in Trees Using Dynamic Programming

In this section, we present a technique using dynamic programming to solve the MaxIS on trees in $O(n)$ time using n agents. To the best of our knowledge, this is the first work that uses dynamic programming to solve a problem using mobile agents. Our algorithm idea is similar to the sequential algorithm presented in [27].

Let $\mathcal{T}$ be a tree with n nodes and n agents be positioned at a single node u. Our algorithm runs in three phases. The agents perform dispersion using the DFS technique in phase 1 of our algorithm. Phase 2 computes the size of a MaxIS and in phase 3 the agents learn whether the nodes they occupy are in the MaxIS. Below we provide a detailed description of each phase after providing a list of the parameters maintained by each agent r_v that is settled at a node v.

- $r_v.parent$- This variable stores the port used by an agent, say r_v, to enter into a node, say v, for the first time before settling there during dispersion. It is initialized to -1.
- $r_v.phase$- This variable stores the value of the current phase. It can take values from $\{1, 2, 3\}$ and is initialized to 1.

- $A[r_v]$- This variable stores the value of $\max\{|S| \mid S \subseteq V(T_v),\ S$ is an independent set of T_v such that $v \notin S\}$. It is initialized to -1. Here T_v is the subtree of T rooted at v.
- $B[r_v]$- This variable stores the value of $\max\{|S| \mid S \subseteq V(T_v),\ S$ is an independent set of T_v such that $v \in S\}$.
- $C[r_v]$- This variable stores the value of $\max\{A[v], B[v]\}$.
- $r_v.computed$- This is an indicator variable and can take values from $\{0, 1\}$. It is initialized to 0.
- $r_v.round$- This variable stores the current round number.
- $r_v.prt\_in$- This variable stores the port used by agent r_v to enter into the current node. It is initialised to -1.
- $r_v.selected$: This is a binary variable and can either be 0 or 1. It is initialized to be -1. If v is selected to be in MaxIS, then r_v sets $r_v.selected = 1$. Else, it is set to 0.

Algorithm for Phase 1: The algorithm for dispersion on trees uses the depth-first-search (DFS) approach. As discussed in Sect. 3.1, dispersion can be achieved on trees in $2n$ rounds [26]. When $r_i.round = 2n$, the agents execute the algorithm for phase 2 by updating $r_i.phase = 2$. Each agent knows the value of n since it is a rooted configuration.

Algorithm for Phase 2: Let an agent r_v be settled at a node v after dispersion is achieved. We call v the *original node* of r_v. In this phase, r_v computes $A[r_v]$, $B[r_v]$, and $C[r_v]$. The algorithm executed by the agents is as follows:

Let the agent r_v be present at a node v of degree $\delta(v)$. If the agent r_v has $r_v.computed = 1$, then it stays at its original node. However, if $r_v.computed = 0$, then the following two cases arise.

- The node v is not the root node and $\delta(v) = 1$: In this case, v must be a leaf. The agent r_v that is settled at the node v, computes the values $A[r_v]$, $B[r_v]$, and $C[r_v]$. After computing these values, it moves through $r_v.parent$ (recall that, r_v has already computed its $r_v.parent$ during phase 1) to reach node u and provide its computed A, B, and C values to the agent settled at u. It stays at its parent node unless there are $\delta(u) - 1$ many agents present at u.
- The node v is either the root node or $\delta(v) \geq 2$: In this case, the agent settled at the node v, i.e. r_v checks if $\delta(v) - 1$ agents are present at the node except r_v itself. This means the computations for all its children are done and the agent r_v can now perform the computations for itself. In this scenario, r_v computes its values for $A[r_v]$, $B[r_v]$, and $C[r_v]$. Further, the agents r_is at the node v except r_v, update $r_i.computed = 1$ and return to their original position by moving through $r_i.prt\_in$.

This can be seen as a bottom-top technique since the computations are performed from the leaf nodes, ending with the computations at the root node. Finally, after the agent settled at the root node (say r_r) performs its computations of $A[r_r]$, $B[r_r]$, and $C[r_r]$, it sets $r_r.phase = 3$ and initiates phase 3 of the algorithm. The algorithm executed by the agents in phase 3 is given below.

Algorithm for Phase 3: In this phase, a MaxIS is computed by the agents. The agent r_r initiates the phase 3 when $r_r.phase = 3$. The algorithm executed by the agent r_r is given below.

If $B[r_r] > A[r_r]$, then agent r_r sets $r_r.selected = 1$. This implies the node where r_r is settled is a part of the MaxIS. However, if $B[r_r] < A[r_r]$, then r_r sets $r_r.selected = 0$. Further, it moves through each of its ports one by one and meets with all its one-hop neighbors to let them know if it is selected or not. Finally, after traversing through all its ports, it settles at its original node.

When a settled agent r_i meets with its parent r_j with $r_j.phase = 3$, it sets $r_i.phase = 3$ as well. Further decisions are made based on the following cases:-

- If $r_j.selected = 1$: This implies that the parent of r_i i.e. r_j is selected in MaxIS. Thus, r_i sets $r_i.selected = 0$. Further, it moves through all its ports one by one except its parent port to let them know if it is selected or not. Finally, it returns to its original node after visiting through all of them.
- If $r_j.selected = 0$: In this case, r_j is not a part of MaxIS. Hence, r_i checks values of $A[r_i]$ and $B[r_i]$. If $A[r_i] < B[r_i]$, then $r_i.selected = 1$. Else if $A[r_i] > B[r_i]$, then $r_i.selected = 0$. In both cases, r_i moves through its ports one by one except its parent port and finally returns to its original position.

Hence, after phase 3, the set $I = \{v \in V \mid r_v.selected = 1\}$ forms a MaxIS.

Correctness and Analysis: Here we justify the correctness and runtime of our dynamic programming-based approach.

Theorem 4. *The Algorithm MaxIS_Trees correctly computes a MaxIS in trees[3].*

Theorem 5. *A set of n agents having $O(\log n)$ memory each, can compute MaxIS in trees in $O(n)$ time starting from a rooted initial configuration.*

Proof. Our algorithm runs in three phases. The phase 1 involves dispersion. We use the dispersion algorithm of [26] as a subroutine in our algorithm. The algorithm of [26] requires $O(n)$ time complexity to achieve dispersion on a tree. Each agent r_i maintains the round counter in variable $r_i.round$. As each agent knows n, when $r_i.round = 2n$, phase 1 terminates. The agents settled at the leaf nodes (with respect to the DFS tree) initiate the phase 2 of the algorithm. They perform their computations and move to their parent node. Phase 2 of the algorithm ends when the agent settled at the root node (r_r) performs its computations. An agent r_v settled at a node v moves through its parent port only after $\delta(v)-1$ many agents are present at v except r_v. Since the maximum distance between any node and r_r is bounded by n, thus upcasting the information from leaf nodes to the root node requires $O(n)$ time complexity. After the agent r_r performs its computations, r_r updates $r_r.phase = 3$. In this phase, each agent r_v settled at a node v moves through all its ports one by one to inform about its decision to all the neighboring agents. Thus, the time complexity required to execute phase 3 is $\sum_{i=1}^{n} \delta(v_i) = O(n)$. Hence, agents solve the MaxIS problem on a tree in $O(n)$ time complexity.

---

[3] The proof can be found in the full version.

The variables $r_i.prt\_in$ and $r_i.parent$ require $O(\log \Delta)$ bits of memory. The variables $A[r_i]$, $B[r_i]$, $C[r_i]$ require at most $O(\log n)$ bits of memory. The variables $r_i.selected$ and $r_i.phase$ require $O(1)$ bits. Thus, the agents require $O(\log n)$ bits of memory to execute the algorithm.   □

5   Maximum Clique and Chromatic Number

The maximum clique problem and the minimum coloring problem in chordal graphs can be solved after finding a PEO [25].

Maximum Clique Finding in Chordal Graphs: Maximum clique problem demands finding the maximum size clique in G which is also a sub-graph of G. This is a hard problem in general graphs. Here we solve for chordal graphs. We first restate the following theorem from Gavril et al. [25].

Theorem 6. *[25] Given a chordal graph $G = (V, E)$ and its PEO $v_1, v_2, \ldots, v_n$, every clique C in G is of the form $N_i[v_i]$, for some $i \in [n]$, where $N_i[v_i] = \{v_j \in N[v_i] \mid j \geq i\}$.*

Using Theorem 6, it can be concluded that a maximum clique is also of the form $N_i[v_i]$ for some i. A maximum clique can be computed as follows. While a node v joins PEO (refer Sect. 3.1), recall that, $r_v.count$ is the size of the clique formed by r_v and its one-hop neighbors who are not already selected in PEO. Let $C = \{u_1, u_2, \ldots, u_s\}$ be a maximum clique. Let u_q where $q \in [1, s]$ be the first to be added in the PEO. Then the agent settled at u_q, i.e., r_{u_q} must have $r_{u_q}.count = s$. So, after the PEO computation is done, by finding a such that $a.count$ is the maximum among all the settled agents, it is possible to know the maximum clique size. The following can be done after this to find a maximum clique. Let r_v be the agent settled at a node v such that $r_v.count$ is maximum among all agents. The agent r_v moves to each of v's neighbors. Any neighbor of v, say u that has an agent r_u with $r_u.PEO > r_v.PEO$ becomes a part of the maximum clique. Therefore finding a maximum clique requires at most $O(\Delta)$ rounds along with the time required to find the PEO as in Sect. 3. The correctness is as follows. Let w be a neighbor of v such that $r_w.PEO > r_v.PEO$, but w is not a part of the maximum clique. It contradicts that v was added in the PEO before w. We have the following result.

Theorem 7. *Given a chordal graph $G = (V, E)$ and n agents are initially positioned at a single node of G, the agents can compute the maximum size of the clique and the maximum clique itself in $O(mn \log \Delta)$ time provided the agents are equipped with $O(\log n)$ memory.*

Coloring a Chordal Graph with Minimum Color: Given a graph $G = (V, E)$, a k-coloring of the vertex set V is a function $f : V \to [1, k]$, which satisfies the property that $f(u) \neq f(v)$, if $(u, v)ki \in E$. The chromatic number of G is defined to be $\chi(G) = min\{k \mid G \text{ has a } k\text{-coloring }\}$. In this section, we give the high-level idea of an algorithm that computes $\chi(G)$ for a chordal graph G as well as colors the graph using $\chi(G)$ many colors.

We define a parameter $a.color$ for every agent a and initialize it as $a.color = 0$ for all a. After the PEO is computed, every node v has a settled agent a_v that knows its order in the PEO (that is stored in $a_v.PEO$). After this, at $i\Delta$ round, the agent a with $a.PEO = n - i + 1$ decides its color for $i \in [1, n]$. This is how it decides it's color: $a.color = j$, where $j = min\{k \in [1, n] \mid a_u.color \neq k, u \in N(v)\}$. Hence the time complexity of the algorithm (including computing the PEO) is $O(mn \log(\Delta))$. Our algorithm is similar to the sequential algorithm provided in [25] and thus it correctly color G with minimum number of colors. Our final result is as follows.

Theorem 8. *Given a chordal graph $G = (V, E)$ and n agents are initially positioned at a single node of G, the agents can color G using the least number of colors required to color G. The agents can achieve this in $O(mn \log \Delta)$ time given the agents are equipped with $O(\log n)$ memory.*

6   Conclusion

We design an algorithm to compute a perfect elimination ordering for a chordal graph using mobile agents. This helps us to find the maximum independent set, maximum clique in chordal graphs and to color any chordal graph with a minimum number of colors. We provide a linear time algorithm to find the maximum independent set in trees by running a dynamic programming-based approach distributedly using mobile agents. To the best of our knowledge, this is the first such attempt. Improving the run time in chordal graphs to compute MaxIS can be a further study.

Acknowledgements. Tanvir Kaur and Kaustav Paul acknowledge the support from the CSIR, India (Grant No. 09/1005(0048)/2020-EMR-I and 09/1005(0043)/2020-EMR-I). Kaushik Mondal acknowledges the ISIRD grant provided by IIT Ropar.

References

1. Klosowski, J.T., Held, M., Mitchell, J.S.B., Sowizral, H., Zikan, K.: Efficient collision detection using bounding volume hierarchies of k-DoPs. IEEE Trans. Visual Comput. Graphics **4**, 21–36 (1998)
2. Verweij, B., Aardal, K.: An optimisation algorithm for maximum independent set with applications in map labelling. In: Nešetřil, J. (ed.) ESA 1999. LNCS, vol. 1643, pp. 426–437. Springer, Heidelberg (1999). https://doi.org/10.1007/3-540-48481-7_37
3. Montemanni, R., Smith, D.H., Chou, X.C.: Maximum independent sets and supervised learning. J. Oper. Res. Soc. China **11**, 957–972 (2023)
4. Ghafari, S.M., Tjortjis, C.: A survey on association rules mining using heuristics. WIREs Data Min. Knowl. Discovery **9**, e1307 (2019)
5. Alon, N., Babai, L., Itai, A.: A fast and simple randomized parallel algorithm for the maximal independent set problem. J. Algorithms **7**, 567–583 (1986)

6. Linial, N.: Locality in distributed graph algorithms. SIAM J. Comput. **21**, 193–201 (1992)
7. Luby, M.: A simple parallel algorithm for the maximal independent set problem. SIAM J. Comput. **15**, 1036–1053 (1986)
8. Pattanayak, D., Bhagat, S., Chaudhuri, S.G., Molla, A.R.: Maximal independent set via mobile agents. In: ICDCN 2024, pp. 74–83 (2024)
9. Gorain, B., Kaur, T., Mondal, K.: Distance-2-dispersion with termination by a strong team. In: CALDAM, vol. 14508, pp. 44–58 (2024)
10. Chand, P.K., Molla, A.R., Sivasubramaniam, S.: Run for cover: dominating set via mobile agents. In: ALGOWIN, vol. 14061, pp. 133–150 (2023)
11. Barenboim, L., Elkin, M., Pettie, S., Schneider, J.: The locality of distributed symmetry breaking. J. ACM **63**, 20:1–20:45 (2016)
12. Fischer, M., Noever, A.: Tight analysis of parallel randomized greedy MIS. In: SODA, pp. 2152–2160 (2018)
13. Ghaffari, M.: An improved distributed algorithm for maximal independent set. In: SODA, pp. 270–277 (2016)
14. Harris, D.G., Schneider, J., Su, H.H.: Distributed $(\Delta+1)$-coloring in sublogarithmic rounds. In: STOC, pp. 465–478 (2016)
15. Kuhn, F., Moscibroda, T., Wattenhofer, R.: Local computation: lower and upper bounds. J. ACM **63**, 17:1–17:44 (2016)
16. Bodlaender, M.H.L., Halldórsson, M.M., Konrad, C., Kuhn, F.: Brief announcement: local independent set approximation. In: PODC, pp. 93–95 (2016)
17. Czygrinow, A., Hańćkowiak, M., Wawrzyniak, W.: Fast distributed approximations in planar graphs. In: DISC, pp. 78–92 (2008)
18. Halldórsson, M.M., Konrad, C.: Distributed large independent sets in one round on bounded-independence graphs. In: DISC, pp. 559–572 (2015)
19. Schneider, J., Wattenhofer, R.: An optimal maximal independent set algorithm for bounded-independence graphs. Distrib. Comput. **22**, 349–361 (2010)
20. Molla, A.R., Pandit, S., Roy, S.: Optimal deterministic distributed algorithms for maximal independent set in geometric graphs. J. Parallel Distributed Comput. **132**, 36–47 (2019)
21. Turau, V., Köhler, S.: A distributed algorithm for minimum distance-k domination in trees. J. Graph Algorithms Appl. **19**, 223–242 (2015)
22. Pramanick, S., Samala, S.V., Pattanayak, D., Mandal, P.S.: Distributed algorithms for filling MIS vertices of an arbitrary graph by myopic luminous robots. TCS **978**, 114187 (2023)
23. Kamei, S., Tixeuil, S.: An asynchronous maximum independent set algorithm by myopic luminous robots on grids. Comput. J. **67**, 57–77 (2024)
24. Rose, D.J.: Triangulated graphs and the elimination process. J. Math. Anal. Appl. **32**, 597–609 (1970)
25. Gavril, F.: Algorithms for minimum coloring, maximum clique, minimum covering by cliques, and maximum independent set of a chordal graph. SIAM J. Comput. **1**, 180–187 (1972)
26. Augustine, J., Moses Jr, W.K.: Dispersion of mobile robots: a study of memory-time trade-offs. In: ICDCN 2018, pp. 1:1–1:10 (2018)
27. Chen, G., Kuo, M., Sheu, J.P.: An optimal time algorithm for finding a maximum weight independent set in a tree. BIT **28**, 353–356 (1988)

Faster Leader Election and Its Applications for Mobile Agents with Parameter Advice

Ajay D. Kshemkalyani[1] , Manish Kumar[2]([✉]) , Anisur Rahaman Molla[3] , and Gokarna Sharma[4]

[1] University of Illinois Chicago, Chicago, USA
ajay@uic.edu
[2] Indian Institute of Technology Madras, Chennai, India
manishsky27@gmail.com
[3] Indian Statistical Institute, Kolkata, India
[4] Kent State University, Kent, USA
sharma@cs.kent.edu

Abstract. Leader election is a critical and extensively studied problem in distributed computing. This paper introduces the study of leader election using mobile agents. Consider n agents initially placed arbitrarily on the nodes of an arbitrary, n-node, m-edge graph G. These agents move autonomously across the nodes of G and elect one agent as the leader such that the leader is aware of its status as the leader, and the other agents know they are not the leader. The goal is to minimize both time and memory usage.

We study the leader election problem in a synchronous setting where each agent performs operations simultaneously with the others, allowing us to measure time complexity in terms of rounds. We assume that the agents have prior knowledge of the number of nodes n and the maximum degree of the graph Δ.

We first elect a leader deterministically in $O(n \log^2 n + D\Delta \log n)$ rounds with each agent using $O(\log n)$ bits of memory, where D is the diameter of the graph. Leveraging this leader election result, we then present a deterministic algorithm for constructing a minimum spanning tree of G in $O(m+n \log n)$ rounds, with each agent using $O(\Delta \log n)$ bits of memory.

Finally, using the same leader election result, we improve time and memory bounds for other key distributed graph problems, including gathering, maximal independent set, and minimal dominating set. For all the aforementioned problems, our algorithms remain memory-optimal.

Keywords: Distributed algorithms · mobile agents · local communication · leader election · MST · MIS · gathering · minimal dominating set · time and memory complexity · graph parameters

M. Kumar—Supported by CyStar at IIT Madras.
A. R. Molla—Supported, in part, by ANRF-SERB Core Research Grant, file no. CRG/2023/009048 and R. C. Bose Centre's internal research grant.

Q. Bramas et al. (Eds.): ICDCIT 2025, LNCS 15507, pp. 108–123, 2025.
https://doi.org/10.1007/978-3-031-81404-4_9

1   Introduction

Leader election is one of the fundamental and well-studied problems in distributed computing due to its significance in various applications, including resource allocation, reliable replication, load balancing, synchronization, membership management, and crash recovery. It can also be viewed as a form of symmetry breaking, where a single designated process or node (the leader) is responsible for making the critical decisions. In this paper, we explore the graph-level task of leader election in a distributed network under the agent-based model. In the agent-based model, the leader election problem involves a group of agents operating within a distributed network, where the goal is for exactly one agent to declare itself as the leader.

The agent-based model is particularly valuable in scenarios like private military networks or sensor networks in remote areas, where direct access to the network may be challenging, but small, battery-powered, relocatable devices can traverse the environment to gather information about the network's structure for management purposes. Significant applications of the agent-based model in network management can be found in areas such as underwater navigation [6], network-centric warfare in military systems [15], social network modeling [25], and the study of social epidemiology [8]. Moreover, limited storage capacity reduces the risk of sensitive network information being exposed if a device is compromised. Additionally, mobility in these devices enhances communication security by mitigating concerns over message interception.

Recent applications of the agent-based model have emerged in various areas. A notable example is the work by Martinkus et al. [16], which introduces AgentNet-a graph neural network (GNN) architecture where a group of relocatable (neural) devices, referred to as neural agents, 'walk' across the graph and collaboratively classify graph-level tasks such as detecting triangles, cliques, and cycles. In this model, neural agents can gather information from the nodes they occupy, neighboring nodes they visit, and other co-located devices. Moreover, a recent study [4] demonstrated that a fundamental graph-level task can be solved in the agent-based model using a deterministic algorithm within $O(\Delta \log n)$ rounds, with each device requiring only $O(\Delta \log n)$ bits of storage.

We present a deterministic algorithm for leader election that offers provable guarantees on two key performance metrics in the agent-based model: the solution's *time complexity* and the storage requirements for each agent. We focus specifically on deterministic algorithms, as they may be more appropriate for relocatable devices. In the agent-based model, storage requirements are treated as a primary performance metric alongside time complexity. The objective in the agent-based model is to minimize storage usage, ideally keeping it as small as the size of a device identifier, typically $O(\log n)$ bits per device. The limited storage prevents relocatable devices from first traversing the graph to learn the topology and then performing graph computation as a separate step. Our goal is to develop an algorithm that is storage-optimal.

Building on our deterministic leader election algorithm, which guarantees both time and storage efficiency, we present improved algorithms for several fun-

Table 1. Summary of Our Results - Leader Election, MST, MIS, MDS and Gathering.

Summarizing Results of This Paper			
Algorithm	Knowledge	Time	Memory (optimal)
Leader Election	n, Δ	$O(n \log^2 n + D\Delta \log n)$	$O(\log n)$
MST	Leader, Dispersed	$O(m + n \log n)$	$O(\Delta \log n)$
MIS	Leader, Dispersed	$O(n \log \Delta)$	$O(\log n)$
MDS	Leader, Dispersed	$O(n \log \Delta)$	$O(\log n)$
Gathering	Leader, Dispersed	$O(n \log \Delta)$	$O(\log n)$

damental distributed graph problems, including minimum spanning tree (MST), maximal independent set (MIS), minimal dominating set (MDS), and gathering. A summary of these results, detailing their time and memory complexities along with the required knowledge, is provided in Table 1. Our leader election algorithm requires prior knowledge of the number of nodes/agents, denoted as n, and the maximum degree of the graph, Δ. We assume that the number of agents equals the number of nodes in the graph, which directly applies to graph problems such as MST, MIS, MDS, and gathering. Furthermore, the results presented in Table 1, aside from the leader election algorithm, assume that the leader is known-that is, each agent is aware of whether they are the leader. Additionally, our leader election process disperses the agents, so we assume each agent is positioned at a distinct node. The aforementioned problem has been studied by Kshemkalyani et al. [11], where no prior knowledge of global parameters was assumed. In contrast, our approach, with prior knowledge of the number of nodes and the maximum degree of the graph, achieves faster and memory-optimal results [1]. A comparative analysis of our results is presented in Table 2.

1.1 Our Results

We examine the leader election problem in a synchronous setting where all agents operate simultaneously, allowing us to measure time complexity in terms of rounds. We assume that the agents have prior knowledge of both the number of nodes n and the maximum degree Δ of the graph. We show the following main results.

1. **Leader Election** - Given any configuration of n agents positioned initially arbitrarily on the nodes of a n-node graph G, there is a deterministic algorithm that elects a leader in $O(n \log^2 n + D\Delta \log n)$ rounds with $O(\log n)$ bits of memory per agent for a known value of n and Δ.

2. **Minimum Spanning Tree (MST)** - Given any configuration of n agents positioned initially arbitrarily on the nodes of a n-node graph G, there is a deterministic algorithm that finds an MST of G in $O(m + n \log^2 n + D\Delta \log n)$ rounds with $O(\Delta \log n)$ bits per agent for a known value of n and Δ.

3. **Maximal Independent Set (MIS)** - Given any configuration of n agents positioned initially arbitrarily on the nodes of a n-node graph G, there is a deterministic algorithm that finds an MIS of G in $O(n \log^2 n + D\Delta \log n)$ rounds with $O(\log n)$ bits per agent for a known value of n and Δ.

4. **Minimal Dominating Set (MDS)** - Given any configuration of n agents positioned initially arbitrarily on the nodes of a n-node graph G, there is a deterministic algorithm that finds an MDS of G in $O(n \log^2 n + D\Delta \log n)$ rounds with $O(\log n)$ bits per agent for a known value of n and Δ.

5. **Gathering** - Given any configuration of n agents positioned initially arbitrarily on the nodes of a n-node graph G, there is a deterministic algorithm that collects all n agents to a node in G not fixed a priori in $O(n \log^2 n + D\Delta \log n)$ rounds with $O(\log n)$ bits per agent for a known value of n and Δ.

The rest of the paper is organized as follows.

Paper Organization: Sect. 2 states our distributed computing model. Section 3 discusses the closely related work. Section 4 presents the leader election algorithm, which is the main contribution of the paper. Section 5 explores some graph-related applications of the leader election with improved time/memory complexity. Lastly, Sect. 6 concludes the paper with some interesting future work.

2   Computational Model

We model the network as a connected, undirected graph $G = (V, E)$ with $|V| = n$ nodes and $|E| = m$ edges. Each node $v_i \in V$ has δ_i ports corresponding to each incident edge, labeled $[1, \ldots, \delta_i]$. We consider a set $\mathcal{R} = \{r_1, r_2, \ldots, r_n\}$ of n agents, initially positioned on the nodes of G[1]. The agents have unique IDs within the range $[1, n^c]$, for some constant, c and agents know the value of c.

Initially, a node may host zero, one, or multiple agents. An agent at a node can communicate with other agents present at the same node but cannot communicate with agents at different nodes (this is the *local communication* model). An agent can move from node v to a neighboring node u via the edge e_{vu}. Following standard message-passing models, such as in [10], we assume that an agent can traverse an edge within a single round, regardless of the edge's weight, even in weighted graphs. When an agent moves from v to u along port p_{vu}, it learns the corresponding port p_{uv} upon arrival at u. Furthermore, at any node v, the agent is aware of the weight $w(e)$ (if G is weighted) of the edge e_{vu} connecting v to its neighbor u. We assume no correlation between the two port numbers of an edge. Multiple agents can traverse an edge simultaneously, as the agent-based model imposes no restrictions on how many agents may move across an edge at the same time.

The agents operate in a synchronous setting, similar to the standard $\mathcal{CONGEST}$ model: In each round, an agent r_i at node v_i can perform local

---

[1] Certain graph problems may be solvable with $k < n$ agents, but not all, such as the Minimum Spanning Tree (MST), where computing the MST with $k < n$ agents will yield the MST of a subgraph of G.

Table 2. Summary of previous and our results in the agent-based model. M is the memory required for the Universal Exploration Sequence (UXS) [24] and γ is the number of clusters of agents in the initial configuration. '−' means no prior knowledge of any parameter is required.

Comparative Analysis of the Closely Related Work			
Algorithm	Knowledge	Time	Memory
Leader Election			
Sect. 4	n, Δ	$O(n \log^2 n + D\Delta \log n)$	$O(\log n)$
Kshemkalyani et al. [11]	−	$O(m)$	$O(n \log n)$
MST			
Sect. 5	n, Δ	$O(m + n \log^2 n + D\Delta \log n)$	$O(\Delta \log n)$
Kshemkalyani et al. [11]	−	$O(m + n \log n)$	$O(n \log n)$
MIS			
Sect. 5	n, Δ	$O(n \log^2 n + D\Delta \log n)$	$O(\log n)$
Pattanayak et al. [19]	n, Δ	$O(n\Delta \log n)$	$O(\log n)$
Kshemkalyani et al. [11]	−	$O(n\Delta)$	$O(n \log n)$
MDS			
Sect. 5	n, Δ	$O(n \log^2 n + D\Delta \log n)$	$O(\log n)$
Chand et al. [5]	n, Δ, m, γ	$O(\gamma\Delta \log n + n\gamma + m)$	$O(\log n)$
Kshemkalyani et al. [11]	−	$O(m)$	$O(n \log n)$
Gathering			
Sect. 5	n, Δ	$O(n \log^2 n + D\Delta \log n)$	$O(\log n)$
Molla et al. [17]	n	$O(n^3)$	$O(M + m \log n)$
Kshemkalyani et al. [11]	−	$O(m)$	$O(n \log n)$

computations based on its stored information and the (unique) port labels at its current node, and then decide to either remain at the node or move to a neighboring node via a port. Before leaving, the agent may write information to the storage of another agent at the same node. An agent exiting a node always reaches another node by the end of the round (agents are never positioned on edges at the end of a round).

The agents are assumed to wake up simultaneously at the beginning of the execution. The time complexity is measured in the number of rounds required to reach a solution, while the memory complexity is the number of bits stored by each agent during the execution.

At any round, the agent distribution on G may satisfy one of the following configurations:

- *Dispersed*: each of the n agents occupies a distinct node,
- *Rooted*: all n agents are gathered at a single node,
- *General*: the configuration is neither dispersed nor rooted.

3   Related Work

The leader election problem was first stated by Le Lann [14] in the context of token ring networks, and since then it has been central to the theory of distributed computing. Gallager, Humblet, and Spira [9] provided a deterministic algorithm for any n-node graph G with time complexity $O(n \log n)$ rounds and message complexity $O(m \log n)$. Awerbuch [2] provided a deterministic algorithm with time complexity $O(n)$ and message complexity $O(m + n \log n)$. Peleg [20] provided a deterministic algorithm with optimal time complexity $O(D)$ and message complexity $O(mD)$. Recently, an algorithm is given in [12] with message complexity $O(m)$ but no bound on time complexity, and another algorithm with $O(D \log n)$ time complexity and $O(m \log n)$ message complexity. Additionally, it was shown in [12] the message complexity lower bound of $\Omega(m)$ and time complexity lower bound of $\Omega(D)$ for deterministic leader election in graphs. Leader election was not studied in the agent-based model before, except for [11]. See Table 2.

For MST, the algorithm in Gallager, Humblet, and Spira [9] is the first deterministic algorithm in the message-passing model with time complexity $O(n \log n)$ and message complexity $O(m \log n)$. Time was improved to $O(n)$ in [2] and to $O(\sqrt{n} \log^* n + D)$ in [10,13]. Furthermore, a time lower bound of $\Omega(\sqrt{n}/\log n + D)$ was given in [21]. MST was not studied in the agent-based model before, except for [11]. See Table 2.

For MIS in the message-passing model, the best-known deterministic distributed algorithms have time complexity $O(2^{\sqrt{\log n}})$ [3,18]. For MDS, Deurer *et al.* [7] gave two algorithms with an optimal approximation ratio of $(1 + \epsilon)(1 + \log(\Delta+1))$ running respectively in $O(2^{O(\sqrt{\log(n) \log(\log(n))})})$ and $O(\Delta \operatorname{polylog}(\Delta) + \operatorname{polylog}(\Delta) \log^\star(n))$ rounds for $\epsilon > \frac{1}{\operatorname{polylog}(\Delta)}$. MIS and MDS were solved in the agent-based model in [5,19] with time and memory complexities reported in Table 2 assuming n, Δ (additionally m, γ for MDS) are known to agents a priori. [11] improved these results w.r.t. time/memory complexities as well as lifted the parameter assumptions, see Table 2.

Gathering is a very old problem and has been studied extensively in the agent-based model. The recent results are [17,24] (detailed literature in [17]). [24] provided a $\tilde{O}(n^5 \log \beta)$ time solution to gather $k \leq n$ agents in arbitrary graphs, where $\tilde{O}$ hides polylog factors and β is the smallest label among agents. Molla *et al.* [17] provided improved time bounds for large values of k assuming n is known but not k: (i) $O(n^3)$ rounds, if $k \geq \lfloor \frac{n}{2} \rfloor + 1$ (ii) $\tilde{O}(n^4)$ rounds, if $\lfloor \frac{n}{2} \rfloor + 1 \leq k < \lfloor \frac{n}{3} \rfloor + 1$, and (iii) $\tilde{O}(n^5)$ rounds, if $\lfloor \frac{n}{3} \rfloor + 1 > k$. Each agent requires $O(M + m \log n)$ bits of memory, where M is the memory required to implement the universal traversal sequence (UXS) [24]. [11] lifted the assumption of known n and improved time bound for $k = n$ case from $O(n^3)$ to $O(m)$ and additionally the memory bound.

Finally, there is a model, called *whiteboard* [22], related to the agent-based model. The whiteboard model considers (limited) storage at the network nodes in addition to (limited) storage per device. Other aspects remain the same as in the agent-based model, for example, devices have identifiers, computation ability, and communication through relocation. It is immediate that any solution designed in the agent-based model works in the whiteboard model without any change but the opposite may not be true.

4 Leader Election

In this section, we present our deterministic leader election algorithm which, starting from any initial configuration (dispersed, rooted, or arbitrary) of n agents on an n-node graph G, ensures that one agent is elected as a leader. Initially, we disperse the agents on the graph with the help of the algorithm discussed in [23]. After dispersing the agents, we elect the leader. The running time of our algorithm depends on the starting configuration, increasing from the dispersed configuration to the rooted configuration, and finally to the general configuration. Our primary goal is to minimize the round complexity by keeping the optimal memory (in bits) per agent.

4.1 Challenges and High-Level Idea for Leader Election

We are given a set $\mathcal{R}$ of n agents with unique IDs positioned initially arbitrarily on the nodes of an n-node, m-edge graph G such that n and Δ is known to the agents. We also assume that the range $[1, n^c]$ of the IDs is known to the agents for any constant $c > 1$. We aim to elect a unique leader; the pseudocode is given in Algorithm 1. Initially, we disperse all the agents (if not dispersed already) with a well-known algorithm [23]. Then each agent iteratively passes the information of a higher known ID to its neighbors, and finally, the agent with the highest ID agent becomes the leader. The algorithm (after dispersion) uses $O(D\Delta \log n)$ rounds and $O(\log n)$ bits of memory per agent. Our leader election following dispersion presents three key challenges to the aforementioned complexity: (i) The graph diameter is unknown, making it difficult to terminate the algorithm. (ii) Since agents are mobile entities, therefore, meeting neighboring agents is challenging. (iii) The algorithm assumes each agent has only $O(\log n)$ bits of memory, making it difficult to track all the information passed by neighboring agents.

On a high level, we deal with all the above challenges in the following ways (in order): (i) Based on a voting mechanism, our algorithm ensures that the agents have passed the information (about the highest ID) from one end of the graph to another. (ii) Based on ID, our algorithm makes sure that each neighbor meets all of its neighbors in a definite interval of time/rounds. (iii) Based on the child-parent relationship, our algorithm makes sure only each child keeps track of its parent rather than the parent keeps track of all its children which requires $\Delta \log n$ memory.

4.2   Detailed Description of the Algorithm

We disperse the agents in $O(n \log^2 n)$ rounds[2] with the help of the dispersion algorithm for the general configuration, given in [23]. Their algorithm does not have the termination time, therefore, with the help of a known parameter of n all the agents get to know the dispersion time. After dispersing all the agents, the algorithm operates in phases of $2\Delta \log n$ rounds each. In a phase, each agent meets all its neighbors in $O(\Delta \log n)$ time. Each agent tries to figure out the

---

Algorithm 1: Leader Election

Input   : A set $\mathcal{R}$ of n agents with unique IDs positioned initially arbitrarily on the nodes of an n-node, m-edge graph G such that n and Δ is known to the agnets.

Output: An agent in $\mathcal{R}$ is elected as a leader with status *leader*.

1 Disperse the agents in $O(n \log^2 n)$ rounds with the help of an arbitrary dispersion algorithm in [23].   ▷ Takes $O(n \log^2 n)$ rounds.

2 A phase consists of $O(\Delta \log n)$ rounds, in which agent r_u meets all its neighbors, follows from Lemma 1.

3 Each agent r_u does nothing for a phase of $c\Delta \log n$ rounds.

4 **while** *agent r_u is unaware about the leader* **do**

5   **if** *agent r_u has not sent its highest ID known from the previous phase* **then**

6   Agent r_u sends its highest known ID to all the neighbors

7   **if** *r_u receives higher ID from neighbour r_v* **then**

8   r_u considers r_v as its parent and becomes the child of r_v

9   **if** *r_v remains parent of r_u for next two phases* **then**

10   r_u sends "undecided" vote to r_v for next two phases
               `// Initialization of ''undecided'' vote.`

11   **if** *r_u received "yes" vote and did not receive the vote "undecided" from all its children (if any), in the previous phase, after two phases of proposal* **then**

12   r_u sends the vote "yes" to its parent (if any)

13   **else**

14   r_u sends the vote "undecided" to its parent (if any)

15   **if** *r_u does not have child* **then**

16   r_u keeps sending a vote "yes" to its parent until it gets to know about the leader // r_u `did not receive a vote from any neighbor.`

17   **if** *r_u received its own proposed ID from all its children with a "yes" vote in the previous phase* **then**

18   r_u becomes the leader and informs its ID to all neighbors

19   **if** *r_u knows the leader ID from the previous phase* **then**

20   r_u informs the leader ID to all its neighbors

---

[2] Our approach uses the algorithm as it is and considers the constant as in [23] throughout the paper.

highest ID agent—in phase k the highest ID in a k-hop neighborhood is identified. The highest ID agent eventually becomes the leader.

Meeting with Neighboring Agents: The approach is based on the ID of the agent, whose size is $O(\log n)$, i.e., $c \log n$ since the highest ID is n^c (n is known parameter for the Algorithm 1) and the known value of Δ. Each agent r_u keeps the ID length $c \log n$; if ID is shortened by x bits then x number of bits with value 0 is prepended as MSB (Most Significant Bit). Starting from the LSB (Least Significant Bit) of an agent r_u's ID, each agent r_u decides whether it would visit its neighbor or not. If LSB is 1 then the agent r_u visits its neighboring nodes one by one based on port numbering (in increasing order) which takes $2\delta_{r_u}$ rounds (two rounds to visit a neighboring node—back and forth) to explore all the neighbors, where δ_{r_u} is the degree for the agent r_u. If LSB is 0 for an agent r_u then agent r_u waits for 2Δ rounds at its node. After 2Δ rounds, r_u decides based on the next bit in its ID whether it would explore its neighboring nodes or would stay at its node. Notice that if $\delta_{r_u} < \Delta$ then r_u completes visiting its neighboring agents in less than 2Δ rounds for bit value 1 in its ID. Therefore, r_u stays at its node for the remaining rounds $(2\Delta - 2\delta_{r_u})$. Lemma 1 shows that agent r_u meets with all its neighbors at least once in $O(\Delta \log n)$ rounds.

Election of the Highest ID Agent as Leader: After dispersing every agent such that each node possesses only one agent, each agent r_u does nothing for a phase of $O(\Delta \log n)$ rounds. We consider *Meeting with Neighboring Agents* as a phase that takes $2\Delta \log n$ rounds. In this phase, we keep our algorithm deliberately ideal to simplify the flow of the algorithm, i.e., to pass the updated information in the next phase that was received in the prior phase.

The following statements and conditions are executed by agent r_u until r_u gets to know the leader and informs all its neighbors:

In the very first phase, each agent already has its own ID which would be passed during the next phase. Each agent r_u passes its ID to neighboring agents if that is the highest ID known to r_u. Therefore, if agent r_u has not sent (earlier) its highest ID known from the prior phase then agent r_u sends its highest known ID to all the neighbors.

If r_u receives a higher ID from neighbor r_v then r_u considers r_v as its parent and becomes the child of r_v. This is required since due to memory limitation r_u can not keep track of all its neighbors to whom it passes the higher ID. Therefore, each receiving agent (child) keeps the track of sender (parent) which is not more than 1 in numbers. In case of a tie—(i) more than one agent sends the same ID which is not less than the earlier known ID, an agent r_u gives priority to the agent that was the parent in the prior phase. Notice that this condition is more than breaking a tie since in another case—giving priority to the latest sending agent, an agent might keep changing its parent forever. (ii) If there is more than one agent that proposes the same ID in the same phase then priority (to be considered as parent) is given to the higher ID proposer. Additionally, if r_v remains the parent of r_u for the next two phases then r_u sends an "undecided" vote to r_v for the next two phases. In this way, the initialization of the "undecided" vote takes place. The vote "undecided" is sent to the parent by its child if it received the "undecided" vote from any of its children or r_v becomes the parent two phases before. In these two phases, r_u's children (if any) receive the ID and send their vote. Therefore, r_u sends an "undecided" vote in the first two phases irrespective of its children's vote. From the next phase onwards, r_u receives its children's vote and considers them for voting to its parent.

In case, if r_u received "yes" vote from all its children (if any) and did not receive the vote "undecided", in the previous phase, after two phases of the proposal then r_u sends the vote "yes" to its parent (if any). An agent r_u considers a neighbor its child only if it sends the vote either "yes" or "undecided". An agent r_u sends a "yes" vote to its parent only if it has received a "yes" vote from all its children (if any) and it has not received any "undecided" vote from its neighbors. Otherwise, r_u sends the vote "undecided" to its parent (if any). Notice that if agent r_u does not possess any child, in that case, r_u does not receive any "yes" or "undecided" vote. This implies that r_u does not have any child and r_u initiates the vote "yes" to its parent after two phases of passing the highest ID known to its neighbors. A child always responds with a vote of "yes" or "undecided". If r_u does not have a child then r_u keeps sending a vote "yes" to its parent until it gets to know about the leader.

Whenever r_u receives its own proposed ID from all its children with a "yes" vote in the prior phase then r_u becomes the leader and informs its ID to all neighbors. If r_u knows the leader ID from the prior phase, in that case, r_u informs the leader ID to all its neighbors.

Now, we present the above claims formally. In Lemma 1, we show the number of rounds required to meet any two neighbors. Lemma 2 shows the time and memory complexity required by Algorithm 1. Further, Lemma 3 shows the correctness of the Algorithm 1 such that it elects a unique leader.

Lemma 1. *After dispersion, every agent requires at most $O(\Delta \log n)$ rounds to meet all its neighbors.*

Proof. To prove our lemma, we prove the results for agent r_u and any neighboring agent r_v. Each agent r_u has a unique ID with length $O(\log n)$ bits. Therefore, there exists at least one index between r_u and any neighboring agent r_v such that their bits are different. Furthermore, each agent explores its neighboring nodes in the interval of 2Δ rounds based on the next bit (starting from the LSB). This implies during the different bit for a certain index either r_u would visit r_v or vice versa. Henceforth, each r_u meets all its neighbors in $O(\Delta \log n)$ rounds. Hence, the lemma.   □

Lemma 2. *Algorithm 1 takes $O(n \log^2 n + D\Delta \log n)$ rounds and $O(\log n)$ memory to elect the leader.*

Proof. For round complexity, Line 1 takes $O(n \log^2 n)$ rounds to disperse all the n agents [23]. Furthermore, Lemma 1 takes $O(\Delta \log n)$ rounds to meet its neighbor. Therefore, to pass the information one hop away takes $O(\Delta \log n)$ rounds. The farthest agent is D hops away from any other agent which takes overall $O(D\Delta \log n)$ rounds to know the highest ID agent in the graph. Then it takes $O(D\Delta \log n)$ rounds for the "yes" votes to propagate back to the highest ID agent. After that, it takes $O(D\Delta \log n)$ rounds required to inform all the agents in the graph about the highest ID agent, i.e., the leader. This shows the overall round complexity for leader election is $O(n \log^2 n + D\Delta \log n)$. In case of memory complexity, Line 1 takes $O(\log n)$ memory [23]. On the other hand, after dispersion, knowing the highest ID also takes $O(\log n)$ bits to store the information of ID, parent, highest ID known, and Leader ID. Hence, the lemma.   □

Lemma 3. *Algorithm 1 correctly elects a unique agent as the leader.*

Proof. For the sake of contradiction, let us suppose Algorithm 1 elects more than one leader, namely, ℓ_1 and ℓ_2 such that $\ell_1 > \ell_2$, i.e., ℓ_1's ID is higher than ℓ_2. In such case, ℓ_2's children voted "yes" for ℓ_2 and so did their children and their children's children, and so on. Therefore, ℓ_1 which is an agent situated at the graph also voted for ℓ_2 which is not possible. Hence, there exists a unique leader with the highest ID.   □

From the above discussion, we have the following result.

Theorem 1. *Given any configuration of n agents positioned initially arbitrarily on the nodes of a n-node graph G, there is a deterministic algorithm that elects a leader in $O(n \log^2 n + D\Delta \log n)$ rounds with $O(\log n)$ bits of memory per agent for a known value of n and Δ.*

Remark 1. For the rooted configuration, dispersion takes $O(n \log n)$ rounds in Line 1 of Algorithm 1 as shown in [23]. Therefore, round complexity becomes $O(n \log n + D\Delta \log n)$. On the other hand, for the case of already dispersed configuration, round complexity is $O(D\Delta \log n)$. Furthermore, memory complexity remains unchanged in both configurations, i.e., $O(\log n)$ bits per agent.

5   Applications to Additional Graph Problems

We leverage the leader election result (Theorem 1) to enhance existing solutions for MST, MIS, MDS, and Gathering problems in the agent-based model. The improvements over previous results (discussed in Table 2) are achieved either by optimizing time or memory. All our solutions are memory-optimal, with most offering significant reductions in round complexity as well.

5.1   Minimum Spanning Tree

A **Minimum Spanning Tree (MST)** of a graph $G = (V, E)$ with n nodes is a subgraph $T = (V, E')$ such that $w(e)$ represents the weight of an edge e and for the MST T:

$$T = \arg\min_{T' \subseteq G} \sum_{e \in T'} w(e)$$

subject to the constraints that T' is connected, acyclic, and spans all n nodes in G.

Kshemkalyani et al. [11] constructed the MST in $O(m + n \log n)$ rounds and $O(\Delta \log n)$ bits per agent from a given dispersed configuration in the presence of a leader. From Sudo et al. [23], we can disperse all the n agents in $O(n \log^2 n)$ rounds and $O(\log n)$ memory. Their protocol does not have termination [23], therefore, knowledge of n provides the dispersed configuration in $O(n \log^2 n)$ rounds. From the above discussion and Theorem 1, we have the following result.

Theorem 2 (MST). *Given any configuration of n agents positioned initially arbitrarily on the nodes of a n-node graph G, there is a deterministic algorithm that finds an MST of G in $O(m + n \log^2 n + D\Delta \log n)$ rounds with $O(\Delta \log n)$ bits per agent.*

Remark 2. In an MST, an agent might have to track all its neighboring edges as the MST edge that requires $O(\Delta \log n)$ bits of memory. Therefore, Theorem 2 is memory optimal.

5.2 Maximal Independent Set (MIS)

Suppose n agents are initially located arbitrarily on the nodes of an n-node anonymous graph $G = (V, E)$. The goal in the maximal independent set (MIS) problem is to relocate the agents autonomously to find a subset $S \subset V$ of nodes such that S forms an MIS of G.

Description of the MIS Algorithm: We construct the MIS from a dispersed configuration and known leader in Algorithm 2. In this, the leader becomes the MIS agent and converts all its neighbors non-MIS in $O(\log \Delta)$ rounds with the help of the Helping-Each-Other (HEO) technique introduced by [23]. In this, each agent r_u having the token visits its neighbor by port 1 and comes back with the agent situated across port 1. Now, these two agents visit ports 2 and 3 individually and come back with one agent each. Similarly, after every 2 rounds the number of agents becomes double, and for the degree δ_{r_u}, it takes $2 \log \delta_{r_u}$ rounds to gather all the neighboring agents at r_u's node. During the MIS algorithm, we run a variant of Depth-First-Search (DFS) with the help of a token. We run the MIS algorithm until some neighbor of agent r_u remains unexplored. We call an agent r_u as unexplored if it never held the token. Specifically, if the leader's neighbor remains unexplored, we run the following protocol for any agent r_u. If agent r_u has the token and it is neither an MIS nor a non-MIS agent, in that case, r_u collects all the agents using HEO technique and figures out the status of all other agents. If none of the neighboring agents is an MIS agent only then r_u becomes the MIS agent. Otherwise, r_u becomes a non-MIS agent. If agent r_u has the token and it is either an MIS or a non-MIS agent and there exists any unexplored port then r_u passes the token to the next unexplored port (in increasing order) and becomes the parent of the node across the port. Otherwise, r_u sends the token to the parent node. In this protocol, each agent stores its own ID and parent's port number. It requires $O(\log n)$ memory. Furthermore, the token reaches all the n nodes and takes at most $O(\log \Delta)$ rounds to run HEO. Therefore, the overall time complexity to run the MIS algorithm is $O(n \log \Delta)$ rounds and $O(\log n)$ memory.

Below, we show the correctness of Algorithm 2.

Lemma 4. *Algorithm 2 generates an MIS.*

Proof. We prove the lemma by considering two cases: (i) The token is passed to each agent r_u. (ii) Either the agent r_u is part of the MIS or one of its neighbors is.

We prove both cases by contradiction. For case (i), let us assume the token is not passed to agent r_u. Then, it is also not passed to r_u's parent, grandparent, and so forth, due to Line 13 of Algorithm 2. This implies that the token was not passed by the leader, contradicting Line 2. For case (ii), given that the token reaches all agents, suppose there exists an agent at a node that is neither part of the MIS nor has any neighbors in the MIS. This would mean that Line 8 in Algorithm 2 was not executed, contradicting the assumption.   □

From the above discussion and Theorem 1 of leader election, we have the following result.

Algorithm 2: MAXIMAL INDEPENDENT SET

Input   : A set $\mathcal{R}$ of n agents with unique IDs dispersed on a graph of n nodes with known leader's ID.
Output: MIS configuration.

1 Helping-Each-Other (HEO) technique to gather all the neighboring agents at a node as discussed in [23]. A HEO phase consists of $O(\log \Delta)$ rounds, in which, agent r_u meets all its neighbors.
2 The leader becomes the MIS agent and converts all its neighbors in non-MIS in $\log \Delta$ rounds with the help of HEO, passes the token via port 1, and becomes the parent of the across-the-port node.
3 **while** *agent r_u's neighbors are unexplored* **do**
4   **if** *agent r_u has the token* **then**
5   **if** r_u *is neither an MIS nor a non-MIS agent* **then**
6   r_u collects all the agents using HEO technique and figures out the status of all other agents
7   **if** *none of the neighboring agents is an MIS agent* **then**
8   r_u becomes the MIS agent
9   **else**
10   r_u becomes a non-MIS agent
11   **if** r_u *is either MIS or Non-MIS* **then**
12   **if** *any unexplored port exists* **then**
13   r_u passes the token to the next unexplored port (in increasing order) and becomes the parent of the node across the port
14   **else**
15   r_u sends the token to the parent node

Theorem 3 (MIS). *Given any configuration of n agents positioned initially arbitrarily on the nodes of a n-node graph G, there is a deterministic algorithm that finds an MIS of G in $O(n \log^2 n + D\Delta \log n)$ rounds with $O(\log n)$ bits per agent.*

5.3   Minimal Dominating Set (MDS)

Suppose n agents are initially located arbitrarily on the nodes of an n-node anonymous graph $G = (V, E)$. A *dominating set* of G is a subset $DS \subset V$ of nodes such that for any $v \notin DS$, v has a neighbor in DS.

For the sake of completeness, we prove the following lemma to show every MIS is an MDS. Therefore, the result of MIS holds for MDS as it is.

Lemma 5. *Every MIS is an MDS.*

Proof. We prove this by contradiction. Let us suppose there exists a neighbor in MIS that is not covered by any of the MIS agents then there exists an agent r_u which is neither MIS nor its neighbor which contradicts the assumption that it is an MIS. Hence, the proof.   □

From the Lemma 5 and Theorem 3, we have the following result.

Theorem 4 (MDS). *Given any configuration of n agents positioned initially arbitrarily on the nodes of a n-node graph G, there is a deterministic algorithm that finds an MDS of G in $O(n \log^2 n + D\Delta \log n)$ rounds with $O(\log n)$ bits per agent.*

5.4   Gathering

Suppose n agents are initially located arbitrarily on the nodes of an n-node anonymous graph $G = (V, E)$. The goal of the gathering problem is to relocate the agents autonomously to position all of them to a node in G not fixed a priori (n agents at a node of G).

Algorithm 2 can be adapted to gather all the agents at the leader's node. In Algorithm 2 (Line 15), when an agent passes the token to its parent, the parent agent keeps the account of the number of children. Therefore, after $O(n \log \Delta)$ rounds all the agents are traversed, and MIS is formed. The agent without children gathers at its parent node. When the parent finds all its children in its place, the parent moves to its parent with all of its children. This process occurs recursively and eventually all the agents are gathered at the leader's node. In the worst case, an agent can be at most n hop away from its leader. Therefore, it takes at most $O(n)$ rounds to gather all the agents. Notice that an agent only counts its number of children other than the memory used for MIS, therefore, the memory complexity remains unchanged, i.e., $O(\log n)$.

From the above discussion and Leader Election Algorithm 1, we have the following result.

Theorem 5 (Gathering). *Given any configuration of n agents positioned initially arbitrarily on the nodes of a n-node graph G, there is a deterministic algorithm that collects all n agents to a node in G not fixed a priori in $O(n \log^2 n + D\Delta \log n)$ rounds with $O(\log n)$ bits per agent.*

6 Conclusions

We solved leader election in the agent-based model in $O(n \log^2 n + D\Delta \log n)$ time with optimal memory of $O(\log n)$ bits per agent for general initial configurations. Furthermore, the memory complexities of the existing results on MST, MIS, MDS, and Gathering on the agent-based model were improved using the leader election result, and we achieved the optimal memory complexity bits per agent for all the aforementioned problems. Our result also solved near-linear time complexity for MIS, MDS, and Gathering problems after leader election in a dispersed setting in $O(n \log \Delta)$ rounds (see Table 1). It would be interesting to improve the time complexity of our leader election, which would directly help to improve the complexity of the other graph-related problems. It would also be interesting to see whether these results can be achieved without any prior knowledge of the parameter.

References

1. Augustine, J., Moses Jr, W.K.: Dispersion of mobile robots: a study of memory-time trade-offs. In: ICDCN, pp. 1:1–1:10 (2018)
2. Awerbuch, B.: Optimal distributed algorithms for minimum weight spanning tree, counting, leader election and related problems (detailed summary). In: Aho, A.V. (ed.) STOC, pp. 230–240. ACM (1987). https://doi.org/10.1145/28395.28421
3. Awerbuch, B., Goldberg, A.V., Luby, M., Plotkin, S.A.: Network decomposition and locality in distributed computation. In: FOCS, vol. 30, pp. 364–369. Citeseer (1989)
4. Chand, P.K., Das, A., Molla, A.R.: Agent-based triangle counting and its applications in anonymous graphs. CoRR abs/2402.03653 (2024). https://doi.org/10.48550/arxiv.2402.03653
5. Chand, P.K., Molla, A.R., Sivasubramaniam, S.: Run for cover: dominating set via mobile agents. In: ALGOWIN, pp. 133–150. Springer, Cham (2023)
6. Cong, Y., Changjun, G., Zhang, T., Gao, Y.: Underwater robot sensing technology: a survey. Fundam. Res. **1** (2021). https://doi.org/10.1016/j.fmre.2021.03.002
7. Deurer, J., Kuhn, F., Maus, Y.: Deterministic distributed dominating set approximation in the congest model. In: Proceedings of the 2019 ACM Symposium on Principles of Distributed Computing, pp. 94–103 (2019)
8. El-Sayed, A., Scarborough, P., Seemann, L., Galea, S.: Social network analysis and agent-based modeling in social epidemiology. Epidemiol. perspect. Innov. EP+I **9**, 1 (2012). https://doi.org/10.1186/1742-5573-9-1
9. Gallager, R.G., Humblet, P.A., Spira, P.M.: A distributed algorithm for minimum-weight spanning trees. ACM Trans. Program. Lang. Syst. **5**(1), 66–77 (1983). https://doi.org/10.1145/357195.357200

10. Garay, J.A., Kutten, S., Peleg, D.: A sub-linear time distributed algorithm for minimum-weight spanning trees (extended abstract). In: FOCS, pp. 659–668. IEEE Computer Society (1993). https://doi.org/10.1109/SFCS.1993.366821
11. Kshemkalyani, A.D., Kumar, M., Molla, A.R., Sharma, G.: Brief announcement: agent-based leader election, MST, and beyond. In: DISC 2024. LIPIcs, vol. 319, pp. 50:1–50:7 (2024). https://doi.org/10.4230/LIPICS.DISC.2024.50
12. Kutten, S., Pandurangan, G., Peleg, D., Robinson, P., Trehan, A.: On the complexity of universal leader election. J. ACM **62**(1), 7:1–7:27 (2015)
13. Kutten, S., Peleg, D.: Fast distributed construction of small k-dominating sets and applications. J. Algorithms **28**(1), 40–66 (1998)
14. Lann, G.L.: Distributed systems - towards a formal approach. In: Gilchrist, B. (ed.) Information Processing, Proceedings of the 7th IFIP Congress 1977, Toronto, Canada, 8–12 August 1977, pp. 155–160. North-Holland (1977)
15. Lee, J., Shin, S., Park, M., Kim, C.: Agent-based simulation and its application to analyze combat effectiveness in network-centric warfare considering communication failure environments. Math. Probl. Eng. **2018**, 1–9 (2018). https://doi.org/10.1155/2018/2730671
16. Martinkus, K., Papp, P.A., Schesch, B., Wattenhofer, R.: Agent-based graph neural networks. In: The Eleventh International Conference on Learning Representations, ICLR 2023, Kigali, Rwanda, 1–5 May 2023. OpenReview.net (2023). https://openreview.net/pdf?id=8WTAh0tj2jC
17. Molla, A.R., Mondal, K., Moses Jr, W.K.: Fast deterministic gathering with detection on arbitrary graphs: the power of many robots. In: IEEE International Parallel and Distributed Processing Symposium, IPDPS, pp. 47–57. IEEE (2023)
18. Panconesi, A., Srinivasan, A.: On the complexity of distributed network decomposition. J. Algorithms **20**(2), 356–374 (1996)
19. Pattanayak, D., Bhagat, S., Chaudhuri, S.G., Molla, A.R.: Maximal independet set via mobile agents. In: ICDCN, pp. 74–83. ACM (2024)
20. Peleg, D.: Time-optimal leader election in general networks. J. Parallel Distrib. Comput. **8**(1), 96–99 (1990). https://doi.org/10.1016/0743-7315(90)90074-Y
21. Peleg, D., Rubinovich, V.: A near-tight lower bound on the time complexity of distributed minimum-weight spanning tree construction. SIAM J. Comput. **30**(5), 1427–1442 (2000). https://doi.org/10.1137/S0097539700369740
22. Sudo, Y., Baba, D., Nakamura, J., Ooshita, F., Kakugawa, H., Masuzawa, T.: A single agent exploration in unknown undirected graphs with whiteboards. In: Proceedings of the 3rd International ACM Workshop on Reliability, Availability, and Security, WRAS 2010, vol. E98.A (2010). https://doi.org/10.1145/1953563.1953570
23. Sudo, Y., Shibata, M., Nakamura, J., Kim, Y., Masuzawa, T.: Near-linear time dispersion of mobile agents. In: Alistarh, D. (ed.) 38th International Symposium on Distributed Computing, DISC 2024, October 28 to November 1, 2024, Madrid, Spain. LIPIcs, vol. 319, pp. 38:1–38:22. Schloss Dagstuhl - Leibniz-Zentrum für Informatik (2024). https://doi.org/10.4230/LIPICS.DISC.2024.38
24. Ta-Shma, A., Zwick, U.: Deterministic rendezvous, treasure hunts, and strongly universal exploration sequences. ACM Trans. Algorithms **10**(3), 12:1–12:15 (2014). https://doi.org/10.1145/2601068
25. Zhuge, C., Shao, C., Wei, B.: An agent-based spatial urban social network generator: a case study of Beijing, China. J. Comput. Sci. **29** (2018). https://doi.org/10.1016/j.jocs.2018.09.005

A Novel Protocol for Mitigating Wormhole Attack in Multi-hop Payment Channels

Rohan Mariyala[1]([envelope]) [iD] and Susmita Mandal[2] [iD]

[1] University of Hyderabad, Hyderabad, Telangana, India
mariyalarohankumar@gmail.com
[2] Institute for Development and Research in Banking Technology, Hyderabad,
Telangana, India
susmitamandal.nitrkl@gmail.com

Abstract. The rapid advancement of blockchain technology has highlighted critical issues, such as slow transaction speeds, which impede
its widespread adoption. To address these limitations, layer-two protocols have been developed to process transactions off-chain, reserving the
blockchain for dispute resolution. Among these, Payment Channel Networks offer a promising solution by enabling efficient multi-hoppayments
through off-chain mechanisms. These networks utilize Hash Time-Locked
Contracts to ensure secure conditional payments, releasing funds only
when predefined conditions are met and ensuring that all transaction segments either succeed or fail together. However, traditional approaches to
PCNs face significant security challenges, including Wormhole Attacks,
Griefing Attacks, Bribery Attacks, and Balance Security issues. This
study presents a novel cryptographic protocol designed to mitigate
wormhole attack within multi-hopPCNs. By integrating HTLCs, Elliptic Curve Cryptography, and Schnorr signatures, the proposed solution
enhances transaction security by locking funds and releasing them only
after verifying the identities and actions of all involved parties. This
research contributes a practical approach to improving the security of
multi-hop payments, offering a robust defense against intermediary col-
lusion and enhancing the overall reliability of blockchain-based financial
transactions.

Keywords: Blockchain · Layer-two Protocols · Off-chain
Transactions · Payment Channel Networks (PCNs) · Multi-hop
Payments · Hash Time-Locked Contracts (HTLCs) · Wormhole
Attacks · Schnorr Signatures · Elliptic Curve Cryptography (ECC)

1 Introduction

Payment channels [1] are a type of Layer-two scaling solution [2] designed to
enhance the transaction throughput and reduce the latency of blockchain networks [3]. Payment channels leverage the capabilities of smart contracts in

Q. Bramas et al. (Eds.): ICDCIT 2025, LNCS 15507, pp. 124–139, 2025.
https://doi.org/10.1007/978-3-031-81404-4_10

blockchain technology to facilitate transactions between two parties. These channels are established by locking funds within a smart contract, which utilizes the concept of Hash Time-Locked Contracts (HTLCs) to manage and secure the transaction process. They allow users to transact directly with one another without recording each transaction on the blockchain, thereby reducing the load on the network. Only the opening and closing transactions are recorded on-chain, which drastically reduces the number of transactions the blockchain has to process, leading to lower fees and faster transactions.

The concept of payment channel is fundamental to the development of PCNs [4], where multiple payment channels are connected to form a network. This enables multi-hop payments [5], where a payment can be routed through several intermediaries before reaching the final recipient, further enhancing the scalability [6] and efficiency of blockchain networks.

Despite the advantages of Payment Channel Networks, they are susceptible to several security vulnerabilities, particularly in the context of multi-hop payments. One of the major issues is the wormhole attack, where an adversary can intercept and manipulate the transaction process, causing financial loss and undermining the trust in the network. This poses a significant security challenge for PCNs, as it discourages honest participation and undermines the network's overall functionality. Mitigating wormhole attack is crucial for ensuring the viability and widespread adoption of multi-hopPCNs. This research aims to develop a solution that effectively prevents or significantly hinders wormhole attack within multi-hop PCNs. This solution will contribute towards building secure and reliable PCNs, fostering secure payment processing, and achieving atomicity within blockchain ecosystems.

The primary motivation of this work is to enhance the security of PCNs, particularly focusing on the vulnerabilities associated with multi-hop payments. Wormhole attack is worsened by malicious relaying nodes that may collude to bypass the release of funds. To address this vulnerability, we are motivated to develop mechanisms that prevent malicious nodes in the PCN from bypassing the release of funds by sharing secrets with colluding nodes. A key aspect of our approach is the design of a communication protocol that ensures transactions are conducted with both atomicity and security. This protocol is essential for maintaining the integrity of multi-hop PCNs, thereby enhancing security and achieving atomic transactions in blockchain ecosystems.

The paper is organized as follows: Sect. 2 presents a literature survey on wormhole attack and existing mitigation techniques. Section 3 outlines the proposed methodology, and Sect. 4 presents the experiment design. Section 5 depicts the results, and finally, Sect. 6 offers the conclusion and future work.

2 Background and Related Work

2.1 Payment Channel Networks

PCNs [1] are a Layer-two scaling solution for blockchain networks that enable off-chain transactions between parties. PCNs allow users to conduct numerous

transactions without recording each one on the blockchain, thus reducing congestion and improving transaction speed and cost efficiency. The basic idea is that
two parties can open a payment channel by locking a certain amount of cryp-
tocurrency into a smart contract. They can then exchange signed transactions
off-chain, updating the balance within the channel. Only the opening and closing
transactions need to be recorded on the blockchain, significantly reducing the
number of on-chain transactions. This mechanism allows for multiple transactions to occur off-chain, reducing the load on the blockchain and enabling faster
and cheaper transactions between the participants.

2.2   Challenges in Payment Channel Networks

There exist several challenges [7] in PCNs, such as Wormhole attacks, Griefing
attacks, Bribery attacks, and Balance security issues.

In a wormhole attack [8], two malicious nodes on opposite ends of the network
act as this tunnel. They trick other nodes into routing payments through them,
appearing as a normal path. The attacker can then steal funds by manipulating
the payment information mid-transit. This disrupts the network's core principle:
secure, multi-hop payments. While rare, wormhole attack pose a threat as they
can be hard to detect and exploit vulnerabilities in the routing system. Developers are constantly working on methods to identify and prevent these attacks,
safeguarding the integrity of PCNs.

In a Grieving attack [9], a malicious actor makes a payment but intentionally
withholds the secret key needed to claim the funds. This locks up other users'
money in channels, preventing them from using it for legitimate transactions.
Griefing attacks disrupt the network's flow, harming its efficiency. While attackers gain nothing directly, they can hinder the network's overall usability. Several
attempts have been made by researchers to develop solutions, such as penalty
systems, to deter such attacks and enhance the security of payment channels.

A malicious actor tempts miners on the underlying blockchain with bribes in
Bribery attacks [10]. These bribes incentivize miners to prioritize the attacker's
transactions over legitimate ones. In the context of time-locked contracts, this
could allow the attacker to steal funds by manipulating the order in which transactions are processed. The success of such an attack depends on factors like the
bribe amount and network congestion. Researchers are constantly developing
methods to discourage bribery and protect the integrity of these networks.

PCNs offer faster transactions compared to traditional blockchains, but balancing security with efficiency can be tricky. While cryptography like Hash Locks
ensures secure transfers, users can't easily top up channels off-chain. This creates a need for "rebalancing", where funds shift between channels. However,
keeping this process private can be challenging. Revealing too much information
about channel balances can hinder user privacy and routing efficiency. Finding
the right balance between transparency and privacy is crucial for building trust
and ensuring the network's long-term success. Addressing these vulnerabilities is
crucial for the broader adoption and trust in blockchain-based payment systems.

2.3   Related Work

In 2016, J. Poon et al. [11] introduced the Lightning Network (LN) to address Bitcoin's scalability limitations, enabling off-chain payments through bidirectional micropayment channels, which reduce the blockchain's load and periodically settle transactions on-chain. Moreno-Sanchez et al. [12] later proposed Anonymous Multi-Hop Locks (AMHLs) in 2018 to enhance security and privacy in PCNs, addressing threats like wormhole attack. In 2020, Tripathy and Mohanty [13] presented MAPPCN, which uses elliptic curve cryptography to mitigate wormhole attack while preserving privacy. Mohanty and Tripathy [8] followed with the Neo-Hashed Time-Lock Commitment (n-HTLC) protocol in 2021, ensuring off-chain transaction integrity by preventing wormhole attack. Aumayr et al. [14] introduced Blitz in 2021, a secure multi-hop payment (MHP) protocol that improves efficiency by avoiding two-phase commits, while Liu et al. [15] in 2022 developed GMHL (Generalized Multi-Hop Locks) to enhance privacy and atomicity in PCNs using adaptor signatures and randomizable puzzles. Despite these advances, research gaps persist, as MAPPCN lacks path privacy, HTLC remains vulnerable to wormhole attack, Blitz offers only moderate security, and GMHL, while effective, incurs high computational costs, underscoring the need for more robust and efficient solutions for securing PCNs.

3   Proposed Solution

In this section, we present the proposed communication protocol designed to enhance the payment process within payment channels. The protocol is structured into three distinct phases, each addressing specific aspects of the payment transaction. Table 1 describes the symbols, notations, and their descriptions used in the protocol. The first phase involves the initial setup and symmetric key sharing through the Diffie-Hellman Key Exchange protocol. Each participant in the path specifically the sender (U_A), the receiver (U_D), and any intermediary nodes (U_B and U_C) generates their respective public and private keys. This is a crucial step to ensure secure and verifiable communication between all parties involved in the transaction.

The second step involves using HTLCs to lock the funds. These contracts essentially lock the money until the agreed-upon conditions for the transaction are fulfilled. The third phase focuses on the verification of the transaction and the release of funds, ensuring both authenticity and integrity. Finally, upon successful verification, the funds are transferred to the appropriate parties.

Figure 1 illustrates step 1, which belongs to the setup phase of the protocol, while Fig. 2 illustrates steps 2 to 7, which belong to the remaining phases of the protocol. The proposed methodology is based on the assumption that both the sender and receiver are honest.

Setup: In step 1, the receiver (U_D) sends the hash of a secret v, denoted as $H(v)$, to the sender (U_A) as shown in Fig. 1. This hash will later be used to

Table 1. Notation and Description

Notation	Description
U	Users (e.g., U_A, U_B)
C	Ciphertext
v	A random secret generated by U_D
$H(v)$	The hash of the secret v
Pk	Public key (e.g., Pk_A, Pk_B)
sk	Secret key (e.g., sk_A, sk_B)
k	Random chosen value (e.g., k_A, k_B)
G	Generator point for the elliptic curve group
(s, R)	Schnorr signature
	For instance, (s_A, R_A) represents the Schnorr signature of U_A, and (s_{AB}, R_{AB}) represents the aggregate Schnorr signature of U_A and U_B
R	Commitment or Nonce
s	Response or Signature

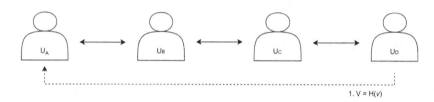

1. V = H(v)

Fig. 1. Transmission of Secret's Hash by Receiver

unlock the funds from the HTLC (Hashed Time-Lock Contract). Using a routing algorithm, U_A obtains the public keys of the intermediary nodes (U_B and U_C) and the receiver (U_D). Next, U_A and U_D perform a Diffie-Hellman key exchange to generate a shared symmetric key. Using this symmetric key, U_A encrypts $H(v)$ with AES-256 encryption, resulting in the ciphertext C_1.

Lock: In the lock phase, HTLC is used to lock funds. Steps 2 to 4, as depicted in Fig. 2, illustrate the lock phase.

U_A initiates the payment by creating an HTLC, locking the specified funds into this contract with a condition to claim the funds. U_A includes C_1, along with their Schnorr signature pair s_A, R_A, and the public keys of U_A, U_B and U_C in a message and forwards it to U_B.

Upon receiving the message from U_A, U_B verifies (s_A, R_A) and attempts to decrypt C_1. Failing to decrypt, U_B realizes that they are not the final recipient and that the message must be forwarded to the next node, U_C, as indicated by the routing algorithm. U_B then aggregates their Schnorr signature pair with that

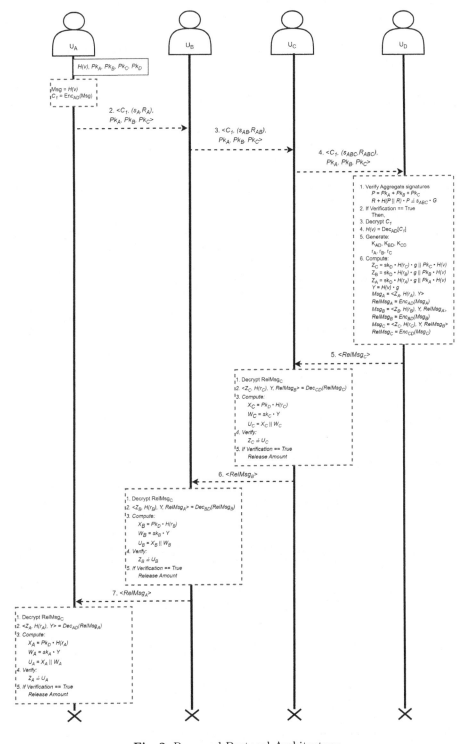

Fig. 2. Proposed Protocol Architecture

of U_A and forwards the HTLC by creating a new one with U_C by deducting the forwarding fee. U_C follows the same procedure, attempting to decrypt C_1 and, upon failure, forwarding the message to U_D and creating a HTLC by deducting the forwarding fee.

Verification and Release:

- **At the receiver: Schnorr Signature verification**
  - The combined public key P is derived from the individual public keys of the signers (U_A, U_B and U_C):

$$P = Pk_A + Pk_B + Pk_C \tag{1}$$

where,

$$Pk_A = sk_A \cdot G \tag{2}$$
$$Pk_B = sk_B \cdot G \tag{3}$$
$$Pk_C = sk_C \cdot G \tag{4}$$

  - The combined value R is computed from the individual random values (R_A, R_B and R_C):

$$R = R_A + R_B + R_C \tag{5}$$

where,

$$R_A = k_A \cdot G \tag{6}$$
$$R_B = k_B \cdot G \tag{7}$$
$$R_C = k_C \cdot G \tag{8}$$

  - The combined signature component s_{ABC} is the sum of the individual signature components (s_A, s_B and s_C):

$$s_{ABC} = s_A + s_B + s_C \tag{9}$$

where,

$$s_A = k_A + H(P||R) \cdot sk_A \tag{10}$$
$$s_B = k_B + H(P||R) \cdot sk_B \tag{11}$$
$$s_C = k_C + H(P||R) \cdot sk_C \tag{12}$$

Upon receiving the aggregated signature (s_{ABC}, R), U_D verifies $R + H(P||R) \cdot P \overset{?}{=} s_{ABC} \cdot G$.

- U_D calculates the hash $H(P||R)$ using the received P and R.
- U_D then computes $H(P||R) \cdot P$.
- U_D adds R to the result obtained in the previous step.

- Finally U_D calculates $s_{ABC} \cdot G$ using the received signature component s_{ABC} and compares the sum obtained with the sum obtained earlier.

If the verification returns true, then the signature is valid.

This implies that the signature was indeed generated by the private keys corresponding to Pk_A, Pk_B and Pk_C.

To understand how this verification works, consider the definitions of s_A, s_B, and s_C, mentioned in Eqs. (10), (11) and (12). Thus, the value of s_{ABC} can be calculated as:

$$
\begin{aligned}
s_{ABC} &= s_A + s_B + s_C \\
&= (k_A + k_B + k_C) + H(P||R) \cdot (sk_A + sk_B + s_C)
\end{aligned}
\tag{13}
$$

Since,

$$
\begin{aligned}
R &= R_A + R_B + R_C \\
&= k_A \cdot G + k_B \cdot G + k_C \cdot G \\
&= (k_A + k_B + k_C) \cdot G
\end{aligned}
\tag{14}
$$

Multiplying both sides by G, we have Eq. (13) as:

$$
s_{ABC} \cdot G = (k_A + k_B + k_C) \cdot G + H(P \parallel R) \cdot (sk_A + sk_B + sk_C) \cdot G \tag{15}
$$

Since,

$$
\begin{aligned}
P &= Pk_A + Pk_B + Pk_C \\
&= sk_A \cdot G + sk_B \cdot G + sk_C \cdot G
\end{aligned}
\tag{16}
$$

we have,

$$
s_{ABC} \cdot G = R + H(P \parallel R) \cdot P \tag{17}
$$

Therefore, the verification of $R + H(P||R) \cdot P \overset{?}{=} s_{ABC} \cdot G$ confirms that if the equality holds, the signature is valid. This ensures that the signature was created by the signers with the corresponding private keys.

If the verification of the aggregate signature is successful, U_D then tries to decrypt C_1 with the shared symmetric key, which was obtained after the Diffie-Hellman key exchange with U_A during the setup phase. Upon decrypting C_1, U_D extracts the hash value and compares it with the hash previously sent to U_A in step 1. This comparison verifies the authenticity of the hash, confirming that it was indeed sent by U_A.

After the hash is verified, then U_D generates session keys K_{AD}, K_{BD} & K_{CD} and random nonces r_A, r_B & r_C for all the users in the path. then U_D computes:

$$
Z_C = sk_D \cdot H(r_C) \cdot g \parallel Pk_C \cdot H(v) \tag{18}
$$

$$
Z_B = sk_D \cdot H(r_B) \cdot g \parallel Pk_B \cdot H(v) \tag{19}
$$

$$
Z_A = sk_D \cdot H(r_A) \cdot g \parallel Pk_A \cdot H(v) \tag{20}
$$

and also,

$$Y = H(v) \cdot g \tag{21}$$

Then, U_D constructs release messages for each user, which consists of Z, $H(r)$, Y, and an encrypted release message to be forwarded to the next user. Z, $H(r)$ are unique for each user, whereas Y is common. These release messages are encrypted using the session keys generated in the previous step. The release messages are constructed in this format:

$$Msg_A = < Z_A, H(r_A), Y >$$
$$RelMsg_A = Enc_{AD}(Msg_A)$$
$$Msg_B = < Z_B, H(r_B), Y, RelMsg_A >$$
$$RelMsg_B = Enc_{BD}(Msg_B)$$
$$Msg_C = < Z_C, H(r_C), Y, RelMsg_B >$$
$$RelMsg_C = Enc_{CD}(Msg_C)$$

and are encrypted by AES-256 encryption using the session keys generated. To unlock the funds U_D sends $RelMsg_C$ to U_C.

– **At intermediaries and sender:**
  • U_C Upon receiving the release message, $RelMsg_C$ is decrypted using the session key K_{CD}, through which Z_C, $H(r_C)$, Y and $RelMsg_B$ are obtained. Then, the following components are computed:

$$X_C = Pk_D \cdot H(r_C) \tag{22}$$
$$W_C = sk_c \cdot Y \tag{23}$$
$$U_c = X_C \parallel W_C \tag{24}$$

and verifies $Z_C \overset{?}{=} U_C$. If true, the amount locked in the HTLC between U_C and U_D is released. U_C then forwards the release message obtained during decryption to the next user, i.e., U_B.
  • U_B Upon receiving the release message, $RelMsg_B$ is decrypted by AES-256 decryption using the session key K_{BD}, through which Z_B, $H(r_B)$, Y and $RelMsg_A$ are obtained. Then, the following components are computed:

$$X_B = Pk_D \cdot H(r_B) \tag{25}$$
$$W_B = sk_B \cdot Y \tag{26}$$
$$U_B = X_B \parallel W_B \tag{27}$$

and verifies $Z_B \overset{?}{=} U_B$. If true, the amount locked in the HTLC between U_B and U_C is released.U_B then forwards the release message obtained during decryption to the next user, i.e., U_A.

• U_A Upon receiving the release message, $RelMsg_A$ is decrypted using the session key K_{AD}, through which Z_A, $H(r_A)$ and Y are obtained. Then, the following components are computed:

$$X_A = Pk_D \cdot H(r_A) \tag{28}$$

$$W_A = sk_A \cdot Y \tag{29}$$

$$U_A = X_A \parallel W_A \tag{30}$$

and verifies, $Z_A \stackrel{?}{=} U_A$. If true, the amount locked in the HTLC between U_A and U_B is released.

Release messages are constructed and encrypted using the session keys, ensuring the integrity and confidentiality of the transaction data. Session keys are unique to each transaction session, making it impossible for unauthorized or colluding nodes to decrypt or alter the messages without detection. This encryption process is crucial in preventing a wormhole attack, where malicious nodes attempt to intercept and manipulate the transaction data.

The rigorous verification process ensures that all nodes in the transaction chain are actively participating and adhering to the protocol. By doing this, it prevents any colluding nodes from bypassing the verification steps, which would otherwise allow them to manipulate the transaction. The involvement of each node in the verification process adds multiple layers of security, making the network resilient to attacks and ensuring the trustworthiness of the transaction.

4   Experiment Design

This section presents the experiments conducted to evaluate the proposed communication protocol for payment channels and the results obtained. The protocol leverages a HTLC written in Solidity, a programming language specifically designed for writing smart contracts on the Ethereum blockchain, for fund locking, encrypted message storing, and release of funds. Solidity contracts interact with the Ethereum network using gas, which is a unit that measures the computational work required for operations on the blockchain and incurs a cost for contract execution. Other essential cryptographic operations and verifications are handled off-chain using Python. The experiments were executed in a controlled environment using Truffle to build and deploy smart contracts and Ganache as a local Ethereum blockchain test network to simulate real-world scenarios. The experiments were conducted on a system with the following hardware requirements: Processor: 12th Gen Intel(R) Core(TM) i5-1235U, 1300 MHz, 10 Core(s), 12 Logical Processor(s) and RAM 16 GB. Python, Solidity, Truffle, Ganache GUI, and Web3.py are the software tools and programming languages used in the experiment.

To validate the proposed methodology for secure and efficient payment transactions within payment channels and to avoid wormhole attack during multi-hop

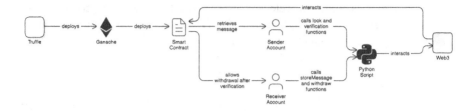

Fig. 3. Process Flow of the Proposed Work

payments, a comprehensive experiment was designed and executed. The experiment involves three primary components: key generation and encryption, smart contract interaction, and the verification and release of funds.

The experimental design, as illustrated in Fig. 3, details the process of deploying the protocol and interacting with a smart contract within a blockchain environment. Using Truffle, a smart contract is deployed to a local blockchain simulated by Ganache. Once deployed, the smart contract interacts with two accounts: the sender account and the receiver account. The sender account calls lock and verification functions, while the receiver account calls storeMessage and withdraw functions. A Python script utilizing the Web3 library facilitates automated interactions with the smart contract, ensuring seamless execution of the lock, verification, store, and withdraw processes of the funds. This setup provides a structured approach to testing smart contract functionality in a controlled environment.

5   Results

The proposed protocol was tested between two parties, successfully demonstrating the secure and efficient execution of payment transactions within payment channels and effectively preventing Wormhole attacks during multi-hop payments. The key results from the experiment are as follows:

Successful Key Generation and Exchange: All users were able to generate their public and private keys correctly. The Diffie-Hellman key exchange was successfully performed between the sender and receiver, resulting in a shared symmetric key. The key generation for each user was completed in 1.168 ms, and the Diffie-Hellman key exchange took 2.05 ms to execute.

Accurate Schnorr Signature Aggregation and Verification: The Schnorr signature pairs generated by individual users were accurately aggregated. The aggregated Schnorr signature was successfully verified, ensuring the integrity and authenticity of the transaction. The generation of Schnorr signatures for each user requires 5.2 ms, and the aggregate signature verification process was executed in 1.7 ms.

Efficient Message Encryption and Decryption: Hash of the pre-image, $H(v)$, is successfully encrypted and decrypted using AES-256. All messages were correctly encrypted using AES-256 and the generated session keys. All messages were successfully decrypted by the intended recipients, ensuring secure communication throughout the transaction. The AES-256 encryption process took 0.1 ms, whereas decryption took 0.3 ms for each encryption and decryption, respectively.

Smart Contract Interaction: The smart contract was successfully compiled using Truffle (Fig. 4) and deployed (Fig. 5) on the Ganache test network and its address was used for interacting with the Python script (Fig. 6). The smart contract accurately locks the funds (Fig. 7) upon receiving the initial transaction details.

The encrypted release message was correctly stored and retrieved from the smart contract. The verification flag was set to True upon successful verification of the release message, allowing the receiver to withdraw the locked funds. Deploying the HTLC smart contract consumed 1,471,572 units of gas. Locking of funds required 121,609 units of gas while storing messages consumed 593,264 units of gas. Withdrawing funds required 82,197 units of gas

Secure and Efficient Fund Release: Release messages were constructed, encrypted, and forwarded to the respective users. Each user successfully decrypted and verified their release message, leading to the release of the locked funds in a secure and efficient manner.

```
2_deploy_contract.js
====================

    Replacing 'HashedTimelockContract'
    --------------------------------------
    > transaction hash:    0xf06518239089d6166cede049ca3f3068bdb4b29536a2ddb4889ee4a8910fcefa
    > Blocks: 0            Seconds: 0
    > contract address:    0x0DD1c4646280566075c6ae071c4827C52ae6474e
    > block number:        1
    > block timestamp:     1721125746
    > account:             0x49830ab4a1899b143f41565c789F84622A352e7d
    > balance:             99.9950334445
    > gas used:            1471572 (0x167454)
    > gas price:           3.375 gwei
    > value sent:          0 ETH
    > total cost:          0.0049665555 ETH

    > Saving artifacts
    --------------------------------------
    > Total cost:          0.0049665555 ETH

Summary
=======
> Total deployments:    1
> Final cost:           0.0049665555 ETH
```

Fig. 4. Smart Contract Deployed Using Truffle

The constructed release messages, encrypted using session keys, effectively prevented any colluding nodes from intercepting and altering the transaction. Each intermediary and the sender verified their respective release messages by computing specific cryptographic components, ensuring the active participation

Fig. 5. Smart Contract Deployed on Local Test Network

```
# truffle development blockchain address
blockchain_address = 'http://127.0.0.1:7545'
# Client instance to interact with the blockchain
web3 = Web3(HTTPProvider(blockchain_address))
# Set the default account (so we don't need to set the "from" for every transaction call)
web3.eth.defaultAccount = web3.eth.accounts[0]

# Path to the compiled contract JSON file
compiled_contract_path = 'build/contracts/HashedTimelockContract.json'
# Deployed contract address (see 'migrate' command output: 'contract address')
deployed_contract_address = '0x0DD1c4646280566075c6ae071c4827C52ae6474e'
```

Fig. 6. Python Code Snippet Using Web3.py to Interact With a Deployed Smart Contract

of all nodes and preventing any bypassing of the verification process. This meticulous verification mechanism ensured that the system was protected against Wormhole attacks, as every node's involvement was authenticated, and no node could fraudulently claim to have received or forwarded a release message without undergoing the proper cryptographic checks.

5.1 Performance Metrics

– **Execution Time:**
  1. Key Generation for each user: 1.168 ms
  2. Diffie-Hellman Key Exchange: 2.05 ms
  3. Schnorr Signature generation for each user: 5.2 ms
  4. Aggregate signature verification: 1.7 ms
  5. AES-256 Encryption: 0.1 ms
  6. AES-256 Decryption: 0.3 ms
– **Gas Consumption:**
  1. Deploy HTLC smart contract: 1,471,572 units of gas.

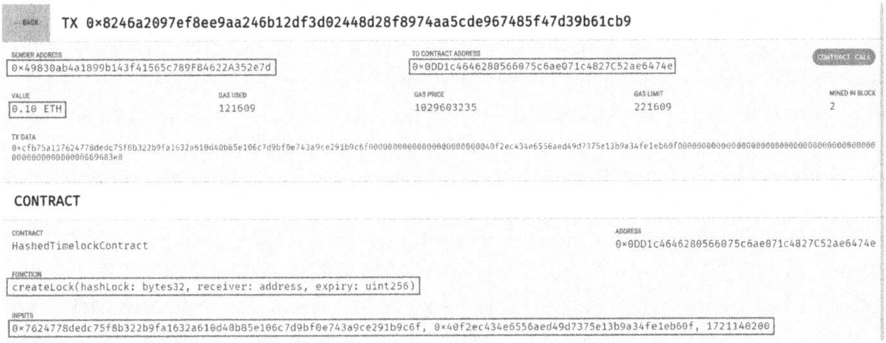

Fig. 7. Transaction of Lock Created Between Sender and Receiver for 0.1 ETH

2. Lock of funds: 121,609 units of gas.
3. Store Message: 593,264 units of gas.
4. Withdraw funds: 82,197 units of gas.

5.2 Comparative Analysis of PCN Solutions

This section compares four different technologies, MAPPCN [13], HTLC [11], Blitz [14], and GMHL [15], along with the proposed work. Table 2 compares these technologies across five features: The Technique Used, Atomicity, Path Privacy, Prevention of wormhole attack, and Security Level. Low security includes basic locking; Moderate has some encryption; High uses advanced cryptography; Yes indicates full atomicity, path privacy, or wormhole attack prevention, while No lacks these features.

Table 2. Comparison Table

Feature/Aspect	MAPPCN [13]	HTLC [11]	Blitz [14]	GMHL [15]	Proposed Work
Technique Used	ETLC	HTLC	UTXO	Guillon-Quisquater-based adaptive signature + RSA	HTLC + ECC + Schnorr signature
Atomicity	✓	✕	✓	✓	✓
Path Privacy	✕	✕	✕	✓	✓
Wormhole Attack	✓	✓	✕	✕	✕
Security Level	Moderate	Low	Moderate	High	High

✓: Yes, ✕: No, +: Combination

The technique used by MAPPCN [13] is ETLC (Elliptic Curve-based Time Lock Contracts), HTLC [11] is Hash Time-Locked Contracts (HTLCs), Blitz

[14] is UTXO (Unspent Transaction Output), GMHL [15] is Guillou-Quisquater based adaptive signature along with RSA cryptosystem and, the proposed work uses HTLC, Schnorr signature Elliptic Curve Cryptography (ECC). The atomicity feature is achieved by MAPPCN [13], Blitz [14], GHML [15], and the proposed work, while HTLC [11] does not have atomicity. The path privacy is a crucial feature achieved by GHML [15] and the proposed work. The other mechanisms fail to achieve path privacy. The main focus of this work is to mitigate the wormhole attack with a high-security and less complex model. The techniques MAPPCN [13] and HTLC [11] are vulnerable to wormhole attack, while Blitz [14], GHML [15], and the proposed work are able to mitigate the same. The security level of MAPPCN [13] is identified as moderate because it has an encryption technique and locking mechanism. The HTLC [11] mechanism possesses only locking. Hence, it is classified under low security. The Blitz mechanism uses UTXO-based transactions, which support locking and signature schemes and no encryption techniques. Hence, the security category of Blitz [14] is treated as Moderate. GHML [15] and the proposed mechanism offer locking mechanisms, encryption techniques, and signature schemes. However, the GHML [15] mechanism uses the RSA cryptosystem for encryption, while the proposed mechanism uses ECC. This will reduce the computational complexity of the proposed mechanism with the same level of security.

6   Conclusion and Future Work

This research addresses the critical security challenge of Wormhole attacks in Payment Channels Networks. While PCNs offer scalability advantages, their vulnerability to such attacks poses significant risks. To mitigate this, we propose a novel communication protocol combined with Hash Time-Locked Contracts. Advanced cryptographic techniques, including Elliptic Curve Cryptography and Schnorr signatures, underpin our approach. Through practical experiments using Solidity and Python, we demonstrate the effectiveness of our solution in enhancing PCN security and achieving transaction atomicity. Our work contributes to the development of more secure, efficient, and scalable blockchain networks by addressing key vulnerabilities and improving overall system reliability.

Future research should focus on scaling our solution for larger networks, as well as addressing other security threats like Griefing and Briber attacks. Continued exploration of advanced cryptography and protocol optimizations will be crucial for enhancing PCN security and performance. Rigorous testing in real-world conditions will provide valuable insights into the system's resilience and pave the way for widespread adoption of PCNs.

Acknowledgment. This work is supported by Ministry of Electronics and Information Technology (MeitY), Government of India under Grant No. 4(4)/2021-ITEA. We would also like to extend our thanks to the Ph.D student Sravan S S for proofreading the manuscript.

References

1. Malavolta, G., Moreno-Sanchez, P., Kate, A., Maffei, M., Ravi, S.: Concurrency and privacy with payment-channel networks. In: Proceedings of the 2017 ACM SIGSAC Conference on Computer and Communications Security, pp. 455–471. ACM (2017)
2. Gudgeon, L., Moreno-Sanchez, P., Roos, S., McCorry, P., Gervais, A.: SoK: layer-two blockchain protocols. In: Bonneau, J., Heninger, N. (eds.) FC 2020. LNCS, vol. 12059, pp. 201–226. Springer, Cham (2020). https://doi.org/10.1007/978-3-030-51280-4_12
3. Nakamoto, S.: Bitcoin: A Peer-to-Peer Electronic Cash System (2008)
4. Papadis, N., Tassiulas, L.: Blockchain-based payment channel networks: challenges and recent advances. IEEE Access **8**, 227596–227609 (2020)
5. Di Stasi, G., Avallone, S., Canonico, R., Ventre, G.: Routing payments on the lightning network. In: 2018 IEEE International Conference on Internet of Things (IThings) and IEEE Green Computing and Communications (GreenCom) and IEEE Cyber, Physical and Social Computing (CPSCom) and IEEE Smart Data (SmartData), pp. 1161–1170. IEEE (2018)
6. Decker, C., Russell, R., Osuntokun, O.: eltoo: A Simple Layer2 Protocol for Bitcoin. White paper (2018). https://blockstream.com/eltoo.pdf
7. Pérez-Solà, C., Ranchal-Pedrosa, A., Herrera-Joancomartí, J., Navarro-Arribas, G., Garcia-Alfaro, J.: LockDown: balance availability attack against lightning network channels. In: Bonneau, J., Heninger, N. (eds.) FC 2020. LNCS, vol. 12059, pp. 245–263. Springer, Cham (2020). https://doi.org/10.1007/978-3-030-51280-4_14
8. Mohanty, S.K., Tripathy, S.: n-HTLC: neo hashed time-lock commitment to defend against wormhole attack in payment channel networks. Comput. Secur. **106**, 102291 (2021)
9. Jourenko, M., Larangeira, M., Tanaka, K.: Payment trees: low collateral payments for payment channel networks. In: Borisov, N., Diaz, C. (eds.) FC 2021. LNCS, vol. 12675, pp. 189–208. Springer, Heidelberg (2021). https://doi.org/10.1007/978-3-662-64331-0_10
10. Judmayer, A., et al.: Pay to win: cheap, cross-chain bribing attacks on PoW cryptocurrencies. In: Bernhard, M., et al. (eds.) FC 2021. LNCS, vol. 12676, pp. 533–549. Springer, Heidelberg (2021). https://doi.org/10.1007/978-3-662-63958-0_39
11. Poon, J., Dryja, T.: The Bitcoin Lightning Network: Scalable Off-Chain Instant Payments (2016)
12. Malavolta, G., Moreno-Sanchez, P., Schneidewind, C., Kate, A., Maffei, M.: Anonymous multi-hop locks for blockchain scalability and interoperability. Cryptology ePrint Archive (2018)
13. Tripathy, S., Mohanty, S.K.: MAPPCN: multi-hop anonymous and privacy-preserving payment channel network. In: Bernhard, M., et al. (eds.) FC 2020. LNCS, vol. 12063, pp. 481–495. Springer, Cham (2020). https://doi.org/10.1007/978-3-030-54455-3_34
14. Aumayr, L., Moreno-Sanchez, P., Kate, A., Maffei, M.: Blitz: secure multi-hop payments without two-phase commits. In: 30th USENIX Security Symposium (USENIX Security 2021), pp. 4043–4060 (2021)
15. Liu, Z., Yang, A., Weng, J., Li, T., Zeng, H., Liang, X.: GMHL: Generalized Multi-Hop Locks for Privacy-Preserving Payment Channel Networks. Cryptology ePrint Archive (2022)

Unleashing Multicore Strength for Efficient Execution of Blockchain Transactions

Ankit Ravish$^{(\boxtimes)}$ ⓘ, Akshay Tejwani ⓘ, Piduguralla Manaswini ⓘ,
and Sathya Peri ⓘ

Indian Institute of Technology Hyderabad, Telangana, India
{cs21resch11014,cs21mtech12015,cs20resch11007}@iith.ac.in,
sathya_p@cse.iith.ac.in

Abstract. Blockchain technology is characterized by its distributed, decentralized, and immutable ledger system which serves as a fundamental platform for managing smart contract transactions (SCTs). However, these SCTs undergo sequential validation within a block which introduces performance bottlenecks in blockchain. In response, this paper introduces a framework called the Multi-Bin Parallel Scheduler (MBPS) designed for parallelizing blockchain smart contract transactions to leverage the capabilities of multicore systems. Our proposed framework facilitates concurrent execution of SCTs, enhancing performance by allowing non-conflicting transactions to be processed simultaneously while preserving deterministic order. The framework comprises of three vital stages: conflict detection, bin creation, and execution. We conducted an evaluation of our MBPS framework in Hyperledger Sawtooth v1.2.6, revealing substantial performance enhancements compared to existing parallel SCT execution frameworks across various smart contract applications. This research contributes to the ongoing optimization efforts in blockchain technology demonstrating its potential for scalability and efficiency in real-world scenarios.

Keywords: Blockchain · Smart Contracts · Parallel Execution · Conflict Detection

1 Introduction

Blockchain [7] is a decentralized digital ledger offering secure and tamper-resistant record-keeping, with applications in finance, supply chain, and identity verification. Despite its advantages, blockchain scalability remains a challenge due to sequential smart contract execution. To address this, we propose the Multi-Bin Parallel Scheduler (MBPS) framework, enabling parallel smart contract execution to improve throughput and reduce transaction execution times.MBPS addresses the issue of transaction conflicts that can arise from parallel processing, ensuring consistent block validation across participants.

Funded by Meity India: No. 4(4)/2021-ITEA & 4(20)/2019-ITEA. This is part of the National (Indian) Blockchain Framework Project.

Numerous strategies have been explored to improve the efficiency of blockchain technology, particularly in terms of scalability, security, and consensus mechanisms. Sharding is a notable approach, dividing the blockchain network into smaller units or shards, which handle transactions independently to increase throughput by allowing concurrent transaction execution across shards. Dickerson et al. [5] proposed a speculative parallel execution model for miners and validators, utilizing software transactional memory to allow non-conflicting transactions to execute concurrently in a deterministic fork-join program. Similarly, Saraph et al. [10] introduced a concurrent execution model in Ethereum, dividing transactions into bins for parallel and serial processing based on their read and write sets. Optimistic Software Transactional Memory systems have also been leveraged for concurrent smart contract execution, demonstrating performance gains over sequential execution [2,3]. A direct acyclic graph (DAG)-based parallel scheduler has been proposed to enhance blockchain performance by improving the parallelism in smart contract execution [8]. Liu et al. [6] introduced an architecture where consensus nodes are separated from execution nodes, supporting asynchronous transaction ordering and parallel execution. The DiPETrans framework by Baheti et al. [4] enables distributed transaction execution with a collaborative PoW approach. Additionally, Yan et al. [11] presented an SCC-VS algorithm, optimizing concurrency within shards based on transaction characteristics like execution time and conflict rate. This paper presents three MBPS variations (Standard, Assisted, and Lockfree) and analyzes their effectiveness in improving throughput and preserving transaction order.

2 Proposed Framework

This section presents the design of our proposed Multi-Bin Parallel Scheduler (MBPS) framework, detailing its architecture and key components. The proposed MBPS framework facilitates parallel transaction execution while preserving a deterministic order, thereby leveraging the capabilities of multicore systems to enhance the efficiency of blockchain ecosystems. This framework introduces three distinct versions to address specific aspects of smart contract execution in blockchain ecosystems: Standard MBPS, Assisted MBPS, and Lockfree MBPS.

Each MBPS framework undergoes three crucial stages: *Conflict Detection, Bin Assignment, and Transaction Execution*. In **Conflict Detection**, conflicts between transactions T_i and T_j are identified if one transaction reads a data item that the other writes, or if both write to the same data item, as detailed in the paper [9]. During **Bin Assignment**, transactions are assigned to bins such that transactions within the same bin are independent, ensuring no conflicts within bins. The procedure for compact bin allocation is outlined in Algorithm 1. Finally, in **Transaction Execution**, non-conflicting transactions in each bin are executed sequentially, bin by bin, starting from Bin 1. All algorithms related to the frameworks discussed above are detailed in the paper [9].

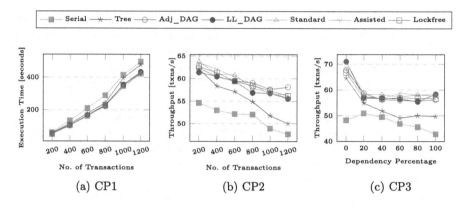

Fig. 1. Simple Wallet Smart Contracts - Baseline Performance Analysis

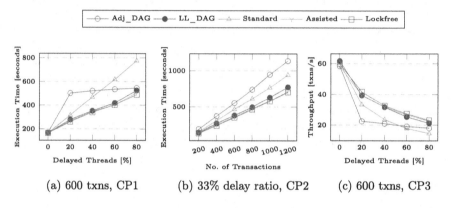

Fig. 2. Simple Wallet Smart Contracts - Threads Latency Analysis

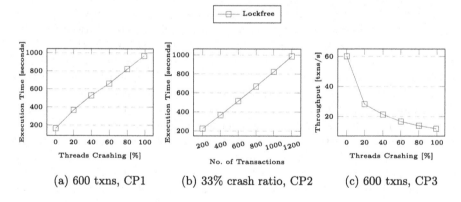

Fig. 3. Simple Wallet Smart Contracts - Threads Crashing Analysis

The **Standard MBPS** framework employs synchronization barriers for parallel smart contract execution, comprising two phases: conflict set identification and bin number assignment. During conflict set identification, transactions are grouped based on conflicts (write-write, read-write, write-read) through input and output address analysis, allowing each transaction to be allocated to a conflict set in parallel. Subsequently, bin numbers are assigned to ensure that conflicting transactions are placed in separate bins, facilitating parallel execution. The **Assisted MBPS** enhances blockchain transaction execution by incorporating a barrier mechanism and helper threads to boost efficiency, particularly during thread crashes or latency. Similar to the Standard MBPS, it consists of conflict set identification and bin number assignment phases, augmented by helper threads to further optimize performance. In contrast, the **Lockfree MBPS** framework advances blockchain transaction parallelism by utilizing lock-free data structures, circumventing traditional synchronization methods like mutexes and barriers. This framework also includes the conflict set identification and bin number assignment phases, where helper threads and atomic operations create a lock-free environment. Algorithm 1 illustrates the bin assignment process using helper threads, enabling each thread to independently claim transactions, detect conflicts, and assign bins in parallel, thereby enhancing scalability and performance in blockchain execution.

3   Analysis of Experiments

In this section, we analyze the experiments conducted to evaluate our framework's performance with the Hyperledger Sawtooth blockchain [1]. We selected Sawtooth due to its parallelism support and inbuilt parallel scheduler. Although Sawtooth is Python-based, we implemented our multi-threaded MBPS framework in C++ for its low-level control over parallelism through threads, mutexes, and atomic operations. We conducted the experiments on an x86_64 machine with 56 CPUs, 2 threads per core, and 14 cores per socket (Intel Xeon CPU E5-2690 v4 @ 2.60GHz). Our MBPS framework's performance was compared with Sawtooth's parallel tree and serial schedulers, as well as the *ADJ_DAG* and *LL_DAG* frameworks [8]. Three experiment types were conducted: Baseline Performance Evaluation, Threads Latency Impact Analysis, and Threads Crash Resilience Analysis. The baseline performance evaluation compares execution times and throughput across frameworks, establishing standard metrics. The threads latency impact analysis explores how thread delays influence performance. Additionally, the threads crash resilience analysis focuses on performance under thread crashes, with particular attention to the lockfree bin scheduler, as it uniquely supports threads crash-handling compared to other schedulers. For these experiments, we used three conflict parameters (CP) defined in [8].

Algorithm 1. Bin Number Assignment Algorithm - Helper Threads

```
 1: function BINNUMASSIGNHELPER
 2:     processedTxns ← 0
 3:     localCount ← 0
 4:     flag ← 0
 5:     while processedTxns < |Txns| do
 6:         i ← atomicFetchAdd(i2, 1) mod |Txns|
 7:         if initialBin[i] = −1 then
 8:             localCount ← 0
 9:             if flag = 1 then
10:                 atomicFetchAdd(threadCounter2, −1)
11:             end if
12:             allotedBin ← CALCULATEBINHELPER(i)
13:             if allotedBin = −1 then
14:                 continue
15:             end if
16:             localVal ← allotedBin
17:             set¡int¿ * copy1, *copy2, *tempCopy
18:             repeat
19:                 copy1 ← binArray[allotedBin]
20:                 if copy1 = NULL then
21:                     (*tempCopy).insert(i)
22:                     copy2 ← tempCopy
23:                 else
24:                     if i ∈ *copy1 then
25:                         break
26:                     end if
27:                     for a ∈ *copy1 do
28:                         (*copy2).insert(a)
29:                     end for
30:                     (*copy2).insert(i)
31:                 end if
32:             until binArray[allotedBin].CAS(copy1, copy2)
33:             temp1 ← −1
34:             if initialBin[i].CAS(temp1, localVal) then
35:                 atomicFetchAdd(processedTxns, 1)
36:             end if
37:         else
38:             localCount ← localCount + 1
39:             if localCount = |Txns| and flag = 0 then
40:                 flag ← 1
41:                 atomicFetchAdd(threadCounter2, 1)
42:             end if
43:         end if
44:         if (threadCounter2 = numThreads) or (localCount = |Txns|) then
45:             atomicStore(processedTxns, |Txns|)
46:         end if
47:     end while
48: end function
```

4   Conclusion and Future Work

This paper introduces the MBPS framework for parallelizing blockchain smart contract transactions on multicore systems, featuring three variants: Standard, Assisted, and Lockfree MBPS. Each variant optimizes transaction execution while ensuring deterministic ordering. Experimental results on Hyperledger Sawtooth show notable improvements in throughput and execution time. Lockfree MBPS proved resilient to thread crashes, while Assisted MBPS effectively reduced latency via helper threads. Our future objective is to extend MBPS to distributed environments, addressing challenges like network latency, communication overhead, and synchronization. We also aim to optimize conflict detection and bin assignment to enhance efficiency.

References

1. Hyperledger Sawtooth Whitepaper. https://8112310.fs1.hubspotusercontent-na1. net/hubfs/8112310/Hyperledger/Offers/Hyperledger_Sawtooth_WhitePaper.pdf
2. Anjana, P.S., Attiya, H., Kumari, S., Peri, S., Somani, A.: Efficient concurrent execution of smart contracts in blockchains using object-based transactional memory. In: Networked Systems, pp. 77–93. Springer International Publishing, Cham (2021)
3. Anjana, P.S., Kumari, S., Peri, S., Rathor, S., Somani, A.: Optsmart: A space efficient optimistic concurrent execution of smart contracts. Distrib Parallel Databases (2022). https://doi.org/10.1007/s10619-022-07412-y
4. Baheti, S., Anjana, P.S., Peri, S., Simmhan, Y.: DiPETrans: a framework for distributed parallel execution of transactions of blocks in blockchain. Concurrency Comput. Pract. Experience n/a, e6804 (2022). https://doi.org/10.1002/cpe.6804, https://onlinelibrary.wiley.com/doi/abs/10.1002/cpe.6804
5. Dickerson, T., Gazzillo, P., Herlihy, M., Koskinen, E.: Adding Concurrency to Smart Contracts, pp. 303–312. PODC '17, ACM, New York, NY, USA (2017)
6. Liu, J., Li, P., Cheng, R., Asokan, N., Song, D.: Parallel and asynchronous smart contract execution. IEEE Trans. Parallel Distrib. Syst. 33(5), 1097–1108 (2022). https://doi.org/10.1109/TPDS.2021.3095234
7. Nakamoto, S.: Bitcoin: A peer-to-peer electronic cash system. Cryptography Mailing list at https://metzdowd.com (2009)
8. Piduguralla, M., Chakraborty, S., Anjana, P.S., Peri, S.: Dag-based efficient parallel scheduler for blockchains: Hyperledger sawtooth as a case study. In: Cano, J., Dikaiakos, M.D., Papadopoulos, G.A., Pericàs, M., Sakellariou, R. (eds.) Euro-Par 2023: Parallel Processing, pp. 184–198. Springer Nature Switzerland, Cham (2023)
9. Ravish, A., Tejwani, A., Manaswini, P., Peri, S.: Unleashing multicore strength for efficient execution of transactions (2024). https://arxiv.org/abs/2410.22460
10. Saraph, V., Herlihy, M.: An Empirical Study of Speculative Concurrency in Ethereum Smart Contracts. Tokenomics '19 (2019)
11. Yan, W., Li, J., Liu, W., Tan, A.: Efficient concurrent execution of smart contracts in blockchain sharding. Secur. Commun. Netw. 2021, 1–15 (2021). https://doi.org/ 10.1155/2021/6688168

Enhancing QR Decomposition: A GPU-Based Approach to Parallelizing the Householder Algorithm with CUDA Streams

Uppu Eshwar, Soumyajit Chatterjee$^{(\boxtimes)}$, and Sathya Peri

Indian Institute of Technology Hyderabad, Hyderabad 502285, Telangana, India
{ch21btech11034,ai22mtech02005}@iith.ac.in, sathya_p@cse.iith.ac.in

Abstract. Linear algebra algorithms, such as the Householder QR decomposition, are pivotal in various applications including signal processing, optimization, and numerical solutions to systems of linear equations. Traditional sequential implementations of the Householder algorithm face significant limitations in terms of performance and scalability when applied to large matrices. To overcome these constraints, this paper explores the parallelization of the Householder QR algorithm on Graphics Processing Units (GPUs) using CUDA, a parallel computing platform and programming model developed by NVIDIA. Our method ensures the availability of critical intermediate data, distinguishing it from standard libraries like cuSOLVER, which modify the processing order and often discard important intermediate computations. By leveraging CUDA streams, we achieve enhanced parallelism without compromising the integrity of the algorithm's sequence or the accessibility of intermediate data. Our performance analysis reveals that our implementation achieves efficiency comparable to cuSOLVER, making it a viable option. This study not only presents a novel implementation but also extends the potential for GPU-accelerated linear algebra procedures to benefit a wider range of scientific and engineering applications.

Keywords: QR Decomposition · Parallel Computing · General Purpose GPU programming · CUDA streams

1 Introduction

The goal of any constrained optimization method is to find the values of the decision variables that optimize the objective function while adhering to the given constraints [16,24]. The solution obtained must satisfy both the optimization objective and the constraints simultaneously.

Techniques to solve constrained optimization problems include mathematical programming, linear programming [17], quadratic programming [13], nonlinear programming [22], and more specialized methods such as interior point methods [21] and evolutionary algorithms [23]. Numerical methods like Sequential

---

This work is supported in part by the MeitY-sponsored research project: No. 4(4)/2021-ITEA.

Q. Bramas et al. (Eds.): ICDCIT 2025, LNCS 15507, pp. 146–161, 2025.
https://doi.org/10.1007/978-3-031-81404-4_12

Quadratic Programming (SQP) [2] solve non-linear programming problems with both equality and inequality constraints and has been widely applied in various fields, including engineering design, optimal control, and operations research. It is effective for solving non-linear programming problems with moderate-sized dimensions and smooth objective functions and constraints.

However when solving optimization problems using Sequential Quadratic Programming (SQP) involving high dimensional data, the computational complexities can become significant. Some challenges and associated complexities include:

- High-dimensional decision variables: As the number of decision variables increases, the size of the quadratic programming sub-problem grows quadratic-ally. The computational complexity of solving a quadratic programming problem is generally $O(n^3)$ where n represents the number of decision variables.
- Storage requirements: Large-scale optimization problems may require substantial memory for storing matrices and vectors used in the quadratic programming sub-problem. As the dimensionality increases, the memory requirements can become a limiting factor, especially if the problem involves dense matrices.
- Evaluation of gradients and Hessians: Computing gradients and Hessians of the objective function and constraint functions is essential for solving the quadratic programming subproblem. In large-scale problems, evaluating these derivatives can be time-consuming, particularly if the derivatives need to be computed numerically or if the functions are complex and computationally expensive.
- Numerical stability: The numerical stability of SQP can become an issue in large-scale problems due to the accumulation of rounding errors and ill-conditioning of the matrices involved. This can lead to numerical instabilities, convergence issues, and inaccurate results.
- Scalability: The scalability of SQP in terms of both computation time and memory usage can become problematic with large-scale dimensions. The time required for each iteration may be quite large, and memory limitations can prevent the use of direct methods for solving the quadratic programming sub-problem.

Prior works like [11] suggests mathematical variations on the standard SQP iteration with [15] proposing a further improvement to it which leads to a faster rate of convergence. While works like [19] suggest alternative methods for the approximation of Quasi-Newton matrices, works like [5] and [8] tackle the storage requirements for computing the Hessian in large scale problems. Also methods like [1] try to effectively utilize the sparsity of high dimensional matrices involved in the problem.

In our work we tackle the problem of scalability by optimizing the QR factorization subroutine which is used in iterations of the SQP algorithm where QR decomposition is utilized to transform the equality constraints into an orthogonal form, which simplifies the formulation and solution of the Karush-Kuhn-Tucker

(KKT) [4] system of equations. QR decomposition is also used to determine the active set of constraints at each iteration of SQP. By decomposing the constraint Jacobian matrix using QR factorization, the linear independence of the constraints can be assessed. The active set, which includes the constraints that are most likely to be active at the solution, can be identified based on the QR factorization. This information helps in constructing the working set of constraints and updating the constraint active set efficiently. QR decomposition can also be used in Hessian approximation and its inverse or in reduced Hessian approximation methods [3] to approximate only the portion of the Hessian matrix relevant to the current iteration of SQP.

Our contribution proposes improvements to the QR factorization kernel used in the Sequential Least Squares Quadratic Programming (SLSQP) [14] algorithm implemented in NLopt [12], a widely used open source software package, using parallel GPU programming methods.

2 Background

QR factorisation is an essential algorithm in linear algebra that decomposes a matrix of any size into the product of two matrices, Q and R, where Q is unitary [9], and R is upper triangular [9]. This technique is widely used in solving several problems such as systems of linear equations, least squares approximations, eigenvalue computation, matrix rank determination, orthogonalisation etc. Hence, developing an efficient solution for QR factorisation can benefit these applications.

The algorithm used in the NLopt [12] library to perform QR factorization is Householder Transformation as given in the Algorithm 1 below.

Algorithm 1. HouseHolder Transform

```
 1: for pivot = 0 to m do
 2:    (x, y, z) = update_pivot(pivot row in mat)
 3:    mat[pivot][pivot] = x
 4:    for j = 1 to pivot-1 do
 5:       sm = dot_product(jth row, pivot row)
 6:       if sm ≠ 0 then
 7:          for k = pivot+1 to n do
 8:             mat[j][k] += sm * mat[pivot][k]
 9:          end for
10:       end if
11:    end for
12: end for
```

The implementation of the Householder transformation within the library accepts a matrix of arbitrary size as input and transforms it into an upper triangular matrix in-place. The computational process within the for loop can be divided into two primary subroutines: the update_pivot kernel and the dot_product kernel. The update_pivot kernel is responsible for processing the pivot row and updating the pivot element. The pivot row is the row utilized to update all other rows, excluding itself, during a single iteration of the for loop in Line 1 of Algorithm 1. The pivot element corresponds to the first element of the pivot row in the initial iteration, the second element in the subsequent iteration, and so forth. This is because, in each iteration of the for loop, not only is each row sequentially selected as the pivot in the matrix, beginning with the first row, but one column is also skipped after each iteration. The remaining submatrix is then used for further computations in the subsequent iterations.

After processing the pivot row and updating its pivot element, the algorithm proceeds to compute the dot product between the pivot row and each of the remaining rows in the matrix. The scalar value obtained from the dot product between the pivot row and any other row is then utilized to update the corresponding row in the matrix, as illustrated in Line 8 of Algorithm 1. The algorithm concludes once the last row of the matrix has been processed as the pivot row and its corresponding pivot element has been updated. Since no rows remain after the final row, no further computations occur following the processing of the last pivot row.

The algorithm exhibits a sequential nature due to the presence of two critical dependencies. The first dependency occurs within the same iteration: the algorithm cannot proceed to update the other rows until the pivot row has been fully processed. The second dependency spans across iterations: a row cannot be updated in the current iteration until its update from the previous iteration is complete, as each iteration's matrix update relies on the matrix produced in the prior iteration. These inter-dependencies present a significant challenge when attempting to parallelize the Householder Algorithm, as described in Algorithm 1.

3   Methodology

3.1   Introduction to Parallel GPU Programming and CUDA

The advent of Graphics Processing Units (GPUs) has revolutionized computational methods in fields such as scientific computing and optimization. Unlike Central Processing Units (CPUs), which excel at sequential processing, GPUs are designed with numerous smaller cores capable of parallel thread execution. This architecture is ideal for data-parallel tasks, where the same operation is performed across multiple data elements simultaneously [18]. CUDA (Compute Unified Device Architecture) by NVIDIA extends C/C++ to harness GPU power, offering fine-grained control over thread hierarchy, memory access, and synchronization. In CUDA's model, threads are organized into blocks (up to 1024 threads each) and further into grids, enabling scalable parallel computations [25].

Linear algebra is fundamental to many optimization techniques, including Sequential Least Squares Quadratic Programming (SLSQP), which requires efficient matrix operations like QR decomposition and matrix multiplications.

GPUs, with their parallel architecture, are well-suited for these tasks [10]. Libraries like cuBLAS and cuSOLVER optimize these computations for GPUs, with cuBLAS providing accelerated BLAS routines [6] and cuSOLVER offering solvers for linear systems, eigenvalue problems, and matrix factorizations. As a GPU extension of LAPACK, cuSOLVER simplifies the integration of GPU-optimized solvers into existing codebases [7].

3.2   Limitations of Traditional QR Factorization in CuSOLVER

cuSOLVER's QR factorization algorithm is highly optimized for parallel execution on GPUs, using batched operations to maximize memory efficiency and computational throughput. It designed as an extension of the LAPACK library for GPUs and typically employs a "left-looking" approach for general-purpose QR decomposition [20], which updates the matrix in-place, focusing on the leftmost columns first. This method is efficient for batch processing but may not align well with algorithms requiring iterative updates with preserved intermediate states. This inherent limitation is why direct application of cuSOLVER's QR routines might not be suitable for the optimization context discussed in this research, where maintaining and utilizing intermediate values is critical.

To account for the limitations of cuSOLVER's QR decomposition routines, particularly its inability to preserve the iteration order and intermediate values required for iterative algorithms, we propose a novel approach that leverages the parallel processing capabilities of GPUs while maintaining intermediate states essential for iterative computations.

3.3   Parallelization Strategy for QR Factorization

The sequential QR factorization algorithm, as previously described, involves two primary computations: (1) updating the pivot element of the pivot row and (2) computing the dot product of each row below the pivot row with the pivot row, followed by updating each row using the scalar value obtained from the dot product. Our approach to QR factorization centres on exploiting potential parallelism within the existing sequential code. Since each scalar product calculation of each row is independent of the others, these operations can be executed concurrently across multiple GPU processing elements. This parallel execution significantly reduces the overall computational time. Furthermore, the update for a next iteration's pivot element does not depend on the completion of all row updates in the current iteration. Instead, the update for the next pivot element can commence as soon as the scalar product involving the immediate next row is completed. This overlapping of computations enables a seamless transition between iterations, minimizing idle time on GPU processing units. To implement this, we utilized CUDA streams, which allow for asynchronous execution of these operations.

To efficiently parallelize these computations on a GPU, we divided the algorithm into two distinct CUDA kernels.

3.4   Kernel Design for Pivot Element Update

Algorithm 2. UpdatePivotElement Kernel

1: **Kernel** UpdatePivotElement(Matrix, PivotRow, NumCols)
2: Shared TempArray[512], SumOfSquares
3: Initialize TempArray[ThreadIndex] $\leftarrow$ 0
4: Initialize SumOfSquares $\leftarrow$ 0
5: **Synchronize** Threads
6: Compute Iterations $\leftarrow$ (NumCols + BlockDim - 1) / BlockDim
7: **for** each iteration it from 0 to Iterations-1 **do**
8:    Calculate ColumnIndex $\leftarrow$ it * BlockDim + ThreadIndex + PivotRow

9:    **if** ColumnIndex < NumCols **then**
10:      Load Matrix[PivotRow * NumCols + ColumnIndex] into TempValue
11:      TempArray[ThreadIndex] $\leftarrow$ TempValue^2
12:    **end if**
13:    **Synchronize** Threads
       /*Before performing the reduction, ensure that the shared memory is fully loaded */
14:    Perform Reduction of TempArray to SumOfSquares
15: **end for**
16: **Synchronize** Threads
    //Only a single thread writes into the shared variable to avoid race conditions

17: **if** ThreadIndex == 0 **then**
18:    PivotValue $\leftarrow$ sqrt(SumOfSquares)
19:    **if** Matrix[PivotRow * NumCols + PivotRow] > 0 **then**
20:      PivotValue $\leftarrow$ -1 * PivotValue
21:    **end if**
22:    Update Matrix[PivotRow * NumCols + PivotRow] $\leftarrow$ PivotValue
23:    Store Matrix[PivotRow * NumCols + PivotRow] - PivotValue in UpdatedPivot
24: **end if**

The first kernel is designed to update the pivot element by calculating the sum of squares of the matrix row elements. This computation is executed using a single block of threads, with the number of threads dynamically determined based on the matrix row size. The kernel loads the elements from the global memory and stores the squared values in shared memory, which is a faster on-chip memory space accessible by all threads within a block. Given that the block size may be smaller than the row size of the matrix, the kernel processes the row in chunks, iterating through each chunk, since a single block of threads is used to avoid atomics. After loading and squaring the elements, the kernel performs a reduction sum on the shared memory array to compute the total sum of squares for the row. This value is then used to update the pivot element by taking its square root. The design of this kernel allows for efficient memory access and minimizes the number of global memory transactions, thereby enhancing performance.

3.5   Kernel Design for Row Update via Dot Product Computation

The second kernel focuses on the computation of the dot product between the pivot row and the remaining rows, followed by updating the rows using the dot product. This kernel is designed, keeping in mind the two-dimensional structure of thread blocks. Each block processes a fixed number of rows and columns, where the y-dimension handles rows and the x-dimension handles columns as shown in Fig. 1. By allocating multiple blocks along the y-dimension in the grid, the kernel exploits the independence of row updates among the rows which allows rows to be processed in chunks avoiding the need for explicit synchronization or atomic operations.

Algorithm 3. UpdateMatrix Kernel

 1: **Kernel** UpdateMatrix(Matrix, PivotRow, NumRows, NumCols)
 2: /* ThreadX - runs from 0 to ColsPerBlock
 3: ThreadY - runs from 0 to RowsPerBlock*/
 4:
 5: Shared PivotValues[ColsPerBlock]
 6: Shared TempResults[RowsPerBlock][ColsPerBlock]
 7: Shared RowSums[RowsPerBlock]
 8: Initialize TempResults[ThreadY][ThreadX] ← 0
 9: Initialize RowSums[ThreadY] ← 0
10: **Synchronize** Threads
11:
12: RowIndex ← PivotRow + BlockIdxY * BlockDimY + ThreadY + 1
13: **if** RowIndex ≥ NumRows **then**
14:     **Exit** Kernel
15: **end if**

The algorithm begins by storing pivot row elements in shared memory for rapid access by all threads within a block. The kernel then calculates the dot product between the pivot row and each remaining row below the pivot row, by iterating column-wise with each thread computing the product of corresponding elements. These results are stored in shared memory, followed by a reduction sum to obtain the final dot product for each row, which is then used to update the rows. This efficient use of shared memory and thread/block organization minimizes latency and maximizes GPU throughput.

Algorithm 3. UpdateMatrix Kernel CONTD.

1: Iterations ← (NumCols - PivotRow + ColsPerBlock - 1) / ColsPerBlock
2: **for** it = 0 to Iterations - 1 **do**
3:    Compute ColStart ← PivotRow + it * BlockDimX
4:    **if** ThreadY == 0 **and** ColStart + ThreadX < NumCols **then**
5:       PivotValues[ThreadX] ← Matrix[(PivotRow) * NumCols + ColStart + ThreadX]
6:    **end if**
7:    **Synchronize** Threads
8:    **if** ColStart + ThreadX < NumCols **then**
9:       TempResults[ThreadY][ThreadX] ← Matrix[RowIndex * NumCols + ColStart + ThreadX] * PivotValues[ThreadX]
10:   **else**
11:      TempResults[ThreadY][ThreadX] ← 0
12:   **end if**
13:   **Synchronize** Threads
14:   Reduce TempResults[ThreadY] to RowSums[ThreadY]
15:   **Synchronize** Threads
16: **end for**
17:
18: **if** ThreadX == 0 **then**
19:    RowSums[ThreadY] ← RowSums[ThreadY] + Matrix[RowIndex * NumCols + PivotRow] * UpdatedPivot[PivotRow]
20:    **if** RowSums[ThreadY] ≠ 0 **then**
21:       ScalingFactor ← 1 / RowSums[ThreadY]
22:       Matrix[RowIndex * NumCols + PivotRow - 1] ← Matrix[RowIndex * NumCols + PivotRow] + ScalingFactor * UpdatedPivot[PivotRow]
23:    **end if**
24: **end if**
25: **Synchronize** Threads
26:
27: **for** it = 0 to Iterations - 1 **do**
28:    Compute ColIndex ← it * BlockDimX + ThreadX + PivotRow
29:    **if** ColIndex < NumCols **then**
30:       Matrix[RowIndex * NumCols + ColIndex] ← Matrix[RowIndex * NumCols + ColIndex] + RowSums[ThreadY] * Matrix[(PivotRow) * NumCols + ColIndex]
31:    **end if**
32: **end for**

3.6 Host Function and Streams-Based Execution

In our parallelized QR factorization implementation, the host function is integral in managing the execution flow across multiple CUDA streams, ensuring

Columns processed in chunks

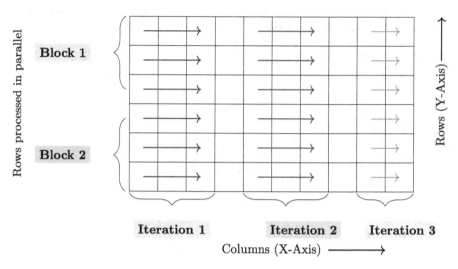

Fig. 1. Illustration of Algorithm 3: Parallel row processing with iterative column processing in chunks. Blocks process rows in parallel, with columns processed in chunks over multiple iterations.

efficient parallel processing. This function is responsible for memory allocation, data transfer between host and device, and synchronization of the various computational tasks executed by the GPU. By leveraging CUDA streams, we achieve concurrent kernel execution, significantly reducing idle time and enhancing overall computational efficiency.

Algorithm 4. Stream-based Execution of Kernels for Matrix Update

---

1: **Input:** Matrix A, Number of rows m, Number of columns n
2: **Initialize:** CUDA streams: `Stream 1`, `Stream 2`
3: **Initialize:** CUDA events: `Event 1`, `Event 2`
4: // Kernel 1 stands for update pivot element kernel and kernel 2 stands for update matrix kernel
5: // parameters for kernel 1 are Matrix, PivotRow, NumCols
6: // parameters for kernel 2 are Matrix, PivotRow, NumRows, NumCols
7: // Initial kernel launch to update the first pivot element
8: `kernel1`$<<<gridDim,BlockDim,stream>>>$$(A,\ \ 0,\ \ n)$ `on default stream`
9: `cudaDeviceSynchronize()`

The implementation strategically utilizes two CUDA streams-designated as Stream 1 and Stream 2-to orchestrate the execution of the two kernels. Stream

1 is tasked with executing the kernel that updates the pivot element, along with executing the kernel responsible for processing the row immediately following the pivot row. Concurrently, Stream 2 handles the updates for the remaining rows, specifically excluding the row next to pivot row which is getting updated concurrently in the Stream 1.

Algorithm 4. Stream-based Execution of Kernels for Matrix Update CONTD.

1: **for** $lpivot = 1$ to m **do**
2:    **if** $lpivot == 1$ **then**
3:       // Stream 1 processes the next row after the pivot row
4:       kernel2<<<$gridDim,BlockDim,stream$>>>($A,lpivot,m,n$)   **on**
         Stream 1
5:       // Stream 2 processes the remaining rows
6:       /* compute grid computes the number of blocks required to process
         (m - lpivot - 1) rows in y-direction and n-lpivot coloumns in x-direction
         for a fixed number of threads per block in x and y directions*/
7:       gridDim = computeGrid($m - lpivot - 1$)
8:       kernel2<<<$gridDim,BlockDim,stream$>>>($A,\ lpivot,\ m,\ n$) **on**
         Stream 2
9:       cudaEventRecord(Event 2, Stream 2)
10:      kernel1<<<$gridDim,BlockDim,stream$>>>($A,\ lpivot + 1,\ m,\ n$) **on**
         Stream 1
11:      cudaEventRecord(Event 1, Stream 1)
12:   **else**
13:      // wait for events to complete to ensure correct execution order
14:      cudaStreamWaitEvent(Stream 1, Event 2, 0)
15:      kernel2<<<$gridDim,BlockDim,stream$>>>($A,\ lpivot,\ m,\ n$) **on**
         Stream 1
16:      cudaStreamWaitEvent(Stream 2, Event 1, 0)
17:      kernel2<<<$gridDim,BlockDim,stream$>>>($A,\ lpivot,\ m,\ n$) **on**
         Stream 2
18:      cudaEventRecord(Event 2, Stream 2)
19:      kernel1<<<$gridDim,BlockDim,stream$>>>($A,\ lpivot + 1,\ m,\ n$) **on**
         Stream 1
20:      cudaEventRecord(Event 1, Stream 1)
21:   **end if**
22: **end for**

During the initial iteration, Streams 1 and 2 function independently. However, as factorization advances, inter-stream dependencies are established to ensure data consistency through CUDA event synchronization mechanisms, such as cudaEventRecord and cudaStreamWaitEvent. This synchronization prevents Stream 2 from initiating operations until the required computation in Stream 1 is complete, and vice versa as shown in Fig. 2. Given that the kernel in Algorithm 3 is sufficiently large to achieve 100% GPU occupancy, the decision to limit the implementation to two streams optimizes GPU utilization while mitigating resource contention and operational complexity. Although incorporating additional streams could theoretically enhance parallelism, it would also introduce greater complexity and diminish cache efficiency. Therefore, the use of two streams represents an optimal balance between performance and complexity.

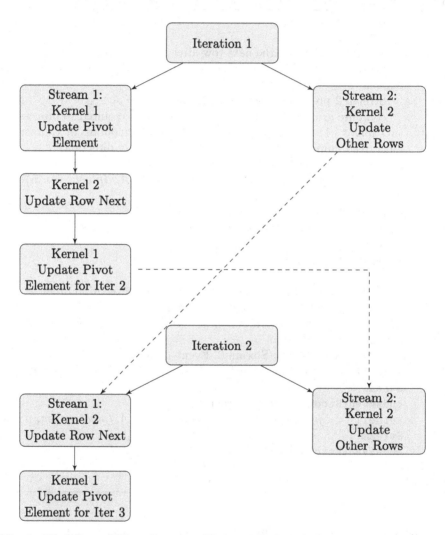

Fig. 2. Workflow of Host Function Using Two CUDA Streams: Dependencies Across Iterations. Stream 1 handles the pivot element and updating the next row, while Stream 2 concurrently processes the remaining rows. The streams synchronize using events recorded at the end of their execution.

4   Results

In this section, we present the results of our experiments, which were designed to optimize the kernel in Algorithm 3. We conducted four key experiments: first, we explored the optimal configuration of threads per block for Algorithm 3; second, we investigated the trade-offs between block dimensions in a 2D thread structure; third, we compared the performance of our approach with optimised configuration against the cuSOLVER library across varying matrix sizes; and finally we demonstrate the improvements in the original SLSQP algorithm [14] of the NLopt Library [12], using our proposed method.

4.1   Experimental Setup

The experiments were conducted on an Nvidia Quadro RTX 5000 GPU server, equipped with 48 Streaming Multiprocessors (SMs) supporting CUDA Compute Capability 7.5. Each multiprocessor can handle up to 1024 threads, distributed across multiple blocks, with a maximum of 64 active warps per SM. The server also includes 16 GB of GDDR6 memory, providing substantial bandwidth to support high-performance computation.

4.2   Experiment 1

In the first experiment, we aimed to identify the optimal number of threads per block for Algorithm 3 by varying the thread count and observing its effect on GPU performance. For the experiment, we perform QR decomposition on a matrix of size 1024×1024 using our proposed approach. Figure 3 presents the performance metrics for different thread configurations.

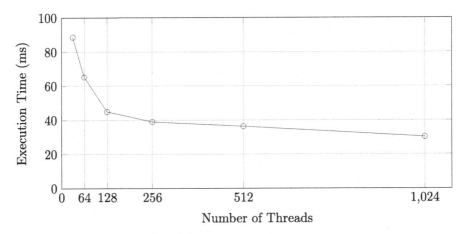

Fig. 3. Execution Time vs. Number of Threads

Our experiment demonstrated that utilizing the maximum number of threads per block i.e. 1024 was optimal, achieving 100% utilization of the GPU. It is important to note that while a block size of 512 threads allowed two active blocks per multiprocessor, the 1024-thread configuration resulted in only one active block per multiprocessor. However, the performance was not solely dictated by the number of active blocks. Despite the reduction in active blocks, the configuration with 1024 threads per block yielded better performance. This suggests that other factors, such as reduced scheduling overhead and improved memory bandwidth utilization, played a significant role in optimizing Algorithm 3's execution. Therefore, we concluded that 1024 threads per block is the optimal configuration for Algorithm 3 in our setup.

4.3   Experiment 2

In this experiment, we focused on further optimizing the kernel in Algorithm 3. Building on the results from the previous experiment, we kept the number of threads per block as 1024 and explored variations in the distribution of threads across the X and Y directions while performing the QR decomposition. Figure 4 presents the performance metrics for different configurations.

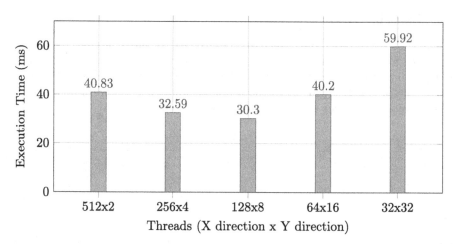

Fig. 4. Scaling with Threads in X and Y Direction for UpdateMatrix Kernel (1024 × 1024 Dataset)

Our primary objective was to identify an optimal balance between the number of blocks, influenced by the thread count in the Y direction, and the number of iterations each block needs to perform in the X direction to process all columns. The experimental findings suggest that the optimal thread configuration for the X and Y directions is (128 × 8).

4.4   Experiment 3

Based on the results obtained from the previous experiments, we conducted a comparative analysis of the QR decomposition algorithm from libraries like cuSolver(GPU), LAPACK(CPU) and PLASMA(CPU) against our proposed approach, across various square matrices of different sizes. The results are illustrated in Fig. 5.

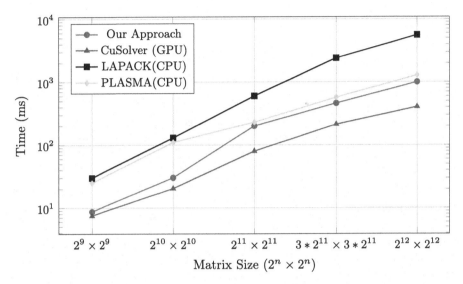

Fig. 5. Performance comparison for different matrix sizes

The graphical analysis of the results clearly demonstrates that our approach outperforms LAPACK (CPU) and PLASMA (CPU), while achieving performance comparable to cuSolver within a close margin. Additionally, as the matrix size increases, our method continues to maintain its efficiency, indicating that it scales effectively with larger datasets.

4.5   Experiment 4

In this study, we evaluated the performance of our optimized GPU-based method by integrating it into the SLSQP algorithm in the NLOPT library and comparing it with the original SLSQP algorithm. The goal was to assess the scalability and efficiency of our approach in managing large-scale matrices compared to the original sequential implementation. The experiment consists of measuring the execution time to complete the entire optimization process for a constrained non-linear problem. The dimensions of problem involves matrices with sizes: 640, 1250, 1728, and 2240. The results are illustrated in Fig. 6.

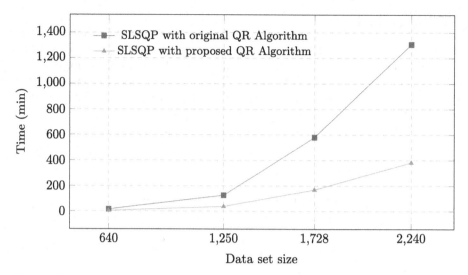

Fig. 6. Performance comparison Between the original SLSQP algorithm and Proposed QR decomposition algorithm on GPU for varying data set sizes

5   Conclusion

Our experimental results show that our approach outperforms LAPACK and PLASMA, and achieves performance comparable to cuSOLVER. Additionally, we demonstrate the effectiveness of our algorithm by integrating it into the SLSQP method in the NLOPT library, where QR factorization is frequently invoked. Replacing the existing QR factorization kernel with our proposed kernel results in significant performance improvements over the original algorithm.

References

1. Betts, J.T., Frank, P.D.: A sparse nonlinear optimization algorithm. J. Optim. Theory Appl. **82**, 519–541 (1994)
2. Boggs, P.T., Tolle, J.W.: Sequential quadratic programming. Acta Numerica **4**, 1–51 (1995)
3. Boggs, P.T., Tolle, J.W.: Sequential quadratic programming. Acta Numerica **4**, 24–25 (1995)
4. Boyd, S., Vandenberghe, L.: Convex Optimization. Cambridge University Press, Cambridge (2004)
5. Byrd, R.H., Nocedal, J., Schnabel, R.B.: Representations of quasi-newton matrices and their use in limited memory methods. Math. Program. **63**(1–3), 129–156 (1994)
6. NVIDIA Corporation. The API reference guide for cublas, the cuda basic linear algebra subroutine library (2024). https://docs.nvidia.com/cuda/cublas/# introduction

7. NVIDIA Corporation. The API reference guide for cusolver, a GPU accelerated library for decompositions and linear system solutions for both dense and sparse matrices (2024). https://docs.nvidia.com/cuda/cusolver/index.html#:~:text=The%20intent%20of,shared%20sparsity%20pattern

8. Gill, P.E., Murray, W., Saunders, M.A.: SNOPT: an SQP algorithm for large-scale constrained optimization. SIAM Rev. **47**(1), 99–131 (2005)

9. Golub, G.H., Van Loan, C.F.: Matrix Computations. Johns Hopkins Studies in the Mathematical Sciences. Johns Hopkins University Press (2013)

10. Heidari, A.A., Mirjalili, S., Faris, H., Aljarah, I., Mafarja, M., Chen, H.: Harris hawks optimization: algorithm and applications. Futur. Gener. Comput. Syst. **97**, 849–872 (2019)

11. Herskovits, J.N., Carvalho, L.A.V.: A successive quadratic programming based feasible directions algorithm. In: Bensoussan, A., Lions, J.L. (eds.) Analysis and Optimization of Systems, pp. 93–101. Springer, Heidelberg (1986)

12. Johnson, S.G.: The NLopt nonlinear-optimization package (2007). https://github.com/stevengj/nlopt

13. Wright, S.J., Nocedal, J.: Numerical Optimization. Springer, New York (2006)

14. Kraft, D.: Algorithm 733: TOMP-fortran modules for optimal control calculations. ACM Trans. Math. Softw. **20**, 262–281 (1994)

15. Lawrence, C.T., Tits, A.L.: A computationally efficient feasible sequential quadratic programming algorithm. SIAM J. Optim. **11**(4), 1092–1118 (2001)

16. Joaquim, R.R.A.: Martins and Andrew Ning. Engineering Design Optimization. Cambridge University Press, Cambridge (2021)

17. Nemhauser, G., Wolsey, L.: Linear Programming, chap. I.2, pp. 27–49. Wiley (1988)

18. Nickolls, J., Buck, I., Garland, M., Skadron, K.: Scalable parallel programming with Cuda. In: ACM SIGGRAPH 2008 Classes, SIGGRAPH 2008. Association for Computing Machinery, New York (2008)

19. Nocedal, J.: Updating quasi-newton matrices with limited storage. Math. Comput. **35**(151), 773–782 (1980)

20. Joe Eaton NVIDIA Corporation. Parallel direct solvers with cusolver: Batched qr (2015). https://developer.nvidia.com/blog/parallel-direct-solvers-with-cusolver-batched-qr/#:~:text=cuSOLVER%20provides%20batch,deliver%20decent%20performance

21. Potra, F.A., Wright, S.J.: Interior-point methods. J. Comput. Appl. Mathe. **124**(1), 281–302 (2000). Numerical Analysis 2000. Vol. IV: Optimization and Nonlinear Equations

22. Ruszczyński, A.: Nonlinear Optimization. Princeton University Press, Princeton (2006)

23. Slowik, A., Kwasnicka, H.: Evolutionary algorithms and their applications to engineering problems. Neural Comput. Appl. **32**(16), 12363–12379 (2020)

24. Sun, W., Yuan, Y.-X.: Optimization Theory and Methods: Nonlinear Programming, vol. 1. Springer, Heidelberg (2006)

25. Wikipedia contributors. Thread block (Cuda programming) — Wikipedia, the free encyclopedia (2024). Accessed 24 Aug 2024

Source Sets in Temporal Graphs

Saksham Yadav[1]([✉]), Srinibas Swain[2]([✉])[iD], and Subhrangsu Mandal[3]([✉])[iD]

[1] Software Development Engineer, Delightful Gourmet Pvt. Ltd., Bengaluru, India
sakshamyadav751@gmail.com
[2] Department of Computer Science and Engineering, Indian Institute of Information
Technology, Guwahati, India
srinibas@iiitg.ac.in
[3] Department of Computer Science and Engineering, Indian Institute of Technology
(ISM), Dhanbad, India
santu.cst@gmail.com

Abstract. Temporal graphs are introduced to model different networks with time-dependent topologies where edge and/or vertex sets of the network change with time. Addressing different graph problems on these types of networks are important to provide efficient solutions to fundamental problems in distributed systems such as information spreading, routing, broadcasting, etc. In this paper, we address the problem of constructing minimum source sets for a given set of vertices in a temporal graph. In particular, for a given set of vertices, we construct a minimum cardinality subset of source vertices such that each vertex in the given set is reachable from at least one vertex in the source set. We have proved that this problem is NP-complete. We have developed a novel $O(n^2)$ time algorithm to address minimum source set problem for static directed bipartite graphs with n vertices and each vertex with fixed in-degree 2 and out-degree 2. Leveraging this solution, we extended our approach to develop a $O((mn(\log \mathcal{T} + \log n)) + n^2)$ time algorithm for the minimum source set problem in a restricted class of temporal graphs with n vertices, m edges, lifetime $\mathcal{T}$ such that each vertex can reach exactly 2 other vertices and can be reached from exactly 2 other vertices.

Keywords: minimum source set · source set · temporal source set · temporal graphs · dynamic graphs

1 Introduction

Temporal graphs extend traditional graphs by incorporating time as a key element, allowing them to model dynamic networks where connections between nodes change over time. In distributed systems, they are crucial for representing evolving network topologies, communication patterns, and resource management. Challenges include maintaining synchronization and consistency amidst these changes, as well as efficiently processing temporal data. Techniques such as temporal path-finding, reachability, and coverage are used to address these

Q. Bramas et al. (Eds.): ICDCIT 2025, LNCS 15507, pp. 162–178, 2025.
https://doi.org/10.1007/978-3-031-81404-4_13

challenges. Real-world networks like delay tolerant networks (DTN), vehicular ad-hoc networks (VANET), social networks, etc. are examples of networks with dynamic topologies. Due to the dynamic nature of the graph topology, traditional problem definitions and algorithms designed to address those problems on static graphs do not directly hold for temporal graphs. For example, in a communication network modeled using a connected static graph, any vertex can communicate with another vertex. But in a scenario when the communication channels between vertices are available only at certain timesteps, communication between those vertices is possible at those timesteps only. Thus, a source vertex in such a network can communicate with another destination vertices when there is a sequence of edges from the source to the destination and those edges exist in increasing order of timesteps. These types of paths in a temporal graph are referred to as journey [24]. Several works have been done to address traditional graph problems like computing shortest paths and trees [15,24], finding minimum dominating sets [14], answering reachability queries [2], finding maximum matching [16], etc. on temporal graphs.

In a temporal graph, a vertex v is reachable from another vertex u if there is a journey from u to v. Thus, any information available to vertex u can be sent to vertex v only when v is reachable from u. We call u as a source vertex of vertex v. In this paper, we explore the problem of finding the minimum cardinality source vertex set for a given set of vertices in a given temporal graph. This minimum set of vertices is referred to as the *minimum source set (MSS)* for the given set of vertices. As any information available to the vertices in an MSS of a particular target set of vertices can be propagated to that target set, finding MSS for a particular target set of vertices is important to address the problem of information spreading among those vertices in the target set. Similarly, if we want to add new vertices in the target set we need to add edges in such a way that these newly added vertices are reachable from the MSS. Thus an already computed MSS plays a significant role in reducing the number of required edge establishments with newly added vertices in the target set.

In this paper, we have addressed the problem of finding the minimum source set for a given set of target vertices in a temporal graph. We have also investigated the problem of determining the minimum source set in static directed bipartite graphs. Our research reveals some noteworthy connections between this problem and the problem of identifying minimum source set on temporal graphs. The particular contributions of this paper are as follows:

1. We prove that the problem of finding the minimum source set for a given set of target vertices in a temporal graph is NP-complete.
2. We prove that the problem of finding the minimum source set for static directed bipartite graphs is NP-complete. We also prove that this problem of finding the minimum source set remains NP-complete on static directed bipartite graphs even when edges of the bipartite graph are directed only from one set to another set and out-degree of any vertex is bounded by 3.
3. A polynomial time algorithm for finding minimum source set for static directed bipartite graphs with fixed in-degree and out-degree. We later used

this to develop a $O((mn(\log \mathcal{T} + \log n)) + n^2)$ time algorithm for finding the minimum source set for a given set of target vertices in temporal graphs where each vertex v can reach 2 other vertices and v can be reached from 2 other vertices. Here, m represents the number of edges, n denotes the number of vertices, and $\mathcal{T}$ refers to the lifetime of the temporal graph.

The rest of the paper is organised as follows. Section 2 discusses some relevant related literature on temporal graphs. After that, Sect. 3 clearly describes the system model used for this work. The formal problem definition and the definition of other relevant terminologies related to temporal graphs are described in Sect. 4. Section 5 presents the results related to finding the MSS problem. Finally Sect. 6 concludes the paper.

2   Related Work

In recent decades, the study of temporal graphs has garnered significant attention for its ability to model dynamic systems. Several models have been proposed to represent temporal graphs, with one of the early models being *evolving graphs* [10], where the temporal graph is depicted as a discrete sequence of static graphs. A more generalized approach is the *time-varying graphs* model, which can accommodate continuous time domains [4]. Other models include *time-dependent graphs* [20], *time-expanded networks* [9], and *time-aggregated graphs* [12].

Research into finding the minimum source set in temporal graphs is closely related to the problems involving journeys or time-dependent paths and reachability in these graphs. In temporal graphs, paths differ from static graphs as an edge can only be traversed if it is available at the time of traversal [16], leading to the concept of time-respecting paths [22] or journeys [24]. Introduced by the authors of [24], journeys are categorized into different types such as *foremost, fastest, and shortest,* with polynomial time algorithms available for computing these types in temporal graphs modeled by evolving graphs. Additionally, Wu et al. [22] expanded the journey types to include *latest departure journeys* and developed algorithms for all four types in directed temporal graphs. Kempe et al. [13] highlighted that classical Menger's theorem does not hold in temporal graphs, making the computation of vertex-disjoint source-to-destination journeys NP-complete. Although a recent reformulation of the theorem has been proposed [17] which holds for all temporal graphs. Further, Casteigts et al. [5] examined minimum cost journeys under waiting time constraints, while Danda et al. [6] developed a near-linear time algorithm for computing the shortest fastest journey.

Due to the dynamic nature of graph topology in temporal graphs, the definition of reachability changes significantly. For a source vertex to reach a destination vertex in a temporal graph, there must be a path between them with edges appearing in strictly increasing order of time. This temporal requirement introduces non-symmetry and non-transitivity in reachability, contrasting with static graph reachability [18]. Wu et al. [23] proposed an efficient indexing-based approach to address reachability and time-dependent path queries in temporal graphs. Whitbeck et al. [21] introduced temporal reachability graphs to represent communication opportunities within a temporal graph. A temporal reachability graph is a directed graph where an edge from a source to a destination is added at time t if there is a journey starting at t from the source to the destination in the original temporal graph. Enright et al. [8] explored the problem of computing the reachable set of vertices from a given vertex, aiming to minimize the set's cardinality by managing the temporal order of edge existence. Similarly, Deligkas et al. [7] focused on optimizing the reachable set by controlling edge occurrence times, which in turn affects delays at vertices. Other studies [1–3, 19] have examined reachability under various constraints in temporal graphs.

In this paper, we address the problem of finding the minimum source set for a given set of vertices in a temporal graph. To the best of our knowledge, there is no work in literature that addresses this problem.

3 System Model

We represent a temporal graph $\mathcal{G}$ using *Time-Varying Graphs (TVG)* [4] model. In this model, $\mathcal{G}$ is represented as a finite sequence of static graphs, where each static graph is an undirected graph representing the state of the temporal graph at a discrete timestep. The length of this discrete finite sequence is called *lifetime* of the temporal graph. Let $\mathcal{T}$ be the lifetime of the temporal graph, then $\mathcal{G}$ exists for the time interval $[0, \mathcal{T})$. Let $G_t = (V_t, E_t)$ be an undirected graph at timestep t. Therefore, $\mathcal{G}$ is a sequence of static (undirected) graphs $G_0, G_1, \cdots, G_{\mathcal{T}-1}$, where $G_{i < \mathcal{T}}$ represents the undirected graph G_i at timestep i. We assume that the vertex set which is denoted by $\mathcal{V}$ remains unchanged throughout the lifetime of the temporal graph. Only the edge set $\mathcal{E}$ of the temporal graph changes with time. These changes in $\mathcal{E}$ are known beforehand. Since the edge set changes with respect to time, we use an indicator function $\rho : \mathcal{E} \times \mathcal{T} \longrightarrow \{0, 1\}$ indicating the presence or absence of an edge at time $t \in \mathcal{T}$. To denote the presence of an edge, sometimes we associate non-overlapping intervals with edges. Thus, an edge $e \in \mathcal{E}$ can also be denoted as $e(u, v, (s_1, f_1), (s_2, f_2), \cdots, (s_k, f_k))$ where e is incident on $u, v \in \mathcal{V}$, and for any $t \in [s_1, f_1) \cup [s_2, f_2) \cup \cdots \cup [s_k, f_k)$, $\rho(e, t) = 1$. For simplicity, we assume the traversal time of an edge in $\mathcal{E}$ is one timestep. Thus, we represent a temporal graph $\mathcal{G}$ using TVG as $\mathcal{G} = (\mathcal{V}, \mathcal{E}, \mathcal{T}, \rho, \zeta)$, where $\mathcal{V}$ is the vertex set, $\mathcal{E}$ is the edge set and $\mathcal{T}$ is the lifetime of $\mathcal{G}$, ρ is the indicator function defined earlier, and $\zeta : \mathcal{E} \times \mathcal{T} \longrightarrow \mathbb{Z}^+$ is the function which returns the edge traversal time/latency time. In our case, we assume $\zeta(e, t) = 1$ if $e \in \mathcal{E}$ and $\rho(e, t) = 1$, $\zeta(e, t) = \infty$ otherwise.

Other than the assumptions stated in the previous paragraph, we assume that during any traversal waiting at a vertex is allowed. This means that, while traversing a series of vertices following a journey, after reaching any vertex v, it can wait at v for any amount of time before moving to the next vertex in the journey.

4   Problem Definition

In this section, we formally define the problem of finding the minimum source set (MSS) on a given temporal graph, $\mathcal{G} = (\mathcal{V}, \mathcal{E}, \mathcal{T}, \rho, \varsigma)$. Before defining the problem of finding MSS, we define a few terminologies related to temporal graphs that are required to define the finding MSS problem.

Definition 1. *Journey* [4]: *A journey (or time-respecting path) on a temporal graph $\mathcal{G} = (\mathcal{V}, \mathcal{E}, \mathcal{T}, \rho, \varsigma)$ is an alternating sequence of vertices and times $(u_1, t_1, u_2, t_2, u_3, t_3, \cdots, t_{n-1}, u_n)$ such that $(u_i, u_{i+1}) \in \mathcal{E}$, $\rho((u_i, u_{i+1}), t_i) = 1$, for all $1 \leq i \leq n - 1$ and $t_i \leq t_{i+1}$, for all $1 \leq i \leq n - 2$ and no vertices are repeated in the sequence. In this sequence, u_1 is the source vertex and u_n is the destination vertex of the journey. Timestep t_1 is the departure time and $t_{n-1} + 1$ is the arrival time of the journey.*

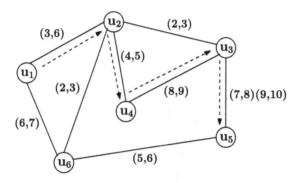

Fig. 1. A temporal graph where dashed arrows indicate a journey.

Definition 2. *Temporal Reachability* [23]: *A vertex $v \in \mathcal{V}$ in a temporal graph $\mathcal{G} = (\mathcal{V}, \mathcal{E}, \mathcal{T}, \rho, \varsigma)$, is said to be able to reach another vertex $u \in \mathcal{V}$ within a time interval $[t_i, t_k]$ such that $t_i < t_k$ and $t_k \leq \mathcal{T}$, if their exists a journey in $\mathcal{G}$ from v to u with departure time $t_1 \geq t_i$ and arrival time $t_2 \leq t_k$. We call that u is reachable from v in $\mathcal{G}$ within the time interval $[t_i, t_k]$.*

In the temporal graph shown in Fig. 1 $(u_1, 3, u_2, 4, u_4, 8, u_3, 9, u_5)$ is a journey from source vertex u_1 to destination vertex u_5 (shown with dashed arrows). The departure time of this journey is 3 and the arrival time is 10. Due to this journey, u_5 is reachable from u_1 within time interval $[3, 10]$. Similarly u_2, u_3, u_4 are reachable from u_1 within time interval $[3, 10]$. But when time interval is $[1, 9]$, u_5 is not reachable from u_1 but u_2, u_3, u_4 are reachable.

Definition 3. *Set of Influence* [4]: *The set of influence of a vertex $v \in \mathcal{V}$ in a temporal graph $\mathcal{G} = (\mathcal{V}, \mathcal{E}, \mathcal{T}, \rho, \varsigma)$, is the set of all vertices that can be reached from v through a journey in $\mathcal{G}$.*

Figure 2a shows the set of influence of vertex u_4 in a temporal graph. Vertices in the set of influence of vertex u_4 are coloured with gray.

Definition 4. Source Set of a vertex [4]: *The source set S_v of a vertex $v \in \mathcal{V}$ in a temporal graph $\mathcal{G} = (\mathcal{V}, \mathcal{E}, \mathcal{T}, \rho, \varsigma)$, is defined as $S_v \subseteq (\mathcal{V} \setminus \{v\})$ such that v is reachable from any $u \in S_v$ within a given time interval $[t_i, t_k]$ such that $t_i < t_k$ and $t_k \leq \mathcal{T}$.*

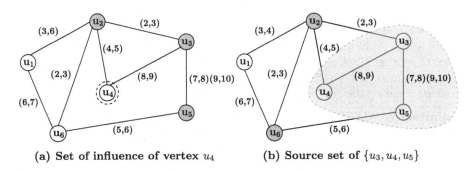

(a) **Set of influence of vertex u_4**   (b) **Source set of $\{u_3, u_4, u_5\}$**

Fig. 2. Set of influence and source set in a temporal graph

Definition 5. Source Set of a Set of Vertices: *Source set of a set of vertices $K \subseteq \mathcal{V}$ denoted by S_K is defined as $S_K \subseteq (\mathcal{V} \setminus K)$ such that for any vertex $v \in K$ there is a vertex $u \in S_K$ such that v is reachable from u within a given time interval $[t_i, t_k]$ such that $t_i < t_k$ and $t_k \leq \mathcal{T}$.*

Definition 6. Minimum Source Set of a Set of Vertices(MSS): *Minimum source set of a set of vertices $K \subseteq \mathcal{V}$ for a given time interval $[t_i, t_k]$, denoted by MSS_{K, t_i, t_k}, is the source set of K with minimum cardinality.*

In Fig. 2b, the set of vertices $\{u_2, u_6\}$, coloured with gray are the source set of set of vertices $\{u_3, u_4, u_5\}$ in time interval $[0, 8]$. This is the minimum source set of set of vertices $\{u_3, u_4, u_5\}$ in time interval $[0, 6]$ also. But in time interval $[0, 8]$, $\{u_2\}$ is the minimum source set of set of vertices $\{u_3, u_4, u_5\}$. In this paper, when no time interval is specified for any source set or minimum source set, we assume that the time interval is $[0, \mathcal{T}]$.

In the next section, we explore the problem of finding the minimum source set for a given set of vertices in a temporal graph.

5   Finding Minimum Source Set on Temporal Graphs

In this section, we address the problem of finding the minimum source set (MSS) for a given set of vertices on a given temporal graph. For this MSS problem on a given temporal graph $\mathcal{G} = (\mathcal{V}, \mathcal{E}, \mathcal{T}, \rho, \zeta)$, there is a given set of vertices $K \subset \mathcal{V}$, we need to minimum sized set S such that $S \subseteq \mathcal{V} \setminus K$ and for each vertex $v \in K$, there is a vertex $u \in S$ and v is reachable from u. For any vertex v in a temporal graph, we can find the set of vertices which are reachable vertices by using the algorithm proposed in [24] in $O(m(\log \mathcal{T} + \log n))$ time where $m = |\mathcal{E}|$, $n = |\mathcal{V}|$ and $\mathcal{T}$ is the lifetime of $\mathcal{G}$. We can construct a bipartite graph $G = (V, E)$ where $V = A \cup B$ by including all vertices of K in B and all vertices of $\mathcal{V} \setminus K$ in set A. Then construct the edge set E by connecting a directed edge (u, v) from $u \in A$ and $v \in B$ if v is in the reachable set of vertices of u. Next, if we find the minimum cardinality subset S' of A such that for each vertex v in B, there is at least one vertex u in S' such that $(u, v) \in E$, then this is the minimum source set for K in $\mathcal{G}$. This process of constructing the directed bipartite graph takes $O(mn(\log \mathcal{T} + \log n))$ time where $|\mathcal{V} \setminus K| \le n^1$. This problem of finding the minimum subset of A is referred to as *minimum static source set problem on bipartite graphs (MSSB)*. Next, we formally define this problem.

Definition 7. MSSB: *Given a directed static bipartite graph $G = (A \cup B, E)$ where direction of each edge is from the vertices in A to the vertices in B, the MSSB problem is to find the minimum cardinality set $C \subseteq A$ such that for all $v \in B$ there exists at least a vertex $u \in C$ such that $(u, v) \in E$.*

In the next subsection, we investigate the computational complexity of the problem of finding the minimum source set for a given set of vertices in a given temporal graph.

5.1   Complexity of the Finding MSS Problem

We prove that the finding MSS problem is NP-complete. First, we prove that the problem of finding MSSB is NP-complete even when the maximum out-degree of any vertex in the bipartite graph is bounded above by 3 or more. We prove this by showing that there is a polynomial time reduction from the decision version of *k-Set Cover* problem referred to as *D-k-SCP* to the decision version of the MSSB problem on directed bipartite graphs when the maximum out-degree of any vertex is bounded by δ referred to as *D-MSSB-δ*. The D-k-SCP problem is known to be NP-complete even when $k \le 3$ [11]. We first formally define the D-k-SCP problem and the D-MSSB-δ problem.

Definition 8. D-k-SCP: *Given a set of elements U, a collection of f sets S where the size of each set is bounded by k such that union of all sets in S is U and $c \in \mathbb{Z}^+$, does there exist a collection $R \subseteq S$ of size c such that union of all sets in R is U.*

Definition 9. D-MSSB-δ: *Consider a directed static bipartite graph $G = (A \cup B, E)$ where direction of each edge is from vertices in A to vertices in B, out degree of each vertex in A is bounded by δ, and $p \in \mathbb{Z}^+$. The D-MSSB-δ problem is to find the existence of a set $C \subseteq A$ of size p such that for all $v \in B$ there exists $u \in C$ such that $(u, v) \in E$.*

---

[1] We run the algorithm proposed in [24] for each vertex in A.

Theorem 1. *The D-MSSB-δ problem is NP-complete even when $\delta \leq 3$.*

Proof. We first show that the D-MSSB-δ problem is in NP. Given any instance of the D-MSSB-δ problem with $G = (A \cup B, E)$ a directed bipartite graph with an out-degree of each vertex in A is bounded by $\delta \leq 3$, the direction of each edge in E is from the vertices of the vertex set A to the vertices of the vertex set B and an integer p. Consider a certificate $C \subseteq A$. Whether $|C| = p$ can be easily checked in polynomial time. We verify whether C is a source set of B or not as follows. Pick each edge $(u, v) \in E$, if $u \in C$ we put v in a set T when $v \notin T$. When all edges in E are processed, C is an MSSB for G if $T = B$, C is not an MSSB for G otherwise. This whole procedure will take polynomial time. Hence, the problem belongs to NP.

Next, we prove that there exists a polynomial time reduction from the D-k-SCP problem when $k \leq 3$ to the D-MSSB-δ when $\delta \leq 3$ problem. Given an instance of the D-k-SCP problem with (U, S, c) when $k \leq 3$ we construct an instance of D-MSSB-δ $(A \cup B, E, p)$ problem where out-degree of each vertex is bounded by 3 as follows:

- For each $x \in U$ insert a vertex v_x into B. Thus,
  $B := \{v_x \,|\, \forall x \in U\}$
- For each set $s \in S$ insert a vertex v_s in A. Thus,
  $A := \{v_s \,|\, \forall s \in S\}$
- For each element $e \in s$ add a directed edge (v_s, v_e) in E where $v_e \in B$. Thus,
  $E := \{(v_s, v_e) \,|\, \forall e \in s, \forall s \in S\}$
- Assign $p = c$.

In the above construction as the number of elements in a set $s \in S$ is ≤ 3 the out-degree of any vertex in A is ≤ 3. Figure 3 shows one example of constructing a directed bipartite graph from an instance of the D-3-SCP problem.

We show that if there is a solution for the D-MSSB-δ problem, then there is a solution for the D-k-SCP problem. Given a solution M such that $|M| = p$ we can construct a solution S of size c as follows. For each vertex $v_s \in M$, we add set s to the solution S. Thus, $|S| = p = c$. As the direction of each edge in E is from A to B, M contains only vertices from set A. Thus, $S \subseteq S$. Next, we need to prove that S is a set cover for (U, S, c). We prove this by contradiction. Assume that, there is an element e' which does not belong to any set s' in S. This implies that there is a vertex $v_{e'}$ in B which represents e' for which there is no vertex $v_{s'}$ in M such that $(v_{s'}, v_{e'}) \in E$. Thus, M is not a static source set for G. This is a contradiction.

Next, we need to prove that if there is no solution for the D-MSSB-δ problem, then there is no solution for the D-k-SCP problem. We prove this by showing that, if there is a solution for the D-k-SCP problem then there is a solution for the D-MSSB-δ problem.

Suppose S is a solution for D-k-SCP problem instance given by (U, S, c), $|S| = c$. We construct a solution M for the D-MSSB-δ problem, with $(A \cup B, E, p)$ as follows. For each set, $s \in S$ add a vertex v_s corresponding to set s to M. Thus, $|M| = c = p$. We need to prove that for any vertex $v_x \in B$, there is a

$$U = \{u_1, u_2, u_3, u_4, u_5\}$$
$$S = \{s_1 = \{u_1, u_2\},$$
$$s_2 = \{u_3, u_4, u_5\},$$
$$s_3 = \{u_1, u_3, u_5\},$$
$$s_4 = \{u_2, u_4\}\}$$

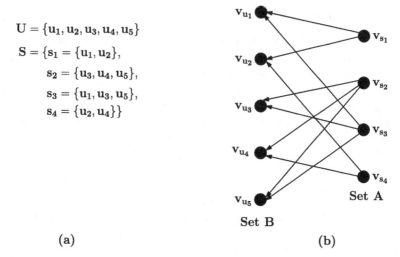

(a)   **(b)**

Fig. 3. Construction of a directed bipartite graph from an instance of k-set cover problem. (a) is an instance of 3-set cover problem, (b) is the constructed directed bipartite graph.

vertex $v_{s_i} \in M$ such that $(v_{s_i}, v_x) \in E$. We again show this by contradiction. Suppose there is a vertex $v_x \in B$ such that there is no vertex v_{s_i} in M such that $(v_{s_i}, v_x) \in E$. This implies that there is an element $x \in U$ which does not belong to any set s_i in $\mathcal{S}$. Hence, $\mathcal{S}$ is not a set cover for (U, S, c). This is a contradiction. Hence, the theorem holds.   □

The following corollary directly follows from Theorem 1.

Corollary 1. *The D-MSSB problem is NP-complete.*

Next, we prove that the problem of finding MSS for a given temporal graph is NP-complete. We prove this by showing that there is a polynomial time reduction from the decision version of the D-MSSB problem to the decision version of the finding MSS problem. First, we formally define the decision version of the MSS problem referred to as *D-MSS* problem.

Definition 10. D-MSS: *Given a temporal graph $\mathcal{G} = (\mathcal{V}, \mathcal{E}, \mathcal{T}, \rho, \zeta)$, a set of vertices $\mathcal{V}' \subseteq \mathcal{V}$, and a given $q \in \mathbb{Z}^+$, does there exist a set $F \subset \mathcal{V}$ such that $|F| = q$ and F is a source set of $\mathcal{V}'$.*

Theorem 2. *The D-MSS problem is NP-complete.*

Proof. First, we show that the D-MSS problem is in NP. Given any instance of the D-MSS problem with a temporal graph $\mathcal{G} = (\mathcal{V}, \mathcal{E}, \mathcal{T}, \rho, \zeta)$, a set of vertices $\mathcal{V}' \subseteq \mathcal{V}$, and a given $q \in \mathbb{Z}^+$. Consider a certificate $F \subseteq \mathcal{V}$. Whether $|F| = q$ can be checked in polynomial time. Next, we verify whether F is a source set of $\mathcal{V}'$ or not as follows. Pick one vertex at a time from F and find the vertices reachable from that vertex. We can do this in polynomial time by the algorithm proposed in [24]. Thus, we find set R, the set of all the vertices reachable from the set of vertices in F, in polynomial time. Then we can check whether $\mathcal{V}' \subseteq R$ in polynomial time. F is a source set of $\mathcal{V}'$ if edge $\mathcal{V}' \subseteq R$. Hence, this problem is in NP.

Next, we prove that there is a polynomial time reduction from the D-MSSB problem to the D-MSS problem. From Corollary 1, we know that the D-MSSB problem is NP-complete. For a given instance of the D-MSS problem with $G = (V = (A \cup B), E)$ a directed bipartite graph such that the direction of each edge in E is from the vertex set A to the vertex set B, and an integer p we can construct an instance of the D-MSS problem as follows:

- First we construct a bipartite temporal graph $\mathcal{G} = (\mathcal{V} = \mathcal{A} \cup \mathcal{B}, \mathcal{E}, \mathcal{T}, \rho, \zeta)$ from the given directed bipartite graph $G = (V = (A \cup B), E)$
  - The vertex set $\mathcal{A}$ of the temporal graph $\mathcal{G}$ includes all the vertices in A and vertex set $\mathcal{B}$ includes all the vertices in B. Thus,
    $$\mathcal{A} := A$$
    $$\mathcal{B} := B$$
    $$\mathcal{V} := \mathcal{A} \cup \mathcal{B}$$
  - To construct the edge set $\mathcal{E}$ of $\mathcal{G}$, for each directed edge $(u, v) \in E$ we add an edge $e = (u, v, (0, 1))$ to $\mathcal{E}$. This means for any edge $e \in \mathcal{E}$, $\rho(e, 0) = 1$ Thus,
    $$\mathcal{E} := \{(u, v, (0, 1)) \mid \forall (u, v) \in E\}$$
  - Lifetime $\mathcal{T}$ of $\mathcal{G}$ is 1. Thus,
    $$\mathcal{T} = 1$$
  - Edge traversal time is one timestep. Thus, for any edge $e \in \mathcal{E}$, $\zeta(e, 0) = 1$.
- The given subset $\mathcal{V}'$ of $\mathcal{V}$ is the set of vertices in $\mathcal{B}$. Thus,
  $$\mathcal{V}' := \mathcal{B}$$
- We assign $q = p$.

We prove that if there exists a solution for the D-MSS problem, then there is a solution for the D-MSSB problem. Given a solution H such that $|H| = q$ for the D-MSS problem, we construct a solution M for the D-MSSB problem as follows. For all vertices in H, add the corresponding vertex in V to M. Thus, $|M| = q = p$. As the lifetime of the temporal graph $\mathcal{G}$ is 1 and edge traversal time is one timestep, only one hop journey is possible in $\mathcal{G}$. As $\mathcal{G}$ is a bipartite temporal graph and $\mathcal{V}' = \mathcal{B}$, from the definition of source set, all the vertices in H are in $\mathcal{A}$. Thus, all the vertices in M are in A. Assume that M is not a static source set for G and u is a vertex in B such that there is no (v, u) in E and $v \in M$. This implies that for the vertex corresponding to u in $\mathcal{B}$ there is no vertex in H from which u is reachable in $\mathcal{G}$. Hence, H is not a source set for $\mathcal{G}$. This is a contradiction.

Next, we need to prove that if there is no solution for the D-MSS problem, then there is no solution for the D-MSSB problem. We prove this by showing that, if there is a solution for the D-MSSB problem then there is a solution for the D-MSS problem.

Suppose M is a solution for the D-MSSB problem instance. We construct a solution H for the D-MSS problem as follows. For each vertex in M add the corresponding vertex from $\mathcal{A}$ to H. Thus, $|H| = p = q$. We need to prove that H is a source set for $\mathcal{G}$. We show this by contradiction. Suppose there is a vertex $u \in \mathcal{V}'$ such that there is no vertex in H with a journey to u. As $\mathcal{V}' = \mathcal{B}$, $u \in \mathcal{B}$. This implies that there is a vertex in B that corresponds to $u \in \mathcal{B}$ such that there is no vertex v in M and $(u, v) \in E$. This is a contradiction. Hence, the theorem holds.   □

In the next section, we study the MSSB of some special classes of graphs. We also present a polynomial time algorithm to compute an MSSB for one of the special classes of graphs.

5.2   MSSB with Fixed Degree

Let $G = (A \cup B, E)$ be a static connected directed bipartite graph. Here we assume, $|A| = |B| = n$, and the out-degree of each vertex in A and the in-degree of each vertex in B are equal (to 2). In this section, we present Lemma 1 and a polynomial time algorithm to compute MSSB for the aforementioned graph.

Lemma 1. *Let G be a bipartite graph, then $|MSSB|$ for B is at least $n/2$.*

Proof. We know that the in-degree of every vertex in B is 2 and the the out-degree of every vertex of A is 2. Therefore, by assumption, $2 * |A| = 2 * |B|$. By the definition of MSSB, and pigeonhole principle, $|MSSB| > |A|/2 - 1 = n/2 - 1$. Therefore, $|MSSB|$ for B is at least $n/2$.   □

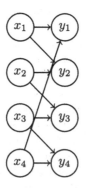

Fig. 4. An example of static bipartite graph with every vertex of A having out-degree 2 and every vertex B with in-degree 2.

We first present an algorithm to compute an MSSB for the aforementioned bipartite graph with every vertex of (in/out)-degree 2. Later we prove the correctness of our proposed algorithm and compute its time complexity.

5.3   Algorithm for Finding MSS

We find an MSSB of a connected static directed bipartite graph $G(A \cup B, E)$ with a fixed out-degree of every vertex $(= 2)$ in A and a fixed in-degree of every vertex $(= 2)$ in B, by iteratively traversing the graph. We keep track of the source set of B through two different sets (say) S_1, S_2. Both S_1 and S_2 are updated as we traverse each vertex of B in G. A vertex $u \in A$ is *visited* if all its neighbors in B have been traversed. Therefore, we assume all vertices of A are *unvisited* at the beginning.

We first select a vertex u from A and store it in S_1 and keep track of its neighbours (say $v_i, v_j \in B$) in a queue B_q. We then mark u as visited. For each vertex v in B_q, we find unvisited vertices u_i, u_j in A such that $u_i v, u_j v \in E$. We store u_i, u_j in S_2 and remove the corresponding vertex v from B_q. Then we find the neighbors of u_i and u_j in B. We store those neighbors in B_q and mark u_i and u_j as visited. We keep repeating the aforementioned process and update S_1 and S_2 alternately until all vertices in B have been traversed.

We formally describe the pseudocode of our approach in Algorithm 1. We demonstrate the execution of Algorithm 1 using an input graph presented in Fig. 5. A vertex $u_1 \in A$ is selected at first, the updation of S_1 and B_q is presented in Fig. 6. The next step of the iteration is presented in Fig. 7. The updation of B_q with respect to S_2 is presented in Fig. 8. The last step of the execution where all the vertices of A have been visited and all vertices in B have been traversed is demonstrated in Fig. 9. Since $|S_1| > |S_2|$, so S_1 is returned as a MSSB of the graph presented in Fig. 5.

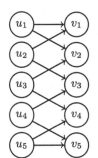
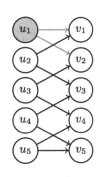
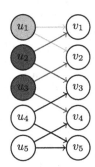

Fig. 5. $S_1 = \emptyset$ $S_2 = \emptyset$ $B_q = \emptyset$

Fig. 6. $S_1 = \{u_1\}$ $S_2 = \emptyset$ $B_q = \{v_1, v_2\}$

Fig. 7. $S_1 = \{u_1\}$ $S_2 = \{u_2, u_3\}$ $B_q = \emptyset$

5.4   Proof of Correctness of Algorithm 1

Lemma 2. *If S_1 and S_2 are the two sets generated by Algorithm 1, then $S_1 \cap S_2 = \emptyset$.*

Algorithm 1: Find an MSSB of a bipartite graph with degree 2

```
      /* ***************************************************
         Input : A connected directed graph G(A ∪ B, E) with fixed degree= 2.
         Output:   MSSB of G.
         ***************************************************           */
 1   S₁ = ∅
 2   S₂ = ∅
 3   Queue Bq = ∅
 4   ∀u ∈ A visited[u] = 0
 5   Let uᵢ ∈ A
 6   S₁.append(uᵢ)
 7   visited[uᵢ] = 1
 8   for all v ∈ B such that  (uᵢ, v) ∈ E do
 9   │   Bq.enqueue(v)
10   end
11   while (Bq ≠ ∅) do
12   │   appendSet(S₂, Bq, visited)
13   │   appendSet(S₁, Bq, visited)
14   end
15   if |S₁| > |S₂| then
16   │   return S₁
17   │   else
18   │   │   return S₂
19   │   end
20   end
      /* ***** Description of Subroutine appendSet() *****            */
21   def appendSet(T, Bq, visited):
22   Queue qnew = ∅
23   while (Bq ≠ ∅) do
24   │   v = Bq.dequeue()
25   │   for (each u ∈ A : (u, v) ∈ E and visited[u] = 0) do
26   │   │   T.append(u)
27   │   │   visited[u] = 1
28   │   │   qnew.enqueue(u)
29   │   end
30   end
31   for each u ∈ qnew do
32   │   for all v ∈ B  such that  (u, v) ∈ E do
33   │   │   Bq.enqueue(v)
34   │   end
35   end
```

Proof. We prove this lemma by contradiction. Assume that $S_1 \cap S_2 \neq \emptyset$. Let $u \in S_1 \cap S_2$. By, the construction of S_1 and S_2, only unvisited vertices are added to S_1 or S_2. Note that a vertex cannot be added to both S_1 and S_2 simultaneously. Let u has been added to S_1 in the ith iteration and to S_2 in the

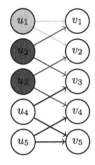

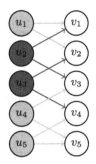

Fig. 8. $S_1 = \{u_1\}$ $S_2 = \{u_2, u_3\}$ $B_q = \{v_1, v_2, v_3, v_4\}$

Fig. 9. $S_1 = \{u_1, u_4, u_5\}$ $S_2 = \{u_2, u_3\}$ $B_q = \emptyset$

j^{th} iteration (w.l.o.g $i < j$) during the execution of Algorithm 1. However, the addition of u at iteration i would mark u as visited, therefore u cannot be added to S_2, which contradicts our assumption. $\square$

Lemma 3. *Let* $|A| = |B| = 2 * k + 1$ *for some* $k \in \mathbb{N}$. *Let* c_1 *and* c_2 *be the cardinalities of* S_1 *or* S_2 *between two successive updates. Then* $c_2 - c_1$ *is 2.*

Proof. Let i and j ($i < j$) be the iterations for successive updates of S_2. If all the vertices of A are visited before the jth iteration, then there are no more vertices to add to S_2, hence $c_2 - c_1$ is 0. Similarly, $c_2 - c_1$ cannot be 1 as that implies the input graph is a disconnected graph. Since every vertex of B has in-degree 2, by the construction of S_2, $c_2 - c_1$ is 2. Using similar arguments this can be proved for S_1. $\square$

Note that if $|A| = |B| = 2 * k$ then the above lemma holds for every iteration except the last one, where $c_2 - c_1 = 1$, which is the last unvisited vertex in A.

Theorem 3. *If* S *is the solution produced by Algorithm 1, then* S *is an MSSB of* G.

Proof. Let S be the solution produced by Algorithm 1. We first show that S is a source set for G and then we show that S is a MSSB.

Suppose S is not a source set for G. This implies there exists a vertex $v \in B$ which is not covered by S. Since the in-degree of v is 2, then there are un-visited vertices $u_1, u_2 \in A$, such that $u_1 v, u_2 v \in E(G)$. We know that Algorithm 1 terminates when all vertices A are visited, therefore, S cannot be a solution produced by Algorithm 1.

From Algorithm 1, we know that the sets S_1 and S_2 are updated alternately. From Lemma 3, it is clear that successive updations in S_1 or S_2 marks 2 un-visited vertices of A as visited. Since $|A| = n$ and S is the set with maximum cardinality between S_1 and S_2, therefore by Lemma 1 and Lemma 2, $|S| = n/2$. Therefore, S is an MSSB of G. $\square$

Theorem 4. *The time complexity of Algorithm 1 is $O(n^2)$ where n is the number of vertices in the bipartite graph G.*

Proof. The function **appendSet**() generates the candidate solutions S_1 and S_2. In this function, we iteratively select and list the vertices of A which covers all the vertices of B. Therefore the time complexity of this function is $O(n)$. This function is called $O(n)$ times. Therefore, the time complexity of Algorithm 1 is $O(n^2)$. □

Theorem 5. *Finding a minimum source set problem for temporal graphs where each vertex v can reach 2 vertices $(\neq v)$ and v can be reached from 2 vertices $(\neq v)$ can be solved in polynomial time.*

Proof. Let $\mathcal{G} = (\mathcal{V}, \mathcal{E}, \mathcal{T}, \rho, \zeta)$ be a temporal graph where each vertex v can reach 2 other vertices and v can be reached from 2 other vertices. Let $|\mathcal{V}| = n$ and $|\mathcal{E}| = m$. We first convert $\mathcal{G}$ into a static directed bipartite graph G using the method described in Sect. 5. This construction process takes $O(mn(\log \mathcal{T} + \log n))$ time. By using Algorithm 1, we find a MSSB for G, which is a MSS for $\mathcal{G} = (\mathcal{V}, \mathcal{E}, \mathcal{T}, \rho, \zeta)$. Therefore, the time complexity for finding MSS is $O((mn(\log \mathcal{T} + \log n)) + n^2)$. Hence, finding MSS for the aforementioned temporal graph takes polynomial time. □

6   Conclusion

In this paper, we have defined a minimum source set problem for temporal graphs and a minimum source set problem for static directed bipartite graphs. We have proved that both these problems are NP-complete. We further developed a polynomial time $(O(n^2))$ solution for minimum source set problem for static directed bipartite graphs with fixed in-degree 2 and out-degree 2. We used this solution to develop a polynomial time $(O((mn(\log \mathcal{T} + \log n)) + n^2))$ solution for minimum source set problem for temporal graphs where each vertex v can reach exactly 2 other vertices and v can be reached from exactly 2 other vertices. An extension of this work is to consider the minimum source set problem on different models of temporal graphs.

References

1. Brito, L.F., Albertini, M.K., Casteigts, A., Travençolo, B.A.: A dynamic data structure for temporal reachability with unsorted contact insertions. Soc. Netw. Anal. Min. **12**(1), 1–12 (2022)
2. Casteigts, A., Corsini, T., Sarkar, W.: Simple, strict, proper, happy: a study of reachability in temporal graphs. In: International Symposium on Stabilization, Safety, and Security of Distributed Systems (SSS), pp. 3–18 (2022)

3. Casteigts, A., Corsini, T., Sarkar, W.: Simple, strict, proper, happy: a study of reachability in temporal graphs. Theoret. Comput. Sci. **991**, 114434 (2024)
4. Casteigts, A., Flocchini, P., Quattrociocchi, W., Santoro, N.: Time-varying graphs and dynamic networks. Int. J. Parallel Emergent Distrib. Syst. **27**(5), 387–408 (2012)
5. Casteigts, A., Himmel, A.S., Molter, H., Zschoche, P.: Finding temporal paths under waiting time constraints. Algorithmica **83**(9), 2754–2802 (2021)
6. Danda, U.S., Ramakrishna, G., Schmidt, J.M., Srikanth, M.: On short fastest paths in temporal graphs. In: International Workshop on Algorithms and Computation (WALCOM), pp. 40–51 (2021)
7. Deligkas, A., Potapov, I.: Optimizing reachability sets in temporal graphs by delaying. Inf. Comput. 104890 (2022)
8. Enright, J., Meeks, K., Skerman, F.: Assigning times to minimise reachability in temporal graphs. J. Comput. Syst. Sci. **115**, 169–186 (2021)
9. Ferrati, M., Pallottino, L.: A time expanded network based algorithm for safe and efficient distributed multi-agent coordination. In: IEEE Conference on Decision and Control (IEEE CDC), pp. 2805–2810 (2013)
10. Ferreira, A.: On models and algorithms for dynamic communication networks: the case for evolving graphs. In: 4^e Rencontres Francophones sur les Aspects Algorithmiques des Telecommunications (ALGOTEL), pp. 155–161 (2002)
11. Garey, M.R., Johnson, D.S.: Computers and Intractability: A Guide to the Theory of NP-Completeness. Freeman, W. H (1979)
12. George, B., Shekhar, S.: Time-aggregated graphs for modeling spatio-temporal networks. In: Journal on Data Semantics XI, pp. 191–212 (2008)
13. Kempe, D., Kleinberg, J., Kumar, A.: Connectivity and inference problems for temporal networks. In: ACM Symposium on Theory of Computing (STOC), pp. 504–513 (2000)
14. Mandal, S., Gupta, A.: Approximation algorithms for permanent dominating set problem on dynamic networks. In: International Conference on Distributed Computing and Internet Technology (ICDCIT), pp. 265–279 (2018)
15. Mandal, S., Gupta, A.: Convergecast tree on temporal graphs. Int. J. Found. Comput. Sci. **31**(03), 385–409 (2020)
16. Mandal, S., Gupta, A.: Maximum 0–1 timed matching on temporal graphs. Discret. Appl. Math. **319**, 310–326 (2022)
17. Michail, O., Chatzigiannakis, I., Spirakis, P.G.: Naming and counting in anonymous unknown dynamic networks. In: Symposium on Self-Stabilizing Systems (SSS), pp. 281–295 (2013)
18. Molter, H., Renken, M., Zschoche, P.: Temporal reachability minimization: delaying vs. deleting. In: International Symposium on Mathematical Foundations of Computer Science (MFCS), pp. 76:1–76:15 (2021)
19. Thejaswi, S., Lauri, J., Gionis, A.: Restless reachability problems in temporal graphs. arXiv preprint arXiv:2010.08423 (2020)
20. Wang, Y., Yuan, Y., Ma, Y., Wang, G.: Time-dependent graphs: definitions, applications, and algorithms. Data Sci. Eng. **4**(4), 352–366 (2019)
21. Whitbeck, J., Dias de Amorim, M., Conan, V., Guillaume, J.L.: Temporal reachability graphs. In: International Conference on Mobile Computing and Networking (MOBICOM), pp. 377–388 (2012)
22. Wu, H., Cheng, J., Huang, S., Ke, Y., Lu, Y., Xu, Y.: Path problems in temporal graphs. Proc. VLDB Endowm. **7**(9), 721–732 (2014)

23. Wu, H., Huang, Y., Cheng, J., Li, J., Ke, Y.: Reachability and time-based path queries in temporal graphs. In: IEEE International Conference on Data Engineering (ICDE), pp. 145–156 (2016)
24. Xuan, B.B., Ferreira, A., Jarry, A.: Computing shortest, fastest, and foremost journeys in dynamic networks. Int. J. Found. Comput. Sci. **14**(02), 267–285 (2003)

Team Formation Based on the Degree Distribution of the Social Networks

Bobby Ramesh Addanki[1,2]($\boxtimes$) and S. Durga Bhavani[2]

[1] B V Raju Institute of Technology, Vishnupur, Narsapur, Medak, Telangana 502313, India
ramesh.ab@bvrit.ac.in
[2] School of Computer and Information Sciences, University of Hyderabad, Prof. CR Rao Road, Gachibowli, Hyderabad, Telangana 500046, India
{17mcpc02,sdbcs}@uohyd.ac.in

Abstract. The challenge of the Team Formation Problem (TFP) is to select an effective team for a given task with minimum communication cost and time. The heuristic as well as the recent evolutionary approaches to team formation focus on optimizing one communication cost, yet do not yield teams in a reasonable amount of time. Our study proposes a novel approach to solve the TFP by considering the topology of the underlying social network. We propose two heuristic algorithms: TPLRandom and TPLClosest, that use the degree distribution of the social network to solve TFP. The proposed approach utilizes the power law followed by the degree distribution as well as the skill distribution of the experts to compose an effective team. This idea optimizes not only more than one communication cost but also time. Extensive experimentation is carried out on the large well-known real-world DBLP dataset and all the subnetworks of DBLP. Empirically it is observed that the proposed algorithm TPLClosest is 3, 10, 27, and 65 times faster than Genetic algorithm, MinSD, Cultural algorithm and MinLD algorithm respectively. Further our algorithms are found to be significantly scalable. The results are shown empirically on different sized networks of DBLP.

Keywords: LeaderDistance · team formation · degree centrality · power law · DBLP network

1 Introduction

Real-world projects like community-based software development or the challenges thrown open by major conferences are examples of tasks requiring multiple skills that can only be tackled as a team. As given in project management statistics for 2024 [5], only 35% of projects successfully completed with respect to time, budget, and quality. Studies like [5,9] show that insufficient communication and ineffective management are some of the reasons for project failure. Kashyap [13], claims that most of the technology implementation projects fail

Q. Bramas et al. (Eds.): ICDCIT 2025, LNCS 15507, pp. 179–194, 2025.
https://doi.org/10.1007/978-3-031-81404-4_14

because of people, and not due to technology. These studies conclude that an effective team formation plays a crucial role in project sucess rate.

Given a task and the set of available experts, the *team formation problem (TFP)* is to find a subset of experts, who have the skill set required for the task, and who can work together efficiently. Most of the work in the literature adopts a skill-centric approach. For each skill of the given task, they choose an expert closest to the team being formed. This approach involves many shortest-path calculations which slow down the algorithms [10–12]. Existing algorithms focus on reducing communication cost which forms the main component of the time complexity of the TFP algorithms [4,10,11,14,18]. Clearly, there is a trade-off between the quality of the solution and the speed of the algorithm.

In recent times, algorithms based on evolutionary approach like Cultural algorithm [17,20] have been proposed for the team formation problem. Multi-objective variant of TFP is addressed in the recent literature. They optimize different parameters like workload, personnel cost, communication cost, etc. [21]. Majority of these algorithms focus on skill-centric approach and minimize one communication cost.

Since social networks are rapidly increasing over time, scalability is a challenge faced by the team formation algorithms. The algorithms in the literature fail to scale on these evolving large networks. We adopt an approach that considers the topological properties of the network so that it can scale on large networks and also run in a reasonable amount of time and perform well with respect to many cost measures. In this work we address TFP in which three communication costs are being minimized.

The organization of the paper is as follows. The related literature is given in Sect. 2. The problem statement and the communication cost measures are discussed in Sect. 3. In Sect. 4, the insights of the network analysis and proposed algorithms *TPLRandom* and *TPLClosest* are explained. In Sect. 5, the benchmark data set, the experimentation carried out and the results obtained for the algorithms in terms of execution time and the various communication cost measures are given. Conclusion and future work are given in Sect. 6.

2   Literature

Lappas et al. [14] introduced the "Team Formation Problem" in a social network context, aiming to identify a team of specialists with the necessary abilities to complete a task with minimum communication cost. They proposed *Rarestfirst* algorithm to minimize *Diameter* communication cost. In the same year, Wi et al. [24] proposed an algorithm based on finding a team leader who then identifies the team members. Wi et al. used a multi-objective fuzzy model giving importance to both interpersonal collaboration and technical skills for team formation. Bredereck et al. [4] analyzed the computational complexity of TFP with respect to the parameters of task size, cardinality and the communication costs namely, *Diameter* and *SumDistance*. They concluded that computational complexity of a TFP algorithm strongly depends on the communication cost used. Rehman et al. [18] employed search space reduction in the team formation problem for qucik processing. Similarly for quick processing Berktas et al. [3] applied Branch-and-bound method for TFP to solve small and medium instances with respect to *Diameter*.

Kargar et al. [10] proposed two new communication cost measures to evaluate the team, namely, *LeaderDistance* and *SumDistance* that are defined in Sect. 3.1. Kargar et al. proposed an algorithm *MinLD* that aims at minimizing the *LeaderDistance* of a team. The *LeaderDistance* partially captures collaborations among the team members, the algorithm is extremely slow. In the same paper, *SumDistance* is proposed that sums up pairwise collaborations of all experts representing the skills for all combinations of skills of the task. *SumDistance* captures collaborations among team members better than *Diameter* distance and *LeaderDistance*. The objective of the *MinSD* algorithm is to minimize the *SumDistance*. This algorithm requires more time but is faster than *MinLD*. There are many other communication cost measures that have been proposed in the literature like bottleneck cost [15], SteinerTree cost [14], LeaderSumDistance [10], and greedy approaches that minimize the respective measures to form a team. Since each of these algorithms minimizes a specific distance measure, there is a need for an approach which is fast as well as that minimizes more than one communication cost measure in order to obtain efficient teams with high collaboration which is the main focus of our work. Many other variants of TFP have been proposed in the literature: minimizing the workload of experts [1], balancing the workload of experts [2], placing constraints on capacity of the expert [15], communication load constraint [22], the overall budget of a team [11], and the personnel budget of team members [11], allocating distinct teams for multiple tasks [8], team formation based on reliability of experts [6]. A column generation approach for swapping the members of existing teams to form new teams is studied [16].

In this paper, we focus on presenting an efficient approach for the team formation problem that aims at finding a balance between the processing time and different communication costs. In particular, we aim to find teams that minimize three costs *Diameter*, *SumDistance*, and *LeaderDistance*. Hence, the algorithms proposed in this paper have been compared for performance with a few of the classical algorithms, namely *RarestFirst* of [14], *MinLD* and *MinSD* of [10] that are best at minimizing *Diameter*, *LeaderDistance* and *SumDistance* costs respectively. Further, comparison is shown with a few recent approaches based on genetic algorithm given in [17] and [20].

3   Preliminaries

A social network is modeled as a graph $G(V, E)$. The experts are considered as nodes and their mutual interactions are depicted as edges. The edge weights are given by a distance measure that is based on the strength/weakness of the interaction.

Table 1: Notation used for the team formation problem

Symbol	Meaning
G	Graph representation of a network
V	Set of experts as nodes of G
E	Set of weighted edges of G
S	Universal set of skills of V
T	Task $T \subseteq S$, the subset of skills required
S_v	Set of skills possessed by an expert $v \in V$
V_s	Set of experts having a skill $s \in S$
V_A	Set of experts, a skill $s \in A$ is represented by at least one expert $\cup_{s \in A} V_s, A \subseteq S$
λ	Parameter to select candidate leaders
X	Team $X : V_T = X, X \subseteq V$

3.1   Communication Cost Measures

A few of the popular communication cost functions that measure the quality of a team formation algorithm as given in a survey of [23] are described below. Let $sp(u, v)$ denote the weight of the shortest path found between nodes u and v in the graph G. Let $X \subseteq V$ denote the team obtained for a given task T.

- *Diameter* [14]: The *Diameter* of a team X is defined as the weight of the longest among the shortest paths between all pairs of nodes of the team X.

$$Diameter(X) = max_{u,v \in X}(sp(u, v)) \tag{1}$$

- *LeaderDistance* [10]: *LeaderDistance* of a team X is defined as the sum of the distances from a designated leader L in the team to the other members of the team.

$$LD(X) = \sum_{v \in X} sp(v, L) \tag{2}$$

where L is leader and $v, L \in X$.

- *SumDistance* [10]: This measure computes the sum of distances between each pair of skills (i.e. experts chosen by the algorithm for the skill) of task T.

$$SD(X) = \sum_{i=1}^{|T|} \sum_{j=i+1}^{|T|} sp(v_{s_i}, v_{s_j}) \tag{3}$$

where v_{s_i} and v_{s_j} are experts in X responsible for skills s_i and s_j respectively in T. Since one expert may be responsible for more than one skill, the calculation may have repeated occurrence of the experts.

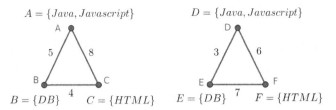

Fig. 1: Toy example: The subgraphs corresponding to two teams {A, B, C} and {D, E, F} are shown for the task T = {Java, Javascript, HTML, DB}. The skills possessed by each team member are given at the node along with pairwise distances.

For example, Fig. 1 shows a scenario for picking a team for a website development task. The required skills are {Java, Javascript, HTML, DB}. Clearly, the feasible teams are {A, B, C} and {D, E, F}.

The *Diameter* cost of the team {A, B, C} is 8, and that of {D, E, F} is 7. So *Rarestfirst* algorithm, which aims at minimizing the *Diameter* cost, would select the team {D, E, F} having least *Diameter* cost. *MinLD* algorithm which minimizes *LeaderDistance* both teams {A, B, C} and {D, E, F} stand equal with LeaderDistance is 9 as B and D as leaders respectively. Finally if *SumDistance*(SD) cost is considered then SD({A, B, C}) is equal to 30. Similarly, SD({D, E, F}) is equal to 25 by considering the distance between all the pairs of skills. Hence *MinSD* would choose the team as {D, E, F}.

3.2   Problem Statement

Given a set of experts V in G and a universal set of skills S, an expert $v \in V$ possesses skill set represented as S_v and given a task $T = \{s_1, s_2, ..., s_k\}$ contained in S, *team formation* problem is to find a team $X \subseteq V$ such that the communication costs of *LD(X), SD(X) and Diameter(X)* are minimized subject to the constraint that

$$\left(\bigcup_{v \in X} S_v \right) \supseteq T \tag{4}$$

Our algorithms imitate the real-world process of team formation in which a team leader is identified first, then the team leader chooses the team members possessing the maximum necessary skills from their neighbourhood. The idea of the proposed approach is to reduce the shortest path calculations by restricting the search space to decrease the processing time. Choosing high-degree nodes and their neighbors covering many skills required for the task reduces the search space and thus leads to a potentially fast and scalable algorithm.

4   Proposed Approach

The degree distribution of a real-world social network exhibits a typical heavy tail since it satisfies the power law as shown in Fig. 2a. The heavy tail in the degree distribution consists of a few high degree nodes, motivating us to select these nodes as team leaders. With this motivation, we define H_λ as the set containing nodes with degree greater than $\lambda \times$ avg-deg(G). Clearly H_λ is non-empty for $\lambda = 1$. Figure 2a shows H_λ, for $\lambda = 1$ using stars that can be chosen as leaders. Figure 2b shows the skill coverage of the experts from H_λ, for $\lambda = 1$ and 2. We can observe that almost 90% of the skills are covered by experts from $H_\lambda(\lambda = 1)$ and 75% of skills are covered by the experts from H_λ $(\lambda = 2)$. Hence our algorithms employ H_λ to pick the leaders of the teams. So these are named as Teams based on Power Law (TPL).

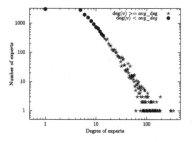
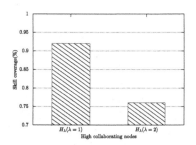

(a) Experts having high collaborations represented using stars and those with low collaborations represented using circles in DBLP network at $\lambda = 1$.

(b) Percentage of skill coverage of experts in H_λ, the set of high collaborating experts, having degree at least $\lambda*$(average degree), $\lambda = 1$ and 2.

Fig. 2: Degree distribution of the DBLP network and skill coverage of the experts in H_λ.

4.1   TPLRandom and TPLClosest Algorithms

We propose two algorithms, namely, *TPLRandom* and *TPLClosest*. *TPLRandom* algorithm is given in Algorithm 1.

Here we explain the proposed *TPLRandom* algorithm. Each leader from H_λ starts forming a team by choosing members from their own p-hop neighbourhood having the necessary skills. *Nbd* (in line 8) denotes the p-hop neighbourhood of the leader that is used to choose the other members of the team. The expert with maximum coverage of skills is chosen (in line 11) and added to the team then T_{NC} is updated by removing the skills covered. These steps(lines 10–15) are repeated until T_{NC} is empty or maximum skill coverage of T is achieved. Let T_{NC} be the set of the remaining skills that are not yet covered by *Nbd*. If the leader and *Nbd* are chosen well, T_{NC} will be much smaller in size than

T. *TPLRandom* and *TPLClosest* algorithms differ with respect to the selection mechanism given in line 17 by which the experts are added for the skills in T_{NC}.

- In the case of *TPLRandom* algorithm, for each skill $s \in T_{NC}$, an expert $v_s \in V_s$ is chosen randomly and added to the team.
- For the *TPLClosest* algorithm, for each skill $s \in T_{NC}$, an expert v_s is chosen for which $sp(v_s, leader)$ is minimum.

In the final steps of the algorithm in lines 21–24, the *LeaderDistance* is computed for the different teams formed by the leaders from H_λ. The algorithm returns the best team with the minimum *LeaderDistance* as the best team by the algorithm.

Algorithm 1 TPLRandom

Require: *Network G, Task T, hops p, and* parameter to select high-degree nodes λ

Ensure: *Team X*

1: **procedure** $TPLRandom(G, T, p, \lambda)$
2:     $bestTeam \leftarrow \emptyset$
3:     $bld \leftarrow \infty$
4:     $H_\lambda \leftarrow \{v \in G \mid k_v \geq \lambda * d_{avg}(G)\}$
5:     **for** $leader \in H_\lambda :\mid S_{leader} \cap T \mid > 0$ **do**
6:         $team \leftarrow \emptyset$
7:         $team \leftarrow team \cup \{leader\}$
8:         $Nbd \leftarrow \{v \mid v \in G, \mid d(v, leader) \mid \leq p\}$ ▷ p-hop Neighbourhood
9:         $T_{NC} \leftarrow T$
10:        **while** $\{S_{Nbd} \cap T_{NC}\} \neq \emptyset$ **do**
11:            $expert \leftarrow argmax_{v \in Nbd}(\mid T_{NC} \cap S_v \mid)$
12:            $team \leftarrow team \cup \{expert\}$
13:            $T_{NC} \leftarrow T_{NC} \setminus S_{expert}$
14:            $Nbd \leftarrow Nbd \setminus \{expert\}$
15:        **end while**
16:        **while** $\{T_{NC}\} \neq \emptyset$ **do**   ▷ Skills not yet covered by Nbd
17:            $expert \leftarrow$ Choose-Randomly $(V_{T_{NC}})$
18:            $team \leftarrow team \cup \{expert\}$
19:            $T_{NC} \leftarrow T_{NC} \setminus S_{expert}$
20:        **end while**
21:        **if** $LD(team) \leq bld$ **then**   ▷ LD(X) : Leader distance of team X
22:            $bld \leftarrow LD(team)$
23:            $bestTeam \leftarrow team$
24:        **end if**
25:    **end for**
26:    **return** $bestTeam$
27: **end procedure**

Choice of Parameters. The algorithm has two parameters: λ, which helps in choosing high degree nodes as leaders; and p denoting the hop-size of the neighbourhood around the leader. If λ is chosen such that H_λ is empty, then the proposed algorithms fail to return a team. Note that the algorithms always work for $\lambda = 1$. Higher values of λ may be chosen based on the given data set ensuring H_λ to be non-empty.

The small-world property of the real-world networks forces us to choose $p = 1$ and $p = 2$ as reasonable sizes of the neighbourhood. $p > 2$ may cover almost the entire network which makes the algorithm computationally inefficient.

Time Complexity. The line 4 of Algorithm 1 finds high degree nodes that requires $O(|V + E|)$ time. The time intensive step in line 8 involves visiting vertices that are within p hop distance. Hence BFS of the p-hop neighbourhood of H makes the time complexity of the algorithm to be $O(|H_\lambda| ((|V|+|E|) |T|+|T|) = O(|T||H_\lambda||V|)$ as $|E|$ is $O(|V|)$ for social networks. Though the time complexity of the algorithm is $O(|T||H_\lambda||V|)$, where T is the task chosen for the team formation, since $|H_\lambda| <<|V|$, empirically the algorithm is much faster than $O(|T||V|^2)$.

5   Experimentation and Results

In this paper, we focus on presenting efficient algorithms for the classical team formation problem and not its variants. Hence, the algorithms proposed in this paper have been compared with the classical algorithms and a few recent algorithms. The results are compared with the classical algorithms, namely *Rarest-First* of Lappas et al. [14], *BestLeaderDistance* and *BestSumDistance* of Kargar et al. [10]; and the evolutionary algorithms, namely, Genetic algorithm [17] and Cultural algorithm [20]. We adopt the methods *MinLD* and *MinSD* proposed in [23] based on *BestLeaderDistance* and *BestSumDistance*.

5.1   Network Construction

We curated a large collaboration network from DBLP database[1]. DBLP data is modeled as an undirected and weighted network. The network is constructed exactly as suggested originally by [14] and followed by [1,2,10,11,15] and is explained below.

Individuals who have published papers in the DBLP are considered as authors. Authors having at least two publications are considered as experts. Experts are taken as nodes of the network. Two experts v_i and v_j are connected by an edge if they have at least two joint publications indexed in DBLP. The amount of collaboration between v_i and v_j is calculated by using Jaccard distance measure which is taken as edge weight w_{ij}, given by $1 - \frac{|P_{v_i} \cap P_{v_j}|}{|P_{v_i} \cup P_{v_j}|}$ where

---

[1] https://dblp.uni-trier.de/xml/.

P_{v_i} represents the number of papers published by v_i. Hence in the network lesser the Jaccard distance is, more their collaboration and vice-versa.

We consider the largest connected component(LCC) of the network, having 32,477 nodes and 115938 edges.

5.2 Problem Setting

The skill set of an expert v consists of all non-trivial words from the titles of the papers authored by v. Union of all such skill sets of the experts from DBLP form the universal skill set S. A task is any random subset of S. The problem is to find a team of experts X from the DBLP data set having the required skills T, incurring minimum communication cost.

5.3 Experiments

Given the set of skills S, random subsets of S of size k are chosen as tasks T. We generate tasks of sizes $4 \leq k \leq 20$. And for each size k, we generate 10 tasks of size k. The algorithms are implemented for these tasks T to find teams. The average communication cost of the teams obtained for the 10 tasks is tabulated for each k. We compare *TPLRandom* and *TPLClosest* algorithms with classical algorithms namely, *Rarestfirst*, *MinLD*, *MinSD* and recent algorithms, namely, Cultural algorithm [20] and Genetic algorithm [17] with respect to communication cost and processing time. *TPLClosest* algorithm has been implemented with $\lambda = 1$ and 2 and are named as *TPL-1* and *TPL-2* respectively. For both *TPL-1* and *TPL-2*, experiments are conducted for the values of $p = 1, 2$.

5.4 Results

The algorithms have been implemented in Python on Intel(R) Core(TM) i7-4300M CPU @ 2.60 GHz. It is to be noted that the optimizing criterion for *Rarestfirst* algorithm is *Diameter* distance, *LeaderDistance* for *MinLD* algorithm and *SumDistance* for *MinSD* algorithm. Hence, to keep the comparison fair, the results are organized as follows:

(A) Comparison of team size obtained by the proposed algorithms against the classical and recent algorithms in the literature.
(B) The proposed algorithms *TPL-1*, *TPL-2* and *TPLRandom* are compared with *Rarestfirst* algorithm with respect to the *Diameter* distance and execution time.
(C) Comparison of proposed algorithms with *MinLD* algorithm with respect to *LeaderDistance* and execution time.
(D) Comparison of proposed algorithms with *MinSD* algorithm with respect to *SumDistance* and execution time.
(E) Comparison of proposed algorithms with Genetic and Cultural algorithms with respect to *SD* and execution time.

Team Size. Figure 3a shows the average team size obtained by the proposed algorithms compared against the algorithms from the literature. We observe that all the algorithms yield similar team sizes for tasks upto size 12. For tasks of size more than 12, both TPL Random and *TPL-2* appear to give smaller teams for the tasks.

In order to confirm the significance, we perform the ANOVA test to analyze the results obtained by all the algorithms. The p-value of 0.98 at 95% confidence level confirms that the difference between average team sizes yielded by algorithms in Fig. 3 is not significant.

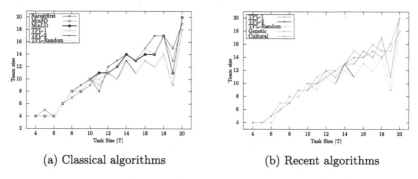

(a) Classical algorithms   (b) Recent algorithms

Fig. 3: Comparison of average team size obtained by *TPL-1*, *TPL-2* and *TPLRandom* against the classical and recent algorithms.

Communication Cost: Diameter. Figure 4a shows that the communication cost obtained by all the algorithms seem to be similar. We computed Pearson's correlation coefficient between *TPL-2* and *Rarestfirst* algorithm and obtained a value of 0.97 confirming the closeness of the results.

The plot in Fig. 4b shows that *Rarestfirst* algorithm is faster than the proposed algorithms in terms of execution time. *TPLRandom* is seen to be faster than *TPL-2* and *TPL-1*.

Rarestfirst algorithm is only designed to optimize *Diameter* distance, unlike the proposed algorithms that are designed to optimize *LeaderDistance* and *SumDistance* along with *Diameter*. Hence, in addition, we compare the proposed algorithms with *Rarestfirst* algorithm for the communication costs of LeaderDistance and *SumDistances*.

Communication Cost: LeaderDistance (LD). The proposed algorithms are compared with the *MinLD* algorithm in terms of the communication cost of *LeaderDistance*. As all these algorithms are designed to optimize *LeaderDistance*, intuitively, the *LeaderDistance* values of the proposed algorithms match with the *MinLD* algorithm. In Fig. 5a we can observe that *TPLRandom* and *TPL-1*

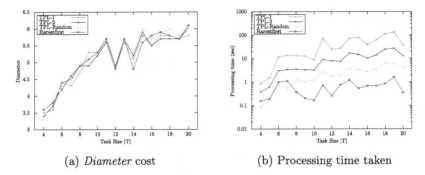

(a) *Diameter* cost   (b) Processing time taken

Fig. 4: The average *Diameter* cost and the processing time taken by the proposed algorithms *TPL-1*, *TPL-2* and *TPLRandom* are compared with *Rarestfirst* algorithm.

give higher communication cost as compared to TPL-2 and *MinLD*. The costs achieved by *TPL-2* seem to be close to *MinLD*. We compute Pearson's correlation coefficient between *TPL-2* and *MinLD* and obtained a value of 0.67 that confirms a significant matching of the results. The unpaired t-test confirmed no statistical significance between the *LeaderDistance* values for teams generated by *TPL-2* and *MinLD* with a p-value of 0.4126 at 95% confidence.

Figure 5b shows that the proposed algorithms, *TPL-2* and *TPL-1* are significantly faster than the *MinLD* algorithm. The slowness of *MinLD* is due to the computations involved when it considers every expert in the network to be a leader. As the Leader Distance of *TPL-2* is closest to *MinLD*, we conduct unpaired t-test for these algorithms with respect to time. A p-value of 10^{-6} is obtained in the t-test that confirms that *TPL-2* is significantly faster than *MinLD*.

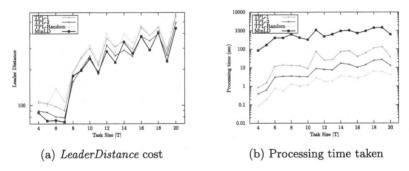

(a) *LeaderDistance* cost   (b) Processing time taken

Fig. 5: *TPL-2* matches *MinLD* algorithm with respect to *LeaderDistance* cost. Proposed algorithms *TPL-1*, TPL-2 and *TPLRandom* are clearly much faster than *MinLD* algorithm.

Communication Cost: SumDistance (SD). Figure 6a shows the *SumDistances* yielded by the proposed algorithms and *MinSD* algorithm. *MinSD* seems to give slightly lower communication cost for tasks of size greater than 12. Hence we conducted both Pearson's correlation coefficient and t-test to test for the matching.

Pearson's correlation coefficient of 0.99 is obtained between *SumDistances* of teams yielded by *TPL-2* and *MinSD* algorithms. The unpaired t-test confirms that the results are not significantly different at 5% significance with a p-value of 0.335.

The proposed *TPL-1*, *TPL-2*, and *TPLRandom* algorithms achieve better processing time compared to *MinSD* algorithm. *TPLRandom* is fastest followed by *TPL-2* as is clearly seen in Fig. 6b. We perform t-test between *TPL-2* and *MinSD* with respect to the processing time. The p-value of 0.0002 at a 95% confidence level confirms that the proposed algorithm *TPL-2* is significantly faster than *MinSD* algorithm.

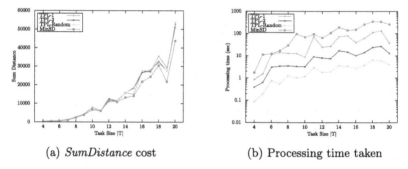

(a) *SumDistance* cost   (b) **Processing time taken**

Fig. 6: Comparison of the proposed algorithms with *MinSD* with respect to *SumDistance* and processing time.

Comparison with Recent Algorithms. In recent times, researchers have been interested in multi-objective variants of TFP. Among them, evolutionary approaches are popular and achieve quality solutions at the cost of computation. We compare our proposed algorithms with these evolutionary approaches by [17] and [20]. We implemented the genetic algorithm-based approach of [17] and the Cultural algorithm [20] to compare with the proposed algorithms. The parameters for implementation are chosen as specified in the algorithm: with adaptive mutation and the size of a population as ten. Parent selection and crossover selection are taken from the existing evolutionary algorithms. *SumDistance* is used as the fitness function as chosen by the authors [19,20]. We have used PyGAD [7] python module to implement these algorithms.

The plot in Fig. 7a indicates that the Genetic and Cultural algorithms show a lower communication cost in some cases when compared to TPL algorithms.

Therefore, we conduct ANOVA test which confirmed that no statistical significance is seen between the *SumDistance* of teams generated by *TPL-2*, Genetic and Cultural algorithms with a p-value of 0.22 at 5% significance level.

The proposed algorithms outperform the Genetic and Cultural algorithms with respect to the processing time as shown in Fig. 7b.

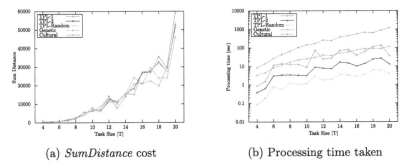

(a) *SumDistance* cost   (b) Processing time taken

Fig. 7: Comparison of the proposed *TPL-1*, TPL-2 and *TPLRandom* algorithms with the recent Genetic and Cultural algorithms with respect to *SumDistance* as well as the processing time.

5.5   Scalability

In order to show the scalability of our algorithms, we perform experiments by taking the subnetworks of DBLP of different order of sizes. We consider VLDB (nodes: 3261, edges: 9912) which is a subset of DB (nodes: 11699, edges: 46127) which is a subset of DBLP that contains 32477 nodes and 115938 edges for the experimentation. The results are shown in Fig. 8.

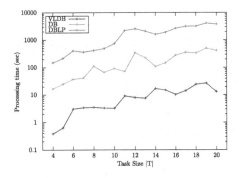

Fig. 8: Scalability of *TPL-2* algorithm is shown by plotting the time taken by the algorithm on smaller to larger networks: VLDB, DB, and DBLP networks.

As shown in Fig. 8, *TPL-2* could complete the larger tasks of size 18 in less than 3500 s on average on DBLP; on DB, in approximately 400 sec; and in about 10 s on VLDB.

Further, comparison of the performance of all the algorithms under consideration is shown with respect to the execution time taken for a task of size 19 for the smaller VLDB network. The results are given in Table 2. These results clearly show the superiority of *TPL-1* and *TPL-2*. TPL-Random is the second fastest algorithm followed by *TPL-2* which is more than 10 times faster than *MinSD* and 32 times faster than Cultural algorithm. In summary, *TPL-2* performs well by giving teams with low *Diameter* and LD costs as well as having low execution time.

Table 2: Comparison of the proposed algorithms against algorithms in the literature with respect to the processing time for an average of 10 runs for an instance of task size $|T| = 19$ from VLDB network. The best result is in boldface, second best is italicized.

Algorithm	Processing time (s)
TPLRandom	5.98
TPL-1	134.78
TPL-2	26.99
Rarestfirst	**1.61**
Genetic	90.78
MinSD	341.74
Cultural	868.34
MinLD	1465.74

5.6 Limitations

It can be seen from Table 2 that our algorithms minimize more than one communication cost, but are not really faster than *Rarestfirst* algorithm. Hence, there is scope for improvement in the processing time obtained by our algorithms. Since most of the social networks satisfy power law, the strategy of choosing high degree nodes helps both in optimizing computational cost as well as time. We need to reassess our strategy for the networks whose degree distributions do not satisfy power law.

6   Conclusion and Future Work

In this work, we proposed two algorithms *TPLRandom* and *TPLClosest* to solve the Team Formation Problem(TFP). To the best of our knowledge, we are the first to utilize network topology and optimize more than one communication cost to solve the TFP faster and more scalable. Among the three implementations of proposed algorithms *TPL-1, TPL-2* of *TPLClosest* and *TPLRandom, TPL-2* performs best with respect to all the three communication costs. *Rarestfirst* algorithm is the fastest in the literature but does not optimize other than *Diameter* distance. As given in Table 2, the processing time for a task size 19, *TPLRandom* and *TPL-2* took 5.98 s and 26.99 s respectively that are next best after the fastest *Rarestfirst* algorithm that has taken 1.61 s.

To show the scalability, we experimented with our best *TPL-2* algorithm on different orders of networks. Figure 8 shows that the *TPL-2* algorithm scales well. Further, on one of the largest DBLP network with 32477 nodes and 115938 edges for a tasksize 16, *TPL-2* could complete in 50 min where as *Genetic, MinSD, Cultural, MinLD* could complete in 1 h, 1 h 46 min, 2 h 51 min, and 6 h 28 min respectively. There is still scope for improvement in speeding up of the proposed algorithms that could be our future work.

In future, it will be interesting to repeat the experimentation for datasets other than DBLP like Bibsonomy, IMDB, Stackoverflow, GitHub etc. Exploring other variants of team formation problems like capacitated TF, TF with personnel cost, TF with budget constraints, etc. will extend the understanding of TFP.

References

1. Anagnostopoulos, A., Becchetti, L., Castillo, C., Gionis, A., Leonardi, S.: Power in unity: forming teams in large-scale community systems. In: Proceedings of the 19th ACM International Conference on Information and Knowledge Management, pp. 599–608 (2010)
2. Anagnostopoulos, A., Becchetti, L., Castillo, C., Gionis, A., Leonardi, S.: Online team formation in social networks. In: Proceedings of the 21st International Conference on World Wide Web, pp. 839–848 (2012)
3. Berktaş, N., Yaman, H.: A branch-and-bound algorithm for team formation on social networks. INFORMS J. Comput. **33**(3), 1162–1176 (2021)
4. Bredereck, R., Chen, J., Hüffner, F., Kratsch, S.: Parameterized complexity of team formation in social networks. Theoret. Comput. Sci. **717**, 26–36 (2018)
5. Dean, E.: Project Management Statistics: 45 Stats You Can't Ignore. Business2Community (2023). https://www.business2community.com/statistics/project-management-statistics-45-stats-you-cant-ignore-02168819
6. Fathian, M., Saei-Shahi, M., Makui, A.: A new optimization model for reliable team formation problem considering experts' collaboration network. IEEE Trans. Eng. Manage. **64**(4), 586–593 (2017)
7. Gad, A.F.: Pygad: an intuitive genetic algorithm python library (2021)
8. Georgara, A., Rodríguez-Aguilar, J., Sierra, C.: Allocating teams to tasks: an anytime heuristic competence-based approach. In: Baumeister, D., Rothe, J. (eds.) Multi-agent Systems, pp. 152–170. Springer, Cham (2022)
9. Gupta, T.: (25) 30 Best Project Management Statistics | LinkedIn (2024). https://www.linkedin.com/pulse/30-best-project-management-statistics-tirtha-gupta-e6fkf. Accessed 26 June 2024

10. Kargar, M., An, A.: Discovering top-k teams of experts with/without a leader in social networks. In: Proceedings of the 20th ACM International Conference on Information and Knowledge Management, pp. 985–994 (2011)
11. Kargar, M., An, A., Zihayat, M.: Efficient bi-objective team formation in social networks. In: Machine Learning and Knowledge Discovery in Databases: European Conference, ECML PKDD 2012, Bristol, 24–28 September 2012. Proceedings, Part II 23, pp. 483–498 (2012)
12. Kargar, M., Zihayat, M., An, A.: Finding affordable and collaborative teams from a network of experts. In: Proceedings of the 2013 SIAM International Conference on Data Mining, pp. 587–595 (2013)
13. Kashyap, V.: Experts Thoughts on Team Collaboration Strategy That Helped Them Save Projects From Failing. ProofHub (2024). https://www.proofhub.com/articles/team-collaboration-strategy
14. Lappas, T., Liu, K., Terzi, E.: Finding a team of experts in social networks. In: Proceedings of the 15th ACM SIGKDD International Conference on Knowledge Discovery and Data Mining, pp. 467–476 (2009)
15. Majumder, A., Datta, S., Naidu, K.: Capacitated team formation problem on social networks. In: Proceedings of the 18th ACM SIGKDD International Conference on Knowledge Discovery and Data Mining, pp. 1005–1013 (2012)
16. Muniz, M., Flamand, T.: A column generation approach for the team formation problem. Comput. Oper. Res. **161**, 106406 (2024)
17. Niveditha, M., Swetha, G., Poornima, U., Senthilkumar, R.: A genetic approach for tri-objective optimization in team formation. In: 2016 Eighth International Conference on Advanced Computing (ICoAC), pp. 123–130 (2017)
18. Rehman, M.Z., et al.: A novel state space reduction algorithm for team formation in social networks. PLoS One **16**(12) (2021)
19. Selvarajah, K., Kobti, Z., Kargar, M.: Cultural algorithms for cluster hires in social networks. Procedia Comput. Sci. **170**, 514–521 (2020)
20. Selvarajah, K., Zadeh, P.M., Kargar, M., Kobti, Z.: Identifying a team of experts in social networks using a cultural algorithm. Procedia Comput. Sci. **151**, 477–484 (2019)
21. Selvarajah, K., Zadeh, P.M., Kobti, Z., Palanichamy, Y., Kargar, M.: A unified framework for effective team formation in social networks. Expert Syst. Appl. **177**, 114886 (2021)
22. Teng, Y.C., Wang, J.Z., Huang, J.L.: Team formation with the communication load constraint in social networks. In: Trends and Applications in Knowledge Discovery and Data Mining, pp. 125–136. Springer, Cham (2014)
23. Wang, X., Zhao, Z., Ng, W.: A comparative study of team formation in social networks. In: Renz, M., Shahabi, C., Zhou, X., Cheema, M.A. (eds.) DASFAA 2015. LNCS, vol. 9049, pp. 389–404. Springer, Cham (2015). https://doi.org/10.1007/978-3-319-18120-2_23
24. Wi, H., Oh, S., Mun, J., Jung, M.: A team formation model based on knowledge and collaboration. Expert Syst. Appl. **36**(5), 9121–9134 (2009)

InVideo Search: Scene Description Clustering and Integrating Image and Audio Captioning for Enhanced Video Search

Almira Asif Khan[1], Muhammed[1], Asher Mathews Shaji[1], Devika Sujith[1], Aneesh G. Nath[1(✉)], and Sandeep S. Udmale[2]🄳

[1] Department of Computer Science and Engineering, TKM College of Engineering, Kollam, Kerala, India
aneeshgnath@tkmce.ac.in
[2] Department of Computer Engineering and Information Technology, Veermata Jijabai Technological Institute (VJTI), Mumbai 400019, Maharashtra, India
ssudmale@it.vjti.ac.in

Abstract. In the digital era, the vast amount of long videos highlights the need for an advanced system to efficiently find specific segments based on text descriptions. The proposed solution aims to develop a video content retrieval system by utilizing established tools in video analysis, image/video captioning, and information retrieval. The work is organized into three modules: Keyframe extraction, Captioning, and Query-based searching. Our primary focus is on effectively identifying key elements within these videos, achieving a semantic understanding of these videos in the form of captions, and establishing precise matches of user queries. In short, users input descriptive text prompts, and the application, equipped with pre-trained models, promptly and accurately identifies and retrieves the video segments. This application carries significant potential across various domains, from enabling efficient scene location in movies to helping extract knowledge from educational lectures. Furthermore, this research fundamentally departs from conventional video search methods that heavily rely on metadata or manually assigned tags, which often fall short of capturing the nuances of video content. This work also focuses on a multimodal captioning strategy to integrate more semantic content. Clustering of captions was also incorporated to improve search performance in the case of long videos. This approach allows us to deliver a robust and efficient solution, taking advantage of the extensive knowledge and research underlying these established technologies. Beyond the immediate applications, this research has broader applications in fields like natural language understanding, multimedia analysis, and information retrieval.

Keywords: Clustering · Keyframe extraction · Natural language processing · Video content retrieval system

© The Author(s), under exclusive license to Springer Nature Switzerland AG 2025
Q. Bramas et al. (Eds.): ICDCIT 2025, LNCS 15507, pp. 195–208, 2025.
https://doi.org/10.1007/978-3-031-81404-4_15

1   Introduction

The digital landscape overflows with video content. Within this seemingly bound-less expanse, navigating to a specific scene feels like searching for a needle in a digital haystack. Traditional search methods, rely on tags and metadata and fail to capture the semantic relationships within video content [1]. We imagine a future where you can simply talk about the scene you want - like a car chase in a long movie, a teacher saying something important and precisely retrieving the desired segment.

The major objectives of this paper include:

– Bridge the Semantic Gap: This paper aims to bridge the semantic gap between user intent and video content through the development of advanced natu-ral language processing models and video analysis techniques. These models go beyond simple keyword matching to understand the deeper meaning and context of user queries, including subtle emotional cues and underlying goals. Simultaneously, it analyzes large videos to automatically extract key elements such as objects, actions, and emotions, along with their relationships and temporal dynamics. The users can locate exact moments within videos with exceptional accuracy and efficiency by generating a semantic description of the video.
– Enhance Retrieval Accuracy: This approach utilizes advanced NLP models to understand the meaning behind user queries by taking into consideration the context and possible ambiguities that can exist.
– Pinpoint precise moments in vast videos, boosting productivity: By narrow-ing down specific moments accurately and efficiently, we empower users to navigate large video datasets with minimal time investment. This novel app-roach transcends traditional search methods, offering significant productivity gains across diverse domains, including research, education, and marketing activities.

Content-based video retrieval (CBVR) has become much relevant in our world where video content is everywhere. Traditional text-based search methods struggle with the complex nature of videos. They often fail to capture the com-plete meaning of the content. CBVR addresses this challenge by automatically analyzing the visual and audio features of videos, enabling retrieval based on the actual content. The advancements in deep learning and natural language processing (NLP) are helping the evolution of CBVR. Deep learning models are capable of extracting high-level semantic features from videos. Capturing not just objects and actions but also emotions and even the overall theme of the video [1, 18]. By combining the advantages of deep learning and NLP, CBVR is on the verge of becoming a truly intelligent system capable of understanding the essence of video content and responding to user intent with remarkable accuracy and efficiency.

Video is a combination of moving images along with auditory and textual features and hence to implement CBVR, the whole process is broken down into keyframe extraction, image frame captioning and text prompt matching using

NLP techniques [18]. Although not extensively explored in past research, frame sampling techniques are now recognised and essential to any CBVR approach. An automatic scene segmentation method for the television series dataset based on the grouping of adjacent shots and relying on a combination of multimodal neural features is proposed in [3]. Extracting keyframes has been the centre focus of many works. The authors of [10] too developed an innovative and intelligent approach for automatically generating summaries of large and diverse video libraries. Ongoing research is continuously improving the accuracy and effectiveness of this framework, paving the way for more intelligent and user-centric video summarization systems [2]. During the initial phase of development in computer vision technology, prime focus was given to image captioning. A generative model for automatic image captioning based on a deep recurrent architecture that combines recent advances in computer vision and machine translation is presented in [16] and that method can be used to generate natural sentences describing an image. The model [1] is trained to maximize the likelihood of the target description sentence given the training image. Similarly, other milestones in the domain of image captioning were achieved with the introduction of ReFormer which is discussed in detail in [17]. It follows a different approach to image captioning by introducing a novel architecture relational transformer to generate features with relation information embedded and to explicitly express the pairwise relationships between objects in the image, thus enabling a more semantic form of image description. Combining the above-discussed domains, the development right now focuses on an effective combination of video segmentation, indexing and caption generation that counters the limitations of traditional image captioning techniques. The approaches to extract keyframes with the inclusion of more semantic data and partial caption generation were discussed in [14,15]. While [14] uses semantic grouping network (SGN), [15] makes use of vector motion-based signatures to describe the visual content and uses machine learning techniques to extract keyframes for rapid browsing and efficient video indexing, most efficient for a larger database.

The most important aspect of the text-based CBVR is covered in the research carried out in [9,13] and [10,13] focuses on question-answer pair for showing prompt-based results and [5] focuses on a part of the speech guidance module and a multimodal-based image captioning model to enhance the lexical diversity of deep learning. These approaches are by far the most efficient and compatible with the models under research and development as they blend in semantic understanding of video data with larger lexical knowledge. The next pivotal step in enhancing the semantic understanding of a video lies in leveraging audio data. By extracting audio from video shots, captions can be generated to describe scenes, providing a more comprehensive depiction of the content. Audio captioning utilizes advanced methods covered in [7] to analyze and interpret auditory information, such as recurrent neural networks (RNNs). These models, like the one proposed in [11], use RNNs that have proven effective in generating accurate captions from audio inputs. Audio captions contribute significantly to the semantic richness of the video content by incorporating auditory cues, thus complementing visual descriptions and offering a more holistic understanding of the scenes.

The CBVR technology holds immense potential for unlocking the wealth of information hidden within video data. However, current CBVR systems face limitations that hinder their performance and widespread adoption. These limitations can be broadly categorized into three areas: feature representation, search efficiency and scalability, and user interaction and relevance evaluation. Challenges related to feature representation include the semantic gap between low-level features and high-level semantic concepts, the limited feature set often neglecting valuable information in audio and textual components, and the domain specificity of feature extraction and retrieval methods. Additionally, limitations in search efficiency and scalability arise from the computational cost of feature extraction, indexing, and similarity search algorithms, the high dimensionality of extracted feature vectors, and the inability to handle dynamic video content effectively. Finally, limitations in user interaction and relevance evaluation stem from the difficulty of formulating effective queries, the lack of robust relevance assessment techniques, and the absence of personalization features in most CBVR systems.

Addressing these limitations is crucial for realizing the full potential of CBVR technology. Ongoing research efforts focus on developing more robust and semantic feature representations, improving search efficiency and scalability, and enhancing user interaction and relevance evaluation. By overcoming these limitations and integrating advances in artificial intelligence, CBVR technology promises to revolutionize the way we interact with and unlock the vast potential of video data.

This work uniquely addresses the challenge of in-video search by implementing a system that directly facilitates query-based retrieval of specific video segments-an innovative approach that surpasses conventional solutions, which are often limited to metadata or tag-based methods and struggle to capture the nuanced, content-rich nature of video data.

The rest of the paper is organized as follows: The proposed framework is described in Sect. 2. The experiments and results are included in the Sect. 3 which provides the details of the experimental settings, data collection process, and the analysis of the results. The Sect. 4 gives the concluding remarks.

2   Proposed Method

The proposed approach in this paper can be primarily divided into the below stages (Fig. 1):

- For each identified shot, a **Keyframe extraction** process will be employed to generate representative frames for each shot containing the essence of the respective shot.
- Subsequently, employing **Image captioning techniques**, captions will be generated for each keyframe, aiming to describe the visual content present.

Methods to increase the quality of generated captions and make them more context-based, such as the multimodal approach, need to be explored.

- Leveraging **Similarity search methodologies**, these generated captions will then be compared with the user's query to identify the most relevant keyframe(s).
- The correspondence between the identified keyframes and their respective shots will provide users with direct access to the relevant segments within the video, effectively addressing the challenge of precise content retrieval.

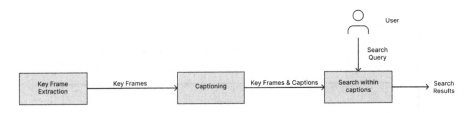

Fig. 1. Working of the project

2.1   Keyframe Extraction

A video is composed of frames, which are organized into shots, and shots are grouped into scenes as shown in Fig. 2. The module focuses on detecting scene cuts, which are points in the video where there is a significant change in content between adjacent frames. Each detected scene cut marks the beginning of a new scene, representing a transition from one continuous sequence of shots to another.

The key frame extraction from videos involves comparing content differences between frames using colour and intensity information in the HSV colour space. This method triggers a scene cut when the difference between adjacent frames exceeds a specified threshold. The method employs various components, each weighted based on their significance in detecting scene changes. This approach excels in detecting fast cuts, setting it apart from methods that primarily focus on identifying slow fades. These steps are detailed in Fig. 3.

- **Frame score calculation**: The method calculates the frame score using the mean pixel distance between the current frame and the previous frame. This is done separately for each component, considering the unique characteristics of hue, saturation, luma, and edges.
- The method utilizes the following components for calculating the frame score:
    1. Delta Hue (ΔH): Represents the difference between pixel hue values of adjacent frames.
    2. Delta Saturation (ΔS): Measures the difference between pixel saturation values of adjacent frames.

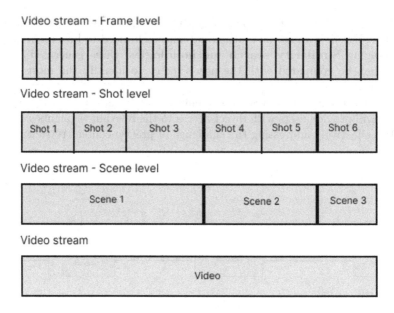

Fig. 2. Structure of a video

3. Delta Luma (ΔL): Captures the difference in pixel luma (brightness) values of adjacent frames.
4. Delta Edges (ΔE): Quantifies the difference between calculated edges of adjacent frames

   The frame score (FS) is calculated using the weighted sum of these components: The formula for FS is given by Eq. (1):

$$FS = \frac{\sum_i (C_i \times W_i)}{\sum_i W_i} \tag{1}$$

   where C_i represents some values and W_i represents weights.

- **Thresholding and Scene Cut Detection**: A user-defined threshold (T) is applied to the frame score. If the frame score exceeds the threshold and a minimum scene length requirement is met, a scene cut is detected, marking the beginning of a new scene.
- **Edge Detection**: The method incorporates edge detection using the Canny algorithm on the luma channel of the frame. The edges are dilated to reduce noise, improving robustness against noise and slow camera movement.

2.2 Captioning

The Image captioning is done using an encoder-transformer approach. The image data is encoded using an image encoder, extracting rich visual features, which is then be passed into a transformer model. This transformer model, leveraging its

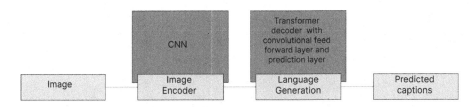

Fig. 3. Steps for Image Captioning

self-attention mechanism and contextual understanding, generates descriptive captions for the images. These steps are detailed in Fig. 4.

Audio in a video segment may frequently carry crucial data that visuals alone may not convey. Hence, capturing these audio cues in the captioning module is necessary to accurately depict the underlying plot. Multimodal captioning seeks to provide a thorough description of a video by including both visual and audio elements.

In the **Audio captioning** part, the audio portion of the video is divided into clips. Each audio clip is passed through an audio encoder, which generates audio embeddings, similar to image embeddings. The audio embeddings are then fed into a transformer. Similar to the image captioning system, the transformer here pays attention to different parts of the audio embedding sequence to generate a caption that describes the audio content.

The CoNeTTE [12] model for audio captioning is used in this project. It utilizes a deep neural network with an encoder-decoder architecture. The encoder part of the model produces frame-level audio embeddings, and the decoder predicts the next word according to the previous ones and the audio representation. The model outputs give the probabilities of the next word that are compared with the ground truth next word using a standard Cross-Entropy (CE) loss.

The video captions and audio captions are then joined together using a large language model (LLM). The LLM can combine the video captions and the audio captions into a single, coherent caption that describes both the visual and auditory content of the video.

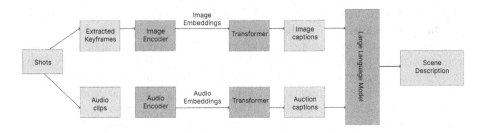

Fig. 4. Multimodal approach to Captioning

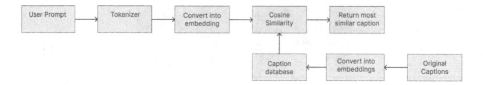

Fig. 5. Steps for Searching within Captions

2.3   Search Within the Captions

The method includes tokenization, bidirectional encoder representations from transformers (BERT) [6] embeddings, and cosine similarity calculation to facilitate efficient keyframe retrieval based on semantic similarity with user prompts (Fig. 5).

- Embedding and Indexing: Along with raw text captions, precompute and store the embeddings for each caption in the database. This enhances efficiency during the similarity search and retrieval steps. To prepare for efficient retrieval, embeddings are generated for each original caption using a robust embedding method such as BERT. Tokenization is performed using the BERT tokenizer, transforming user prompts and captions into sequences of tokens. The BERT embeddings are then computed, capturing semantic information.
- Similarity checking and retrieval: In the similarity-checking phase, a user-provided query caption undergoes seamless embedding using the same methodology applied to the original captions, ensuring a consistent representation in the embedding space. This unified approach sets the stage for efficient similarity assessments.

Caption Clustering for Performance Enhancement. Searching through the subtitles of each movie in a large collection can be both computationally demanding and time-intensive, especially with longer videos. Clustering helps reduce the search space by grouping similar videos, allowing searches to focus on the most relevant clusters first, which significantly speeds up the process and makes it more scalable.

Our approach uses K-means clustering to improve search performance in high-dimensional spaces through centroid-based partitioning. Each cluster's centroid represents the average position of caption embeddings, enabling efficient nearest-neighbor searches to quickly identify clusters relevant to a query. This clustering structure supports adaptive search, where clusters closest to the query embedding are prioritized over others, thus optimizing computational resources. This approach not only accelerates the search process but also retains semantic coherence within clusters, ensuring both rapid and accurate retrieval across large-scale video datasets (Fig. 6).

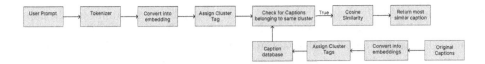

Fig. 6. Incorporating clustering into Search module

3   Experiments and Result Discussions

3.1   Experimental Settings

In the preprocessing phase of the video analysis project, a method to identify significant changes in scenes throughout our video files and to attain keyframes was used. This step was important for getting to the most important parts of the video and improving our analysis. Out of the 10,070 frames in the video, 132 keyframes where major scene changes occurred, which allowed us to identify most relevant segments of the video.

To achieve this, first, the video was loaded and set up a system to manage and analyze it. A technique that detects changes in visual content to determine where scenes begin and end was used, which processed the video and identified the frames where these significant changes took place.

After processing, a list of these key scenes, including the specific frames where each scene starts and ends was obtained. This information was then displayed, which helped us concentrate on the most important moments of the video. This approach helped narrow down the analysis by focusing on the scenes where the most noticeable changes occurred, making it easier to review and interpret the key parts of the video.

In the image captioning module of our project, we conducted testing across varieties of English-language films, over a wide range of genres such as action, drama, comedy and sci-fi. To prepare the dataset of movie frames, we implemented a processes that includes essential augmentation techniques-such as rotation, scaling, and flipping- in order to diversify the dataset and enhance model robustness. Additionally, frames were cropped to focus on relevant visual regions, eliminating extraneous content. This meticulous approach ensures that the model trains on targeted visual information which optimizing its ability to generate accurate and contextually relevant captions.

Furthermore, during the process of storing captions in the database, several data-cleaning measures were implemented. Specifically, any extraneous white spaces are trimmed and any unrecognized or non-standard characters from the captions are removed.

In the preprocessing phase for audio captioning, a critical step involved cleaning audio data to improve the quality and accuracy of the subsequent captioning process. Audio signals often contain various types of noise-such as background chatter, static, and other extraneous sounds-that can interfere with the effectiveness of captioning algorithms. To address this issue, a comprehensive noise reduction strategy was implemented.

By meticulously cleaning the audio data, the quality of the input for the captioning algorithms was significantly enhanced, thereby improving the precision and reliability of the generated captions. This preprocessing step was fundamental in achieving high-quality audio captioning and ensuring that the captions accurately reflect the spoken content of the audio.

In addition to the preprocessing steps, advanced fuzzy matching techniques were employed to refine the selection of captions. Fuzzy methods were utilized to handle the inherent variability and imperfections in textual data. By leveraging algorithms designed to measure similarity between strings, it was able to identify and extract the most appropriate captions from a pool of potential candidates. This resulted in effectively matching the captions with varying degrees of similarity and accuracy, ensuring that the final captions were the most contextually relevant and coherent. The application of fuzzy matching not only improved the precision of caption retrieval but also enhanced the overall quality and consistency of the captioning process.

3.2   Performance Evaluation of the Captioning Module

In evaluating the performance of a captioning module, we use the performance evaluation metrics BLEU (B), ROUGE (R), and METEOR (M) [4]. The BLEU score evaluates the quality of the generated text, known as the candidate, by comparing it to a set of reference texts. The METEOR score is a metric for assessing machine translation by comparing it to human translations. It evaluates the translation's accuracy and fluency while considering the word order. The ROUGE score is a collection of metrics designed to assess the quality of summaries and translations by comparing them to reference texts. For instance, it has been observed that incorporating audio captions results in a 0.12-point improvement in the BLEU score. These findings indicate that audio captions effectively supplement visual data, enhancing the overall quality of the generated captions without introducing inconsistencies (Table 1).

Table 1. Performance Evaluation

Modalities	Values		
	B	M	R
V	14.39	29.51	40.79
V+A	14.51	43.44	47.63

By incorporating details such as facial expressions, vocal tone, and the content of speech, captions generated through this approach offer a more comprehensive understanding of the scene. This is exemplified in Fig. 7, where the caption not only describes the woman's posture and the presence of running water ("Seated at the table with a plate of food in front of her," "The sound of running water adds a dynamic and refreshing element to the scene") but also captures her animated speech and enthusiasm ("speaking animatedly about a topic," "Her voice is expressive and filled with enthusiasm"). This results in a more vivid and engaging portrayal of the video content.

3.3   Comparison with State-of-the-Art Methods for Captioning

We selected Shot2Story as a state-of-the-art baseline for comparison because it shares our objective of enhancing semantic video understanding through detailed shot-level captions and summaries. However, while Shot2Story focuses primarily on summarizing and understanding video narratives across multiple shots, our approach uniquely aims to enable precise, query-based retrieval of specific video segments, integrating image and audio captioning to directly address in-video search-a capability that goes beyond Shot2Story's summarization-focused framework.

In this section, a comparative analysis of the proposed method against another captioning model referred to as "Shot2Story" [8] is presented. The comparison is based on three widely used evaluation metrics: BLEU, METEOR, and ROUGE. The table below summarizes the performance of both models (Table 2).

Table 2. Comparison of BLEU, METEOR, and ROUGE scores for different methods.

Method	BLEU	METEOR	ROUGE
Shot2Story	18.8	24.8	39.0
Ours	14.51	43.44	47.63

Although Short2Story achieves a higher BLEU score, which indicates better precision in matching n-grams with reference captions, our method significantly outperforms both METEOR and ROUGE scores. The higher METEOR score reflects our model's superior ability to capture the semantic meaning of the reference captions, incorporating content relevance. Additionally, the superior ROUGE score demonstrates our model's effectiveness in maintaining the essential content and structure of the references. Therefore, while [8] excels in lexical precision, our method offers a more robust overall performance, especially in preserving semantic accuracy.

3.4   Performance Enhancement on Using Clustering Methods

The implementation of clustering techniques has significantly enhanced search speed within the video datasets. Empirical evidence indicates that the search time was reduced from 0.0335 s to a mere 0.0042 s, representing a remarkable 9.8x improvement. This substantial reduction in processing time illustrates the efficacy of clustering in efficiently navigating large video datasets. By focusing on relevant clusters, the algorithm effectively narrows down the search space, thereby expediting the retrieval process. This improvement not only demonstrates the practical benefits of clustering in managing extensive datasets but also underscores its potential to optimize computational resources and enhance user experience in real-time applications.

Image Caption: there is a women sitting at a table with a plate of food

Audio Caption: a woman is speaking about something while water is running in the background

Scene Description: Seated at the table with a plate of food in front of her, a woman leans forward, speaking animatedly about a topic. Her voice is expressive and filled with enthusiasm. In the background, the sound of running water adds a dynamic and refreshing element to the scene, creating a sense of activity and movement.

Image Caption: a close up of a man with a white hair and a black jacket

Audio Caption: a car engine is started and drives away

Scene Description: camera zooms into a man with white hair wearing black jacket with a serious and focused expression, scene unfolds with sound of car engine starting, reverberates, growing louder, vehicle drives away creates sense movement energy contrasting stillness in man's close shot.

Image Caption: someone is writing in a notebook with a pencil

Audio Caption: a man is speaking

Scene Description: scene captures someone writing notebook pencil scratch creating rhythmic sound meanwhile man's voice is heard speaking words adding depth atmosphere. Audio description notes man engaging in conversation likely sharing thoughts.

Fig. 7. Examples of Generated Captions

4 Conclusion

The proposed video content retrieval system successfully integrates keyframe extraction, captioning, and text-based search modules. We leveraged established techniques within each module, achieving efficient video analysis and retrieval based on user queries. Notably, the captioning module exhibited a significant performance improvement (9.8x) compared to existing models. Additionally, text clustering within the search module further enhanced retrieval efficiency, particularly for long videos.

This system departs from conventional video search methods reliant on metadata or manual tags. By focusing on semantic understanding through captions, the system offers a more robust and nuanced approach. This research also holds promise for advancements in natural language understanding, multimedia analysis, and information retrieval. Beyond the immediate applications, the methodologies and insights gained here contribute significantly to content-based video retrieval.

Acknowledgment. This work was supported by the Centre of Excellence in Artificial Intelligence (CoE AI), Veermata Jijabai Technological Institute (VJTI), Mumbai, India.

References

1. Apostolidis, E., Adamantidou, E., Metsai, A.I., Mezaris, V., Patras, I.: Video summarization using deep neural networks: a survey. Proc. IEEE **109**(11), 1838–1863 (2021)
2. Bae, J.W., Lee, S.H., Kim, W.Y., Seong, J.H., Seo, D.H.: Image captioning model using part-of-speech guidance module for description with diverse vocabulary. IEEE Access **10**, 45219–45229 (2022)
3. Berhe, A., Barras, C., Guinaudeau, C.: Video scene segmentation of tv series using multimodal neural features. Series-Int. J. TV Serial Narratives **5**(1), 59–68 (2019)
4. Blagec, K., Dorffner, G., Moradi, M., Ott, S., Samwald, M.: A global analysis of metrics used for measuring performance in natural language processing. arXiv preprint arXiv:2204.11574 (2022)
5. Chaquet, J.M., Carmona, E.J., Fernández-Caballero, A.: A survey of video datasets for human action and activity recognition. Comput. Vis. Image Underst. **117**(6), 633–659 (2013)
6. Devlin, J., Chang, M.W., Lee, K., Toutanova, K.: Bert: pre-training of deep bidirectional transformers for language understanding (2019). https://arxiv.org/abs/1810.04805
7. Xiao, F., Zhu, Q., Guan, J., Wang, W.: Enhancing audio retrieval with attention-based encoder for audio feature representation. In: EUSIPCO 2023 (2023)
8. Han, M., Yang, L., Chang, X., Wang, H.: Shot2story20k: a new benchmark for comprehensive understanding of multi-shot videos. arXiv preprint arXiv:2311.17043 (2023)
9. Iyer, R.R., Parekh, S., Mohandoss, V., Ramsurat, A., Raj, B., Singh, R.: Content-based video indexing and retrieval using CORR-LDA. arXiv preprint arXiv:1602.08581 (2016)
10. Jadon, S., Jasim, M.: Unsupervised video summarization framework using keyframe extraction and video skimming. In: 2020 IEEE 5th International Conference on Computing Communication and Automation (ICCCA), pp. 140–145. IEEE (2020)
11. Drossos, K., Adavanne, S., Virtanen, T.: Automated audio captioning with recurrent neural networks. In: IEEE Workshop on Applications of Signal Processing to Audio and Acoustics (WASPAA). IEEE (2017)
12. Labb, E., Pellegrini, T., Pinquier, J., et al.: Conette: an efficient audio captioning system leveraging multiple datasets with task embedding. IEEE/ACM Trans. Audio Speech Lang. Process. (2024)

13. Peng, M., Wang, C., Gao, Y., Shi, Y., Zhou, X.D.: Multilevel hierarchical network with multiscale sampling for video question answering. arXiv preprint arXiv:2205.04061 (2022)
14. Ryu, H., Kang, S., Kang, H., Yoo, C.D.: Semantic grouping network for video captioning. In: Proceedings of the AAAI Conference on Artificial Intelligence, vol. 35, pp. 2514–2522 (2021)
15. Saoudi, E.M., Jai-Andaloussi, S.: A distributed content-based video retrieval system for large datasets. J. Big Data **8**(1), 1–26 (2021)
16. Vinyals, O., Toshev, A., Bengio, S., Erhan, D.: Show and tell: a neural image caption generator. In: Proceedings of the IEEE Conference on Computer Vision and Pattern Recognition, pp. 3156–3164 (2015)
17. Yang, X., Liu, Y., Wang, X.: Reformer: the relational transformer for image captioning. In: Proceedings of the 30th ACM International Conference on Multimedia, pp. 5398–5406 (2022)
18. Yoon, H., Han, J.H.: Content-based video retrieval with prototypes of deep features. IEEE Access **10**, 30730–30742 (2022)

Does Data Balancing Impact Stutter Detection and Classification?

Ashita Batra$^{(\boxtimes)}$ ⓘ, Pratyush Shrivastava ⓘ, and Pradip K. Das ⓘ

Indian Institute of Technology Guwahati, Guwahati 781039, India
{b.ashita,pratyush.civ21,pkdas}@iitg.ac.in

Abstract. Stuttering, a speech impediment that significantly impacts an individual's personality and daily life, is a critical research area requiring technological solutions. Therefore, bringing our attention, we analyzed speech utterances of people who stutter, using recordings from the publicly available Sep-28k dataset, which consists of natural conversations from podcasts. A major focus has been put on analyzing the fact that data imbalance plays a role in learning the characteristics of a speech utterance. We have used a sampling technique by considering the middle value of samples calculated from the minority and the majority class and this serves as a combination of up-sampling and down-sampling. This helps us to avoid bias in the class-wise characteristic learning of the model.

The proposed approach focuses on two feature extraction techniques, specifically Mel-Frequency Cepstral Coefficients (MFCCs), del-del MFCC and a comprehensive analysis using the openSMILE toolkit, selecting only the ComParE2016 features. We conducted a comparative study between various machine learning models like random forest (RF), support vector machine (SVM) and time-delayed neural network (TDNN) using both features. Our findings indicated that the stutter class outperformed the no stutter class by a significant margin for each classifier in binary classification. This prompted us to conduct two experiments: one with all classes and another with only stutter classes. The experimental analysis revealed an average F1-score with del-del MFCC features of 85.38% with RF, 90.10% with SVM when all classes are considered. Furthermore, 93.29% with RF, 93.71% with SVM when only stutter classes are considered. On the contrary, when we use ComParE2016 features we achieve an average accuracy of 86.79% with RF and 87.77% with SVM considering all classes. Whereas, 95.10% with RF, 94.34% with SVM when only stutter classes are considered. When TDNN was used with del-del MFCC, we achieved an accuracy of 79.02% and 92% with ComParE2016, implying better performance because of better feature extraction. It is noteworthy that throughout all the experiments, sound repetition is the best performing class indicating consistency in the learning process. The results achieved through this sampling technique improve the stutter detection and classification by a significant margin.

Keywords: Stuttering · Speech disorder · feature extraction · MFCC · ComParE · TDNN · Sep-28k

© The Author(s), under exclusive license to Springer Nature Switzerland AG 2025
Q. Bramas et al. (Eds.): ICDCIT 2025, LNCS 15507, pp. 209–224, 2025.
https://doi.org/10.1007/978-3-031-81404-4_16

1   Introduction

Around 1% of the world population [1], experience atypical patterns in their speech which unable them to produce fluent speech. Stuttering is a neuro-speech disorder which is characterised by pauses/disruptions in the "normal flow of speech" [2]. It is experienced because of tension in the facial muscles, jaw or throat. The disruptions can be in form of exaggerating a character in a word like helllllllo (prolongation), repeating various sounds like s-s-sunlight (sound repetition) or words like stop-stop the car (word repetition), big pauses in between sentences or words (mostly visible through videos) like butter-break-scotch (block) and filler words like uhhh, ummmm, hmmmm etc. (interjections) as described in Table 1. All of these examples are various stutter types. At present, there is a need of automatic stuttering detection & classification (ASDC) in providing individual specific therapies, intelligibility assessment and recovery over a period of time. But ASDC remains a challenge due to the unavailability of enough data and heterogeneous stutter types which varies individual to individual [8]. The time duration of each stutter type varies for each individual. The major reason being, the size of public datasets available which lacks balanced number of samples for each stutter type like SEP-28k [3] where NoStutter (NS) class has the most number of samples. This is the largest corpus with 28,000 speech samples of individuals who stammer (IWS) containing file-level labelling, consisting of natural conversation from multiple podcasts (freely available). There are many datasets publicly available like Uclass [5] which is a clinical dataset, LibriStutter [6] which is synthetically made dataset from Librispeech corpus [7]. Both these dataset contains word-level transcriptions. Due to diverse nature of the datasets, it becomes difficult to combine all the datasets, to balance the classes and subsequently make a large training corpus. To solve the above mentioned problem in the SEP-28k dataset, the objective of our work revolves around coming up with a solution for balancing the classes in the dataset. This helps to improve the detection & classification performance by a significant margin. This works' major contributions are as follows: observing the effect of balancing the number of samples for each class by using a combination of up-sampling and down-sampling technique, ply multiple feature extraction techniques, analyzes the difference in performance of the model when all the classes (NS, B, P, I, SR, WR) are considered, compared to when only stutter classes are considered (B, P, I, SR, WR). A description of types of stutter is shown in Table 1 and pictorial representation of the same in done in Fig. 1.

The rest of the paper is structured as follows: Sect. 2 focuses on the literature done in previous studies on stuttering detection and classification. Section 3 describes about the dataset used. In Sect. 4, the proposed methodology has been discussed in detail. Section 5 presents the experiment and results analysis. At last, Sects. 6 and 7 contains the conclusion & future work.

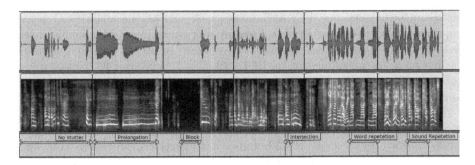

Fig. 1. Speech waveforms and sound spectrograms demonstrating different stutter types of an IWS

Table 1. Description of stutter types

Stuttering Label	Definition and Examples
Prolongation (P)	Stretched syllables. Example: *"S[sss]ee the airplane."*
Block (B)	Pauses or stoppages in speech. Example: *"I am ... so tired!"*
Sound Repetition (SR)	Repeated individual sounds or syllables. Example: *"Look at the [bu-bu-]butterfly."*
Word Repetition (WR)	Repeated words. Example: *"I went [went] there."*
Interjection (I)	Insertion of extra sounds or syllables. Example: *"[Um, uh,] yes we may go!"*

2 Related Work

Much efforts has been done lately to improve the detection of atypical speech like stuttering. As it is not always feasible and affordable to visit the speech language pathologist (SLPs) for keeping track of progress in stuttering from time-to-time. Therefore, ASDC may help SLPs in carrying out the therapy process via application development which automatically detects stuttering, where an IWS has to record their data and do the tasks as mentioned in the application. Post this, a report can be generated by the SLPs to track the progress in their speech. The only constraint in this area is the lack of publicly available data. If there are any datasets available, they are highly imbalanced and of different nature (clinical, natural, synthetic). A review on pathological speech was done in a study [16] covering a variety of atypical speech disorders. In a study, [9] performed four stage syllable repetition identification in stuttered speech which consisted of manual segmentation of stuttered data, feature extraction using MFCC, score matching using DTW and decision logic using SVM. They achieved an accuracy of 93.45%. The dataset consisted of read speech from 15 IWS. A work done by [10] proposed StutterNet architecture which solely relies on acoustic signals exploiting TDNN for capturing the contextual elements of the disfluent speech using only MFCC features on UCLASS dataset. [12] performed spectral features based stutter detection on UCLASS dataset using MFCC, del-del MFCC, pitch and spectral flux to extract dominant feature representation and used multi-layer perceptron for classification achieving an accuracy of 99.2%. In [15], emphasis was put on using a combination on UCLASS [5] & LibriStutter [6] dataset using various machine learning (ML) models, use of sampling technique has also been done which gave an accuracy of 66.46%.

In [11], eight popular ML approaches have been explored for stutter detection on SEP-28k [3] and FluencyBank (FB) [4] datasets. Best performance is achieved using RF with an F1-score of 42% and 34% respectively. Moreover, [13] used SEP-28k and FB dataset for experimentation. Their work included a variety of ML models namely Decision Tree (DT), RF, Gradient boosting, CatBoost and XGBoost. They achieved accuracy in 80s for all the models. A latest work done by [14], explores muti-feature fusion technique using heterogeneous features like pitch, spectral, temporal and ASR based features for SED. MFCC is considered to be common across all the experiments performed for feature extraction and subsequently fused with other features. Their model surpass the state-of -the-art by 4% and 3% in F1-score for SEP-28k and FB respectively. A study done on introducing a therapy based KSoF dataset [17], used ComParE2016 features from OpenSMILE toolkit. They used SVM with gaussain kernel on CompParE features to perform SED.

3   Dataset

3.1   Stuttering in Events Podcast

This is the largest English corpus containing speech samples of IWS with 28,177 samples ($\approx$ 23 h of audio) [3]. The dataset is curated by extracting 3-second clips from natural conversation publicly available podcasts where the host and guest both stutter. It contains five stutter classes, namely B, P, I, SR, WR and a fluent class (NS). File-level labels are assigned to each 3-second file by three annotators who were trained to best find the stuttering event in the audio samples. The dataset contains 56.9% NS, 21.2 % I, 12% B, 10% P, 9.8% WR and 8.3% SR classes in the dataset. The percentage visibly signifies the dominance of NS class in the dataset.

4   Methodology

This section contains a comprehensive analysis of Stuttering event detection (SED) and classification (SEC) using heterogeneous features set. The proposed model primarily consists of finding spectral representation using MFCC, del-MFCC, del-del MFCC and ComParE features using the OpenSMILE toolkit [18]. Random forest (RF) and Support vector machine (SVM) are used to capture feature representation using DT and optimal hyperplane separation in the non-linear data. Time-delay neural networks are used to capture frame-wise contextual information.

Algorithm 1: Training data preparation steps

Input: Audio files, SR = 16000 Hz, WS = 25 ms, HS = 10 ms, n_MFCC
 = 100, ComParE2016=200 out of 6373

Output: Stuttering event detection

1 **Initialize:** del_del_mfcc_data & ComParE as an empty list
2 **for** *each audio file* file.wav *in the input folder* **do**
3   **if** file.wav *is valid* **then**
4   **begin**
5   **Load** the audio file
6   **Skip** the file ($<$1 second)
7   **Extract** Del-Del MFCC features & ComParE from the audio
8   **Compute** and **append** the mean of the extracted features to
         del_del_mfcc_data & ComParE

9 **Normalize** the extracted features
10 **Load and balance** the labels using **Hybrid Sampling**

11 **Train Random Forest (RF) Classifier:**
   – Set n_estimators = 1000, max_depth = 15
   – Perform 10-fold cross-validation
   – **Record** and **store** the classification results

   Train Support Vector Machine (SVM) Classifier:

   – Set C = 10, gamma = 0.01, kernel = rbf
   – Perform 10-fold cross-validation
   – **Record** and **store** the classification results

   Train Time-Delay Neural Network (TDNN) Classifier:
   for *each setting of* include_label_5 *(No Stutter Class) in {True, False}* **do**
     begin
       Load and preprocess the data
       Define and compile the TDNN model:

         – **Conv1D Layer 1:** 64 filters, kernel size 3, ReLU activation
         – **MaxPooling1D Layer 1:** Pool size 2
         – **Conv1D Layer 2:** 128 filters, kernel size 3, ReLU activation
         – **MaxPooling1D Layer 2:** Pool size 2
         – **Flatten Layer**
         – **Dense Layer 1:** 100 units, ReLU activation
         – **Output Dense Layer:** num_classes units, softmax activation

       Train the model for 10 epochs with a batch size of 32
       Evaluate the model and **store** the results

   Generate and print the final classification results including & excluding label
   5 (No Stutter Class)
   return *Final classification results*

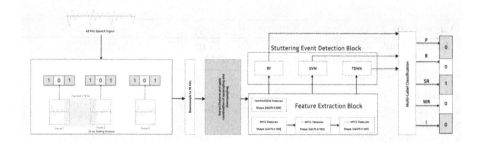

Fig. 2. Proposed Architecture

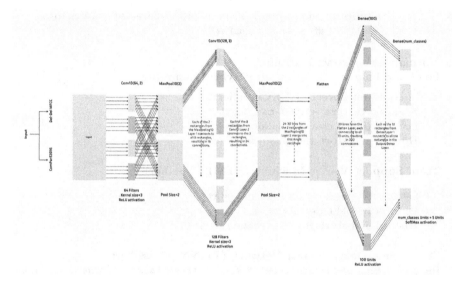

Fig. 3. TDNN Architecture

4.1   Architectural Overview

The proposed architecture overview has been demonstrated in the Fig. 2. It leverages the use of very high-dimensional-based feature representation using del-del MFCC and ComParE. Then, SED and SEC were subsequently performed using RF and SVM. Further, effectively learn frame-wise spectral features of contextual data using TDNN framework. A detailed description of the architecture is given below.

4.2   Learning Spectral Features with MFCC and ComParE

Auditory-based spectral feature extraction using MFCC has been carried out in this work. It has been proved in the literature that MFCC captures features analogous to human auditory system (HAS). The process involves dividing the signal into short segments called frames, followed by applying hamming window on each frame to avoid discontinuity at the beginning and end of each frame. The magnitude spectrum of the signal is found by converting the signal to frequency domain using Fast Fourier Transform(FFT). Subsequently, the Mel-Filter bank is applied to the frequencies obtained through magnitude spectrum which emulates HAS. Finally, mapping these signals on a quasi-logarithmic frequency scale, which resembles how humans perceive loudness. We have explored the potential of observing minute voice transitions in atypical speech patterns by finding the difference between two consecutive frames, in other words the first derivative of the cepstral coefficients (CC) i.e. del-MFCC which helps in identifying the rate of change in speech. Furthermore, also finding the del-del-MFCC which is the difference between del-MFCCs of two neighbor del-MFCC frames. This helps in identifying how quickly the changes are happening in the del-MFCCs. The delta and delta-delta coefficients are of significant importance in stutter event detection in the speech signal as it helps in finding specific temporal patterns related to different stutter types namely SR, WR, P and B. In our experiment, we have used 100 MFCC coefficients with a window size of 25 ms and hop length of 10 ms.

Computational Paralinguistics Challenge Features using openS-MILE [19,20] has been used to perform features representation for SED. The paralinguistics focuses on those parts of speech which is not verbal like stress, emotion etc. This is the reason why this feature set has been used to find stuttering events from the speech samples of IWS because more stress is directly proportional to more stutter. The ComParE 2016 feature is a large set consisting of 6373 features which includes pitch, skewness, variance, low-level descriptors (LLDs) etc. [19], this makes the feature set highly heterogeneous. Also, it covers multiple speech characteristics namely prosody, voice quality, temporality in the samples. In our experiments, it helps us in finding irregular pitch, stress, disruption in the rhythmic speech and loudness variation. All of these characteristics helps us in efficiently differentiating between stuttered and normal speech. Out of 6373 features, we have used 200 features per sample in our experiments.

4.3 Capture Event Detection Using Decision Trees and Separating Hyperplane

Detection and Classification Stutter Event in a Speech Sample is done using an Ensemble Learning Approach i.e. Random Forest (RF) [21]. It works by constructing multiple DT while training. Each tree is randomly chosen from the data as a subset. Each data point goes through the DT process using random set of features. For each data point, we get a target value like whether prolongation is there in the file or not. If the predicted value is high for prolongation, then it is predicted as prolongation. If the predicted value is low, then it is not predicted as prolongation. Now, similarly the process continues for each data point, if more than half of the data point predict the sample as prolongation, then RF predicts it as prolongation. The voting process helps us understand and provides more transparency in the process of classifying. In our experiment, we have used 1000 DT with a maximum depth of 15.

Detection and Classification Stutter Event in a Speech Sample by Separating Hyperplane i.e. Support Vector Machine (SVM) [22]. It handles non-linear data very well by transforming data points into higher dimensional space where it optimally separates the hyperplane. The hyperplane is chosen in such a way that the distance between the two data points is maximized i.e. the support vectors. For best classifying the non-linear data points, radial basis function (rbf) kernel is widely used. to avoid margin calculation, a slack variable is used to maintain a balance between maximizing the distance between the two data points and classification error. Since, stutter feature representation are a little complex to easily identified by the systems, SVM helps in identifying complex feature set. In our experiment, we have used rbf kernel and gamma value as 0.01.

4.4 Capture Event Detection Using Contextual Information

TDNN is majorly used for capturing the temporal and contextual aspects of speech [23,24]. The number of input features i.e. del-del-MFCC is 100 and ComParE is 200 to learn and extract the temporal aspect of stuttering which are separately fed into the TDNN model as shown in Fig. 3 along with all the hyperparameters. The TDNN architecture contains four time delay layers focusing on contextual frames of [t-2, t+2], {t-2, t, t+2}, {t-3, t, t+3}, {t-4, t, t+4} with dilation of 1, 2, 3, 4. This next layer is a statistical pooling layer to correspondingly account for changes in the frame-level transformation of the temporal context, followed by one fully connected (FC) layers for performing multi-class classification. Every hidden layer uses ReLU activation function and 1-D batch normalization apart from statistical pooling layer.

5   Experiments and Results

This section presents the findings of the experiments performed for carrying out SED. SEP-28k dataset [3] has been used for both training and testing. More emphasis has been put on using a sampling technique which is a combination of up-sampling and down-sampling. This sampling technique helps us in finding the appropriate amount of samples for each class. Thus, avoiding the model bias towards the majority class i.e. NS.

SEP-28k is highly imbalanced dataset as clearly demonstrated in Sect. 3.1. Therefore, it impacts the model performance by learning only the characteristics of the dominant class. It became evident after performing comprehensive same set of experiments on the proposed model. Down-sampling and up-sampling was also performed on the dataset, but it didn't increase the learning characteristics of the model by a significant margin when compared with original experiments.

Thereafter, in order to balance the dataset and preserve the characteristics of all the stutter types, minority and majority class samples are identified. Average

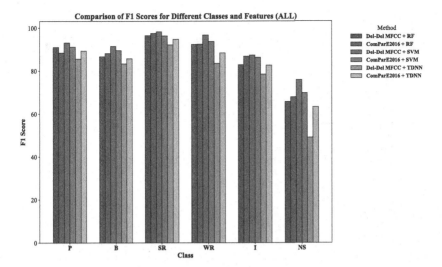

Fig. 4. Comparison of F1-Scores amongst different classes and features including no stutter class.

of these samples is found by dividing these classes by two. It is computed as follows

$$N_{avg} = \frac{N_m + N_M}{2} \tag{1}$$

where N_m is the number of minority samples and N_M is the number of majority samples.

After sampling, we generated 42,528 total samples. Out of which, 7088 samples are used for each of the six classes in experiments.

In this study, six set of experiments are performed to assess and evaluate the SED of stuttered speech by learning spectral features using del-del-MFCC and ComParE. The training data preparation steps are clearly demonstrated in algorithm 1. We have performed a comparative analysis between three different learning techniques namely ensemble learning (RF), machine learning (SVM) and sequence model learning (TDNN).

We performed the experiments in two phases: first phase was aimed to examine whether the proposed model was able to capture stutter classes with no stutter class using binary classification. It was observed that model was able to better capture stutter class characteristics by a significant margin as compared to no stutter class. This motivated us to perform second phase of experiment of multi-class classification. Here, we perform two experiments: one which includes all the classes namely B, P, I, SR, WR, NS and another which contains only stutter classes namely B, P, I, SR, WR. Figure 4 & 5 compares the F1-scores of the experiments and demonstrate which model performs better in which scenario. As evident, del-del MFCC with SVM performs the best when "ALL" the classes are considered the performance slightly differs by a small margin when only stutter classes are considered "MULTI". On the other hand, when we compare class wise

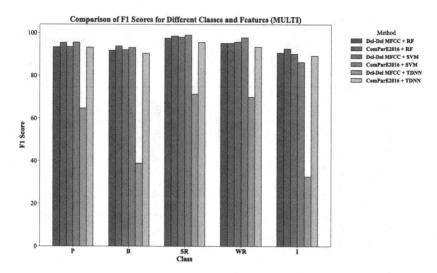

Fig. 5. Comparison of F1-Scores amongst different class and features for only stutter class.

accuracies in all the experiments, SR consistently performs the best irrespective of the model and feature representation being used. This signifies that the rate of change in speech at phoneme and syllable level is captured correctly.

5.1   Model Evaluation

Model's performance has been evaluated in this paper using hold-out and k-fold cross validation. Furthermore, statistical techniques namely F1-score, matthew's correlation coefficient (MCC) and unweighted average recall (UAR) are used for assessing the effectiveness of the model. In 10 fold cross validation, the dataset is randomly segregated into 10 equal sized fold/parts. The model runs for 10 iterations, where in each iteration training and testing both are done using different training and test set. In every iteration, one set is used for testing and rest k-1 are used for training. The results are the average of 10 iterations. The dataset divided into is 80% training and 20% for testing on unseen stuttering samples.

The statistical techniques used for evaluation are:

- *F1-score* represents a balance between correctly predicting false-positives and false-negatives especially in case of imbalanced datasets. It is the weighted average of precision (Pr) and recall (Rc), using the formula

$$\text{F1-Score} = 2 \times \frac{\text{Pr} \times \text{Rc}}{\text{Pr} + \text{Rc}} \qquad (2)$$

- *Matthew's Correlation Coefficient* (MCC) which provides a fair evaluation method for solving data imbalance problems. The values lie in the range -1 to

1, where -1 denotes wrongly predicted values, 0 denotes prediction is random, 1 denotes correctly predicted values. It is computed as

$$\text{MCC} = \frac{(t_p \times t_n) - (f_p \times f_n)}{\sqrt{(t_p + f_p) \times (t_p + f_n) \times (t_n + f_p) \times (t_n + f_n)}} \quad (3)$$

where,

t_p: represents correctly classified true samples,
t_n: represents correctly classified false samples,
f_p: represents wrongly classified false samples,
f_n: represents wrongly classified true samples,

- *Unweighted Average recall* (UAR) takes the average of recall (Rc) for all the classes. Here, unweighted refers to considering all the classes equally regardless of their count. It is calculated as

$$\text{UAR} = \frac{1}{T} \sum_{p=1}^{T} \text{Rc}_p \quad (4)$$

where T represents total number of classes.

Table 2. F1-scores, MCC, and UAR for binary classification in stuttering event detection using RF, SVM, TDNN and del-del MFCC Features with and without hybrid sampling.

Sampling	Method	Stutter	NoStutter	Avg. F1	Avg. MCC	Avg. UAR
WITHOUT	RF	64.28	51.11	59.92	0.16	0.58
	SVM	65.92	54.19	60.12	0.19	0.59
WITH	RF	65.17	71.19	68.19	0.37	0.68
	SVM	60.25	64.18	62.81	0.24	0.62

5.2 Results

The proposed model achieved an exponential increase in the F1-scores, UAR and MCC value with hybrid sampling (which was used to balance the class-wise audio sample of the dataset) and very poor identification without sampling. We have performed experiments in four phases where phase 1 consists of binary classification with and without hybrid sampling (balancing) as shown in to Table 2, in phase 2, results were evaluated without performing sampling as shown in Table 3, in phase 3, results were evaluated using del-del MFCC features with sampling as shown in Table 4, lastly, in phase 4 same experiments were performed using ComParE 2016 feature set as shown in Table 5. The literature

Table 3. F1-scores, MCC, and UAR for stuttering event detection using RF, SVM, TDNN using del-del MFCC Features without hybrid sampling.

Dataset	Method	P	B	SR	WR	I	NS	Avg. F1	Avg. MCC	Avg. UAR
ALL	RF	16.43	13.21	14.25	10.21	10.77	64.69	46.28	0.46	0.17
	SVM	17.63	14.37	18.95	12.22	14.11	64.32	47.22	0.47	0.49
	TDNN	14.28	11.93	13.44	9.34	9.77	63.57	45.26	0.44	0.35
MULTI	RF	24.35	31.42	32.44	23.12	46.14	–	53.57	0.52	0.24
	SVM	30.25	37.51	35.27	27.15	48.21	–	55.67	0.53	0.25
	TDNN	31.43	32.23	25.33	21.36	44.12	–	49.26	0.51	0.23

Table 4. F1-scores, MCC and UAR for stuttering event detection using RF, SVM, TDNN and del-del MFCC Features with hybrid sampling.

Dataset	Method	P	B	SR	WR	I	NS	Avg. F1	Avg. MCC	Avg. UAR
ALL	RF	91.03	86.57	96.45	92.32	82.78	65.67	85.38	0.83	0.86
	SVM	93.12	91.48	98.23	96.65	87.24	75.72	90.10	0.88	0.89
	TDNN	85.48	83.29	92.14	83.43	78.36	48.92	78.60	0.72	0.75
MULTI	RF	93.35	91.76	97.54	95.14	90.65	–	93.29	0.91	0.93
	SVM	93.42	92.11	98.02	95.78	90.22	–	93.71	0.92	0.94
	TDNN	64.63	38.91	71.35	69.89	32.67	–	55.49	0.58	0.60

shows our results are very promising in identifying stutter type when the classes are balanced as evident through the results shown in Table 4 & 5. Referring to Table 4 & 5, when all the classes are considered, using del-del MFCC with RF we achieved an average F1-score of 85.38% where SR performs the best with a score of 96.45% and worst performing class was NS with 65.67% whereas when only stutter classes were included, we observed an increase in the score of each class. The average score increased to 93.29%, with a relative increase of 9.26% considering only stutter classes, which is a significant increase when it comes to detecting atypical speech patterns. SR still gives the best score of 97.54%. When ComParE features were used with RF, a slight increase in the scores was observed when compared to MFCC by a relative margin of 1.65% (ALL), 1.94% (MULTI), considering all classes and only stutter classes respectively. Where SR still performs the best in both cases.

When SVM was used with del-del-MFCC, we observed an average score of 90.10% with all classes and 93.71% with stutter classes. SVM was better able to capture all the stutter classes along with NS, resulting in a relative increase in score of 2.2%, 3.1%, 1.78%, 4.33%, 4.46%, 10.05% for P, B, SR, WR, I, NS respectively. On the other hand, there is no significant difference in RF and SVM performance when only stutter classes are considered. While in ComParE with SVM results much difference was not observed in the class-wise scores. But we observe a significant increase in the score when ComParE was used with TDNN

Table 5. F1-scores, MCC and UAR for stuttering event detection using RF, SVM, TDNN and ComParE2016 Features with hybrid sampling.

Dataset	Method	P	B	SR	WR	I	NS	Avg. F1	Avg. MCC	Avg. UAR
ALL	RF	88.35	88.03	97.50	92.40	86.70	67.80	86.79	0.84	0.87
	SVM	91.15	89.55	96.30	93.70	86.20	69.65	87.77	0.85	0.87
	TDNN	89.27	85.62	94.75	88.29	82.51	63.18	83.93	0.80	0.82
MULTI	RF	95.40	93.80	98.50	95.20	92.60	–	95.10	0.93	0.94
	SVM	95.50	93.15	99.00	97.80	86.25	–	94.34	0.92	0.94
	TDNN	93.18	90.47	95.54	93.47	89.32	–	92.39	0.91	0.92

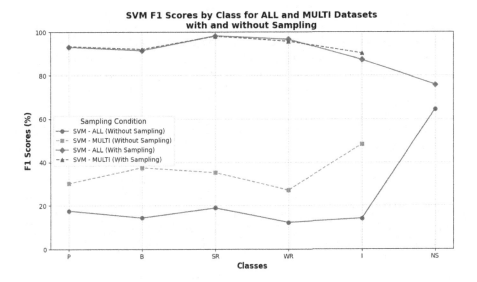

Fig. 6. Comparison of F1-Scores of various classes using del-del MFCC features based on sampling condition.

considering only stutter classes with a relative increase of 63% in the scores indicating that ComParE features aligns effectively with the sequence and context information used by the TDNN. We have also used MCC scores and UAR values, to demonstrate how well is the data aligning with the class samples in determining classes correctly. An overall assessment in all the experiments is that irrespective of the model SR performs the best. This indicates that the stuttering event is learned by the models correctly proving consistency in all results. ComParE 2016 using openSMILE indicate that LLDs can captured phonetic and syllable wise atypicality in the speech along with some modifications in the speech.

It is clearly evident through the results how using data balancing technique helps in better stutter identification. In Fig. 6, best performing classifier i.e. SVM using del-del features shows a comparison between the performance of a classifier with and without data balancing (sampling) technique.

6   Conclusion

This work addresses the imbalanced class problem in the area of stuttering. The problem is addressed by using a hybrid sampling technique, which combines up-sampling and down-sampling and finds a way to handle the bias towards the dominant class in learning the features. By balancing the samples of each class, the attention is given to each class equally. Use of high-dimensional features like ComParE2016, captures the stuttering events very effectively and for equal comparison we kept the MFCC coefficients to 100 per frame. The ComParE2016 feature set focuses on capturing emotions, pitch, loudness or stress, etc., i.e., mainly non-verbal elements. On the other side, del-del-MFCC have been used because they captures the rate of change in speech, which is important for finding stutter type, especially SR or WR. The proposed methodology shows significant improvement in the results in detecting stutter by using data balancing technique.

7   Future Work

The present work can be extended by using data partitioning techniques like leave-one-speaker-out (LOSO) or leave-one-podcast-out (LOPO). This would make the model to be used for multiple purposes. As file-level labeling is given in the dataset, it is not predicted at which instant the stutter is happening in the file. Hence, transcriptions can be provided at which timestamp the stutter takes place. Moreover, transcription of what is spoken in the files is absent in the dataset, manual transcription of the data can be done, making the model's learning process more accurate.

References

1. Al-Banna, A.-K., Edirisinghe, E., Fang, H., Hadi, W.: Stuttering disfluency detection using machine learning approaches. J. Info. Know. Manag. **21**(02) (2022). https://doi.org/10.1142/S0219649222500204
2. A World Health Organization. 2010. ICD-10 Version:2010. http://apps.who.int/classifications/icd10/browse/2010/en#/F98.5. Accessed 23 Feb 2020
3. Lea, C., Mitra, V., Joshi, A., Kajarekar, S., Bigham, J. P.: SEP-28k: a dataset for stuttering event detection from podcasts with people who stutter. In: ICASSP 2021-2021 IEEE International Conference on Acoustics, Speech and Signal Processing (ICASSP), pp. 6798–6802 (2021)
4. Ratner, N.B., MacWhinney, B.: Fluency Bank: a new resource for fluency research and practice. J. Fluency Disord. **56**, 69–80 (2018)
5. Howell, P., Davis, S., Bartrip, J.: The University College London Archive Of Stuttered Speech (UCLASS) (2009)

6. Kourkounakis, T., Hajavi, A., Etemad, A.: FluentNet: end-to-end detection of stuttered speech disfluencies with deep learning. IEEE/ACM Trans. Audio Speech Lang. Process. **29**, 2986–2999 (2021). https://doi.org/10.1109/TASLP.2021.3110146

7. Panayotov, V., Chen, G., Povey, D., Khudanpur, S.: LibriSpeech: an ASR corpus based on public domain audio books. In: 2015 IEEE International Conference on Acoustics, Speech and Signal Processing (ICASSP), IEEE, pp. 5206–5210 (2015)

8. Gillam, R. B., Marquardt, T. P.: Communication Sciences and Disorders: From Science to Clinical Practice. Jones and Bartlett Learning (2019)

9. Ravikumar, K., Rajagopal, R., Nagaraj, H.: An approach for objective assessment of stuttered speech using MFCC. In: The International Congress for Global Science and Technology, Vol. 19 (2009)

10. Sheikh, S.A., Sahidullah, M., Hirsch, F., Ouni, S.: StutterNet: stuttering detection using time delay neural network: In: 2021 29th European Signal Processing Conference (EUSIPCO), Dublin, Ireland, pp. 426–430 (2021). https://doi.org/10.23919/EUSIPCO54536.2021.9616063

11. Al-Banna, A.-K., Edirisinghe, E., Fang, H., Hadi, W.: Stuttering disfluency detection using machine learning approaches. J. Info. Know. Manag. (2022). https://doi.org/10.1142/S0219649222500204

12. Priya, K., Roomi, M.M.M., Senthilarasi, M., Shree, S.K., Anusha, M.: Speech stammer detection by spectral features based artificial neural network. In: International Conference on Smart Generation Computing, Communication and Networking (SMART GENCON), pp. 1–6. https://doi.org/10.1109/SMARTGENCON56628.2022.10084338, 2022

13. Scott, T., Seliya, N.: Stuttering prediction with machine learning. In: IEEE Asia-Pacific Conference on Computer Science and Data Engineering (CSDE), pp. 1–6 (2023)

14. Al-Banna, A.K., Fang, H., Edirisinghe, E.: A novel attention model across heterogeneous features for stuttering event detection. Expert Syst. Appl. **244** 122967 (2024)

15. Batra, A., Shah R., Das, P.K.: Machine learning models based stuttering classification. In: Fourth International Conference on Innovations in Computational Intelligence and Computer Vision (ICICV) (2024)

16. Batra, A., Das, P.K.: A review on automatic assessment and detection of pathological speech. In: Swain, B.P., Dixit, U.S. (eds.) Recent Advances in Electrical and Electronic Engineering. ICSTE. Lecture Notes in Electrical Engineering, vol. 1071. Springer, Singapore (2023). https://doi.org/10.1007/978-981-99-4713-3_40

17. Bayerl, S.P., von Gudenberg, A.W., Hönig, F., Nöth, E., Riedhammer, K.: KSoF: The Kassel state of fluency dataset–a therapy centered dataset of stuttering (2022). arXiv preprint arXiv:2203.05383

18. Eyben, F., Wöllmer, M., Schuller, B.: OpenSMILE: the Munich versatile and fast open-source audio feature extractor. In: Proceedings of the 18th ACM International Conference on Multimedia, pp. 1459–1462 (2010)

19. Schuller, B., Steidl, S., Batliner, A., Hirschberg, J., Burgoon, J. K., Baird, A., ... & Evanini, K. "The interspeech 2016 computational paralinguistics challenge: Deception, sincerity and native language", 2016

20. Karas, V., Schuller, B.W.: Recognising COVID-19 from coughing using ensembles of SVMs and LSTMs with handcrafted and deep audio features (2021)

21. Breiman, L.: Random forests. Mach. Learn. **45**, 5–32 (2001)

22. Boser, B.E., Guyon, I.M., Vapnik, V.N.: A training algorithm for optimal margin classifiers. In: Proceedings of the Fifth Annual Workshop on Computational Learning Theory, pp. 144–152 (1992)
23. Waibel, A., Hanazawa, T., Hinton, G., Shikano, K., Lang, K.J.: Phoneme recognition using time-delay neural networks. In: Backpropagation. Psychology Press, pp. 35–61 (2013)
24. Snyder, D., Garcia-Romero, D., Sell, G., Povey, D., Khudanpur, S.: X-vectors: robust DNN embeddings for speaker recognition. In: 2018 IEEE International Conference on Acoustics, Speech and Signal Processing (ICASSP), pp. 5329–5333 (2018)

Deep Learning-Driven Person Re-identification: Leveraging Color Space Transformations

Riya Jhalke[1], Madan Sharma[2], Nirbhay Kumar Tagore[2(✉)],
Ramakant Kumar[3], and Mukund Pratap Singh[4]

[1] Department of Information Technology, NIT Raipur, Chhattisgarh 492001, India
[2] Department of CSE, RGIPT, Jais, Amethi 229304, U.P., India
`nktagore@rgipt.ac.in`
[3] Department of CEA, GLA University, Mathura 281406, U.P., India
[4] School of CSET, Bennett University, Greater Noida 201310, India

Abstract. Person re-identification (Re-ID) is a critical computer vision job that entails identifying individuals across various images and camera viewpoints. It is very applicable to intelligent transportation systems, security, and surveillance. This study of ours uses cutting-edge color conversion methods and deep learning to give a thorough method for person Re-ID. Our approach improves matching accuracy and feature extraction under a range of lighting situations and camera setups by employing convolutional neural networks (CNNs) and cutting-edge color scheme conversions. We use a solid dataset to assess our model's performance and show that it effectively obtains high re-identification accuracy. The outcomes demonstrate that our method works better than conventional approaches, especially in difficult situations with large color changes and occlusions. Along with discussing how various color spaces affect Re-ID performance, this study also identifies future research areas in this quickly developing topic. Our research advances person-Re-ID technology and provides improved functionality for practical applications. We have evaluated the results and performance of our proposed approach on publicly available datasets i.e., *CUHK_01*, *CUHK_03*, *Market-1501*, and *VIPeR* demonstrating satisfactory improvements in rank-based accuracy.

Keywords: Person Re-identification · Deep Learning-based approach · Spatial feature extraction · Color Space analysis · Siamese Network (ReIDTwin Network)

1 Introduction

Person re-identification, or Re-ID, has gained significant attention in computer vision research lately because of its utility in various security, surveillance, and public safety applications. The process of recognizing and matching individuals in a multi-camera surveillance network from various camera angles is known as

© The Author(s), under exclusive license to Springer Nature Switzerland AG 2025
Q. Bramas et al. (Eds.): ICDCIT 2025, LNCS 15507, pp. 225–239, 2025.
https://doi.org/10.1007/978-3-031-81404-4_17

person re-identification or Re-ID. For many sectors that need to be able to track and identify people from several camera angles, this technology is essential. Re-ID, or person re-identification, is a computer vision task that strives to identify and match different people across various surveillance footage views in different places or at different times. It is important for many applications, such as urban mobility, security, and surveillance, where it is necessary to track a person's motion throughout a network of connections of cameras. It is a challenging issue in computer vision since a lot of variables may alter a person's look from one camera view to another. The job turns substantially more complicated due to variations in lighting circumstances, positions, and perspectives of the cameras. It may be tough to capture consistent features of persons when they are partially concealed by additional things. Differences in frame rates, color calibration, and camera resolution might influence the visual quality and accuracy of shots that are taken. Seasonal changes and changes in day-night cycles can affect how people and places seem throughout time.

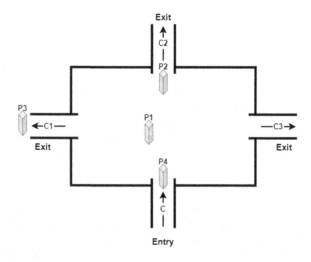

Fig. 1. Illustration of Camera Placement in a surveillance zone

Person Re-ID's worth in ensuring the security of the public has garnered a lot of attention in recent years. Conventional surveillance systems frequently use labor-intensive and prone to error human operators to track persons manually. These difficulties are mitigated by automated Re-ID systems, which offer a scalable and effective method of tracking individuals. The task of person re-identification proves challenging for several reasons: People's appearances can vary depending on what they're wearing, accessorizing, or carrying. A person's look can be dramatically changed by varying camera perspectives and body positions. It is possible for people or items to obscure someone completely or partially. Layouts that are dynamic and diverse can make it more difficult to extract pertinent features. Individuals' looks can be impacted by variations in lighting across various camera angles. Person Re-ID strives for precise identification if a person observed in one camera view is the same person observed in a different one, regardless of the views having differences in space and time. Person Re-ID is an approach that commences with capturing/collecting images of people, followed by analyzing those image frames to extract unique characteristics. Based on those traits, classifiers are developed, which then undergo comparison between various camera angles to figure out whether or not the same person is there. Person Re-ID has many uses, such as: Improving security for the public by automatically identifying people in real-time via numerous cameras, and examining how customers behave and travel around establishments in order to enhance marketing and customer service tactics. Re-ID systems are being integrated into urban infrastructures to streamline public transportation, control pedestrian traffic, and guarantee safety.

The surveillance scenario considered for the proposed approach is shown in Fig. 1. From the figure it can be seen that there is one camera C and three cameras $C1$, $C2$, and $C3$, placed at entry and exit gates respectively, with four people $P1$, $P2$, $P3$, and $P4$ entering at different times from the field of view of the camera C and being captured. As soon as they leave the surveillance zone the cameras $C1$, $C2$, and $C3$ placed at the exit gates will capture their descriptor again to establish the correspondence for matching. The goal is to use the entry and exit cameras to identify and re-identify identities while concentrating on the functionality of various color channels and datasets.

This paper employs a deep learning technique for person re-identification, utilizing several color channels and physical characteristics to assign similarity scores to a pair of images of human beings. With an emphasis on methodological, technical, and practical improvements, these points underline the novelty and significance of our proposed approach in the field of person re-identification:

1. Proposing a new method for Re-ID accuracy and feature extraction using color conversion. Creating a hybrid color conversion model that captures distinct identification elements by combining various color spaces.
2. Improving re-identification accuracy by developing a distinct deep learning framework specifically designed for person Re-identification tasks by implementing a ReIDTwin Siamese network.
3. Developing feature extraction methods that integrate color information and spatial data
4. Presenting a comprehensive comparison with popular state-of-the-art Re-ID techniques in order to emphasize the benefits and advancements of the proposed technique.

The rest of the paper is organized as follows: In Sect. 2, we discussed the recent advancements in the field of person re-identification with a focus, particularly on deep learning models. In the following section, i.e., Sect. 3, we described our method for re-identification utilizing a Siamese network (called ReIDTwin network). Section 4 focuses on defining the datasets and explains the overall performance of the proposed approach. Lastly in Sect. 5, we conclude the paper with the findings and the directions for further research.

2 Related Work

Person re-identification (Re-ID) has long been an important field of study in surveillance and computer vision. These fields' early achievements set the stage for more recent deep learning-based techniques. Below is a quick summary of the groundbreaking discoveries and methods from the early days of Re-ID research:(a) Image-driven person re-identification (b) Person re-identification using videos

2.1 Image-Driven Person Re-identification

Re-ID, or image-based person re-identification, is a computer vision challenge that uses still images to identify and match people from various camera viewpoints. This work is crucial for many sectors of work like security apps, forensic investigations, and surveillance systems where the objective is to follow people as they walk through various areas that are monitored by a collection of cameras.

The foundation of Image-based Re-ID is feature extraction [1], which involves identifying unique visual features from an image, such as Hand-Crafted Features [2–4] and Deep Learning Features. Obtaining crucial visual information, color histograms [2,5–11] were utilized in feature extraction techniques that relied on hand-crafted features. The combination of the Siamese network is the combination of verification and classification model [12]. Additionally, deep learning features-modern methods for automatically acquiring strong features-are included. Convolutional neural networks (CNNs) were used for Re-ID [13,14], greatly enhancing feature extraction capabilities [14]. They have introduced image-based and video-based person Re-ID methods. Described the problems with person Re-ID and the methods employed to fix them [1,15]. Use of dense layer, ReLU activation function, and Maxpooling layer with the convolutional layer [1,16]. Part-based approach for human re-identification that uses a convolutional neural network and semantically divided body component masks [17]. A common evaluation metric in Re-ID is the Cumulative Match Characteristic (CMC) curve [18]; both are utilized in this research. Rank-based accuracy quantifies the proportion of times the right identification is ranked inside the top-K spots [19,20]. The feature fusion network uses color features from multiple color spaces. These color spaces include RGB (Red, Green, Blue), an additive color model that creates colors by combining red, green, and blue light in different intensities; YCbCr (Luma, Blue-difference Chroma, Red-difference Chroma), which is used in television and video compression and splits the image luminance (Y) from chrominance components (Cb and Cr); and HSV (Hue, Saturation, Value), a color space that represents colors based on hue, saturation, and brightness and is frequently used in the selection of colors like devices [21]. In [22] authors improve the resilience and diversity of training data, which aids in the better generalization of models to various settings and camera angles. To make the model more resilient to occlusions, techniques including randomized cropping, flipping up of images in any way (either vertical or horizontal), and chromatic jittery conditions were frequently employed [23]. Research aimed at identifying a better set of traits [24–26] examining a technique for learning Siamese neural networks using a convolutional architecture [1,27], Random erasing is a technique that obscures random areas of an image [23]. Combination of the Siamese network which is the combination of verification and classification model [12], CNN-based pose estimator [28], locating different body parts and joints [29]. Measuring the degree of similarity among pairs of images requires metric learning. Images of the same individual will always be closer together in the feature space because of effective metric learning [5–7,30].

2.2   Person Re-identification Using Videos

Re-ID, or video-based person re-identification, uses time-dependent data from video sequences to increase the resilience and accuracy of person identification from various camera angles. Using time data from video sequences, video-based person re-identification improves the capacity to match individuals across several camera viewpoints. Important elements include multiple levels for extraction of features and aggregation, complex network topologies such as Siamese networks, data augmentation, and assessment measures such as rank-based accuracy and CMC curves. Random Erasing picks a rectangle area at random from an image and uses random values to delete its pixels. Training images with different degrees of occlusion are created during this procedure, which lowers the possibility of occlusion-resistant and prevents over-fitting of the model [23]. Both the Cumulative Match Characteristic (CMC) curve, a common evaluation metric in Re-ID, and rank-based accuracy, which quantifies the percentage of times the correct identification is rated inside the top-K spots, are employed papers article [19,20]. In [31,32], authors proposed an occlusion handling approach for re-identification by exploiting spatiotemporal information from the image sequences, while in [33] authors proposed an ensemble scheme to capture the temporal and spatial features from the input video sequence.

3   Proposed Approach

The proposed work is divided into discrete modules, each of which performs a certain task: 1) Preprocessing: Initial stages of data collection, improvement, preparation, and enhancement. 2) ReIDTwin Siamese Network Architecture: Fundamental network architecture for comparing and extracting features. 3) Feature Refinement using Input Neighborhood Variance and Unified Patch Overview 4) Post-processing: enhancing feature representations. 5) Aggregation of features and Prediction

3.1 Preprocessing

A dataset must be preprocessed before it can be used in any model. Resizing, cleaning, converting, augmenting, splitting, and using various color channels (such as RGB, Yc_bc_r, HSV) are all part of the process of improving the raw data so that it can be used further to train a deep neural network. Effective preprocessing contributes to increased model performance, generalization, and efficacy.

Choosing two input image pairs from the collection that represent the same identity is the first step. The pairs of images(1 and 2) may be positive or negative. A positive image pair is made up of two image frames that depict the same identity and a negative image pair consists of two image frames, each of which represents a distinct person. The ReIDTwin Siamese network, which is intended to ascertain their resemblance, receives these image pairings as input. Next, eliminate any possible artifacts from the inputs. Afterward, make sure every image is the same size required for network consistency and batch processing. Then transforming the images into an appropriate color channel, when the network architecture calls for it. It guarantees that the inputs provided are in optimal condition so that the network can learn efficiently.

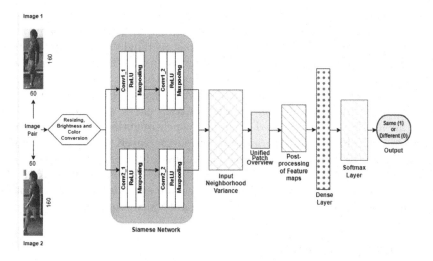

Fig. 2. Block schematics of the proposed network approach for Person-ReIdentification.

3.2 ReIDTwin Network

ReIDTwin stands for Re-identification Twin network. A ReIDTwin Siamese Network is a deep neural network architecture designed specifically for person re-identification (ReID). A Siamese network has been used as it is designed to learn the similarity between pairs of inputs. By using pairs of images, the model can learn from a smaller dataset effectively, making it suitable for tasks like re-identification. In contrast, the approaches that do not rely on pairwise similarity treat each person as a unique class, making it particularly unscalable to unknown identities. Both branches of the Siamese network share the same weights, which enforces consistent feature extraction for both similar and dissimilar pairs. This consistency helps the model to learn robust features invariant to certain transformations. Using the idea of Siamese networks, our architecture is able to acquire discriminative features that allow it to recognize distinct people from a variety of camera angles. ReIDTwin Siamese Networks are deep learning frameworks that combine two or more identical subnetworks (commonly referred to as twins) to facilitate human re-identification. With identical architectures and weights, these subnetworks process two distinct input images concurrently to acquire embeddings that allow for the comparison and identification of people from various camera angles.

Table 1. Layer-wise specification for the Siamese network (ReIDTwin network), and Feature Refinement Network (FRN)

Network	Layer	Size of Filters	# of Filters
ReIDTwin Network	Conv1_1	5x5	20
	Conv1_2	5x5	25
	Conv2_1	5x5	20
	Conv2_2	5x5	25
Feature Refinement Network (Unified Patch Overview)	Conv1_3	5x5	25
	Conv1_4	3x3	25
	Conv2_3	5x5	25
	Conv2_4	3x3	25

In our proposed ReIDTwin Siamese architecture each branch processes one of the input images, and both branches share the same architecture and weights. The layers (refer to Fig. 2) are denoted as Conv'i'_'j' where 'i' is the branch number and 'j' is the layer number within that branch as in Table 1 where Conv1_1 and Conv1_2 deal with Image 1 and Conv2_1 and Conv2_2 deal with Image 2, ensuring that both branches of the network are identical in architecture and parameters.

3.3   Feature Refinement

After the ReIDTwin Network, the output from it is processed by the input neighborhood variance module to analyze local variations and enhance feature extraction. Influenced by the Cross-input Neighborhood layer presented in a prior study [1], we integrated it into our neural network architecture with a few minor adjustments (the Input Neighborhood Variance, specifically). The Cross-input Neighborhood Difference method calculates the difference between an input patch's features and those of its related patches from a nearby region in another input image, enhancing feature extraction.

Our modification improved the model's ability to capture subtle spatial relationships by incorporating local variance estimates into each layer, which improved feature extraction capabilities. The input neighborhood variance layer, which is a convolutional layer, calculates the variance among specific areas (neighborhood feature maps) of the feature map generated by earlier layers. The input neighborhood variance layer is utilized to examine variations or variations within a certain area (neighborhood) of the image. This technique aids in the comprehension and recording of regional patterns, textures, or other characteristics that are beneficial for categorizing images. Input Neighborhood Variance Layer is a layer created to identify and capture local changes in the input image. The statistical variance of the values of each pixel within the chosen neighborhood or patch is computed by this layer.

This method can greatly improve the feature representation for person Re-ID by emphatically capturing and evaluating the differences within the local areas (neighborhoods) of an image. The technique entails computing the statistical variance within each patch after splitting the image into smaller ones. After that, these variance values are either included in the already-existing feature maps from convolutional layers or used as extra descriptors for features. With this method, the model can withstand more frequent obstacles in one-on-one Re-ID, like resemblances in appearance and background.

The specific configuration of layers (conv1_3, conv1_4, conv2_3 and conv2_4) are defined in Table 1. These layers are part of the unified patch overview, which is a critical component of the feature refinement network. This configuration ensures that the extracted features are comprehensive and robust, capturing both local and global patterns essential for accurate person re-identification. These layers contribute to a unified patch overview by refining the features extracted from multiple patches, ensuring that the network can effectively discern patterns and structures necessary for identifying individuals, even under challenging conditions.

The unified patch overview layer processes image patches separately and collectively to create a thorough and reliable depiction of a person's appearance, it gathers specific local features from every patch and analyses the links between them. The unified patch overview layer splits an image into numerous patches and evaluates every single patch individually. This technique enhances the precision and resilience of re-identification systems by acquiring unique and precise details regarding how a person looks. Each layer receives input from the previous layer of their corresponding image.

It highlights the minute nuances and distinctive qualities of particular locales, such as the textures of garments, accessories, or eye-catching patterns. The method guarantees an accurate representation of local differences and thorough information by producing an extensive summary for every patch.

3.4 Post-processing of Feature Maps

Before the extracted features are sent to other layers or modules for additional analysis or final predictions, post-processing of feature maps entails applying numerous operations to improve, filter, and refine the features. These procedures aid in the integration of the collected features and set them up for the identification or classification processes that come next.

Neural network architectures require post-processing of feature maps, which includes concatenation and reshaping. This is particularly significant after a unified patch overview. To get the characteristics collected from various patches ready for the final classification or re-identification task, these processes aid in their integration and refinement. The network can make predictions that are more reliable and accurate by utilizing both local and wider data through the efficient blending and reshaping of the feature maps. The input image is divided into various patches to create feature maps. Convolutional layers have been used to process these patches in order to extract localized features. Along the channel dimension, feature maps from several patches are concatenated. In doing so, the localized features are combined into one feature map that serves as a cohesive summary of the input image. Then a 2D tensor is created by reshaping the concatenated feature map, where each row represents the concatenated features for one input instance. After that Dense layer is applied to the altered features to further incorporate and understand the combined features.

Table 2. Summary of datasets: *CUHK_01*, *CUHK_03*, *Market-1501*, and *VIPeR*

Dataset Name	# of Images	# of Identities	# of Cameras
CUHK_03 [34]	14,097	1,467	6
CUHK_01 [35]	3,884	971	2
Market-1501 [20]	32,668	1,501	6
VIPeR [36]	1,264	632	2

3.5   Aggregation of Features and Prediction

The Dense Layer is used to convert the input data through a sequence of computations involving activation functions, biases, and weights into useful outputs. Every neuron in the dense layer receives input from every other neuron from the previous layer.

A softmax layer is an output layer or we can say that it is the last layer that is utilized in the classification job. It is used to transform the prior layer's raw outputs (the logs) into a probability distribution over multiple categories. A set of probabilities illustrating the chance that each class is the correct class is the softmax layer's output. It is applied when each input requires the model to predict one of several potential classes. The anticipated label, denoted by R in the Eq. 1, can be either 0 or 1. In this case, V_ω stands for the output score from the Softmax layer, and $R = 1$ indicates that the image pairs belong to the same class, while $R = 0$ indicates that they are from distinct classes.

$$L_{contr} = (1 - R)\frac{1}{2}(V_\omega) + (R)\frac{1}{2}max(0, m - V_\omega)^2 \tag{1}$$

For person re-identification, the output of a Siamese network model is a binary prediction that indicates whether the input image pair corresponds to distinct identities ($output = 0$) or the same identity ($output = 1$). The model's performance is evaluated by employing Rank-based accuracy.

4   Datasets and Experimental Results

Here in this section, we present a summary of the assessment circumstances and the datasets along with experimental results of the proposed approach. We used datasets that are available to the public to assess the effectiveness of the re-identification approach. The name of the dataset, the number of still images, the number of identities, and the number of cameras used are all summarized in the Table 2.

We examined our proposed method on the same test sets as other ways that have been reported in different research papers to assess its efficacy. We used the Rank-1, Rank-5, and Rank-10 accuracy values (refer Table 3) as stated in their individual studies with ours to ensure a fair and straightforward comparison.

We compared our model with both deep learning based and non-deep learning based existing methods, as mentioned in the Table 3. Our model outperformed most of the others comparative approaches in the study, demonstrating superior performance across multiple datasets. Specifically, our model achieved a rank-based accuracy of 58.20% on the CUHK03 dataset, 58.24% on the CUHK01 dataset, 31.44% on the Market-1501 dataset, and 71.93% on the VIPeR dataset. These results underscore the effectiveness and robustness of our approach, confirming that our model is the best among those tested. A detailed comparison of Rank-1 accuracy scores for RGB, $Y_{c_b c_r}$, and HSV color channels is shown in Fig. 3 for four well-known datasets: CUHK_03, CUHK_01, Market-1501, and VIPeR.

Table 3. Comparisons with the state-of-the-art person re-ID models on *CUHK_03*, *CUHK_01, Market-1501,VIPeR*

Dataset	Method	R1	R5	R10
CUHK_03	BoW [20]+KISSME [5]	53.80	63.2	69.6
	LOMO [37]+ XQDA [37]	52.55	70.05	84.80
	FPNN [34]	53.10	65.34	85.72
	MSCAN [38]	58.5	73.86	80.23
	SVD-Net [39]	60.25	74.57	82.0
	Ours	58.20	76.22	82.62
CUHK_01	BoW [20]+KISSME [5]	51.80	64.2	71.6
	LOMO [37]+ XQDA [37]	28.75	40.51	52.04
	FPNN [34]	53.1	70.86	82.14
	MSCAN [38]	55.0	62.3	75.52
	SVD-Net [39]	58.23	78.57	88.66
	Ours	58.24	81.83	89.1
Market-1501	BoW [20]+KISSME [5]	30.80	52.2	65.6
	LOMO [37]+ XQDA [37]	28.20	40.8	52.0
	FPNN [34]	30.14	50.6	65.4
	MSCAN [38]	29.6	54.2	65.6
	SVD-Net [39]	33.5	40.6	56.7
	Ours	31.44	56.18	68.59
VIPeR	BoW [20]+KISSME [5]	12.97	20.5	34.79
	LOMO [37]+ XQDA [37]	23.42	40.6	51.96
	FPNN [34]	45.17	52.8	62.04
	MSCAN [38]	48.75	60.0	72.62
	SVD-Net [39]	68.5	83.5	91.8
	Ours	71.93	96.79	99.20

Ablation Study: Table 4 shows an ablation study of our model architecture on CUHK_03, CUHK_01, Market-1501, and VIPeR Datasets in terms of rank-1, rank-5, and rank-10 accuracy(%). In our Baseline, we have used the convolution network (ReID Twin Network) as depicted in Table 1, removing the Input Neighborhood variance and Unified Patch Overview layers. Post-processing of features, Softmax is applied on the logits received from the Baseline to arrive at the output. From Table 4, we can clearly examine that the Feature Refinement part of our network is particularly enhancing the model's ability to learn discriminative features and enhance the results.

Table 4. Ablation study: Quantitative comparison for variants of our model on CUHK_03, CUHK_01, Market-1501 and VIPeR Datasets. Numbers in bold represent the best performance with inclusion of our Feature Refinement Network (Unified Patch Overview) on top of the baseline ReIDTwin Network.

Dataset	Method	R1	R5	R10
CUHK_03	(Baseline) ReIDTwin Network	52.13	70.20	75.32
	⊕ (Input Neighborhood variance and Unified Patch Overview)	**58.20**	**76.22**	**82.62**
CUHK_01	(Baseline) ReIDTwin Network	53.11	76.20	79.89
	⊕ (Input Neighborhood variance and Unified Patch Overview)	**58.24**	**81.83**	**89.1**
Market-1501	(Baseline) ReIDTwin Network	29.75	48.26	59.83
	⊕ (Input Neighborhood variance and Unified Patch Overview)	**31.44**	**56.18**	**68.59**
VIPeR	(Baseline) ReIDTwin Network	64.04	80.02	84.29
	⊕ (Input Neighborhood variance and Unified batch Overview)	**71.93**	**96.79**	**99.20**

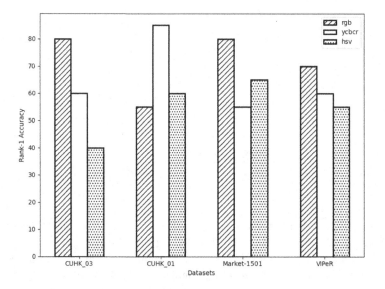

Fig. 3. Comparison of different Datasets with Color channels using Grouped bar chart

5 Conclusions

With an emphasis on deep learning, this research study has examined some approaches and strategies for improving person re-identification (ReID) systems. We have shown notable gains in performance measures like re-identification accuracy and robustness by utilizing color conversion and accuracy representation, which are essential for the accurate and efficient identification of people in a variety of settings and cameras. Our proposed approach has been proven to be effective through rigorous experimentation and evaluation on datasets like *CUHK_01, CUHK_03, VIPeR*, and *Market-1501*. Not only has color-space analysis and layer integration improved the state-of-the-art in-person ReID, but it has also yielded insightful information.

Enabling quick and precise identification in dynamic environments and developing techniques and algorithms suited for real-time human re-identification applications can be considered as one of the future scopes. The incorporation of edge computing platforms and Internet of Things (IoT) devices with person re-identification systems is also a futuristic thought in this direction to enable scalable and dispersed deployments.

References

1. Ahmed, E., Jones, M., Marks, T.K.: An improved deep learning architecture for person re-identification. In: Proceedings of the IEEE Conference on Computer Vision and Pattern Recognition, pp. 3908–3916 (2015)
2. Farenzena, M., Bazzani, L., Perina, A., Murino, V., Cristani, M.: Person re-identification by symmetry-driven accumulation of local features. In: 2010 IEEE Computer Society Conference on Computer Vision and Pattern Recognition, pp. 2360–2367. IEEE (2010)
3. Di, W., et al.: Deep learning-based methods for person re-identification: a comprehensive review. Neurocomputing **337**, 354–371 (2019)
4. Zheng, L., Yang, Y., Hauptmann, A.G.: Person re-identification: past, present and future. *arXiv preprint*arXiv:1610.02984 (2016)
5. Koestinger, M., Hirzer, M., Wohlhart, P., Roth, P.M., Bischof, H.: Large scale metric learning from equivalence constraints. In: 2012 IEEE Conference on Computer Vision and Pattern Recognition, pp. 2288–2295. IEEE (2012)
6. Martinel, N., Micheloni, C., Foresti, G.L.: Saliency weighted features for person re-identification. In: Agapito, L., Bronstein, M.M., Rother, C. (eds.) ECCV 2014. LNCS, vol. 8927, pp. 191–208. Springer, Cham (2015). https://doi.org/10.1007/978-3-319-16199-0_14
7. Li, W., Wang, X.: Locally aligned feature transforms across views. In: Proceedings of the IEEE Conference on Computer Vision and Pattern Recognition, pp. 3594–3601 (2013)
8. Tagore, N.K., Chattopadhyay, P.: SMSNet: a novel multi-scale siamese model for person re-identification. In: ICETE, no. 1, pp. 103–112 (2020)
9. Tagore, N.K., Singh, S.K.: Crowd counting in a highly congested scene using deep augmentation based convolutional network. In: International Conference on Advances in Engineering Science Management & Technology (ICAESMT)-2019, Uttaranchal University, Dehradun, India (2019)
10. Tagore, N.K., Medi, P.R., Chattopadhyay, P.: Deep pixel regeneration for occlusion reconstruction in person re-identification. Multimedia Tools Appl. **83**(2), 4443–4463 (2024)
11. Tagore, N.K., Singh, A., Manche, S., Chattopadhyay, P.: Person re-identification from appearance cues and deep siamese features. J. Vis. Commun. Image Represent. **75**, 103029 (2021)

12. Zheng, Z., Zheng, L., Yang, Y.: A discriminatively learned CNN embedding for person reidentification. ACM Trans. Multimedia Comput. Commun. Appl. (TOMM) **14**(1), 1–20 (2017)
13. Wang, K., Wang, H., Liu, M., Xing, X., Han, T.: Survey on person re-identification based on deep learning. CAAI Trans. Intell. Technol. **3**(4), 219–227 (2018)
14. Chahar, H., Nain, N.: A study on deep convolutional neural network based approaches for person re-identification. In: Shankar, B.U., Ghosh, K., Mandal, D.P., Ray, S.S., Zhang, D., Pal, S.K. (eds.) PReMI 2017. LNCS, vol. 10597, pp. 543–548. Springer, Cham (2017). https://doi.org/10.1007/978-3-319-69900-4_69
15. Mathur, N., Mathur, S., Mathur, D., Dadheech, P.: A brief survey of deep learning techniques for person re-identification. In: 2020 3rd International Conference on Emerging Technologies in Computer Engineering: Machine Learning and Internet of Things (ICETCE), pp. 129–138. IEEE (2020)
16. Javid, A.M., Das, S., Skoglund, M., Chatterjee, S.: A ReLU dense layer to improve the performance of neural networks. In: ICASSP 2021-2021 IEEE International Conference on Acoustics, Speech and Signal Processing (ICASSP), pp. 2810–2814. IEEE (2021)
17. Aksu, F.: Person re-identification using convolutional neural networks. Master's thesis, Middle East Technical University (2021)
18. Hirzer, M., Beleznai, C., Roth, P.M., Bischof, H.: Person re-identification by descriptive and discriminative classification. In: Heyden, A., Kahl, F. (eds.) SCIA 2011. LNCS, vol. 6688, pp. 91–102. Springer, Heidelberg (2011). https://doi.org/10.1007/978-3-642-21227-7_9
19. Hermans, A., Beyer, L., Leibe, B.: In defense of the triplet loss for person re-identification. arXiv preprint arXiv:1703.07737 (2017)
20. Zheng, L., Shen, L., Tian, L., Wang, S., Wang, J., Tian, Q.: Scalable person re-identification: a benchmark. In: Proceedings of the IEEE International Conference on Computer Vision, pp. 1116–1124 (2015)
21. Wu, S., Chen, Y.-C., Li, X., Wu, A.-C., You, J.-J., Zheng, W.-S.: An enhanced deep feature representation for person re-identification. In: 2016 IEEE Winter Conference on Applications of Computer Vision (WACV), pp. 1–8. IEEE (2016)
22. Krizhevsky, A., Sutskever, I., Hinton, G.E.: Imagenet classification with deep convolutional neural networks. Commun. ACM **60**(6), 84–90 (2017)
23. Zhong, Z., Zheng, L., Kang, G., Li, S., Yang, Y.: Random erasing data augmentation. In: Proceedings of the AAAI Conference on Artificial Intelligence, vol. 34, pp. 13001–13008 (2020)
24. Yang, Y., Yang, J., Yan, J., Liao, S., Yi, D., Li, S.Z.: Salient color names for person re-identification. In: Fleet, D., Pajdla, T., Schiele, B., Tuytelaars, T. (eds.) ECCV 2014. LNCS, vol. 8689, pp. 536–551. Springer, Cham (2014). https://doi.org/10.1007/978-3-319-10590-1_35
25. Zhao, R., Ouyang, W., Wang, X.: Learning mid-level filters for person re-identification. In: Proceedings of the IEEE Conference on Computer Vision and Pattern Recognition, pp. 144–151 (2014)
26. Zhang, Z., Chen, Y., Saligrama, V.: A novel visual word co-occurrence model for person re-identification. In: Agapito, L., Bronstein, M.M., Rother, C. (eds.) ECCV 2014. LNCS, vol. 8927, pp. 122–133. Springer, Cham (2015). https://doi.org/10.1007/978-3-319-16199-0_9
27. Koch, G., Zemel, R., Salakhutdinov, R., et al.: Siamese neural networks for one-shot image recognition. In: ICML Deep Learning Workshop, Lille, vol. 2 (2015)

28. Wei, S.-E., Ramakrishna, V., Kanade, T., Sheikh, Y.: Convolutional pose machines. In: Proceedings of the IEEE Conference on Computer Vision and Pattern Recognition, pp. 4724–4732 (2016)
29. Zhao, H., et al.: Spindle net: person re-identification with human body region guided feature decomposition and fusion. In: Proceedings of the IEEE Conference on Computer Vision and Pattern Recognition, pp. 1077–1085 (2017)
30. Li, Z., Chang, S., Liang, F., Huang, T. S., Cao, L., Smith, J.R.: Learning locally-adaptive decision functions for person verification. In: Proceedings of the IEEE Conference on Computer Vision and Pattern Recognition, pp. 3610–3617 (2013)
31. Tagore, N.K., Kumar, R., Yadav, N., Jaiswal, A.K.: Occlusion reconstruction for person re-identification. In: Proceedings of Data Analytics and Management: ICDAM 2022, pp. 161–172. Springer, Cham (2023)
32. Tagore, N.K., Chattopadhyay, P.: A bi-network architecture for occlusion handling in person re-identification. SIViP 16(4), 1071–1079 (2022)
33. Tagore, N.K., Chattopadhyay, P., Wang, L.: T-man: a neural ensemble approach for person re-identification using spatio-temporal information. Multimedia Tools Appl. 79(37), 28393–28409 (2020)
34. Li, W., Zhao, R., Xiao, T., Wang, X.: Deepreid: deep filter pairing neural network for person re-identification. In: Proceedings of the IEEE Conference on Computer Vision and Pattern Recognition, pp. 152–159 (2014)
35. Li, W., Zhao, R., Wang, X.: Human reidentification with transferred metric learning. In: Lee, K.M., Matsushita, Y., Rehg, J.M., Hu, Z. (eds.) ACCV 2012. LNCS, vol. 7724, pp. 31–44. Springer, Heidelberg (2013). https://doi.org/10.1007/978-3-642-37331-2_3
36. Gray, D., Brennan, S., Tao, H.: Evaluating appearance models for recognition, reacquisition, and tracking. In: Proceedings of IEEE International Workshop on Performance Evaluation for Tracking and Surveillance (PETS), vol. 3, pp. 1–7 (2007)
37. Liao, S., Hu, Y., Zhu, X., Li, S.Z.: Person re-identification by local maximal occurrence representation and metric learning. In: Proceedings of the IEEE Conference on Computer Visión and Pattern Recognition, pp. 2197–2206 (2015)
38. Li, D., Chen, X., Zhang, Z., Huang, K.: Learning deep context-aware features over body and latent parts for person re-identification. In: Proceedings of the IEEE Conference on Computer Vision and Pattern Recognition, pp. 384–393 (2017)
39. Liu, X., et al.: Hydraplus-net: attentive deep features for pedestrian analysis. In: Proceedings of the IEEE International Conference on Computer Vision, pp. 350–359 (2017)

An Ensembled Parking Space Classifier Across Diverse Weather Conditions

Navpreet$^{(\boxtimes)}$ ⓘ, Rajendra Kumar Roul ⓘ, and Saif Nalband ⓘ

Thapar Institute of Engineering and Technology, Patiala, Punjab, India
navpreet705@gmail.com, {raj.roul,saif.nalband}@thapar.edu

Abstract. The rapid pace of urbanization and the growing number of vehicles has driven the demand for advanced parking management systems. However, a significant challenge remains in maximizing the efficiency of parking space utilization. While deep learning algorithms have proven effective in detecting available parking spots, their accuracy can be compromised by obstacles such as partial obstructions and varying lighting conditions. These issues are particularly pronounced under foggy or hazy weather, leading to a noticeable drop in performance. This research article presents an innovative approach that combines the strengths of Convolutional Neural Networks (CNN) with Kernel Extreme Learning Machine (KELM) to improve accuracy and reduce training time in parking space classification. The core advancement lies in substituting the fully connected layer of the CNN with KELM, which eliminates the need for backpropagation, thereby cutting down the training duration. The proposed approach is validated on the PKLot dataset, and a custom-built dataset designed to classify parking spaces under hazy conditions is used. The images from this hazy dataset are first preprocessed with Light-DehazeNet (LD-Net) to mitigate the impact of haze. Then, the CNN is trained on the dehazed dataset to extract features and produce a feature vector. This vector is then fed into the KELM to classify the parking spaces as occupied or vacant. Compared to standalone CNN, KELM, other machine learning classifiers, and similar models, the proposed approach demonstrates superior performance and enhanced computational efficiency. The study illustrates that the combination of CNN and KELM offers a promising solution for accurately classifying parking spaces, even in challenging weather conditions.

Keywords: Classification · CNN · Hazy · Kernel ELM · Parking Space · PKLot

1 Introduction

Approximately 30% of vehicular traffic in densely populated cities continuously seeks parking slots, as indicated by previous research [2]. This continuous hunt for parking places has put immense stress on parking management systems, resulting in increased commute times as drivers struggle to find parking spots [16].

ⓒ The Author(s), under exclusive license to Springer Nature Switzerland AG 2025
Q. Bramas et al. (Eds.): ICDCIT 2025, LNCS 15507, pp. 240–256, 2025.
https://doi.org/10.1007/978-3-031-81404-4_18

Efficient parking classification techniques play a pivotal role in addressing this challenge. These techniques provide critical information about parking space availability, enabling effective parking lot management. By informing drivers about the number of vacant parking spaces, these systems can substantially reduce long waiting queues, enhance scalability, and reduce the duration needed to find a parking space. This challenge is exacerbated during hazy weather conditions, as reduced visibility makes it difficult for drivers to assess the size and configuration of parking spaces and obstacles around their vehicles.

Many research studies have already been done for parking space classification under non-hazy conditions. Parking space classification systems were either manually keeping track of vehicles leaving/entering or sensor-based [8]. Manual-based tracking of vehicles is a time-consuming process. The problem with using sensors is that it is not suitable for large parking areas, require time-consuming tasks for installing sensor updates, have high installation and maintenance costs, are susceptible to physical tampering, and raise cyber security concerns [17].

Image processing techniques are better options to deal with the shortcomings mentioned earlier about sensors [7,17,21,22]. Deep learning techniques have already been employed to classify parking spaces under clear or non-hazy conditions [6]. Vision-based techniques can experience a decline in performance due to obstacles in parking spots like trees and adverse weather conditions (i.e., haze), where the fog is an obstacle for sensors or cameras. Also, Real-time datasets for parking space classification under hazy conditions are unavailable. Hence, researchers have not considered parking space classification under foggy conditions.

Fully connected layers in a CNN typically have many parameters and involve backpropagation to adjust parameters. The backpropagation computes gradients and updates the layer weights based on these gradients, which leads to longer training times and increased computational complexity. As a result, a very high computational time is required to train CNN.

Huang GB et al. [14] proposed a Kernel Extreme Learning Machine (KELM), a simple and efficient solution for the backpropagation process. KELM offers significant advantages over traditional Extreme Learning Machine (ELM), particularly in handling non-linear data. KELM maps inputs to a higher-dimensional space by utilizing kernel functions, effectively managing non-linearly separable data that traditional ELMs struggle with due to their linear nature [20,23]. This approach improves generalization by creating more flexible and robust decision boundaries and eliminates the need for random weight initialization, resulting in more consistent and reproducible performance. KELM is also more efficient in high-dimensional spaces, avoiding the excessive computational and memory demands that ELMs may face. Furthermore, its natural incorporation of regularization techniques helps reduce overfitting, making it a powerful alternative for complex and high-dimensional data tasks. It has been demonstrated that ELM's training speed is considerably faster than that of most popular machine learning (ML) techniques like RF, SVM, DT, etc. [1,4,13].

Researchers have either improved their model performances or reduced the computational time but have failed to optimize both of these parameters for parking slot classification under non-hazy conditions. This is the first study in which parking space classification has been done for hazy weather. The proposed model has taken care of both these parameters (i.e., model performance and computational time) to a better extent. Due to the advantages mentioned above and the excellent performance of CNN and KELM, the proposed work has combined CNN with KELM to classify the parking space under hazy conditions.

1.1 Our Contribution

The paper's primary contributions are summarized as follows:

- The proposed approach utilizes CNN and KELM for feature extraction and classification, reducing the computational time and increasing the model's performance.
- A custom dataset for parking space classification under hazy conditions is designed and preprocessed.
- The proposed approach undergoes validation on our custom dataset and PKD, with performance assessment conducted in terms of various parameters such as precision, sensitivity, specificity, accuracy, and F1-Score.
- A comparative analysis of the proposed CKELM is performed with ML classifiers. Further, the CKELM model's efficacy is compared with similar existing models.

2 Proposed Model: CKELM

The proposed model comprises CNN, a well-known feature extractor, and a KELM parking slot classifier. Dehazing network and CKELM work together as a single unit and can be employed to get better results in hazy weather.

2.1 CKELM Architecture

The proposed approach integrated CNN with KELM to reduce computational time and enhance model performance. The specific details of each layer in the CKELM architecture are further discussed below and are summarized in Table 1.

- **Input Layer:** Dehazed images of dimensions $227 \times 227 \times 3$ are fed to the input layer.
- **CL:** Images from the input layer are passed to the CL for extracting features such as edges, curves, and shapes by applying filters (kernels) of different sizes.
- **ReLU:** Each CL is followed by a ReLU layer. ReLU aims to get the activation values corresponding to neurons by increasing the non-linearity in the CNN.

Table 1. Architecture details of proposed CKELM

Layer	Kernel size	Filters	Feature Map	Activation Function	Trainable Params
Input	-	-	$227 \times 227 \times 3$	-	-
Conv-layer1	11×11	96	$55 \times 55 \times 96$	ReLU	34944
MaxPool-layer1	3×3	2	$27 \times 27 \times 96$	-	0
Conv-layer2	5×5	256	$27 \times 27 \times 256$	ReLU	614656
MaxPool-layer2	3×3	2	$13 \times 13 \times 256$	-	0
Conv-layer3	3×3	384	$13 \times 13 \times 384$	ReLU	885120
Conv-layer4	3×3	384	$13 \times 13 \times 384$	ReLU	1327488
Conv-layer5	3×3	384	$13 \times 13 \times 256$	ReLU	884992
MaxPool-layer3	3×3	-	$6 \times 6 \times 256$	-	0
Flatten-layer1	-	-	9216	ReLU	0
Fully-connected layer1	-	-	4096	-	37752832
Dropout-layer1	-	-	4096	-	0
Softmax layer	-	-	2	Softmax	8194
Hidden layer	-	-	256	-	-
KELM Classifier	-	-	2	RBF Kernel	-

- **BatchNormalization Layer:** Batch normalization is a normalization technique applied to the intermediate outputs of a neural network, helping to stabilize and accelerate the training process by normalizing inputs and introducing learnable parameters.
- **Flattened Layer:** The flattening layer is introduced to prepare the data for input into the FCL. It takes the output from the convolutional layer (in the form of a 3D array) and transforms it into a one-dimensional vector.
- **FCL:** The proposed model consists of one FCL with 4096 features and the softmax as an activation function.
- **Dropout Layer:** A dropout layer follows the FCL to avoid over-fitting. The dropout rate is decided to be 0.5 based on the experiment.
- **Classifier layer:** KELM is plugged at the FCL of CNN, consisting of the featured map as input, a hidden layer, and a classifier layer. The featured vector generated by CNN is fed to the KELM's input layer. KELM's classifier layer applies the different kernels with varying gamma values.

2.2   Working Principle of CKELM

An in-depth discussion of the proposed model and its working principle is provided in the subsequent subsections. The working principle of the proposed model comprised seven steps, as follows:

1. **Data Collection:** The proposed model is validated on the Hazy parking dataset (HPD) and the PKLot Dataset (PKD) and is discussed as follows:

   (a). **HPD** is constructed and designed for the proposed model. Cameras are used to capture a total of 752 hazy parking images. The dataset is divided into HPD_training and HPD_Testing sets. The HPD_training set includes 70% of the dataset and the remaining in the HPD_Testing set. Table 2 represents the details of the HPD. To demonstrate the proposed dataset, we have kept around 10% of the HPD in GitHub for free download and is available at the link[1].

   (b). **PKD** [9] is an expanded version of the parking lot dataset released earlier in 2013 [5]. The dataset comprises images captured within the parking premises of PUCPR (Pontifical Catholic University of Parana) and UFPR (Federal University of Parana) located in Curitiba, Brazil. In order to reduce the likelihood of occlusion of nearby vehicles, cameras were strategically positioned on the rooftops of buildings. Table 3 represents the summary of the occupied and empty parking slots.

2. **Data Augmentation:** Keras, a deep learning Framework, was applied to augment and preprocess the dataset. The images are flipped, rotated, and cropped to increase the variability of images.
3. **Data Pre-processing:** Captured hazy images are fragmented into individual parking spaces, and each hazy image is pre-processed. A meticulous and thoughtfully devised series of pre-processing steps, such as resizing to a resolution of 224 × 224, converting into a gray color, and normalizing.
4. **Dehazing of Images:** For the dehazing of images, a CNN-based model called LD-Net (Lightweight dehazing network) is used and each hazy image is passed by LD-Net to remove the effects of haze.
5. **Feature Extractor:** The features from dehazed images are extracted using CNN and generated a feature vector to classifier for classification into free or busy classes.
6. **Classifier:** The extracted features are fed as input to KELM and classified into busy or free classes. Kernel ELM eliminates the need for random weight initialization as it directly computes the kernel matrix, leading to more stable and reproducible results. CKELM is good at generalizing, which means it can make accurate predictions on data that hasn't been seen before with less computational overhead and accelerate the learning speed by creating more flexible and robust decision boundaries.

---

[1] https://github.com/GauravS9776/Hazy-parking-system.

7. Performance Evaluation: Finally, results are aggregated, and CKELM is compared with ML classifiers integrated with CNN and with similar existing models in terms of performance metrics and is discussed in detail in the Sect. 3.

Table 2. Summary of HPD

Images Type	Free Slot Images	Busy Slot Images	Total Images
Unaugmented Training Images	150	380	532
Unaugmented Testing Images	100	122	222
Total Unaugmented Images	250	502	752
Augmented Training Images	1900	1500	3400
Augmented Testing Images	1000	610	1610
Total Augmented Images	2500	2510	5010

Table 3. Overview of the PKD

| Parking Lot | Weather Condition | Parking Capacity | | |
		Occupied Parking Slots	Empty Parking Slots	Total Parking Slots
UFPR04	Sunny	32,166	26,334	58,400
	Rainy	2,351	5,607	7,958
	Cloudy	11,608	27,779	39,387
UFPR05	Sunny	57,584	42,306	99,890
	Rainy	6,078	2,851	8,929
	Cloudy	33,764	23,202	56,966
PUCPR	Sunny	96,762	1,11,672	2,08,433
	Rainy	55,104	27,951	83,056
	Cloudy	42,363	90,417	132,780
Total Parking Capacity		3,37,780	3,58,119	6,95,899

2.3 Methodology of the Proposed Model

The proposed model is implemented on the Visual Studio Code IDE and the Python 3.9.9 platform with 12GB RAM and 24GB GPU with an Intel Core i3 processor. The model is trained and validated on the HPD and PKD. Both datasets are partitioned into ratios of 70 and 30. Table 4 lists the parameters used for feature extraction by the CNN. Firstly, images are dehazed by a based model called LD-Net. In the next step, dehazed images are fed to CNN for feature extraction. The extracted feature map is flattened and fed to KELM for classification. KELM is trained on this extracted feature map with a poly kernel and classifies images into output class labels as busy or free.

Table 4. Parameters setting during feature extraction by CNN

Parameter	Value and description
Learning Rate	0.001
Optimization	SGD
Batch Size	32
Epochs	5–20
Iteration Per Epoch	106

3   Results and Discussion

CKELM is trained for 5–20 epochs with different kernels in ELM and is validated on the hazy and non-hazy datasets. The performances are analyzed by plotting the confusion matrix (CM), comparing precision, accuracy, sensitivity, specificity, and F1-Score at different kernels. Finally, a performance comparison is made between CKELM and similar existing models.

3.1   Analysis by Confusion Matrix

Figure 1 illustrates the confusion matrices of the CKELM model for both HPD and PKD. The matrices show the model's performance across different epochs, highlighting the accuracy and misclassification rates for each class.

3.2   Comparison of Performance at Different Kernels

The performance of CKELM is analyzed using different kernel functions. Table 5 represents the accuracy and specificity comparison of CKELM for HPD and PKD with different kernel functions. Figures 2a, 2b, and 2c, respectively, represent Precision, Recall, and F1-Score metrics comparison with different kernel functions for HPD. Figures 3a, 3b, and 3c, respectively, represent Precision, Recall, and F1-Score metrics comparison with different kernel functions for PKD.

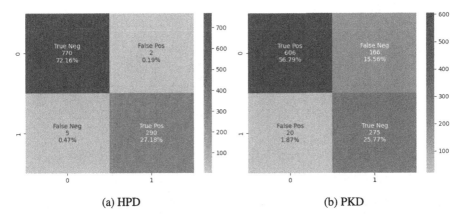

(a) HPD   (b) PKD

Fig. 1. Analysis of Confusion Matrix of CKELM for HPD and PKD

Table 5. Comparison of performance across different Kernels

	HPD		PKD Dataset	
Kernel used	Accuracy (%)	Specificity (%)	Accuracy (%)	Specificity (%)
Linear	94.38	**99.87**	92.36	95.87
RBF	73.01	90.00	69.23	85.65
Poly	**99.34**	97.74	**95.36**	**96.65**

3.3   Performance Comparison of CKELM with ML Classifiers

A performance comparison is made between CKELM and various ML classifiers, including ET, MLP, SVM, LDA, QDA, XgBoost, and DT, among others, combined with CNN. Each model has been trained for ten epochs on a hazy training subset (HPD_Training) and PKD. Table 6 represents the accuracy comparison of CKELM with ml classifiers trained and tested on the hazy and non-hazy datasets. Figures 4a, 4b, and 4c represent the performance metric comparison between CKELM and CNN-ML Classifiers for HPD. Figures 4a, 4b, and 4c represent the performance metric comparison between CKELM and CNN-ML Classifiers for HPD. Figures 5a, 5b, and 5c represent the performance comparison of CKELM with ml classifiers across subsets of PKD.

- The empirical findings demonstrate that CKELM outperforms CNN-ML classifiers in terms of accuracy for the UFPR05 and PUCPR subsets, as illustrated in Table 6. Specifically, CNN-SVM achieved the highest accuracy for the hazy dataset, while CNN-LR achieved the highest accuracy for the UFPR04 dataset.
- CNN-RF has the highest precision compared to CNN-ML classifiers. The reason may be during the construction of decision trees, and ET arbitrarily

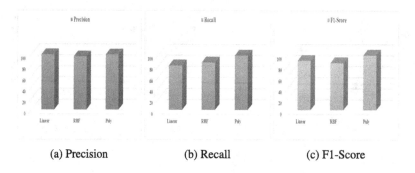

(a) Precision   (b) Recall   (c) F1-Score

Fig. 2. Performance comparison of CKELM for HPD

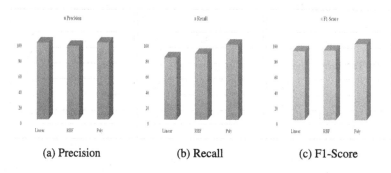

(a) Precision   (b) Recall   (c) F1-Score

Fig. 3. Performance comparison of CKELM on PKD

chooses a subset of features for each node. The randomization process introduces diversity and reduces the correlation between the decision trees. Due
to Randomization, RF captures specific patterns in the data, which exhibits
higher specificity.

- In comparison to other ML classifiers, CKELM achieves the highest specificity
  and F1-Score.
- CNN-LR shows a higher recall than CKELM. The expanded ability of LR
  to effectively capture the relationships between features and classes makes it
  particularly sensitive to identifying positive instances. Although some of the
  classifiers show better results in terms of recall and specificity, their precision,
  accuracy, and F1-score are less than the proposed CKELM model.

3.4   Comparison with Similar Existing Models

Table 7 compares the performance of the proposed model with CNN, KELM,
AOD-Net, and AOD-Net+modified mCNN for HPD. The evaluation was carried
out on the HPD, and the performance metrics were compared. Table 8 compares
the precision and recall values of CKELM with existing deep-learning models for
HPD. Table 9 demonstrates that CKELM outperforms existing models in terms
of accuracy, showcasing its superiority over conventional methods.

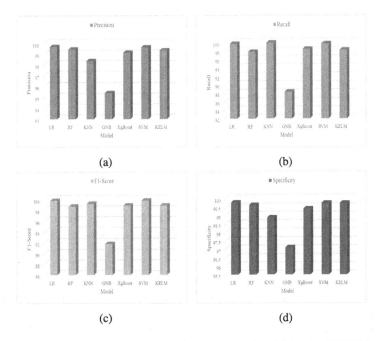

Fig. 4. Comparison of Precision, Recall, F1-Score, and Specificity for CKELM vs CNN-ML Classifiers on HPD

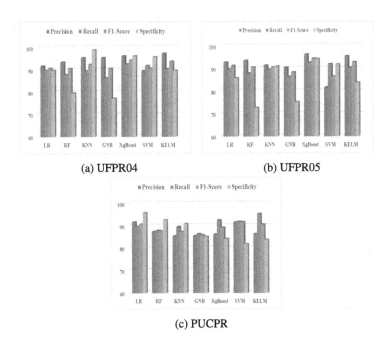

Fig. 5. Comparison of performance for CKELM vs CNN-ML Classifiers on PKD

Table 6. Comparison of Accuracy of CKELM vs CNN-ML classifiers

Model→ Datasets ↓	CNN	KELM	CNN-LR	CNN-RF	CNN-KNN	CNN-GNB	CNN-XgBoost	CNN-SVM	CKELM
HPD	94.65	82.56	99.08	98.93	99.33	93.6	99.06	**99.78**	99.34
UFPR04	92.51	80.23	**99.96**	97.85	87.85	82.56	95.36	94.36	97.68
UFPR05	91.32	85.32	92.56	92.65	82.56	95.36	94.36	97.68	**97.96**
PUCPR	95.26	84.63	99.53	95.65	82.56	95.36	92.36	96.68	**98.54**

- The CKELM performance is compared with existing deep-learning models regarding accuracy. CKELM attained the highest accuracy values when compared with similar existing models for HPD. In Table 8, we comprehensively compare CKELM with established deep-learning models for PKD. The assessment is based on critical performance metrics such as precision and recall. Remarkably, when considering precision and recall, CNN integrated with KELM emerges as the standout performer, boasting the highest scores for recall. Its precision and recall values signify its exceptional ability to identify positive cases precisely while effectively capturing all relevant instances. In essence, Table 8 encapsulates the superior performance of CKELM, showcasing its prowess when pitted against both established benchmarks and contemporary methods.
- CKELM is benchmarked against the existing parking classification models [6,10,18,26]. Table 9 demonstrates that CKELM outperforms existing models in terms of accuracy, showcasing its superiority over conventional methods. CKELM exhibits the highest accuracy across the PKD dataset subsets such as UFPR04\UFPR04 (99.47%), UFPR04\PUCPR (97.77%), PUCPR\PUCPR (99.09%), UFPR05\UFPR05 (99.26%), and remains competitive for other subset combinations. Mean Ensemble from De et al. [10] exhibits superior performance for the subset UFPR04\UFPR05 compared to existing methods. Amato et al.'s mAlexNet [7] excels for the UFPR05\PUCPR and PUCPR\UFPR04. Referring to Table 9, CKELM outperforms other methods for the subsets as UFPR05\UFPR05, UFPR04\UFPR04, UFPR04\PUCPR, and PUCPR\PUCPR with accuracies of 99.26%, 99.47%, 97.77%, and 99.09% respectively and is comparable for other subsets.

3.5   Runtime Analysis

During the training phase, FCL of CNN consumes ten percent of the computation time for adjusting layer parameters [11] and the training time is computed as follows, represented in the Eq. 1.

$$\sum_{l=1}^{k} a_{l-1}.b_l^2.a_l.c_l^2 \tag{1}$$

Table 7. Accuracy Comparison of the CKELM with existing models for HPD

Model	Accuracy (training and testing on hazy)
CNN	94.65%
KELM	82.56%
AOD-Net [25]	86.71%
AOD-Net + modified mAlexnet [25]	88.39%
CKELM (Proposed)	**97.56%**

Table 8. Precision and Recall comparison of CKELM with existing models for PKD

Author(s)	Model	Precision	Recall
Agrawal et al. [3]	Mask R-CNN	95.00%	-
Kolhar et al. [15]	mAlexNet	**97.90%**	-
Mettupally et al. [17]	FMR-CNN	91.90%	-
Polprasert et al. [19]	mAlexNet	79.00%	98.00%
Sairam et al. [24]	Mask R-CNN	92.33%	-
Proposed Model	CKELM	97.32%	**99.32%**

Table 9. Accuracy comparison of CKELM with existing state-of-the-art models

Author(s)	Model	Training	Testing		
			UFPR04	UFPR05	PUCPR
			Accuracy (%)		
		UFPR04	98.27	99.54	93.29
Amato et al. [7]	mAlexnet	UFPR05	92.72	93.69	**99.49**
		PUCPR	**99.90**	98.03	96.00
		UFPR04	84.25	99.55	84.92
De et al. [10]	LPQ, LBP and its variants	UFPR05	87.74	85.76	98.90
		PUCPR	99.58	87.15	82.78
		UFPR04	88.40	**99.64**	88.33
De et al. [10]	Mean Ensemble	UFPR05	89.83	85.53	99.30
		PUCPR	99.61	88.88	84.20
		UFPR04	98.30	95.60	97.60
Nurullayev et al. [18]	CarNet	UFPR05	**98.40**	95.20	97.50
		PUCPR	98.80	94.40	97.70
		UFPR04	**99.47**	98.97	**97.77**
Proposed Model	CKELM	UFPR05	94.90	**99.26**	95.90
		PUCPR	96.83	96.08	**99.09**

where, l is the index of the convets, a_l is the number of kernels at the lth layer, a_{l-1} is the number of input channels of the lth layer, k is the number of convets, b_l is the size of the filter, and c_l is the size of the output feature vector.

Previous work has demonstrated that ELM classifiers require less training time than traditional ML classifiers because ELM is trained in a single iteration, eliminating the need for costly backpropagation [12]. Hence, the FCL of CNN is replaced with KELM, and due to this, CNN exhibits the minimum training and testing time compared with all other models. Table 10 depicts the training time comparison of CKELM with other ML classifiers combined with CNN (bold indicates minimum). As shown in Table 10, CNN obtained the highest training and testing time, which may be due to the following reasons:

- CNN has a deeper architecture of eight layers, including five convolutional and three fully connecting layers. Due to more parameters and complex calculations, each layer exhibits the maximum training time.
- Backpropagation is applied to adjust the output layers' weights in the fully connecting layer. This process entails numerous iterations, which in turn extends the duration of the training process.

Table 10. Training Time Comparison

Model	Training time (in sec)			
	HPD	PKD		
		UFPR04	UFPR05	PUCPR
CNN	4728	9785	8526	9654
KELM	1.669	1.289	1.456	1.401
CNN-LR	1.700	2.451	1.589	1.653
CNN-RF	6.945	1.356	1.326	1.421
CNN-KNN	1.989	1.547	1.897	**1.123**
CNN-GNB	1.451	1.145	1.987	1.235
CNN-XgBoost	1.897	1.564	1.789	1.954
CNN-SVM	0945	4895	9785	8754
CKELM (Proposed)	**0.131**	**1.111**	**1.045**	1.651

3.6 Discussion

CNN attained an accuracy of 94.09% after ten epochs of training. CNN achieved an even greater degree of accuracy when trained for fifty or more epochs with a very high computational time. In the same terms, KELM attained an accuracy of 82.56% with a 'poly' kernel. Further enhancing the accuracy of KELM is achieved by training for more epochs. The proposed model has leveraged the benefits of

CNN and KELM, resulting in a maximum accuracy of 99.34% for HPD and 98.54% for PKD with few training epochs. The model performed better with relatively less training time (discussed in Sect. 3.5).

- Fig. 6 and 7 represents the confusion matrix for CNN, KELM, and CKELM for HPD and PKD datasets.
- Fig. 8a, 8b, and 8c represents precision, recall, and specificity comparison for CNN, KELM, and CKELM for 20 epochs for HPD. Figure 9a, 9b, and 9c represents precision, recall, and specificity comparison for CNN, KELM, and CKELM for 20 epochs for PKD dataset.

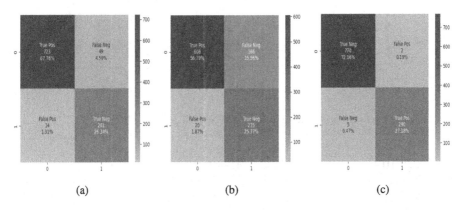

(a)   (b)   (c)

Fig. 6. Confusion Matrix for (a) CNN (b) KELM (c) CKELM for HPD

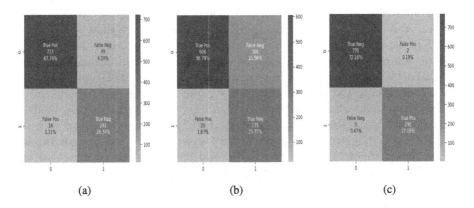

(a)   (b)   (c)

Fig. 7. Confusion Matrix for (a) CNN (b) KELM (c) CKELM for PKD

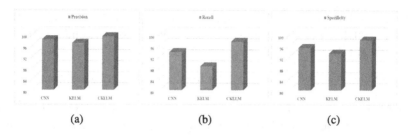

Fig. 8. Performance comparison for CNN, KELM, and CKELM for HPD

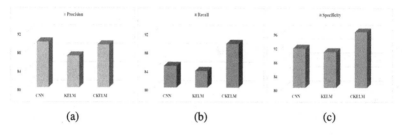

Fig. 9. Performance comparison for CNN, KELM, and CKELM for PKD

4   Conclusion and Future Directions

This study introduces an innovative ensemble approach named CKELM, designed to classify parking spaces under hazy conditions and non-hazy. Firstly, images are dehazed using LD-Net, a CNN-based model. In the second stage, the dehazed image is input into CNN for feature extraction. Finally, the extracted feature vector is passed to the Kernel ELM (KELM) for classification, with KELM is taking the place of the FCL of CNN. To validate the effectiveness of this approach, an HPD was curated, comprising images captured in various hazy conditions, including haze, fog, and snow. The CKELM is tested on the PKD dataset for non-hazy weather conditions. Comparative performance analysis was made with similar existing models. The results demonstrate that CKELM achieved an impressive accuracy rate of 97.56% for HPD and 99.34% for PKD. Additionally, the computational time required for the entire classification process either outperformed or was comparable with similar existing models. These findings underscore the potential of CKELM as a promising approach for accurately classifying parking spaces in hazy and non-hazy weather conditions. Future extensions of this work may encompass optimizing parameters that are essential for the classification operation within the KELM. Furthermore, the utilization of CNN variants for feature extraction presents a possibility of further reduce reducing computational time.

References

1. Huang, G.B.: What are extreme learning machines? Filling the gap between Frank Rosenblatt's dream and John von Neumann's puzzle. Cogn. Comput. **7**(3), 263–278 (2015)
2. Khan, A., et al.: Reducing parking space search time and environmental impacts: a technology driven smart parking case study. IEEE Technol. Soc. Mag. **39**(3), 62–75 (2020)
3. Agrawal, T., Urolagin, S.: Multi-angle parking detection system using mask R-CNN. In: Proceedings of the 2020 2nd International Conference on Big Data Engineering and Technology, pp. 76–80 (2020)
4. Ahmad, I., Basheri, M., Iqbal, M.J., Rahim, A.: Performance comparison of support vector machine, random forest, and extreme learning machine for intrusion detection. IEEE Access **6**, 33789–33795 (2018)
5. Almeida, P., Oliveira, L.S., Silva, E., Britto, A., Koerich, A.: Parking space detection using textural descriptors. In: 2013 IEEE International Conference on Systems, Man, and Cybernetics, pp. 3603–3608. IEEE (2013)
6. Amato, G., Carrara, F., Falchi, F., Gennaro, C., Meghini, C., Vairo, C.: Deep learning for decentralized parking lot occupancy detection. Expert Syst. Appl. **72**, 327–334 (2017)
7. Amato, G., Carrara, F., Falchi, F., Gennaro, C., Vairo, C.: Car parking occupancy detection using smart camera networks and deep learning. In: 2016 IEEE Symposium on Computers and Communication (ISCC), pp. 1212–1217. IEEE (2016)
8. Chiu, M.Y., Depommier, R., Spindler, T.: An embedded real-time vision system for 24-hour indoor/outdoor car-counting applications. In: Proceedings of the 17th International Conference on Pattern Recognition, 2004. ICPR 2004, vol. 3, pp. 338–341. IEEE (2004)
9. de Almeida, P.R., Oliveira, L.S., Britto, A.S., Silva, E.J., Koerich, A.L.: Pklot - a robust dataset for parking lot classification. Expert Syst. Appl. **42**(11), 4937–4949 (2015)
10. De Almeida, P.R., Oliveira, L.S., Britto, A.S., Jr., Silva, E.J., Jr., Koerich, A.L.: Pklot-a robust dataset for parking lot classification. Expert Syst. Appl. **42**(11), 4937–4949 (2015)
11. He, K., Sun, J.: Convolutional neural networks at constrained time cost. In: Proceedings of the IEEE Conference on Computer Vision and Pattern Recognition, pp. 5353–5360 (2015)
12. Huang, G.B., Ding, X., Zhou, H.: Optimization method based extreme learning machine for classification. Neurocomputing **74**(1–3), 155–163 (2010)
13. Huang, G.B., Zhou, H., Ding, X., Zhang, R.: Extreme learning machine for regression and multiclass classification. IEEE Trans. Syst. Man Cybern. Part B (Cybernetics) **42**(2), 513–529 (2011)
14. Huang, G.B., Zhou, H., Ding, X., Zhang, R.: Extreme learning machine for regression and multiclass classification. IEEE Trans. Syst. Man Cybern. Part B (Cybernetics) **42**(2), 513–529 (2012). https://doi.org/10.1109/TSMCB.2011.2168604
15. Kolhar, M.S., Alameen, A.: Multi criteria decision making system for parking system. Comput. Syst. Sci. Eng. **36**(1), 101–116 (2021)
16. Mangiaracina, R., Tumino, A., Miragliotta, G., Salvadori, G., Perego, A.: Smart parking management in a smart city: costs and benefits. In: 2017 IEEE International Conference on Service Operations and Logistics, and Informatics (SOLI), pp. 27–32. IEEE (2017)

17. Mettupally, S.N.R., Menon, V.: A smart eco-system for parking detection using deep learning and big data analytics. In: 2019 SoutheastCon, pp. 1–4. IEEE (2019)

18. Nurullayev, S., Lee, S.W.: Generalized parking occupancy analysis based on dilated convolutional neural network. Sensors **19**(2) (2019)

19. Polprasert, C., Sruayiam, C., Pisawongprakan, P., Teravetchakarn, S.: A camera-based smart parking system employing low-complexity deep learning for outdoor environments. In: 2019 17th International Conference on ICT and Knowledge Engineering (ICT&KE), pp. 1–5. IEEE (2019)

20. Roul, R.K.: Impact of multilayer elm feature mapping technique on supervised and semi-supervised learning algorithms. Soft. Comput. **26**(1), 423–437 (2022)

21. Roul, R.K., Navpreet, Sahoo, J.K.: Ensemble-based road surface crack detection: a comprehensive approach. In: Goyal, V., Kumar, N., Bhowmick, S.S., Goyal, P., Goyal, N., Kumar, D. (eds) Big Data and Artificial Intelligence. International Conference on Big Data Analytics, pp. 166–184. Springer, Cham (2023). https://doi.org/10.1007/978-3-031-49601-1_12

22. Roul, R.K., Navpreet, Sahoo, J.K.: Intelligent ensemble-based road crack detection: a holistic view. In: Devismes, S., Mandal, P.S., Saradhi, V.V., Prasad, B., Molla, A.R., Sharma, G. (eds) Distributed Computing and Intelligent Technology. International Conference on Distributed Computing and Intelligent Technology, pp. 307–323. Springer, Cham (2024). https://doi.org/10.1007/978-3-031-50583-6_21

23. Roul, R.K., Satyanath, G.: A novel feature selection based text classification using multi-layer elm. In: Roy, P.P., Agarwal, A., Li, T., Krishna Reddy, P., Uday Kiran, R. (eds) Big Data Analytics. International Conference on Big Data Analytics, pp. 33–52. Springer, Cham (2022). https://doi.org/10.1007/978-3-031-24094-2_3

24. Sairam, B., Agrawal, A., Krishna, G., Sahu, S.P.: Automated vehicle parking slot detection system using deep learning. In: 2020 Fourth International Conference on Computing Methodologies and Communication (ICCMC), pp. 750–755. IEEE (2020)

25. Satyanath, G., Sahoo, J.K., Roul, R.K.: Smart parking space detection under hazy conditions using convolutional neural networks: a novel approach. Multimedia Tools Appl. **82**(10), 15415–15438 (2023)

26. Simonyan, K., Zisserman, A.: Very deep convolutional networks for large-scale image recognition. arXiv preprint arXiv:1409.1556 (2014)

Classification of Impacted Teeth from Panoramic Radiography Using Deep Learning

Shweta Kharat[1], Sandeep S. Udmale[1]([✉])(iD), Aneesh G. Nath[2],
Girish P. Bhole[1], and Sunil G. Bhirud[3]

[1] Department of Computer Engineering and Information Technology, Veermata
Jijabai Technological Institute (VJTI), Mumbai 400019, Maharashtra, India
{sskharat_m22,gpbhole}@ce.vjti.ac.in, ssudmale@it.vjti.ac.in
[2] Department of Computer Science and Engineering, TKM College of Engineering,
Kollam, Kerala, India
aneeshgnath@tkmce.ac.in
[3] Department of Computer Science and Engineering, COEP Technological
University, Pune 411005, Maharashtra, India
vc@coeptech.ac.in

Abstract. Impacted teeth with a high prevalence rate pose a significant challenge in dental diagnosis and treatment planning. Traditional methods heavily rely on manual assessment, which can be time-consuming and prone to human error for classifying the signs of anomalies. This research proposes a novel approach for impacted teeth analysis using a custom Convolution Neural Network (CNN) architecture. Panoramic radiographs are employed for this research as they cover the whole dental arch, from individual teeth to the maxilla and mandible. It is significantly influenced by the diverse angles and shapes of teeth with non-similar patterns of individuals' impacted teeth. The proposed CNN architecture leverages the power of deep learning to classify impacted teeth from panoramic radiographs automatically. This study evaluated the performance of pre-trained models and YOLO architectures for the teeth dataset. The custom CNN architecture outperforms these models and shows an testing accuracy of 95.99%. Overall, our research showcases the effectiveness of deep learning in revolutionizing the analysis of impacted teeth, paving the way for more efficient and personalized treatment strategies in dentistry.

Keywords: Convolutional Neural Networks (CNNs) · Deep Learning · Impacted Teeth · Panoramic Radiography

1 Introduction

Generally, dental clinics employ various radiographic techniques to acquire multiple properties and visualize the specific region to confirm and prepare the

© The Author(s), under exclusive license to Springer Nature Switzerland AG 2025
Q. Bramas et al. (Eds.): ICDCIT 2025, LNCS 15507, pp. 257–270, 2025.
https://doi.org/10.1007/978-3-031-81404-4_19

treatment accordingly. The widely adopted picturing technique in dentistry is panoramic radiography, which covers a vast region with a remarkably inferior radiation dose. It makes it possible and assists the specialist in diagnosing various abnormalities, injuries, and dental conditions [18,26]. Impaction is most commonly found dental condition in third molars, also known as wisdom teeth, and can be classified based on the classification provided by Winter's classification [10] into Horizontal, Mesioangular, Vertical, Distoangular, and other types. Impacted teeth are a common dental anomaly. The plurality of third molar impacted teeth varies approximately from 17.0% to 68.0%, presenting significant challenges in diagnosis and treatment planning due to their varying positions and orientation within the jaw. This phenomenon often occurs due to factors such as overcrowding of teeth, the jaw being too small to fit the wisdom teeth, abnormal eruption path, or lack of space in the jaw [10,18,26].

Traditional diagnostic methods rely heavily on manual assessment of panoramic radiographs. These methods are often time-consuming and prone to human error, which can vary significantly among dental clinicians due to differences in individual judgment and opinions. With advancements in artificial intelligence (AI) and deep learning, there is a growing interest in integrating these technologies to enhance the efficiency and accuracy of patient care in the dental field [4,14].

Deep learning has revolutionized various fields, including medical and dental imaging, by providing architectures for automated diagnosis and analysis [21]. In the context of impacted teeth, several studies have explored the application of deep learning in diagnosis and treatment planning for impacted teeth [1,14]. Lee et al. (2022) in [15] utilized regional Convolutional Neural Networks (CNNs) to automatically detect and classify 17 categories impacted teeth from DICOM format. The clinical data and X-ray images of patients were employed as input to develop the combined practical predictive model using multilayer perceptron and CNN respectively for identifying mandibular third molar tooth. Vollmer et al. (2022) conducted a systematic review of deep learning in dental imaging and observed an accuracy of 0.75 for ResNet50, 0.75 for VGG16, 0.62 for MobileNetV2, 0.75 for InceptionV3, and 0.70 for custom CNN for RS classification. The study concluded that Custom CNN achieved a higher accuracy of 0.90 on AUC and robustness, making it the preferred choice for classification systems according to their relationship to OAC [25]. Lei et al. (2023) proposed a method of knowledge distillation on YOLOv5 architecture utilizing YOLOv5x as a teacher model and YOLOv5s as a student model to create YOLOv5s-x architecture, which is lightweight and increased mAP by 2.9% compared to original models on 2146 panoramic images leveraging a powerful aspect of deep learning known as transfer learning [16].

In summary, applying deep learning in impacted teeth analysis, particularly for diagnosis and treatment planning, demonstrates significant advantages and potential. Many studies leverage pre-trained CNN for classification and innovative approaches like knowledge distillation. Collectively, these works establish a strong foundation for further research, indicating that deep learning methodologies pave the way for enhanced and efficient patient care. This study proposes a novel approach to impacted teeth analysis using a custom CNN architecture. Panoramic radiography is employed to image modality as it provides a comprehensive view of the dental arch, ranging from individual teeth to the maxilla and mandible. A custom CNN architecture is designed to handle the specific characteristics of panoramic images, ensuring optimal performance even with a relatively small dataset of 96 images (Fig. 1).

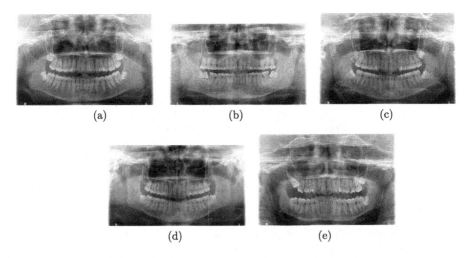

Fig. 1. Dataset with different categories of images: (a) Healthy, (b) Horizontal, (c) Mesioangular, (d) Vertical, and (e) Others.

2   Materials and Methods

Pre-trained models reviewed for this study YOLO, AlexNet, ResNet, Xception, Inception, etc., are commonly trained on large-scale datasets such as ImageNet, which mainly consists of everyday objects such as cats, dogs, and vehicles. However, these models often perform poorly on medical datasets because they are not trained to detect the subtle features needed for medical imaging tasks like identifying impacted teeth. Furthermore, refining these pre-trained models is challenging; thousands of images are often required to detect such tiny patterns and prevent overfitting. Given that our dataset was only 96 original images, using a complex pre-trained architecture was computationally exhaustive and impractical [2,12]. These limitations fueled our motivation to design a custom CNN architecture, which better suits a smaller dataset and allows us to extract relevant information from panoramic efficient X-ray images.

2.1   Image Dataset

The Government Dental College in Nagpur, Dr. Jaiyaswal's Clinic of Dentistry, and the Geriatric Oral Health Care Centre in Nagpur, India, provided support for our research and result confirmation [8,9]. A total of 96 panoramic radiograph images were collected from them and utilized, ensuring a diverse representation of impacted teeth cases. The resolution of PRs was (2706, 1536). PRs were exported in Joint Photographic Experts Group (JPG) format.

Fig. 2. The architecture of custom CNN.

2.2   Data Augmentation

Given the need for large datasets required for model training and feature learning in the deep learning realm, data augmentation proves to be an important aspect of increasing the volume of the dataset. Different augmentation techniques were used for the small dataset of 96 images using TensorFlow's ImageDataGenerator[1], namely vertical flip, horizontal flip, horizontal flip of vertically flipped images, and lastly, outward scaling to obtain a subtotal of 2272 PRs. For the purposes of training, testing, and validation, the augmented dataset was divided into three parts:

– One thousand eight hundred twenty-two images were allocated for training.
– Two hundred twenty-five images were used for testing.
– Another Two hundred twenty-five images were set aside for validation.

2.3   Data Pre-processing

In the image pre-processing stage for this research, a series of essential steps were undertaken. Initially images are resized uniformly to dimensions of (256, 256), to ensure consistency for the dataset. Following this step, datasets are organized in batch of 64 samples each, promoting efficiency during training and evaluation phases. Furthermore, normalization is employed where images are scaled in the range between 0 and 1. Out of many normalization technique min-max scaling was employed. Normalization ensures model's performance remains uninfluenced by the scale of input pixel values [27].

---

[1] https://www.tensorflow.org/api_docs/python/tf/keras/preprocessing/image/ImageDataGenerator.

2.4   Model Architecture

For the classification task for impacted teeth analysis, this study designed a custom Convolutional Neural Network (CNN) architecture, as shown in Fig. 2, which is tailored to the specific needs of our dataset. CNNs are mostly equipped for image recognition tasks due to their ability to capture spatial hierarchies in images through convolutional layers; using this feature, our suggested architecture leverages this potential for efficiency and optimal performance while also keeping the model lightweight.

The custom CNN architecture is composed of several keys for processing the input panoramic X-ray images and producing accurate classification results for impacted teeth analysis. The model architecture begins with an input layer accepting images of shape (256, 256, 3), thus ensuring that all images are uniformly sized. This is followed by the first convolutional layer, which applies 16 filters of kernel size 3x3 using the ReLU activation function. Then, a max-pooling layer is applied, reducing the spatial dimensions by applying a 2x2 pool size. Consequently, the second convolutional layer applied 32 filters with the same kernel size of 3x3 kernel size and ReLU activation, followed by another max-pooling layer with the same 2x2 pool size. The final convolutional layer employs 64 filters with the same kernel size and activation, followed by the final max-pooling layer. Max pooling is employed as it efficiently reduces spatial dimensions and helps emphasize significant features needed for classification.

After all the convolutional and pooling operations, a flattening layer is included, which transforms the 3D feature maps into a 1D feature vector needed for further training. This is followed by three fully connected layers with 256, 128, and 64 units, respectively, all using the ReLU activation function. The final layer of the architecture is a softmax output layer with five units corresponding to the number of classes in the classification task. Using softmax activation facilitates multiclass classification, providing probability interpretations of model outputs, thus enabling efficient training, and ReLU is used for its capacity of nonlinearity, capturing complex patterns and relationships within data, enhancing models' capacity of learning intricate features and thereby increasing the efficacy of classification. Finally, the model is compiled using the Adam optimizer and sparse categorical cross-entropy as the loss function. The accuracy metric is used for evaluation. Training was conducted over 20 epochs with a batch size of 64.

3   Results and Discussion

This study investigated the performance of a custom CNN architecture for image classification in dental applications.

3.1   Software and Hardware

Python 3 is used as the primary programming architecture for the implementation of custom CNN architecture, and TensorFlow as 2.x as a deep learning

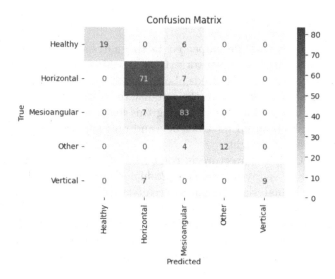

Fig. 3. Confusion matrix of Custom CNN architecture.

framework. Additionally, libraries from Python ecosystems were also employed, such as NumPy for numerical computations and data manipulation and matplotlib for visualization, random for setting the same seed value for NumPy, TensorFlow, and Python to ensure that the random initialization of weights, shuffling of data during training, and other random processes are consistent across runs. This study is executed on a Google Colab[2] runtime environment, utilizing a T4 GPU.

3.2   Evaluation Metric

The evaluation metric used in the study primarily focused on assessing the performance of the developed CNN model for impacted teeth classification. This study employed metrics such as accuracy, precision, recall, and F1-score, which provide insights into the model's ability to correctly classify impacted teeth. Additionally, metrics, like mean Average Precision (mAP) and area under the ROC curve (AUC), were utilized to evaluate the overall performance. These metrics contribute valuable insights to the enhancement of dental image analysis techniques [27].

3.3   Performance Evaluation of Model

The proposed CNN architecture demonstrated strong performance on the testing dataset, achieving a testing accuracy of 95.99%, precision of 0.92, recall of 0.91,

---

[2] https://colab.research.google.com/.

and F1 score of 0.90. These parameters indicate that the model is highly effective in classifying impacted teeth images into their respective categories. The accuracy of 95.99% suggests that the model correctly predicted the labels for a majority of the validation dataset, showcasing its overall effectiveness. A high reliability can be observed as a precision score of 0.92 means that 92.0% of the positive predictions were correct. Additionally, a recall score of 0.91 shows the model's capacity to identify 91.0% of the actual positive cases, demonstrating its sensitivity. Furthermore, the model robustness can be observed with a F1-score of 0.90, which balances precision and recall, making the model accurate and comprehensive predictions. In conclusion, the strong performance metrics achieved by the proposed CNN architecture underscore its effectiveness in accurately classifying impacted teeth images, making it a promising tool for clinical applications in dentistry.

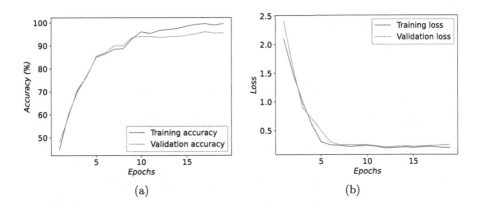

Fig. 4. Training accuracy and loss analysis of proposed model.

In this section, we provide a comprehensive analysis including the confusion matrix, training and validation accuracy, loss curves, and ROC curves to assess the performance and robustness of the proposed custom model. The confusion matrix depicted in the Fig. 3, reveals the custom architecture performance across five classes: Healthy, Horizontal, Mesioangular, Other, and Vertical. The model demonstrated strong performance in identifying Mesioangular and Horizontal impaction, with true positive rates of 83 and 71, respectively. However, there were misclassifications, such as 6 Healthy cases identified as Mesioangular and 7 Horizontal cases misclassified as Mesioangular impactions. The Other and Vertical classes showed higher misclassification rates compared to other classes, indicating a potential class imbalance issue. This finding highlights the need for enhanced class differentiation and acquiring more datasets, especially for less common categories for enhanced accuracy.

The training and validation accuracy/loss graphs, as shown in Fig. 4, highlight the model's strong ability to fit the training data, almost achieving 96.0%

264   S. Kharat et al.

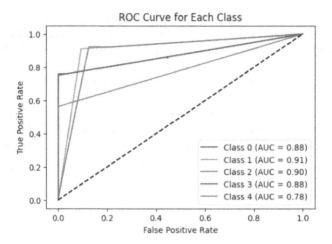

Fig. 5. ROC curve of the proposed method.

testing accuracy. This demonstrates the model's excellent learning capacity and effectiveness in capturing hidden patterns with the training dataset. The fluctuations in validation accuracy indicate that the model faces challenges with unseen data. On the other hand, training loss, as seen in the Fig. 4, remains near zero, while validation loss was consistently high and increased slightly. This suggests a case of overfitting where model performance is exceptional on training data but struggles on validation data. However, with the implementation of techniques such as regularization, balancing the dataset, and inclusion of more images, there is a significant potential to enhance the model's performance, making it even more robust and effective.

The ROC curve depicted in Fig. 5 showcases the model's ability to distinguish between positive and negative cases across different classes. Each line represents the ROC curve for a specific class, with the area under the curve (AUC) metric. The higher AUC values represent better discrimination capacity, and the values closer to 1 represent superior performance. Overall, the model demonstrates strong performance across most classes, with AUC values ranging from 0.78 to 0.91. For class 4, the lowest AUC value is observed at 0.78, indicating that the model is facing a challenge in accuracy distinguishing between positive and negative cases for class 4, and the highest is seen for class 1. Further analysis and implementation need to be done to address the challenge faced by the model for class 4, thereby enhancing the model's performance.

3.4   Performance Comparison

A comprehensive exploration of various deep learning architectures and techniques was conducted to identify suitable approaches for impacted teeth analysis, keeping the system lightweight as well. This exploration encompassed a wide

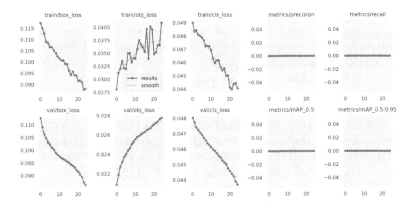

Fig. 6. YOLOv5 Training Performance.

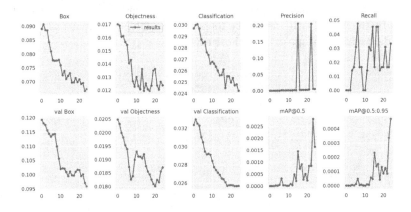

Fig. 7. YOLOv7 Training Performance.

range of state-of-art models, including YOLO (You Only Look Once) [16] versions (specifically YOLO8s, YOLOV8n, YOLOV8m, YOLOV8l, and YOLOV8x, as well as YOLO V5 and YOLO V7) [11]. Additionally, traditional CNN architectures such as VGG16 [20], ResNet [6], AlexNet [13], Google Inception V3 [23], DenseNet [7], Capsnet [17], NASNet [28], EfficientNet [24], Xception [5], SegNet [3], InceptionResNet V2 [22], and UNet [19] were explored. Each model was evaluated based on performance metrics, suitable for specific tasks, training time, and computational capacity required for impacted teeth analysis, paving the way for more informed model selection and development.

In evaluating the performance of YOLOv5 and YOLOv7 for object detection on a dataset consisting of only 96 images, significant advancements were observed in both the training and validation phases, as depicted in Fig. 6 (representing YOLOv5) and Fig. 7 (representing YOLOv7). Despite limited dataset size, both models demonstrated promising progress in training loss, suggesting enhanced capacities for classification. A decrease in validation losses was observed during validation, alongside a general increase in precision and recall metrics. However, the relatively low mAP raises a concern regarding the model's effectiveness in practical applications, potentially questioning its reliability. These results under-score the need for a larger dataset to achieve improved accuracy in the classifi-cation of impacted teeth.

Figure 8 illustrates the performance evaluation of YOLOv8 models based on accuracy and loss trained on a limited dataset of 96 images. YOLOv8x and YOLOv8m emerge as the most efficient, achieving an accuracy of 45.45%, closely followed by YOLOv8l at 36.36%. In contrast, YOLOv8s and YOLOv8n exhibited the lowest accuracies, standing at 9.09%. While YOLOv8x and YOLOv8m out-perform other models in accuracy, they also demonstrate higher computational complexity than YOLOv8s and YOLOv8n, which offer lighter computational demands but achieve lower accuracy. This evaluation highlights the importance of considering model architecture, computational demands, and performance when selecting the most suitable YOLOv8 model for our specific task. These findings further justify the necessity for a custom CNN architecture tailored to limited datasets, as proposed in this study.

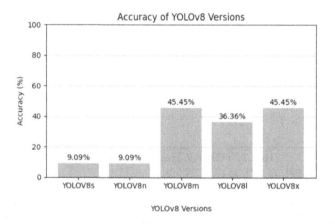

Fig. 8. YOLOv8 Models Training Performance.

Expanding the evaluation to assess the performance metrics of a diverse array of deep learning architectures trained on an augmented dataset while also using the widely adopted transfer learning approach aimed to enhance accuracy. The study, as depicted in Fig. 9, illustrates the impact of employing transfer learning on top of the proposed CNN architecture. Among the models evaluated, Capsnet emerges, achieving an impressive testing accuracy of 95.0%, closely followed by SegNet with an testing accuracy of 94.0%. Conversely, the lowest accuracy was observed with DenseNet, demonstrating a meager testing accuracy of 26.0%.

Model Performance Comparison

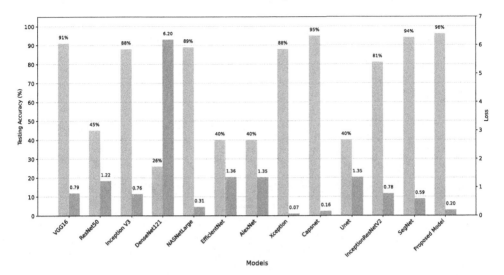

Fig. 9. Other architectures training performance.

Despite the enhanced accuracy, these models exhibit higher computational complexity, demanding substantial resources for training. This presents a significant hurdle, as this study aimed to maintain a lightweight model with respect to training time and computational resources. Through this evaluation, the importance of maintaining a balance between performance and resource efficiency in model selection is highlighted. Figure 10 shows the training time required for each model. This indicates that the proposed model requires less time than the other models. This variation is observed due to the number of trainable parameters employed in each model.

4   Discussion

In this study, we explored the application of various deep learning architectures, including YOLO versions and traditional pre-trained CNNs, for the classification of impacted teeth from panoramic radiographs. Our custom CNN architecture demonstrated promising performance, particularly in capturing hidden patterns in panoramic X-ray images. However, challenges such as overfitting were observed, requiring the implementation of regularization techniques and dataset augmentation to improve generalization. The comparative analysis with YOLO models revealed interesting insights into their performance, with our custom CNN showing competitive results despite the limited dataset size. Moreover, the ROC curve analysis highlighted specific areas, such as the lower AUC for class 4, indicating opportunities for targeted enhancements. Overall, our findings highlight the potential of deep learning in dental image analysis while emphasizing the importance of custom model development through rigorous evaluation

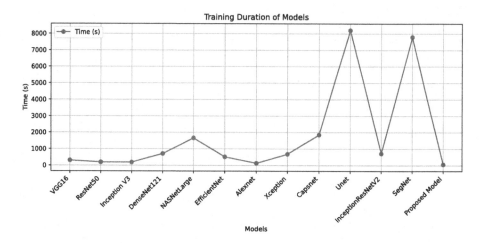

Fig. 10. Compariosn of training time.

methodologies. Future research efforts should focus on expanding the dataset, refining model architectures, and exploring techniques to enhance classification accuracy and efficiency while keeping the architecture lightweight, thereby enhancing patient care in the dental field.

5   Conclusion

In conclusion, this study has presented a novel approach for the analysis of impacted teeth on panoramic radiography using a custom Convolutional Neural Network (CNN) architecture. Through an extensive exploration of various pre-trained deep learning models and techniques, including YOLO versions and traditional CNN architectures, this study designed a custom CNN architecture tailored specifically for limited datasets. The main aim of the study was classification based on types of impacted teeth while keeping architecture simpler and lightweight. Our model demonstrated promising performance in accurately classifying types of impaction from panoramic radiography, achieving an testing accuracy of 95.99%. The evaluation of different normalization techniques and model architecture highlights the importance and need for experimentation for model selection to achieve higher performance. Additionally, the implementation of data augmentation techniques significantly enhanced accuracy and helped vastly improve the training process.

While the proposed architecture showcased higher accuracy, it is essential to acknowledge the limitations faced during this study, one of which is relatively small data. Data acquisition is the biggest challenge faced while incorporating Artificial Intelligence in healthcare, which results in models having some potential bias along with security concerns it raises. Future research efforts could be focused on further enhancing and refining the architecture and exploring larger datasets. Overall, this study highlights the importance of exploring the potential of deep learning in revolutionizing dental diagnosis and treatment planning, paving the way for more efficient and customized patient care in dentistry.

Acknowledgment. This work was supported by the Centre of Excellence in Artificial Intelligence (CoE AI), Veermata Jijabai Technological Institute (VJTI), Mumbai, India.

References

1. Almalki, Y.E., et al.: Deep learning models for classification of dental diseases using orthopantomography X-ray OPG images. Sensors **22**(19), 7370 (2022)
2. Alzubaidi, L., et al.: Towards a better understanding of transfer learning for medical imaging: a case study. Appl. Sci. **10**(13), 4523 (2020)
3. Badrinarayanan, V., Kendall, A., Cipolla, R.: Segnet: a deep convolutional encoder-decoder architecture for image segmentation. IEEE Trans. Pattern Anal. Mach. Intell. **39**(12), 2481–2495 (2017)
4. Chen, S.L., et al.: Detection of various dental conditions on dental panoramic radiography using faster R-CNN. IEEE Access **11**, 127388–127401 (2023)
5. Chollet, F.: Xception: deep learning with depthwise separable convolutions. In: Proceedings of the IEEE Conference on Computer Vision and Pattern Recognition, pp. 1251–1258 (2017)
6. He, K., Zhang, X., Ren, S., Sun, J.: Deep residual learning for image recognition. In: Proceedings of the IEEE Conference on Computer Vision and Pattern Recognition, pp. 770–778 (2016)
7. Huang, G., Liu, Z., Van Der Maaten, L., Weinberger, K.Q.: Densely connected convolutional networks. In: Proceedings of the IEEE Conference on Computer Vision and Pattern Recognition, pp. 4700–4708 (2017)
8. Jaiswal, P., Bhirud, S.: A cropping algorithm for automatically extracting regions of interest from panoramic radiographs based on maxilla and mandible parts. Int. J. Inf. Technol. **15**(7), 3631–3641 (2023)
9. Jaiswal, P., Bhirud, S.: An intelligent deep network for dental medical image processing system. Biomed. Signal Process. Control **84**, 104708 (2023)
10. Jaroń, A., Trybek, G.: The pattern of mandibular third molar impaction and assessment of surgery difficulty: a retrospective study of radiographs in east baltic population. Int. J. Environ. Res. Public Health **18**(11), 6016 (2021)
11. Jiang, P., Ergu, D., Liu, F., Cai, Y., Ma, B.: A review of yolo algorithm developments. Procedia Comput. Sci. **199**, 1066–1073 (2022)
12. Kim, H.E., Cosa-Linan, A., Santhanam, N., Jannesari, M., Maros, M.E., Ganslandt, T.: Transfer learning for medical image classification: a literature review. BMC Med. Imaging **22**(1), 69 (2022)
13. Krizhevsky, A., Sutskever, I., Hinton, G.E.: Imagenet classification with deep convolutional neural networks. In: Advances in Neural Information Processing Systems, vol. 25 (2012)
14. Kwon, D., Ahn, J., Kim, C.S., Kang, D.O., Paeng, J.Y.: A deep learning model based on concatenation approach to predict the time to extract a mandibular third molar tooth. BMC Oral Health **22**(1), 571 (2022)
15. Lee, S., Kim, D., Jeong, H.G.: Detecting 17 fine-grained dental anomalies from panoramic dental radiography using artificial intelligence. Sci. Rep. **12**(1), 5172 (2022)

16. Lei, Y., Chen, X., Wang, Y., Tang, R., Zhang, B.: A lightweight knowledge-distillation-based model for the detection and classification of impacted mandibular third molars. Appl. Sci. **13**(17), 9970 (2023)

17. Mazzia, V., Salvetti, F., Chiaberge, M.: Efficient-capsnet: capsule network with self-attention routing. Sci. Rep. **11**(1), 14634 (2021)

18. Prados-Privado, M., Villalón, J.G., Martínez-Martínez, C.H., Ivorra, C.: Dental images recognition technology and applications: a literature review. Appl. Sci. **10**(8), 2856 (2020)

19. Ronneberger, O., Fischer, P., Brox, T.: U-Net: convolutional networks for biomedical image segmentation. In: Navab, N., Hornegger, J., Wells, W.M., Frangi, A.F. (eds.) MICCAI 2015. LNCS, vol. 9351, pp. 234–241. Springer, Cham (2015). https://doi.org/10.1007/978-3-319-24574-4_28

20. Simonyan, K., Zisserman, A.: Very deep convolutional networks for large-scale image recognition. arXiv preprint arXiv:1409.1556 (2014)

21. Singh, S.K., Singh, R.S., Pandey, A.K., Udmale, S.S., Chaudhary, A.: IoT-based data analytics for the healthcare industry: techniques and applications. Academic Press (2020)

22. Szegedy, C., Ioffe, S., Vanhoucke, V., Alemi, A.: Inception-v4, inception-resnet and the impact of residual connections on learning. In: Proceedings of the AAAI Conference on Artificial Intelligence, vol. 31 (2017)

23. Szegedy, C., Vanhoucke, V., Ioffe, S., Shlens, J., Wojna, Z.: Rethinking the inception architecture for computer vision. In: Proceedings of the IEEE Conference on Computer Vision and Pattern Recognition, pp. 2818–2826 (2016)

24. Tan, M., Le, Q.V.: Efficientnet: rethinking model scaling for convolutional neural networks. arXiv preprint arXiv:1905.11946 (2020)

25. Vollmer, A., et al.: Performance analysis of supervised machine learning algorithms for automatized radiographical classification of maxillary third molar impaction. Appl. Sci. **12**(13), 6740 (2022)

26. Zadrożny, Ł, et al.: Artificial intelligence application in assessment of panoramic radiographs. Diagnostics **12**(1), 224 (2022)

27. Zaki, M.J., Meira, W.: Data mining and analysis: fundamental concepts and algorithms. Cambridge University Press (2014)

28. Zoph, B., Vasudevan, V., Shlens, J., Le, Q.V.: Learning transferable architectures for scalable image recognition. In: Proceedings of the IEEE Conference on Computer Vision and Pattern Recognition, pp. 8697–8710 (2018)

HJCFL: Hashcash and Jaya-Based Communication Efficient Federated Learning

Sudipto Mondal$^{(\boxtimes)}$ (ORCID) and Prasanta K. Jana (ORCID)

Department of Computer Science and Engineering, Indian Institute of Technology
(Indian School of Mines), Dhanbad, India
sudipto.mondal1997@gmail.com, prasantajana@iitism.ac.in

Abstract. Federated Learning (FL) has emerged as an efficient technique to train machine learning (ML) models across decentralized devices without sharing any raw data for preserving privacy. However, it faces challenges in communication overhead and resource constraints, particularly in real-time applications of Internet of Things (IoT). To address these challenges, we propose a novel method called Hashcash and Jaya-based communication efficient Federated Learning (HJCFL). It consists of three main phases: local aggregator selection, clustering of IoT devices and communication efficient FL process. It uses Hashcash for strategically selecting local aggregators and Jaya based algorithm for clustering IoT devices. The usage of Hashcash function has an added advantage over existing aggregator selection techniques because of it's simplicity, proof-of-work and adjustable difficulty level. To the best of our knowledge, none of the existing techniques uses Hashcash for the same. Moreover, unlike most of the existing schemes, the proposed method utilizes all the available devices and therefore it converges faster with significantly less number of global rounds than others. Through extensive simulations, we demonstrate the effectiveness of the proposed HJCFL as compared to two baseline techniques. The result's validity is further confirmed using a widely recognized statistical technique, i.e., analysis of variance (ANOVA), followed by a least significant difference (LSD) post-hoc analysis.

Keywords: Federated learning · Internet of Things · Hashcash function · Clustering · Jaya Algorithm

1 Introduction

In the contemporary landscape of ubiquitous computing, the proliferation of IoT devices has elevated concerns regarding data privacy to unprecedented levels. Users are increasingly worried of sharing sensitive personal information with centralized third-party servers, despite the immense potential of the aggregated data generated by these devices to enhance machine learning (ML) models. Federated learning (FL) [12] has emerged as a promising paradigm (e.g., Gboard's next-word prediction) to navigate this delicate balance between data utility and privacy. FL diverges from traditional centralized ML approaches by enabling

© The Author(s), under exclusive license to Springer Nature Switzerland AG 2025
Q. Bramas et al. (Eds.): ICDCIT 2025, LNCS 15507, pp. 271–287, 2025.
https://doi.org/10.1007/978-3-031-81404-4_20

model training on user devices while transmitting only the resulting model updates (parameters) to a central server. This decentralized approach not only preserves user privacy but also harnesses the collective intelligence of distributed devices to enrich learning models. Nevertheless, FL encounters challenges such as communication and computation overhead [11], particularly in real-time applications such as smart health care, smart transportation, disaster management, or defence where latency is critical. Moreover, the performance of FL algorithms may deteriorate with an increasing number of communication rounds due to resource constraints on client devices. By client devices, we mean those IoT devices which are involved in the FL process. To fully realize the potential of FL across diverse domains, it is imperative to develop innovative solutions that mitigate communication bottlenecks and ensure the seamless operation of FL in decentralized environment.

In this paper, we address the aforesaid issues and propose a novel method, called Hashcash and Jaya-based Communication Efficient Federated Learning (HJCFL) that consists of three basic phases: Hashcash-based aggregator selection, Jaya-based cluster formation and communication efficient FL process. Our approach considers two key factors to optimize the aggregator selection process. First, it prioritizes IoT devices (clients) with strong processing capabilities using Hashcash [3] technique. This ensures efficient aggregation of local models within clusters, allowing for faster and more accurate training. Second, it selects geographically dispersed devices to encourage the formation of well-formed clusters across the network. By leveraging the local aggregators for cluster-level updates and extending the update cycle at that level, our method reduces the frequency of global model updates and thus significantly decreases global communication with the central server.

To the best of our knowledge, none of the exiting techniques uses Hashcash function which is very simple but elegant and fit for limited resource IoT devices for aggregator selection. However, HJCFL has some similarity with [8], which also aims to address the communication related challenges in FL. Nonetheless, the method used in [8] involves data sharing with the fog nodes which is against the core principle of FL. Moreover, the approach involves the usage of fog nodes which is a costlier affair. Further more, unlike the existing techniques that rely on a selected subset of devices, our approach leverages all available devices. This comprehensive participation from all devices accelerates convergence of the global model. The experimental results demonstrate that through aggregation of local models at cluster heads, the proposed algorithm achieves notable communication efficiency, surpassing alternative techniques in comparative analysis.

The remainder of this paper is organized as follows. In Sect. 2, related existing works are reviewed. In Sect. 3, the system model along with a brief of Hashcash and Jaya algorithm are discussed. In Sect. 4, the proposed scheme HJCFL is presented. This is followed by presentation of experimental results and performance analysis in Sect. 5. We wrap up this article and outline avenues for future research in Sect. 6.

2   Related Work

Numerous studies proposing innovative solutions have been conducted, address-ing the communication related challenges in FL. Several methods have been proposed for reducing the communication latency between the server and the devices. For examples, in FedAVG [12], users undertake multiple rounds of local stochastic gradient descent (SGD) to compute the local model before sending it to the server. Despite consuming more computation resources, this method doesn't notably affect FL model convergence. However, in scenarios with non-identical data distribution among user devices, FedAVG significantly decreases convergence rates [19]. Thus, selecting an appropriate number of local rounds becomes challenging due to variations across models and user data distributions. To tackle the communication challenges, sparsification methods have also been explored as follows. Gradient sparsification selectively removes coordinates from the gradient vector, often based on criteria [1,16] like gradient informativeness. Top-K gradient sparsification [15] sends only the top K gradient values from each client to the server. However, using a uniform K across users can lead to bottle-neck for clients with poorer communication. Additionally, it limits each client to one round of SGD before uploading the model, increasing communication costs and missing out on redundant information across users.

Quantization techniques have also been proposed to decrease the entropy of weight updates by mapping all updates to a smaller set of values. For examples, SignSGD [4], quantizes each gradient update to its binary sign, effectively reduc-ing the bit size per update. Alternatively, approaches like TernGrad [17] transmit two bits of information per value. A solution to accommodate the diversity in user resources involves a gradient quantization scheme for FL, as outlined in [5]. This approach enables user devices to quantize their local gradients based on individual quantization budgets.

Clustering and client selection methods have also been proposed to address the communication related issues with FL. The authors in [18], proposed a client selection technique based on reputation for Hierachical FL. Clients with high rep-utation value are selected to particapte in the FL process. However, it's reliance on reputation prediction accuracy may lead to suboptimal node selections if reputation values are inaccurately estimated. In [10], the authors proposed a FL client selection approach based on cluster label information (FedCLS) technique to address Non-IID data affecting global model accuracy and learning speed in real-world dispersed scenarios. However, sharing fault labels in FedCLS can reveal sensitive data about faults and anomalies, raising privacy concerns. In [6], the authors introduce E3CS, a stochastic client selection method that aims to achieve a balance between effective participation and fairness altogether. In [9], authors proposed update control method, FedSAUC, introduces a novel app-roach to FL by incorporating user behavior similarity. The method aimed to save the energy consumption and bandwidth on the edge devices. In [2], authors pro-posed a real-time, on-demand client selection mechanism for FL using DBSCAN clustering based on resources and data quality to improve model accuracy and convergence speed. However, the approach depends on attributes provided by clients, which may be incorrect, resulting in ineffective client assignment and decision-making. In [8], authors proposed Fog Cloud Assisted Federated Learning (FCAFL) which involves clustering IoT devices and selecting efficient Cluster Heads (CHs) based on proximity and energy levels. The scheme reduces latency by parallelizing computational tasks between clients and fog nodes, minimizing data offloading delays and overall communication costs during the FL process. However, sharing data with fog nodes leads to privacy risks and goes against the core principle of FL.

As can be concluded from the previous discussion, researchers have focused mostly on sparsification, quantization, client selection and clustering strategies to tackle communication challenges. While the aforementioned research explores various techniques to address communication challenges in FL, several limitations remain. The existing algorithms, unlike HJCFL, has a reliance on client reported attributes which may be inaccurate. Also, HJCFL incorporates all available devices in the network for model preparation. Furthermore, HJCFL creates clusters with good separation between devices. This ensures a balanced distribution of tasks across all devices.

3   System Architecture and Methods Used

In this section, we give an overview of the system architecture and the methods used for aggregator selection and the cluster formation. Table 1 outlines widely used notations for reader reference. Additionally, arithmetic operations and their symbols are understood element wise.

3.1   System Architecture

Consider a scenario with n deployed IoT devices represented by the set $\mathcal{D} = \{D_i : i = 1, 2, 3, ..., n\}$, where all devices are assumed to be stationary. A central cloud server, denoted by F, coordinates the learning process. The proposed HJCFL method strategically selects k devices from $\mathcal{D}$ to act as aggregators using the Hashcash technique. These k aggregators, denoted by the set $\mathcal{A} = \{A_i : i = 1, 2, 3, ..., k\}$, are responsible for local aggregation within their assigned clusters. The remaining devices are grouped into k clusters around the respective aggregators (see Fig. 1). Since, these aggregator devices become cluster heads(CHs) for their clusters, we use the term aggregators and cluster heads(CHs) interchangeably throughout the remainder of the article to refer to the same device.

Within each cluster, there's a communication cycle that repeats for t iterations. For each of the t iterations, the devices in each cluster send their local model updates to their respective CH. The CH aggregates the received updates from all devices in the cluster. The aggregated model updates are sent back to the devices. Subsequently, after the t-th iteration, the aggregated model updates are sent to the server where it performs global model averaging and broadcasts the averaged model updates back to the devices via the aggregators. This iterative process continues until a predefined global model accuracy is achieved. Figure 1 presents the system model of the proposed HJCFL.

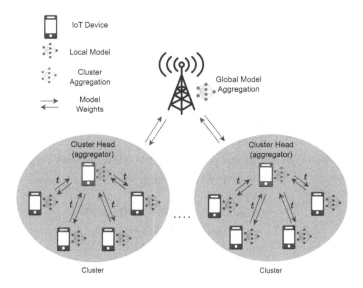

Fig. 1. System Architecture for HJCFL

3.2   Hashcash

Hashcash, introduced by [3], is a cryptographic hash-based proof-of-work mechanism originally designed to combat email spam. It compels senders to expend computational effort in solving a challenge before sending a message. This proof-of-work can be efficiently verified by the recipient, making it a cost-prohibitive endeavor for spammers who traditionally rely on low per-message costs.

Hashcash offers several benefits for aggregator selection in our method. It provides a verifiable proof-of-work mechanism, where devices solve a SHA-256 puzzle, demonstrating processing power without relying on self-reported specifications. Hashcash's difficulty level is adjustable by changing the number of leading zeros in the puzzles. It is efficient for IoT devices with limited resources, as it mainly involves SHA-256 computations. Its simplicity suits both the central server and devices.

Hashcash works as follows: The receiver generates a challenge with a string C and a value j. The sender must find a value R such that the SHA-256 hash of $C + R$ starts with j leading zeros:

$$SHA256(C + R) \text{ starts with } j \text{ zeros}$$

Table 1. List of Notations

Notation	Description
F	Cloud Server
n	Total number of IoT devices deployed
$\mathcal{D}$	The set of the IoT devices deployed
D_i	Device ID of the i-th device
$dis(D_i, D_j)$	Euclidean distance between device D_i and D_j
dis_{max}	Maximum communication range of the devices
k	Number of aggregators to be selected
t	Number of update cycles within a cluster
$\mathcal{A}$	Set of devices which become aggregators
δ	Separation threshold
$CommAgg(D_i)$	Aggregators within D_i's communication range
p	Number of puzzles sent
P_i	i-th puzzle
j_i	0's in SHA-256 hash for i-th puzzle
$\mathcal{P}$	Set of puzzles and their respective solution
R_i	Solution for given puzzle P_i and j_i
t	Iterations of cluster model aggregation

The sender performs a brute-force search to find R. Once found, R is sent to the receiver, who verifies it by computing:

$$SHA256(C + R)$$

If the hash starts with j zeros, the sender's work is valid, and the message is accepted. The value of j determines the puzzle's difficulty, requiring more computational effort for higher j, deterring spam.

3.3 Jaya Algorithm

The Jaya algorithm, proposed by [14], is a population-based optimization technique that draws inspiration from societal concepts of mutual benefit and cooperation. The Jaya algorithm operates on the premise of improving the quality of solutions through cooperation among individuals in a population.

Let F_i denote the ith solution in the population of m solutions, where $i = 1, 2, \ldots, m$. The position update equation for the Jaya algorithm can be represented as follows:

$$F_i(t + 1) = F_i(t) + r \cdot (F_{\text{best}}(t) - |F_i(t)|) + (1 - r) \cdot (F_{\text{worst}}(t) - |F_i(t)|) + \epsilon \quad (1)$$

Here, $F_{\text{best}}(t)$ represents the best solution in the population at iteration t. $F_{\text{worst}}(t)$ denotes the worst solution in the population at iteration t. r is a random coefficient in the range $[0, 1]$ that controls the balance between exploitation and exploration. ϵ is a random number generated from a uniform distribution in the range $[-1, 1]$ to introduce randomness and diversity. The fitness of each solution F_i is evaluated using an objective function specific to the optimization problem being solved. The algorithm iterates through multiple generations, updating the positions of solutions using Eq. 1, until a termination criterion is met (e.g., a maximum number of iterations or convergence of solutions).

4   Proposed Method

An out-sketch of the proposed HJCFL method is depicted in Fig. 2. As it can be seen, HJCFL involves three basic phases. In the first phase, the aggregators are selected from the available IoT devices which is based on their ranking through Hashcash function followed by a proposed algorithm ensuring spatial dispersion. In the second phase, we cluster all the IoT devices surrounding the selected aggregators (CHs) using Jaya algorithm. This is followed by the final phase in which the proposed communication efficient FL process is performed. The details of each phase are described as follows.

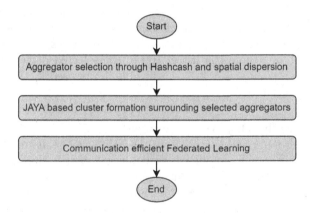

Fig. 2. HJCFL framework consisting of all the phases

4.1   Aggregator Selection

Our methodology depends on selecting the devices which are more computationally powerful. These devices will receive the local model updates from other devices in it's cluster and perform model averaging at the cluster level. Hence, we call these devices as Aggregator devices. The aggregators are also selected in a way such that each cluster contains only one aggregator device, thereby enhancing spatial distribution. Thus there are two steps involved in our aggregator selection method. First, a list of all the devices deployed in the system is obtained by sorting them based on their computational power in decreasing order. Second, from this sorted list, k aggregators are selected, ensuring the separation between them.

Sorting Devices Based on Computational Power: The steps involved, are outlined as follows. Cloud server F, distributes p number of puzzles along with the j value, representing the number of leading zeros as previously discussed, to all the IoT devices. As a result, each device receives a set of puzzles, denoted by $\mathcal{P} = \{\{P_i, j_i\} : i = 1, 2, 3, ..., p\}$. Subsequently, the devices proceed to solve each puzzle (P_i) to find the corresponding R_i. This value should be such that:

$$\text{SHA256}(P_i + R_i) \text{ starts with } j_i \text{ zeros}$$

The solution to these puzzles are communicated back to the server which are then verified. The ability of the device to solve the puzzles quickly and accurately indicates two things. First, it demonstrates the proof-of-work for the device. Secondly, it signifies the computational power of the device. The cloud server F maintains a queue of the solutions, i.e., as and when it receives a solution from a device, it stores the device ID and the solutions, R_i values, for the corresponding puzzles, P_i. For a particular device D_i, it stores in the queue in the form: $\{D_i, \{R_1, R_2, R_3, ..., R_p\}\}$. Upon receiving solutions from all devices, the system verifies it. Devices with correct solutions are then added to a list, maintaining the order from the original queue. The devices with wrong solution are rejected. Let us denote the list of IDs of the selected devices with correct solutions by $\mathcal{L} = \{L_i : i = 1, 2, 3, ..., n\}$. This list is used in the next step to select spatially dispersed aggregators.

Selecting Spatially Dispersed Aggregators: The selection process now involves choosing the k aggregators from the previously generated list $\mathcal{L}$. These aggregators are chosen to maximize their spatial distribution, which in turn enhances the clustering process. The aggregator selection procedure is given in Algorithm 1. Initialization begins by making an empty set of aggregators, denoted by $\mathcal{A}$ in Step 1. The first device in the sorted list $\mathcal{L}$ is then selected as the initial aggregator and added to $\mathcal{A}$, as seen in Step 2. This device possesses the highest computational power. Subsequently, the process starts iterating from the second element in the sorted list $\mathcal{L}$ through Steps 3–17. Step 4 checks if the set $\mathcal{A}$ contains k number of aggregators. If so then the loop breaks at Step 5. Steps 8–16 checks the distances between the devices in the list $\mathcal{A}$ and L_i. If the distance between any of the devices crosses the threshold value δ, then L_i is not considered as an aggregator. Finally, the set of selected aggregators $\mathcal{A}$ is returned in Step 18.

This method incorporates an additional constraint δ to ensure that the selected aggregators are well-separated from each other. A larger value of δ will result in more widely separated aggregators, but it may also limit the number of potential candidates that can be selected, especially in dense deployment scenarios. By enforcing the separation constraint during the selection of aggregators,

Algorithm 1. Aggregator Selection

Input: List of devices sorted by computational power: $\mathcal{L}$
   Number of aggregators to select: k
   Separation threshold: δ
Output: Set of selected aggregators: $\mathcal{A}$
 1: $\mathcal{A} \leftarrow$ empty set
 2: $\mathcal{A} \leftarrow L_0$
 3: **for** L_i in $\mathcal{L}$ where $i = 2, 3, \ldots, n$ **do**
 4:    **if** size of $\mathcal{A}$ is equal to k **then**
 5:       **break**
 6:    **end if**
 7:    $isSeparated \leftarrow$ True
 8:    **for** A_j in $\mathcal{A}$ **do**
 9:       **if** $dis(L_i, A_j) \leq \delta$ **then**
10:          $isSeparated \leftarrow$ False
11:          **break**
12:       **end if**
13:    **end for**
14:    **if** $isSeparated$ **then**
15:       add L_i to $\mathcal{A}$
16:    **end if**
17: **end for**
18: **return** $\mathcal{A}$

---

the technique aims to prevent the situation where two aggregators end up in the same cluster. This will facilitate better inter-cluster separation and ensure that each cluster has only one aggregator node.

4.2   Clustering IoT Devices

The set of aggregators $\mathcal{A}$, selected in the aggregator selection phase is now used in cluster formation. This can be noted that given n IoT devices and k aggregators, the number of possible clusters is k^n. This is an NP-hard problem for a large IoT network [7]. Therefore, the computational complexity for finding optimal clusters is very expensive by means of a brute force approach. This is the rationality behind the use of a metaheuristic approach like Jaya optimization algorithm. Note that, unlike traditional optimization algorithms, Jaya does not rely on complex mathematical operators or parameter tuning. Instead, it employs a simple update mechanism that prioritizes the best-performing individuals while simultaneously improving the weaker members of the population.

   The assignment of an aggregator A_j to an IoT device D_i is represented by b_{ij} as:

$$b_{ij} = \begin{cases} 1 \text{ if device } D_i \text{is assigned aggregator } A_j \\ \quad \forall i, j : 1 \leq i \leq n, 1 \leq j \leq k \wedge D_i \neq A_j \\ 0 \text{ otherwise} \end{cases}$$

   For a device D_i, we define a set of aggregators in it's communication range as follows:

$$CommAgg(D_i) = \{A_j | dis(D_i, A_j) \leq dis_{max} \wedge A_j \in \mathcal{A}\}$$

where $dis(D_i, A_j)$ is the euclidean distance between device D_i and A_j. And dis_{max} is the maximum communication range of the IoT devices. We aim to minimize the average distance between IoT devices and aggregator nodes within their communication range. This distance is defined as follows:

$$AvgDist = \frac{1}{n} \sum_{i=1}^{n} \sum_{j=1}^{k} dis(D_i, A_j)$$

Thus, the optimization problem for cluster formation is as follows:

$$\text{Maximize} \quad H = \frac{1}{AvgDist} \tag{2}$$

Algorithm 2. Clustering

Input: IoT devices: $\mathcal{D} = \{D_1, D_2, \ldots, D_n\}$,
    Aggregators: $\mathcal{A} = \{A_1, A_2, \ldots, A_k\}$,
    Maximum communication range: dis_{max},
    Termination threshold distance: $dis_{threshold}$,
    Population size: m
Output: Assignment matrix: $\mathbf{B} = [b_{ij}]_{n \times k}$
    initialization;
1: $l \leftarrow 0$ {Iteration counter}
2: Initialize population of assignment matrices $\{\mathbf{B}_i^{(0)}\}_{i=1}^{m}$ {Each $\mathbf{B}_i^{(0)}$ is a random valid assignment matrix}
3: **for** each solution i in the population **do**
4:     $F_i^{(0)} \leftarrow$ evaluate objective function using $\mathbf{B}_i^{(0)}$
5: **end for**
6: **repeat**
7:     $l \leftarrow l + 1$
8:     **for** each solution i in the population **do**
9:         **for** each device D_i **do**
10:             $CommAgg(D_i) \leftarrow \{A_j | dis(D_i, A_j) \leq dis_{max} \wedge A_j \in \mathcal{A}\}$
11:             $index_i \leftarrow \lfloor |CommAgg(D_i)| \times r \rfloor$ {r is a random number in $[0, 1]$}
12:             $A_{best} \leftarrow CommAgg(D_i)[index_i]$
13:             Update $\mathbf{B}_i^{(l)}$ by assigning D_i to the aggregator A_{best}, ensuring the assignment matrix remains valid
14:         **end for**
15:         $F_i^{(l)} \leftarrow$ evaluate objective function using $\mathbf{B}_i^{(l)}$
16:     **end for**
17:     Identify $F_{best}^{(l)}$ and $F_{worst}^{(l)}$ in the population
18:     **for** each solution i in the population **do**
19:         Update $\mathbf{B}_i^{(l+1)}$ using Jaya update rule:
20:         $F_i(l+1) = F_i(l) + r \cdot (F_{best}(l) - |F_i(l)|) + (1-r) \cdot (F_{worst}(l) - |F_i(l)|) + \epsilon$
21:         {Apply this update to the assignment matrix $\mathbf{B}_i^{(l+1)}$}
22:     **end for**
23: **until** $\max_i dis(D_i, A_{best}) \leq dis_{threshold}$ **or** $l \geq l_{max}$
24: **return** $\mathbf{B}_i^{(l)}$ corresponding to $F_{best}^{(l)}$ {Return the best assignment matrix}

subject to:

$$dis(D_i, A_j) \leq dis_{max} \tag{3}$$

$$\sum_{i,j \in n} b_{ij} = 1 \tag{4}$$

where constraint (3) ensures that A_j must be within the communication range of D_i. And constraint (4) ensures that the device D_i, for all $1 \leq i \leq n$, can be assigned to one and only one aggregator.

The proposed Jaya-based clustering algorithm to solve the aforesaid optimization problem is given in Algorithm 2 and briefly explained here. The algorithm begins in Step 2 with the initialization of the population of assignment matrices $\{\mathbf{B}_i^{(0)}\}_{i=1}^m$. Each $\mathbf{B}_i^{(0)}$ represents a different solution in the population. In Step 3, the objective function $F_i^{(0)}$ is evaluated for each initial assignment matrix $\mathbf{B}_i^{(0)}$. Steps 7–23, consists of the main iteration loop. These steps consists of an inner loop from Steps 9–14 iterating over each solution in the population. For each device D_i, all reachable aggregators $CommAgg(D_i)$, is found. An aggregator A_{best} for D_i based on a random index is then selected. The assignment matrix $\mathbf{B}_i^{(t)}$ for the solution is then updated. After updating the assignments for each solution, the objective function $F_i^{(t)}$ is recalculated in Step 15. The best $(F_{best}^{(t)})$ and worst $(F_{worst}^{(t)})$ solutions in the population are identified next. Steps 18–22, update each solution $\mathbf{B}_i^{(t+1)}$ using the Jaya update rule. Finally, the process is terminated when the maximum distance of any device to its assigned aggregator is below $dis_{threshold}$ or a maximum number of iterations $t_{\max}$ is reached.

4.3   Communication Efficient Federated Learning Algorithm

Following the cluster formation with designated aggregator nodes, the federated learning process commences. The proposed procedure of FL is presented in Algorithm 3. The process is repeated for t rounds from Steps 1–20. Devices within a cluster transmit their local model updates to their respective CH in Steps 2–5. Each CH, aggregates the received updates in Steps 6–8. For $t - 1$ rounds, the aggregated model updates are transmitted back to the devices in the clusters by their respective CHs. After the t-th round, CHs transmit the aggregated updates directly to the server which performs global model averaging in Steps 9–14. The globally averaged update is then disseminated back to the devices through the CHs. This entire loop iterates until a pre-defined global model accuracy is attained.

5   Experiments

In this section, we present the performance evaluation of HJCFL for different scenarios through simulation runs and comparing the results with two baseline algorithms as follows.

Algorithm 3. Communication Efficient Federated Learning

Input: Number of communication rounds t,
   Aggregators/Cluster Heads: $\mathcal{A} = \{A_1, A_2, \ldots, A_k\}$ obtained from Algorithm 1,
   Cluster information obtained from Algorithm 2
Output: Globally averaged model w_{global}
1: **for** $j = 1, 2, \ldots, t$ rounds **do**
2:    **for** each device i in a cluster **do**
3:       Train local model w_i on local data
4:       Send local model update Δw_i to its CH
5:    **end for**
6:    **for** each CH c **do**
7:       Aggregate local model updates:
         $w_c = \sum_{i \in cluster(c)} \Delta w_i$
8:    **end for**
9:    **if** $j == t$ **then**
10:       **for** each CH c **do**
11:          Send aggregated update w_c to the server
12:       **end for**
13:       Server performs global averaging:
          $w_{global} = \frac{1}{C} \sum_{c=1}^{C} w_c$ (C: number of CHs)
14:       Server broadcasts w_{global} to all CHs
15:    **else**
16:       **for** each CH c **do**
17:          Broadcast w_c to all devices in its cluster
18:       **end for**
19:    **end if**
20: **end for**
21: **return** Distribute w_{global} to all devices through CHs

---

5.1   Simulation Setup

We use the MNIST dataset for evaluating system performance, consisting of 70,000 images, with 60,000 for training and 10,000 for testing. Each image represents digits from 0 to 9 and is of 28 × 28 pixels. Experiments were conducted on a Ubuntu Server with 8 NVIDIA Tesla V100-SXM2 GPUs (32GB each). The code was written in Python, using TensorFlow GPU and Keras. We compare our approach with two methods: FedAvg and FedSAUC. FedAvg involves random selection of a set of devices to share model updates with the central server. FedSAUC is an FL process which groups devices into clusters with the aim of enhancing communication efficiency. In the simulation, 500 IoT devices each receive 1,000 training samples randomly. Each device trains for 1 epoch per round with a batch size of 32. We select 10 geographically dispersed, computationally powerful devices to form clusters with balanced workloads. The FL process runs for 100 communication rounds, comparing our approach against baseline algorithms. We also examine the impact of different aggregator selection sizes.

5.2   Result and Analysis

Figure 3a shows HJCFL outperforms FedAvg and FedSAUC in model accuracy consistently. We achieve a 10.61% improvement over FedSAUC and 34.29% over FedAvg after the initial global model averaging round. Even after 10 iterations, our model demonstrates a 2% and 4% accuracy gain over FedSAUC and FedAvg, respectively. By the 10th round, our accuracy reaches 90.56%. After 100 rounds, we marginally surpass FedSAUC by 0.05% and FedAvg by 0.56%.

In Fig. 3b, we observe a similar trend of improved model performance compared to the baseline methods in terms of model loss.

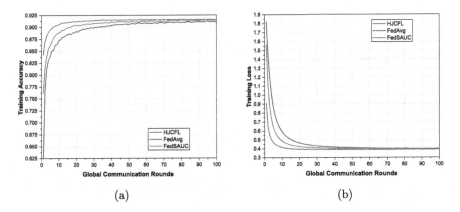

(a)   (b)

Fig. 3. Comparison results with existing approaches on MNIST dataset in terms of: (a) training accuracy, (b) training loss

The notable performance advantage of HJCFL stems from its inclusive approach, where all devices actively participate in model training for FL. Unlike FedAvg and FedSAUC, which involve only a subset of clients communicating updates to the central server, HJCFL ensures every device contributes to refining the model. This collaborative method enables richer information exchange and more comprehensive updates. Additionally, HJCFL incorporates cluster-level model aggregation, enhancing robustness and convergence speed. Employing this approach accelerates the model's accuracy convergence and reduces the need for frequent communication with the central server for global averaging, streamlining the training process and enhancing efficiency.

Figure 4a compares the accuracy of HJCFL across different FL selection strategies over 20 rounds. We evaluate scenarios with 10, 20, and 30 aggregators selected from 500 devices. Results consistently show improved accuracy with more aggregators. By the 10th round, the 30-aggregator model achieves a 2.2% and 2% accuracy gain over 10 and 20 aggregators, respectively. This trend continues, with the 30-aggregator model outperforming the others by 2.4% and 2.28% by the 20th round. This suggests that more aggregators lead to better model performance over time.

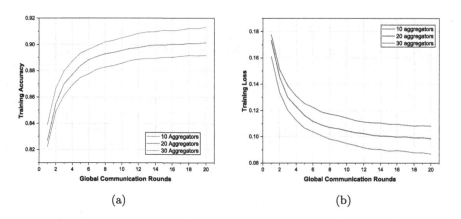

Fig. 4. Comparison results with variable number of selected aggregators on MNIST dataset in terms of: (a) training accuracy, (b) training loss

Figure 4b demonstrates a similar trend in model loss over 20 rounds for scenarios with 10, 20, and 30 aggregators.

Increasing the number of clusters while keeping the number of devices constant improves model performance. This is due to smaller, more homogeneous device groups, allowing for more specialized learning. Additionally, workload distribution among clusters improves communication and resource utilization, enhancing overall performance.

Table 2. ANOVA test results

Source of variation	Sum of square	df	Mean square	p-value	F-critical	F-statistic
Between groups	0.014	2	0.007	0.000	3.0262	11.753
Within groups	0.178	297	0.001			
Total	0.192	299				

Table 3. LSD post hoc analysis results

Between(A-B)	Mean difference(A-B)	Upper bound	Lower bound	Standard Error
HJCFL - FedAvg	0.0168	0.0236	0.0100	0.0035
HJCFL - FedSAUC	0.0077	0.0145	0.0009	0.0035

5.3   Statistical Test Using ANOVA

Here, we validate the simulation results statistically using a one-way ANOVA test
[13]. The test examines two cases: a) Null hypothesis (H_0), and b) Alternative
hypothesis (H_1):

$$H_0 : \mu_{HJCFL} = \mu_{FedAvg} = \mu_{FedSAUC} \tag{5}$$

$$H_1 : \mu_{HJCFL} \neq \mu_{FedAvg} \neq \mu_{FedSAUC}. \tag{6}$$

It indicates that the means of distinct groups differ by accepting H_1 and
rejecting H_0. Criteria for accepting H_1 involves: 1) p-value less than the significance level i.e., $\alpha = 0.05$ and 2) F-critical value smaller than the F-statistic.
These values are derived from the aforesaid experimental analysis. We assess
model convergence for the three different techniques by conducting the ANOVA
test.

The results of the ANOVA tests are presented in Table 2. From the table,
it can be observed that the p-value is less than 0.5 and the F-critical value is
lower than F-statistic. Hence, H_1 is accepted. In other words, the means for the
model convergence of HJCFL, FedAvg and FedSAUC are significantly different
from each other. The LSD post hoc analysis is performed on the outcomes of
the ANOVA test. Table 3 depicts the 95% confidence interval for the difference
between the means of the model convergence.

6   Conclusion

In this paper, we have presented a novel method for FL, called HJCFL, using
an efficient scheme of aggregator selection and Jaya-based clustering to mitigate
communication overhead problem. The superiority of HJCFL has been demonstrated through extensive simulations and by comparing results with two existing
FL techniques, namely FedAvg and FedSAUC. Specifically, we have shown that
HJCFL has 10.61% improvement over FedSAUC and 34.29% improvement over
FedAvg in terms of global model accuracy after the initial global communication round. By the 10th round, the accuracy of HJCFL reaches 90.56% which
is much higher than that of the FedAvg and FedSAUC at this round. We have
also shown that HJCFL consistently improves accuracy with the increase in the
number of aggregators. The proposed work establishes a foundation for efficient
aggregator selection in FL. However, it lacks investigating strategies for dynamic
network conditions and fluctuating resource availability, which will be the focus
of our future research work.

References

1. Aji, A.F., Heafield, K.: Sparse communication for distributed gradient descent. In:
Proceedings of the 2017 Conference on Empirical Methods in Natural Language
Processing. Association for Computational Linguistics (2017). https://doi.org/10.
18653/v1/d17-1045

2. Arisdakessian, S., Wahab, O.A., Mourad, A., Otrok, H.: Towards instant clustering approach for federated learning client selection. In: 2023 International Conference on Computing, Networking and Communications (ICNC), pp. 409–413 (2023).
https://doi.org/10.1109/ICNC57223.2023.10074237

3. Back, A.: Hashcash - a denial of service counter-measure (2002)

4. Bernstein, J., Wang, Y.X., Azizzadenesheli, K., Anandkumar, A.: signSGD: com-
pressed optimisation for non-convex problems. In: International Conference on
Machine Learning, pp. 560–569. PMLR (2018). https://doi.org/10.48550/arXiv.
1802.04434

5. Chang, W.T., Tandon, R.: Communication efficient federated learning over multiple access channels. arXiv preprint arXiv:2001.08737 (2020)

6. Huang, T., Lin, W., Shen, L., Li, K., Zomaya, A.Y.: Stochastic client selection
for federated learning with volatile clients. IEEE Internet Things J. 9(20), 20055–
20070 (2022). https://doi.org/10.1109/JIOT.2022.3172113

7. Kuila, P., Jana, P.K.: Energy efficient clustering and routing algorithms for wireless
sensor networks: particle swarm optimization approach. Eng. Appl. Artif. Intell.
33, 127–140 (2014). https://doi.org/10.1016/j.engappai.2014.04.009

8. Kumari, N., Jana, P.K.: Communication efficient federated learning with data
offloading in fog-based IoT environment. Futur. Gener. Comput. Syst. 158, 158–
166 (2024). https://doi.org/10.1016/j.future.2024.04.051

9. Lee, M.L., Chou, H.C., Chen, Y.A.: FedSAUC: a similarity-aware update control
for communication-efficient federated learning in edge computing. In: 2021 Thir-
teenth International Conference on Mobile Computing and Ubiquitous Network
(ICMU), pp. 1–6 (2021). https://doi.org/10.23919/ICMU50196.2021.9638814

10. Li, C., Wu, H.: FedCLS: a federated learning client selection algorithm based on
cluster label information. In: 2022 IEEE 96th Vehicular Technology Conference
(VTC2022-Fall), pp. 1–5 (2022). https://doi.org/10.1109/VTC2022-Fall57202.
2022.10013064

11. Li, T., Sahu, A.K., Talwalkar, A., Smith, V.: Federated Learning: challenges, methods, and future directions. IEEE Signal Process. Mag. 37(3), 50–60 (2020). https://
doi.org/10.1109/MSP.2020.2975749

12. McMahan, B., Moore, E., Ramage, D., Hampson, S., Arcas, B.A.Y.:
Communication-efficient learning of deep networks from decentralized data. In:
Proceedings of the 20th International Conference on Artificial Intelligence and
Statistics. Proceedings of Machine Learning Research, vol. 54, pp. 1273–1282.
PMLR (2017). https://doi.org/10.48550/arXiv.1602.05629

13. Muller, K.E., Fetterman, B.A.: Regression and ANOVA: An Integrated Approach
Using SAS Software. Wiley-SAS (2003)

14. Rao, V.: Jaya: a simple and new optimization algorithm for solving constrained
and unconstrained optimization problems. Int. J. Ind. Eng. Comput. 7(1), 19–34
(2016). https://doi.org/10.5267/j.ijiec.2015.8.004

15. Stich, S.U., Cordonnier, J.B., Jaggi, M.: Sparsified SGD with memory. In: Advances
in Neural Information Processing Systems, vol. 31. Curran Associates, Inc. (2018)

16. Wangni, J., Wang, J., Liu, J., Zhang, T.: Gradient sparsification for
communication-efficient distributed optimization. In: Advances in Neural Information Processing Systems, vol. 31. Curran Associates, Inc. (2018)

17. Wen, W., et al.: Terngrad: Ternary gradients to reduce communication in distributed deep learning. In: Advances in Neural Information Processing Systems,
vol. 30. Curran Associates, Inc. (2017)

18. Xin, S., Zhuo, L., Xin, C.: Node selection strategy design based on reputation mechanism for hierarchical federated learning. In: 2022 18th International Conference on Mobility, Sensing and Networking (MSN), pp. 718–722 (2022). https://doi.org/10.1109/MSN57253.2022.00117
19. Zhao, Y., Li, M., Lai, L., Suda, N., Civin, D., Chandra, V.: Federated learning with Non-IID data (2018). https://doi.org/10.48550/arXiv.1806.00582

Machine Learning for Sensor-Based Handwritten Character Recognition: A Brief Survey

Shashank Kumar Singh and Amrita Chaturvedi$^{(\boxtimes)}$

Department of Computer Science and Engineering, IIT (BHU), Varanasi 221005,
Uttar Pradesh, India
shashankkrs.rs.cse17@itbhu.ac.in, amrita.cse@iitbhu.ac.in

Abstract. Handwriting recognition technologies have evolved significantly, with recent advancements incorporating wearable devices such as smartpens, smartwatches, and smartphones to capture motion and gesture data. This paper reviews various efficient handwriting recognition models that utilize inertial sensors, visual sensors, EMG sensors, and acoustic and Wi-Fi signals. Inertial sensor-based approaches often use accelerometers and gyroscopes to collect three-dimensional data during handwriting, with models achieving high accuracy in recognizing digits and alphabets. Visual sensor-based techniques, leveraging cameras and image processing, have been fundamental in developing Optical Character Recognition (OCR), further enhanced by deep learning algorithms. EMG sensors have been explored for their potential to capture muscle activity for gesture recognition. At the same time, acoustic and Wi-Fi signal-based methods offer innovative ways to recognize handwriting through sound and signal variation. Despite the progress, challenges such as sensor drift, data generalization, and computational requirements persist. Integrating multi-modal sensors and advanced machine learning techniques holds promise for overcoming these limitations and improving the accuracy and usability of handwriting recognition systems across diverse applications.

Keywords: Inertial Sensor · Machine Learning · Visual Sensors

1 Introduction

Despite the rapid advancements in digital technology, handwritten characters continue to play a vital role in various fields such as education [14,42], communication [23], biometric signature verification [22], and healthcare [18]. These domains often necessitate converting handwritten characters and associated hand movements into digital format for accurate analysis and comprehension. This requirement for digitization underscores the need for developing advanced models capable of recognizing, reconstructing, and identifying handwriting motions.

Q. Bramas et al. (Eds.): ICDCIT 2025, LNCS 15507, pp. 288–305, 2025.
https://doi.org/10.1007/978-3-031-81404-4_21

Handwriting movements arise from intricate cognitive functions driven by bioelectric signals generated within the nervous system. Essentially, these movements are initiated by bioelectric signals within the neural pathways, which are then relayed to the muscular system [2,65].

Additionally, the contribution of machine learning approaches in handwritten character recognition is significant. Machine learning techniques enhance the accuracy and efficiency of recognizing handwritten characters by employing algorithms that can learn from and adapt to data patterns. These approaches leverage deep learning methods, such as convolutional neural networks (CNNs) and recurrent neural networks (RNNs), which excel in handling the spatial and temporal dependencies in handwriting data. Furthermore, machine learning models can integrate data from multiple sensor modalities, improving recognition performance by capturing diverse signal characteristics. By incorporating advanced feature selection methods and optimizing classification algorithms, machine learning substantially advances the field of handwritten character recognition, enabling more robust and reliable systems.

This article explores various sensor-based handwriting recognition techniques, discussing their advantages and disadvantages. To the best of our knowledge, this survey is among the initial works that offer insights into the field of handwriting character recognition based on sensor deployment. The rest of the paper is organized as follows: Sect. 2 describes the taxonomy of handwriting gesture recognition and recent research developments. Section 2.1 covers work using inertial sensors, while Sect. 2.2 highlights major contributions involving visual sensors. Section 2.3 provides details on EMG-based approaches, and Sect. 2.4 summarizes research using WiFi-based methods. Section 3 offers a detailed discussion, followed by conclusions in Sect. 4.

2   Related Work

Driven by the advancements in machine learning approaches, several surveys have been conducted to summarize methods for handwritten character recognition. These surveys have largely summarized the various new machine learning/deep learning algorithms used, mainly focusing on image-based approaches. Among these is the comprehensive work by Remaida et al. [48], in which the authors reviewed handwriting recognition literature summarizing the various artificial neural network models used in this field. Moreover, Al-Taee et al. [3] conducted a review with a primary focus on various deep learning models, highlighting their application to image-based handwritten character recognition. Subsequently, Purohit and Chauhan [54] centered their review on Optical Character Recognition (OCR), exploring image-based techniques such as segmentation and preprocessing methods. AlKendi et al. [5] examined handwriting recognition methods but limited their scope to datasets in French. Later, Sánchez-DelaCruz et al. [52] provided an in-depth analysis across different levels of handwriting recognition (character, word, text line, and text block) and reviewed a range of machine learning algorithms employed for this purpose.

Despite the valuable insights provided by these surveys, limited attention has been given to creating a structured taxonomy that categorizes different sensor-based approaches. Developing such a taxonomy would be beneficial, as it would allow for a detailed examination of each sensor's strengths and limitations, thereby identifying complementary sensor modalities that can be deployed for performing multimodal fusion for handwriting recognition tasks. This would enable future work to harness unique sensor characteristics, contributing to more robust and accurate multimodal fusion methodologies. Recognizing this gap, our survey centers on various sensor-based approaches for handwriting character recognition, aiming to highlight the potential for combining complementary sensor characteristics to improve recognition accuracy.

2.1 Handwriting Analysis and Recognition Using Inertial Data/Sensors

Several powerful handwriting recognition models have emerged in recent years, leveraging inertial sensor data from wearables like smartpens and smartwatches.

Ghosh et al. [24] demonstrated that combining an accelerometer with an RF transmission module and an 8-bit microcontroller on a digital pen can effectively support handwriting digit recognition. They employed acceleration data, transformed into image-based data, to track and identify handwriting trajectories. Patil et al. [44] utilized the wireless IMU unit to recognize handwritten charters in three-dimensional space. The IMU unit consists of a 16-bit accelerometer, gyroscope, and magnetometer to track hand movements while writing different characters. The authors achieved a recognition accuracy of 98.69% for 26 English alphabets. However, the dataset size was limited to 1000 samples and 2600 samples for digits and alphabets, respectively.

Wang et al. [66] used a pen consisting of an accelerometer to recognize handwritten digits and various other gesture trajectories. The triaxial accelerometer was attached to a microcontroller and a wireless transceiver for data recording. The authors extracted various features from acceleration signals and applied a kernel class separability-based approach for feature selection [67]. Using the Probabilistic Neural network [59], their approach was able to recognize the ten digits with 98% accuracy and eight other gestures with 98.75% recognition accuracy. The data collected consisted of 900 and 800 samples corresponding to ten digits and eight gestures.

Oh et al. [43] used input signals from a 3-axis accelerometer and gyroscope for three-dimensional gesture recognition. Using an ensemble recognizer, they achieved a classification accuracy of 95.04%. Amma et al. [6] used an accelerometer and gyroscope signals to recognize different handwriting gestures in the Air. A support vector machine detects the gesture, while the Hidden Markov model decodes the gesture and generates its text representation. The efficiency of their approach was measured by word error rate, which turned out to be 9% for a small vocabulary and 11 % for a comparatively large vocabulary.

Pentelligence, a writing tool embedded with an IMU unit and microphone, was proposed by Schrapel et al. [53] that can identify numerals handwritten on paper. The tool gathered information from pen motion, and writing sounds corresponding to the handwritten characters. Writing sound was processed using the Hilbert method, and the motion data was fed to a neural network for the recognition task. On the Dataset consisting of 9408 handwritten digits, the proposed approach achieved an accuracy of 78.4% using a single sensor.

Agrawal et al. [1] proposed a PhonePoint Pen that utilized the built-in accelerometer to recognize handwritten gestures in the air. The mobile phone was treated as a pen, and the characters were written, considering it a pen. The gestures were transformed into strokes that were eventually recognized as characters. The authors claim that their model achieved the character recognition accuracy of 91.9% for the trained users. Li et al. [35] applied sequential models to recognize six digits and six English alphabets. The authors modified the BiLSTM and BiGRU network using Fisher discriminant analysis and built a Mobile Gesture Database of 5547 sequences. The dataset consists of accelerometer and gyroscope data corresponding to different gestures. The modified BiLSTM and BiGRU achieved an average classification accuracy of 98.04% and 99.15%, respectively. Ardüser et al. [7] used the data from smartwatches to recognize the text written on the Whiteboard. The authors utilized the motion data and acoustic information from the pen to perform segmentation and simulate the orientation of the whiteboard. Using their proposed approach, they were able to achieve a recognition accuracy of 94%.

Lin et al. [38] leveraged the accelerometer and gyroscope data collected from the smartwatch to recognize the handwritten gestures made on horizontal and vertical surfaces. The authors achieved recognition accuracy of 99.8% and 71.3% for the horizontal and vertical surfaces. However, the reported accuracy decreased to 67.5% and 54.1% for horizontal and vertical surfaces, respectively, when the elbow support while writing was altered. Xia et al. [72] illustrate in their work that Smartwatch motion sensors can leak handwriting content if an unauthorized app is installed. They presented MotionHacker, a system that records motions and extracts handwriting features for analysis. The system targets user-independent handwriting recognition and word-level estimation of lowercase print letters. Experimental results show a word recognition accuracy of 32.8% on average for five victims. Moreover, Dash et al. [16] proposed a model, Airscript, which can recognize gestures of digits made in the air. The proposed model consists of a convolution neural network and gated recurrent units to predict the ten-digit hand gestures written in Air. Their framework achieved a recognition accuracy of 96.7% person dependent and 91.7% person independent evaluation. Xu et al. [73] illustrated in their work that motion energy measured using a smartwatch can identify hand and finger gestures. Using the accelerometer and gyroscope sensors embedded in a smartwatch, the authors achieved a classification accuracy of 98% for 37 gestures. These gestures comprised ten arms, fourteen hands, and thirteen finger movements.

Alam et al. [4] proposed a deep learning model to perform digit recognition effectively. The framework applied LSTM & CNN models and used an Intel RealSense SR300 camera and Wiimote device for input data. Wiimote is a hand-held device capable of capturing acceleration and angular speed corresponding to different hand gestures. Using Wiimote, the authors achieved recognition accuracy of 99.32%, corresponding to ten digits.

Jing et al. [32] conducted handwriting recognition using sensors mounted on the fingertips to identify various words, including all 26 lowercase English letters and ten digits. By employing a Support Vector Machine (SVM) classifier, they achieved a notable recognition accuracy of 88%, showcasing the potential of fingertip sensors in capturing fine motor movements essential for distinguishing between different characters. This approach underlines the versatility of wearable sensors in handwriting recognition beyond traditional input devices.

In another study, Jiang et al. [31] explored handwriting recognition with wearable technology, focusing on a smartwatch equipped with accelerometer and gyroscope sensors. The study utilized a multimodal Convolutional Neural Network (CNN) combined with Bidirectional Long Short-Term Memory (BLSTM) layers to capture user-independent features across varying writing styles. The Connectionist Temporal Classification (CTC) method was further employed to enhance accuracy at the character level, ultimately reaching an average recognition accuracy of 64%. This approach underscores the viability of deep learning models in processing complex motion data for handwriting recognition, even in challenging user-independent contexts.

IMU sensors have limitations that impact their accuracy and reliability. They are prone to sensor drift [69], where small measurement errors accumulate over time, leading to inaccuracies in position, velocity, and orientation estimates. Their performance is highly sensitive to orientation [47]; misalignment or improper placement can result in significant measurement errors. External factors like vibrations and magnetic fields introduce noise and interference, reducing measurement precision. Additionally, integrating acceleration over time for position tracking can be inaccurate due to these accumulated errors. Temperature variations can degrade sensor performance, causing additional errors, and regular calibration is necessary to maintain accuracy over prolonged use. To mitigate these issues, combining IMU sensors with other types of sensors in multi-modal approaches can enhance accuracy and reduce dependence on IMU limitations.

2.2 Handwriting Analysis and Recognition Using Visual Data/Sensors

Most handwriting recognition (HCR) techniques rely on visual data/sensors acquired through cameras or mobile devices like smartphones and tablets. These devices capture images or video frames of handwritten characters, providing a rich source of spatial and structural information for recognition algorithms. By leveraging high-resolution visual data, these methods can accurately distinguish subtle differences in character shapes, which is especially useful in complex scripts and cursive writing. HCR using visual sensors can be considered a subfield of Optical Character Recognition(OCR), majorly divided into online and offline systems. The distinction between offline and online systems lies in their input [55]. In offline systems, input data takes the form of scanned images. In online systems, the input is more dynamic and is based on the movement of a pen tip with specific characteristics such as velocity, projection angle, position, and locus point.

In 1974, Ray Kurzweil developed one of the successful and earliest OCR systems, the omni-font OCR. It was capable of recognizing printed text in almost any font. The development of this device was made possible by two key technologies - the CCD flatbed scanner and the text-to-speech synthesizer [27].

Recently, machine learning has enabled OCR systems to recognize handwriting and other non-standard fonts more accurately than earlier systems. By using deep learning algorithms, OCR systems can analyze complex patterns in handwriting and learn to recognize individual characters and words with high accuracy [51].

Most approaches in the field of HCR rely on conventional or manually designed features [19,25,46,63]. However, with the emergence of deep learning techniques, scientists are adopting various models that enable automated feature extraction, such as Convolutional Neural Networks (CNNs). This approach has proven more effective in processing complex medical data and generating accurate results. CNNs can learn to automatically detect features from raw input data such as images or signals, thereby eliminating the need for human-designed features.

Some prominent work includes the method proposed by Roy et al. [49], where the authors utilized camera-based input to capture the characters written in virtual space with six degrees of freedom. Color-based segmentation, followed by processing a video stream using a Convolution neural network, was used to recognize the handwritten literals. The proposed pipeline achieved a recognition accuracy of 97.7% for the English numerals. Moreover, the framework was also able to achieve an accuracy of 95.4% and 93.7% for Bengali and Devnagri languages. Jayasundara et al. [30] applied Capsule networks to deal with the problem of small labeled datasets. The model utilized data augmentation by adjusting the instantiation parameters and achieved an accuracy of 90.46%. Similarly, in [79], the authors achieved high accuracy rates for online and offline handwritten Chinese characters. They combined the direction-decomposed feature map and the variant of CNN.

Tung et al. [64] used a bipartite weighted matching algorithm for handwritten Chinese character recognition. The algorithm was able to enhance the stroke order of handwriting. Image-based character recognition has limitations, such as being sensitive to lighting conditions, high computational complexity, and requiring specialized sensing devices to recognize characters, which incurs additional costs [15,29].

Some benchmark datasets used in this domain are MNINST [8,10,34], CEDAR [60], CHARS74K [17], UCOM [12], IFN/ENIT [45], CENPARMI [33], HCL2000 [76] and IAM [41], corresponding to different languages.

2.3   Handwriting Analysis and Recognition Using Electromyography (EMG) Data/Sensors

Electromyography (EMG) is increasingly used in human-computer interaction (HCI) to capture and interpret muscle activity, enabling systems to respond to user intent based on muscle signals. These bioelectric signals are generated when muscles contract or relax and can be captured using surface electrodes placed on the skin, commonly referred to as surface electromyography (sEMG) [56].

The recorded sEMG data contains finer details about muscle activation patterns, which can be utilized in various fields, including medical diagnostics [81], rehabilitation [21], sports science [61], and more recently, human-computer interaction (HCI) [58].

The pioneering work using sEMG signals for handwritten character recognition and reconstruction was conducted by Linderman et al. [39]. The authors employed EMGS pattern matching with a set of previously recorded EMG sets with which they achieved 90% accuracy. In another work, Huang et al. [28] proposed a method that utilizes template-making and matching for recognizing handwritten digits and Chinese characters and achieved accuracy above 90%.

Li et al. [36] introduced a two-phase approach for creating more efficient templates with enhanced features. Their method prioritized Mahalanobis distance over Euclidean distance, achieving an accuracy of 92.42% in recognizing handwritten characters using four-channel EMG signals. Hernández et al. (2020) utilized the pattern recognition capabilities of deep neural networks, implementing a CNN model for handwritten character recognition. They reported an accuracy 94.85% in detecting falsifications across 26 English alphabet characters and ten handwritten digits using sEMG signals. Recently, Singh and Chaturvedi [57] proposed an EMG-based handwritten character recognition model that utilizes a deep autoencoder to extract advanced features, achieving a classification accuracy of 99.01% for the 26 lowercase English alphabet characters written on a whiteboard. However, the limitation was that their model was resource-intensive, relying on multiple sensors, including an 8-channel EMG and a 13-channel IMU.

While these approaches show high potential, they face several limitations. Muscle fatigue, noise from nearby electrical devices, and sensor placement inconsistencies can affect the accuracy and robustness of recognition systems, which may lead to variability in EMG signals.

Future trends in EMG-based handwriting recognition are likely to focus on enhancing system robustness and portability. Advances may include the development of compact, cost-effective sensors with improved signal processing algorithms that can mitigate noise and adapt to user variability. The application of lightweight deep learning models optimized for edge computing could make EMG-based recognition systems more practical for everyday use, particularly in wearable devices.

2.4 Handwriting Analysis and Recognition Using Acoustic and Wi-Fi Data/Signals

In the last decade, researchers have utilized Wi-Fi and acoustic signals to recognize gestures by tracking motions while writing characters in the air and on a surface [9,40]. Wi-fi-based approaches generally track motion by capturing the variation produced in the signals due to hand movements. Channel state information (CSI) measurements are processed to extract statistical features, then gestures are predicted using classifiers [26,62,70,80]. In a similar work, Cao
et al. [13] proposed Wi-Wri, a WiFi signals-based approach to recognize 26 English letter gestures. The framework utilized the Channel State Information(CSI) of the waveform to identify the motion of the hand and fingers. Their proposed framework was able to achieve 82.7% recognition accuracy for letters. Han et al. [26] proposed a handwriting recognition system, AirDraw, that utilized CSI to predict hand gestures using passive tracking. The framework could track hand positions with a median error of up to 2.2 cm. The limitation of these approaches was that their efficiency was limited by factors such as initial locations and orientations of the hand with respect to the transceiver.

To address these issues, Zhang et al. [77] proposed two features: dynamic phase vector and motion rotation variable. These features provided an efficient representation of handwriting gestures with lesser domain constraints. The approach achieved a recognition accuracy of 95.79% for different characters. Moreover, to provide an alternative way of handwritten character input, recently, few researchers have attempted to predict the handwriting characters using the sound generated by the pen, writing on the table, or writing surface. These approaches exploit the microphone in mobile phones to capture the sound produced by pen writing on solid surfaces. They exploit the present acoustic patterns to identify gestures by deploying machine-learning models. In a similar work, Yin et al. [74] proposed a passive acoustic sensing module to detect and recognize handwritten words. Using a built-in microphone, their framework recorded the acoustic signals generated while writing characters near mobile devices. The recorded signals were segmented using short-time energy and were further recognized using a K-nearest neighbor classifier. In different scenarios, their framework achieved an average accuracy of 93.75%. Li et al. [37] utilized the acoustic signals generated from the textured surfaces while writing using a pen or fingernail. Using Dynamic time wrapping, their framework achieved recognition accuracy of over 80%. In another work, Zhang et al. [78] performed a similar experiment to evaluate the mobile acoustic sensor's capability to recognize handwritten letters. Their framework, SoundWrite, captured the audio signals while writing characters on a wooden table. The framework achieved a classification accuracy of approx. 90%. Another system, WritingHacker [75], could recognize handwritten English words utilizing acoustic and acceleration signals. These signals were collected and transmitted using speakers and microphones. The authors claim their approach can lead to 50–60% word-level recognition accuracy.

Table 1. Summary of Handwriting Recognition Techniques, Sensors, Performance, and Language

Reference	Technique Used	Sensors	Performance	Language
Handwriting Recognition using Inertial Sensors				
Ghosh et al. [24]	Image transformation for digit recognition	Accelerometer	High accuracy for single-stroke digits	Digits
Patil et al. [44]	Wireless IMU unit, feature extraction	Accelerometer, Gyroscope, Magnetometer	99.5% accuracy for digits, 98.69% for alphabets	English
Wang et al. [66]	Kernel class separability, Probabilistic Neural Network	Accelerometer	98% accuracy for digits, 98.75% for gestures	Digits, Gestures
Oh et al. [43]	Ensemble recognizer	Accelerometer (3-axis), Gyroscope	95.04% accuracy	Gestures
Amma et al. [6]	SVM and HMM for Airwriting	Accelerometer, Gyroscope	9% to 11% word error rate	English
Schrapel et al. [53]	Hilbert method, Neural Network	Microphone, IMU	78.4% accuracy for numerals	Digits
Agrawal et al. [1]	Gesture recognition in air	Accelerometer	91.9% accuracy	English
Li et al. [35]	BiLSTM, BiGRU with Fisher Discriminant Analysis	Accelerometer, Gyroscope	98.04% to 99.15% accuracy	English
Ardüser et al. [7]	Motion data and acoustic information	Smartwatch sensors	94% accuracy	English
Lin et al. [38]	Recognition on different surfaces	Accelerometer, Gyroscope	Varies: 99.8% (horizontal), 71.3% (vertical)	Gestures
Xia et al. [72]	Motion feature extraction	Smartwatch sensors	32.8% word recognition accuracy	English
Dash et al. [16]	CNN and GRU for air gestures	-	96.7% person dependent; 91.7% person independent	Digits
Xu et al. [73]	Motion energy for hand and finger gestures	Accelerometer, Gyroscope	98% accuracy for gestures	Gestures
Alam et al. [4]	LSTM and CNN for digit recognition	Intel RealSense SR300 camera, Wiimote	99.32% accuracy	Digits

continued

Table 1. continued

Reference	Technique Used	Sensors	Performance	Language
Handwriting Recognition using Visual Sensors				
Jing et al. [32]	SVM classifier for words	Fingertip sensors	88% accuracy	English
Jiang et al. [31]	Multimodal CNN with BLSTM	Accelerometer, Gyroscope	64% accuracy at character level	English
Roy et al. [49]	CNN, color-based segmentation	Camera	97.7% accuracy for English, 95.4% for Bengali, 93.7% for Devnagri	English, Bengali, Devnagri
Jayasundara et al. [30]	Capsule networks, data augmentation	-	90.46% accuracy	-
Zhang et al. [79]	Direction-decomposed feature map, CNN		High accuracy for Chinese characters	Chinese
Tung et al. [64]	Bipartite weighted matching algorithm		Enhanced stroke order recognition	Chinese
Handwriting Recognition using EMG Sensors				
Linderman et al. [39]	Template matching, Fischer linear discriminant analysis	sEMG	90% accuracy for digits	Digits
Huang et al. [28]	Dynamic Time Warping (DWT)	sEMG	84.26% accuracy	Digits
Li et al. [36]	Improved DWT, Mahalanobis distance	sEMG	92.42% accuracy	Digits
Hernández et al. [11]	Convolutional-recurrent neural networks	sEMG	94.85% accuracy	English
Handwriting Recognition using Acoustic and Wi-Fi Signals				
Bai et al. [9]	Acoustic-based sensing	Microphone	Various applications surveyed	Various
Ma et al. [40]	Wi-Fi sensing with Channel State Information (CSI)	Wi-Fi	Various applications surveyed	Various
Tan et al. [62]	Wi-Fi for fine-grained finger gesture recognition	Wi-Fi	93% accuracy	Gestures
Zheng et al. [80]	Wi-Fi for cross-domain gesture recognition	Wi-Fi	Various applications surveyed	Various

continued

Table 1. continued

Reference	Technique Used	Sensors	Performance	Language
Wu et al. [70]	Sub-wavelength level finger motion tracking	Wi-Fi	Various applications surveyed	Various
Han et al. [26]	AirDraw, Wi-Fi passive tracking	Wi-Fi	Median error up to 2.2 cm	Gestures
Cao et al. [13]	Wi-Wri, Wi-Fi signals for letter gestures	Wi-Fi	82.7% accuracy	English
Zhang et al. [77]	Dynamic phase vector, motion rotation variable	Wi-Fi	95.79% accuracy	Various
Yin et al. [74]	Passive acoustic sensing	Microphone	93.75% accuracy	English
Li et al. [37]	Dynamic time wrapping for acoustic signals	Microphone	Over 80% accuracy	English
Zhang et al. [78]	SoundWrite for audio signals	Microphone	Approx. 90% accuracy	English
Yu et al. [75]	WritingHacker for acoustic and acceleration signals	Microphone, Accelerometer	50–60% word-level accuracy	English
Du et al. [20]	CNN for acoustic signals	Microphone	81% accuracy	English
Wang et al. [68]	AudioWrite with GAN for acoustic signals	Microphone	92.2% accuracy	English
Wu et al. [71]	Fusion of ultrasonic and audio signals	Microphone	95.3% word recognition accuracy	English

In a similar work, Du et al. [20] applied a Convolutional Neural Network on processed acoustic signals collected corresponding to different handwritten letters. Their framework, WordRecorder, achieved a recognition accuracy of 81%. In another work, Wang et al. [68] proposed AudioWrite, which utilized acoustic signals along with a Generative Adversarial Network and achieved a recognition accuracy of 92.2% for 36 English alphabets. Recently, Wu et al. [71] fused ultrasonic and audio signals to recognize handwritten characters. Their framework accommodated the interaction between the two signals and achieved 95.3% word recognition accuracy.

Table 1 summarizes in detail different sensor-based handwritten character recognition approaches.

3 Discussion

Inertial sensors, such as accelerometers and gyroscopes, are widely used in handwriting recognition due to their ability to capture three-dimensional motion data, making them suitable for recognizing a variety of gestures, including those written in the air. These sensors have demonstrated high accuracy, with studies reporting recognition rates of up to 99.5% for digits and 98.69% for alphabets [43]. They can be seamlessly integrated into wearable devices like smartpens and smartwatches, facilitating continuous monitoring and data collection. However, the precision of inertial sensors can be compromised by sensor drift, leading to inaccuracies in position, velocity, and orientation estimation over time. Additionally, the orientation of the sensor significantly affects performance, impacting the consistency of recognition results. The high-dimensional data collected from these sensors also require sophisticated algorithms for accurate feature extraction and classification [43, 65].

Visual sensors, particularly cameras used in Optical Character Recognition (OCR) systems, have been highly effective in character recognition due to their ability to capture detailed spatial information. This is exemplified by a study where a camera-based input achieved a recognition accuracy of 97.7% for English numerals [47]. Integrating deep learning techniques, such as Convolutional Neural Networks (CNNs), enables automated feature extraction, further enhancing accuracy and efficiency. Despite these advantages, visual sensor-based systems are sensitive to environmental factors such as lighting conditions and background noise. Moreover, processing visual data demands significant computational resources, which can be a limitation for real-time applications. High-resolution cameras and the associated processing hardware also increase the overall cost of the recognition system [15].

EMG sensors capture bioelectric signals directly from muscle activity, providing a unique and detailed data source for gesture recognition. These sensors can be embedded in wearable devices, making them suitable for continuous monitoring and real-time applications. Studies have shown that EMG signals can be used to achieve high accuracy in character recognition, with one approach reporting an accuracy of 94.85% using convolutional-recurrent neural networks

[11]. However, EMG signals are susceptible to noise and interference from external sources, affecting the accuracy of recognition systems. Differences in muscle structure and electrode placement among individuals can lead to variability in the captured signals, complicating the development of generalized models. Additionally, the data collected from EMG sensors are often high-dimensional, necessitating advanced feature extraction and selection techniques for efficient processing [2, 61]

Acoustic and Wi-Fi sensors offer innovative approaches to handwriting recognition by capturing sound and signal variations during writing. These sensors are less intrusive compared to other types, as they can capture data without direct contact with the user. Wi-Fi-based systems, in particular, can recognize gestures by tracking hand movements in the air, providing flexibility in data collection environments. However, the performance of these systems can be significantly affected by environmental factors such as background noise and signal interference. Compared to other sensors, acoustic and Wi-Fi methods often achieve lower accuracy, with studies reporting an average accuracy of 93.75% using passive acoustic sensing [62]. The effectiveness of Wi-Fi-based systems can also be constrained by the range and initial positioning of the sensors relative to the user [9].

Each type of sensor used in handwritten character recognition has distinct benefits and limitations. Inertial sensors offer high accuracy and versatility but suffer from sensor drift and orientation sensitivity. Visual sensors provide detailed spatial data and automated feature extraction capabilities but are computationally intensive and environmentally sensitive. EMG sensors capture direct muscle activity with high potential accuracy but face noise, individual variability, and high-dimensional data challenges. Acoustic and Wi-Fi sensors introduce novel, non-intrusive data sources but are affected by environmental factors and generally offer lower accuracy. Integrating multi-modal sensors and advanced machine learning techniques holds promise for mitigating these limitations and enhancing the performance of handwriting recognition systems [1, 11, 24, 31, 39, 50, 74].

4   Conclusion

In conclusion, this survey on machine learning for sensor-based handwritten character recognition illustrates the vast potential of various sensors combined with advanced algorithms to revolutionize handwriting recognition technologies. Machine learning techniques, such as convolutional and recurrent neural networks, have proven instrumental in harnessing sensor data, enabling more accurate and versatile recognition across applications. While each sensor type-inertial, visual, EMG, acoustic, and Wi-Fi-offers unique advantages, they also present specific challenges, such as sensitivity to environmental conditions, noise, and sensor drift.

Recent trends have focused on multi-sensor fusion and lightweight, adaptable models that can operate on wearable devices and in real-time applications. Such innovations promise to create more robust and scalable handwriting recognition systems, with applications spanning from assistive technology and biometrics to virtual reality and beyond. This exploration underscores the role of machine learning as a catalyst in advancing the field. It provides a foundation for further research into sensor-driven recognition models tailored for diverse environments and user needs. Future directions may explore integrating AI with edge computing to enhance efficiency, incorporating adaptive learning mechanisms to accommodate individual variations, and advancing multimodal approaches to increase accuracy and broaden the usability of handwriting recognition technologies.

References

1. Agrawal, S., Constandache, I., Gaonkar, S., Roy Choudhury, R., Caves, K., DeRuyter, F.: Using mobile phones to write in air. In: Proceedings of the 9th International Conference on Mobile Systems, Applications, and Services, pp. 15–28 (2011)
2. Ahsan, M.R., Ibrahimy, M.I., Khalifa, O.O., et al.: EMG signal classification for human computer interaction: a review. Eur. J. Sci. Res. **33**(3), 480–501 (2009)
3. Al-Taee, M.M., Neji, S.B.H., Frikha, M.: Handwritten recognition: a survey. In: 2020 IEEE 4th International Conference on Image Processing, Applications and Systems (IPAS), pp. 199–205. IEEE (2020)
4. Alam, M.S., Kwon, K.C., Alam, M.A., Abbass, M.Y., Imtiaz, S.M., Kim, N.: Trajectory-based air-writing recognition using deep neural network and depth sensor. Sensors **20**(2), 376 (2020)
5. AlKendi, W., Gechter, F., Heyberger, L., Guyeux, C.: Advancements and challenges in handwritten text recognition: a comprehensive survey. J. Imaging **10**(1), 18 (2024)
6. Amma, C., Georgi, M., Schultz, T.: Airwriting: a wearable handwriting recognition system. Pers. Ubiquit. Comput. **18**, 191–203 (2014)
7. Ardüser, L., Bissig, P., Brandes, P., Wattenhofer, R.: Recognizing text using motion data from a smartwatch. In: 2016 IEEE International Conference on Pervasive Computing and Communication Workshops (PerCom Workshops), pp. 1–6 (2016). https://doi.org/10.1109/PERCOMW.2016.7457172
8. Babu, U.R., Chintha, A.K., Venkateswarlu, Y.: Handwritten digit recognition using structural, statistical features and k-nearest neighbor classifier. Int. J. Inf. Eng. Electron. Bus. **6**(1), 62–68 (2014)
9. Bai, Y., Lu, L., Cheng, J., Liu, J., Chen, Y., Yu, J.: Acoustic-based sensing and applications: a survey. Comput. Netw. **181**, 107447 (2020)
10. Baldominos, A., Saez, Y., Isasi, P.: A survey of handwritten character recognition with MNIST and EMNIST. Appl. Sci. **9**(15), 3169 (2019)
11. Beltrán Hernández, J.G., Ruiz Pinales, J., López Rodríguez, P., López Ramírez, J.L., Aviña Cervantes, J.G.: Multi-stroke handwriting character recognition based on sEMG using convolutional-recurrent neural networks. Math. Biosciences Eng. **17**(5), 5432–5448 (2020)
12. Bin Ahmed, S., Naz, S., Swati, S., Razzak, I., Umar, A.I., Ali Khan, A.: UCOM offline dataset-an Urdu handwritten dataset generation (2017)
13. Cao, X., Chen, B., Zhao, Y.: Wi-Wri: fine-grained writing recognition using Wi-Fi signals. In: 2016 IEEE Trustcom/BigDataSE/ISPA, pp. 1366–1373. IEEE (2016)

14. Carter, J.L., Russell, H.L.: Use of EMG biofeedback procedures with learning disabled children in a clinical and an educational setting. J. Learn. Disabil. **18**(4), 213–216 (1985)

15. Chang, Y., Chen, D., Zhang, Y., Yang, J.: An image-based automatic Arabic translation system. Pattern Recogn. **42**(9), 2127–2134 (2009)

16. Dash, A., et al.: AirScript-creating documents in air. In: 2017 14th IAPR International Conference on Document Analysis and Recognition (ICDAR), vol. 1, pp. 908–913. IEEE (2017)

17. De Campos, T.E., Babu, B.R., Varma, M., et al.: Character recognition in natural images. VISAPP **7**(2) (2009)

18. De Stefano, C., Fontanella, F., Impedovo, D., Pirlo, G., di Freca, A.S.: Handwriting analysis to support neurodegenerative diseases diagnosis: a review. Pattern Recogn. Lett. **121**, 37–45 (2019)

19. Deshmukh, S., Ragha, L.: Analysis of directional features-stroke and contour for handwritten character recognition. In: 2009 IEEE International Advance Computing Conference, pp. 1114–1118. IEEE (2009)

20. Du, H., Li, P., Zhou, H., Gong, W., Luo, G., Yang, P.: WordRecorder: accurate acoustic-based handwriting recognition using deep learning. In: IEEE INFOCOM 2018-IEEE Conference on Computer Communications, pp. 1448–1456. IEEE (2018)

21. Fang, C., He, B., Wang, Y., Cao, J., Gao, S.: EMG-centered multisensory based technologies for pattern recognition in rehabilitation: state of the art and challenges. Biosensors **10**(8), 85 (2020)

22. Faundez-Zanuy, M., Fierrez, J., Ferrer, M.A., Diaz, M., Tolosana, R., Plamondon, R.: Handwriting biometrics: applications and future trends in e-security and e-health. Cogn. Comput. **12**, 940–953 (2020)

23. Feder, K.P., Majnemer, A.: Handwriting development, competency, and intervention. Dev. Med. Child Neurol. **49**(4), 312–317 (2007)

24. Ghosh, D., Goyal, S., Kumar, R.: Digital pen to convert handwritten trajectory to image for digit recognition. In: Advances in Communication, Devices and Networking: Proceedings of ICCDN 2017, pp. 923–932. Springer (2018). https://doi.org/10.1007/978-981-10-7901-6_99

25. Graves, A., Liwicki, M., Fernández, S., Bertolami, R., Bunke, H., Schmidhuber, J.: A novel connectionist system for unconstrained handwriting recognition. IEEE Trans. Pattern Anal. Mach. Intell. **31**(5), 855–868 (2008)

26. Han, Z., Lu, Z., Wen, X., Zhao, J., Guo, L., Liu, Y.: In-air handwriting by passive gesture tracking using commodity WiFi. IEEE Commun. Lett. **24**(11), 2652–2656 (2020)

27. Herbert, H.: The history of OCR, optical character recognition. Recognition Technologies Users Association, Manchester Center, VT (1982)

28. Huang, G., Zhang, D., Zheng, X., Zhu, X.: An EMG-based handwriting recognition through dynamic time warping. In: 2010 Annual International Conference of the IEEE Engineering in Medicine and Biology, pp. 4902–4905. IEEE (2010)

29. Islam, N., Islam, Z., Noor, N.: A survey on optical character recognition system. arXiv preprint arXiv:1710.05703 (2017)

30. Jayasundara, V., Jayasekara, S., Jayasekara, H., Rajasegaran, J., Seneviratne, S., Rodrigo, R.: TextCaps: handwritten character recognition with very small datasets. In: 2019 IEEE Winter Conference on Applications of Computer Vision (WACV), pp. 254–262. IEEE (2019)

31. Jiang, H.: Motion eavesdropper: smartwatch-based handwriting recognition using deep learning. In: 2019 International Conference on Multimodal Interaction, pp. 145–153 (2019)

32. Jing, L., Dai, Z., Zhou, Y.: Wearable handwriting recognition with an inertial sensor on a fingernail. In: 2017 14th IAPR International Conference on Document Analysis and Recognition (ICDAR), vol. 1, pp. 1330–1337. IEEE (2017)
33. Khosravi, H., Kabir, E.: Introducing a very large dataset of handwritten Farsi digits and a study on their varieties. Pattern Recogn. Lett. **28**(10), 1133–1141 (2007)
34. LeCun, Y., Bottou, L., Bengio, Y., Haffner, P.: Gradient-based learning applied to document recognition. Proc. IEEE **86**(11), 2278–2324 (1998)
35. Li, C., Xie, C., Zhang, B., Chen, C., Han, J.: Deep fisher discriminant learning for mobile hand gesture recognition. Pattern Recogn. **77**, 276–288 (2018)
36. Li, C., Ma, Z., Yao, L., Zhang, D.: Improvements on EMG-based handwriting recognition with DTW algorithm. In: 2013 35th Annual International Conference of the IEEE Engineering in Medicine and Biology Society (EMBC), pp. 2144–2147. IEEE (2013)
37. Li, W., Hammond, T.: Recognizing text through sound alone. In: Proceedings of the AAAI Conference on Artificial Intelligence, vol. 25, pp. 1481–1486 (2011)
38. Lin, X., Chen, Y., Chang, X.W., Liu, X., Wang, X.: SHOW: smart handwriting on watches. In: Proceedings of the ACM on Interactive, Mobile, Wearable and Ubiquitous Technologies, vol. 1, issue (4), pp. 1–23 (2018)
39. Linderman, M., Lebedev, M.A., Erlichman, J.S.: Recognition of handwriting from electromyography. PLoS ONE **4**(8), e6791 (2009)
40. Ma, Y., Zhou, G., Wang, S.: WiFi sensing with channel state information: a survey. ACM Comput. Surv. (CSUR) **52**(3), 1–36 (2019)
41. Marti, U.V., Bunke, H.: The IAM-database: an English sentence database for offline handwriting recognition. Int. J. Doc. Anal. Recogn. **5**, 39–46 (2002)
42. Neely, L., Rispoli, M., Camargo, S., Davis, H., Boles, M.: The effect of instructional use of an iPad® on challenging behavior and academic engagement for two students with autism. Res. Autism Spectrum Disorders **7**(4), 509–516 (2013)
43. Oh, J., et al.: Inertial sensor based recognition of 3-d character gestures with an ensemble classifiers. In: Ninth International Workshop on Frontiers in Handwriting Recognition, pp. 112–117 (2004). https://doi.org/10.1109/IWFHR.2004.58
44. Patil, S., Kim, D., Park, S., Chai, Y.: Handwriting recognition in free space using WIMU-based hand motion analysis. J. Sens. **2016** (2016)
45. Pechwitz, M., Maddouri, S.S., Märgner, V., Ellouze, N., Amiri, H., et al.: IFN/ENIT-database of handwritten Arabic words. In: Proceedings of CIFED, vol. 2, pp. 127–136. Citeseer (2002)
46. Pradeep, J., Srinivasan, E., Himavathi, S.: Neural network based recognition system integrating feature extraction and classification for English handwritten. Int. J. Eng. **25**(2), 99–106 (2012)
47. Prathivadi, Y., Wu, J., Bennett, T.R., Jafari, R.: Robust activity recognition using wearable IMU sensors. Sensors, 486–489. IEEE (2014)
48. Remaida, A., Moumen, A., El Idrissi, Y.E.B., Sabri, Z.: Handwriting recognition with artificial neural networks a decade literature review. In: Proceedings of the 3rd International Conference on Networking, Information Systems & Security, pp. 1–5 (2020)
49. Roy, P., Ghosh, S., Pal, U.: A CNN based framework for unistroke numeral recognition in air-writing. In: 2018 16th International Conference on Frontiers in Handwriting Recognition (ICFHR), pp. 404–409 (2018). https://doi.org/10.1109/ICFHR-2018.2018.00077
50. Roy, P., Ghosh, S., Pal, U.: A CNN based framework for unistroke numeral recognition in air-writing. In: 2018 16th International Conference on Frontiers in Handwriting Recognition (ICFHR), pp. 404–409. IEEE (2018)

51. Saeed, S., Naz, S., Razzak, M.I.: An application of deep learning in character recognition: an overview. In: Handbook of Deep Learning Applications, pp. 53–81 (2019)
52. Sánchez-DelaCruz, E., Loeza-Mejía, C.I.: Importance and challenges of handwriting recognition with the implementation of machine learning techniques: a survey. Appl. Intell., 1–22 (2024)
53. Schrapel, M., Stadler, M.L., Rohs, M.: Pentelligence: combining pen tip motion and writing sounds for handwritten digit recognition. In: Proceedings of the 2018 CHI Conference on Human Factors in Computing Systems, pp. 1–11 (2018)
54. Singh, L., Sandhu, J.K., Sahu, R., et al.: A literature survey on handwritten character recognition. In: 2023 International Conference on Circuit Power and Computing Technologies (ICCPCT), pp. 1755–1760. IEEE (2023)
55. Singh, S.K., Chaturvedi, A.: Leveraging deep feature learning for wearable sensors based handwritten character recognition. Biomed. Signal Process. Control **80**, 104198 (2023)
56. Singh, S.K., Chaturvedi, A.: A reliable and efficient machine learning pipeline for American sign language gesture recognition using EMG sensors. Multimedia Tools Appl. **82**(15), 23833–23871 (2023)
57. Singh, S.K., Chaturvedi, A.: An efficient multi-modal sensors feature fusion approach for handwritten characters recognition using Shapley values and deep autoencoder. Eng. Appl. Artif. Intell. **138**, 109225 (2024)
58. Singh, S.K., Chaturvedi, A., Prakash, A.: Applying extreme gradient boosting for surface EMG based sign language recognition. In: Machine Learning and Big Data Analytics (Proceedings of International Conference on Machine Learning and Big Data Analytics (ICMLBDA) 2021), pp. 175–185. Springer (2022). https://doi.org/10.1007/978-3-030-82469-3_16
59. Specht, D.F.: Probabilistic neural networks. Neural Netw. **3**(1), 109–118 (1990)
60. Srihari, S.N., Cha, S.H., Arora, H., Lee, S.: Individuality of handwriting. J. Forensic Sci. **47**(4), 856–872 (2002)
61. Taborri, J., et al.: Sport biomechanics applications using inertial, force, and EMG sensors: a literature overview. Appl. Bionics Biomechanics **2020** (2020)
62. Tan, S., Yang, J.: WiFinger: leveraging commodity WiFi for fine-grained finger gesture recognition. In: Proceedings of the 17th ACM International Symposium on Mobile ad Hoc Networking and Computing, pp. 201–210 (2016)
63. Tian, S., et al.: Multilingual scene character recognition with co-occurrence of histogram of oriented gradients. Pattern Recogn. **51**, 125–134 (2016)
64. Tung, C.H., Jean, E.Y.: Stroke-order-free on-line Chinese character recognition by stroke adjustment of two-layer bipartite weighted matching. Futur. Gener. Comput. Syst. **81**, 219–234 (2018)
65. Van Galen, G.P.: Handwriting: issues for a psychomotor theory. Hum. Mov. Sci. **10**(2–3), 165–191 (1991)
66. Wang, J.S., Chuang, F.C.: An accelerometer-based digital pen with a trajectory recognition algorithm for handwritten digit and gesture recognition. IEEE Trans. Industr. Electron. **59**(7), 2998–3007 (2012). https://doi.org/10.1109/TIE.2011.2167895
67. Wang, L.: Feature selection with kernel class separability. IEEE Trans. Pattern Anal. Mach. Intell. **30**(9), 1534–1546 (2008)
68. Wang, L., Zhang, J., Li, Y., Wang, H.: AudioWrite: a handwriting recognition system using acoustic signals. In: 2022 IEEE 28th International Conference on Parallel and Distributed Systems (ICPADS), pp. 81–88 (2023). https://doi.org/10.1109/ICPADS56603.2022.00019

69. Wehbi, M., et al.: Surface-free multi-stroke trajectory reconstruction and word recognition using an IMU-enhanced digital pen. Sensors **22**(14), 5347 (2022)
70. Wu, D., et al.: FingerDraw: sub-wavelength level finger motion tracking with WiFi signals. In: Proceedings of the ACM on Interactive, Mobile, Wearable and Ubiquitous Technologies, vol. 4, issue (1), pp. 1–27 (2020)
71. Wu, Y., Bi, H., Fan, J., Xu, G., Chen, H.: DMHC: device-free multi-modal handwritten character recognition system with acoustic signal. Knowl.-Based Syst., 110314 (2023)
72. Xia, Q., Hong, F., Feng, Y., Guo, Z.: MotionHacker: motion sensor based eavesdropping on handwriting via smartwatch. In: IEEE INFOCOM 2018 - IEEE Conference on Computer Communications Workshops (INFOCOM WKSHPS), pp. 468–473 (2018). https://doi.org/10.1109/INFCOMW.2018.8406879
73. Xu, C., Pathak, P.H., Mohapatra, P.: Finger-writing with smartwatch: a case for finger and hand gesture recognition using smartwatch. In: Proceedings of the 16th International Workshop on Mobile Computing Systems and Applications, pp. 9–14 (2015)
74. Yin, H., Zhou, A., Liu, L., Wang, N., Ma, H.: Ubiquitous writer: robust text input for small mobile devices via acoustic sensing. IEEE Internet Things J. **6**(3), 5285–5296 (2019)
75. Yu, T., Jin, H., Nahrstedt, K.: WritingHacker: audio based eavesdropping of handwriting via mobile devices. In: Proceedings of the 2016 ACM International Joint Conference on Pervasive and Ubiquitous Computing, pp. 463–473 (2016)
76. Zhang, H., Guo, J., Chen, G., Li, C.: Hcl2000-a large-scale handwritten Chinese character database for handwritten character recognition. In: 2009 10th International Conference on Document Analysis and Recognition, pp. 286–290. IEEE (2009)
77. Zhang, J., Li, Y., Xiong, H., Dou, D., Miao, C., Zhang, D.: HandGest: hierarchical sensing for robust-in-the-air handwriting recognition with commodity WiFi devices. IEEE Internet Things J. **9**(19), 19529–19544 (2022)
78. Zhang, M., Yang, P., Tian, C., Shi, L., Tang, S., Xiao, F.: SoundWrite: text input on surfaces through mobile acoustic sensing. In: Proceedings of the 1st International Workshop on Experiences with the Design and Implementation of Smart Objects, pp. 13–17 (2015)
79. Zhang, X.Y., Bengio, Y., Liu, C.L.: Online and Offline handwritten Chinese character recognition: a comprehensive study and new benchmark. Pattern Recogn. **61**, 348–360 (2017)
80. Zheng, Y., et al.: Zero-effort cross-domain gesture recognition with Wi-Fi. In: Proceedings of the 17th Annual International Conference on Mobile Systems, Applications, and Services, pp. 313–325 (2019)
81. Zwarts, M.J., Drost, G., Stegeman, D.F.: Recent progress in the diagnostic use of surface EMG for neurological diseases. J. Electromyogr. Kinesiol. **10**(5), 287–291 (2000)

Author Index

Q. Bramas et al. (Eds.): ICDCIT 2025, LNCS 15507, pp. 307–308, 2025.
https://doi.org/10.1007/978-3-031-81404-4